SURVEYING THE RECORD
North American Scientific Exploration to 1930

Edited by EDWARD C. CARTER II

Philadelphia   *1999*

AMERICAN PHILOSOPHICAL SOCIETY

SURVEYING THE RECORD

North American Scientific

Exploration to 1930

Memoirs
of the
American Philosophical Society
Held at Philadelphia
For Promoting Useful Knowledge
Volume 231

ISBN: 0-87169-231-7
US ISSN: 0065-9738

Library of Congress Cataloging-in-Publication Data

Surveying the record : North American scientific exploration to 1930 /
   [edited by Edward C. Carter II].
      p.   cm. — (Memoirs of the American Philosophical Society Held
   at Philadelphia for Promoting Useful Knowledge, ISSN 0065-9738 ; v. 231)
      Includes bibliographical references and index.
      ISBN 0-87169-231-7
      1. Scientific expeditions—North America—Congresses.   2. North
   America—Description and exploration—Congresses.   3. Discoveries in
   geography—North America—Congresses.   I. Carter, Edward Carlos,
   1928– .   II. Series: Memoirs of the American Philosophical Society; v. 231.
   Q115.S89   1999
   508.7'09'034—dc21   98-50212
                                                                        CIP

Contents

PART II. Oceanic Exploration

PART III. Exploratory Art—Spreading the Image

PART IV. Exploration and Anthropology

PART V. Lewis and Clark

PART VI. New Thoughts on the West

List of Illustrations

RINDGE: *Science and Art Meet in the Parlor*

Introduction and Acknowledgments

Commencing on March 14, 1997 the Library of the American Philosophical Society held a three-day conference on "Surveying the Record: North American Scientific Exploration to 1900" attended by some one hundred and fifty scholars and interested members of the general public who heard twenty-seven presentations organized into nine plenary sessions. Meeting in the Society's Benjamin Franklin Hall under the historic portraits of three American leaders deeply interested and involved in the West and exploration—Benjamin Franklin, our Founder and first President; Thomas Jefferson, our third President; and George Washington, a generous member—the audience heard a variety of informative papers ranging from a major introductory address to a session containing five short work-in-progress reports, with twenty half-hour presentations constituting the greater part of the conference. At the suggestion of the Program Advisory Committee a large number of the participants employed slides and other visual aids which greatly enriched not only their papers, but enhanced the lively audience discussions that followed.

The meeting was intended to examine and, we hoped, illuminate new historical approaches to scientific expeditions and surveys, and to stimulate discussion and intellectual interchange between the new generation of scholars and their more established colleagues. To accomplish these goals the Program Advisory Committee invited participation of historians, art historians, historical geographers, anthropologists, archaeologists, historical botanists and others. We proposed to investigate broad topics that represented both new directions of inquiry and those more traditional ones that should be revisited. **We also stressed the point that the conference schedule would be planned so as to afford ample time for audience participation and informal discussion.** By employing "Surveying the Record" in the conference title, we hoped that participants would look at the actual history of specific expeditions through a variety of disciplinary lenses and also re-evaluate earlier scholars' accounts of the explorative enterprise. "North American Scientific Exploration" was meant to encompass governmental, institutional, corporate, and private expeditions and surveys carried out in the present-day territories of the United States, Canada, and Mexico as well as oceanic, polar, and other extraterritorial exploration undertaken by North Americans.

The early 1990s seemed an appropriate time to think of undertaking such a conference. A resurgence of Western history was underway heightening scholarly and popular interest in scientific expeditions and surveys. Readership in the Society's manuscript and printed exploration and anthropological collections, always vigorous, was on the rise, perhaps helped along by the Library's 1991 publication of William Stanton's *American Scientific Exploration 1803–1865: Manuscripts in Four Philadelphia Libraries*, which highlighted our extensive and varied holdings. The conference program has been reproduced in the Appendix. All the sixteen essays that comprise this volume were drawn from the conference itself; a few appear here nearly as presented; most were revised and somewhat expanded in size, a few in temporal scope, resulting in the volume's terminal date of 1930.

A glance at the Appendix reveals the conference planners' broad structural strategy. Beginning with John Logan Allen's masterful overview of the history of modern American exploration studies, we moved to a consideration of terrestrial cartography followed by, and in a sense paired with, oceanic exploration. Then a double session was devoted to the process and products of expeditionary art after which we returned to the origins of American scientific exploration. "Exploration and Anthropology" largely dealt with issues of Native American culture; the work-in-progress reports highlighted the extraordinary range and variety of research currently underway; a shift from institutional activities was effected in a "Biography of Explorers" session. A stimulating series of papers on "New Dimensions of Exploratory Studies" focusing on future research needs and opportunities brought the proceedings to a successful conclusion.

Certainly "Surveying the Record" achieved its goal of stimulating discussion and intellectual interchange between the new and older generations of scholars. A number of distinguished anthropologists, geographers, historians, historians of art, and representatives of allied disciplines who participated in the program or attended the conference made a point of seeking out and conversing with their younger colleagues. Everyone was delighted that one of America's most renowned senior Western historian, Howard R. Lamar of Yale University, and the nation's dean of exploration studies, William H. Goetzmann of the University of Texas, Austin played important and gracious roles throughout the entire conference. By the conclusion of the program, there was a general consensus that the conference was indeed a success. The many communications received during the succeeding months validated this impression.

In fact, the program worked so well that we decided to retain its structure for this publication. Once again John Logan Allen, University of Connecticut, leads off with his splendid survey of "Where We Are and How We Got There: Surveying the Record of Exploration Studies"; now we conclude with an exciting paper by Donald Worster, University of Kansas, "The Second Colorado River Expedition: John Wesley Powell, Mormonism and the Environment." This essay is what "Surveying the Record" was all about in that Donald Worster, a leading environmental historian, closely reviewed Powell's generally neglected Second Expedition and discerned in the explorer's winter residence experiences among the Mormon pioneers the origins of key elements of his famed 1878 *Report on the Lands of the Arid Region of the United States*. Like the conference, *Surveying the Record* is generously illustrated.

While preparing the book we were saddened to learn from British Columbia of the untimely death of one of our participants, Douglas Cole, of Simon Fraser University. Professor Cole, a regular researcher in the Library's Franz Boas collection, was popular with the staff and the Librarian who respected his inquisitive scholarly diligence and thoroughly enjoyed his dry sense of humor. He is already greatly missed here in Philadelphia as he is throughout the world of anthropology. His friend and Simon Fraser colleague Alex Long's expansion of their original paper is reflected in its new title "The Boasian Anthropological Survey Tradition: The Role of Franz Boas in North American Anthropological Surveys," which is published in memory of Douglas Cole.

Recording ACKNOWLEDGMENTS is always a pleasant task for authors and editors. A number of individuals generously assisted with both the conference and this publication and such effort will be recognized together. In 1992, Howard R. Lamar, Yale University, William Cronon, then of Yale and now the University of Wisconsin, and James P. Ronda, University of Tulsa, assisted in the early planning of the meeting and gave much appreciated encouragement. Professor Lamar kindly chaired the work-in-progress session reporting on his own project "Stephen H. Long's 1820 Expedition: Responses to Native Americans." James Ronda played a key role in every step of the planning of the conference, culminating in his superb summation of the proceedings "Looking Backwards—Looking Forward: Thoughts on the Meaning and Contributions of 'Surviving the Record.'" Professor Ronda joined the Program Advisory Committee which I was to chair and helped me recruit the other two members who brought their outstanding disciplinary knowledge and balanced, judicious advice to our deliberations—John Logan Allen, Geography Department at the University of Connecticut, and Martha A. Sandweiss, Director, Mead Art Museum, Amherst College.

The service of these three highly regarded and incredibly busy scholars was key to our overall success. They suggested topics and appropriate speakers and chairs, reviewed all the paper proposals with me, helped structure the conference, in the case of Professors Allen and Ronda chaired sessions and presented papers themselves, and assisted in the selection of the published papers. Never once did they fail to respond promptly to my numerous, often harried requests for information and assistance. Each deserves our highest praise and warmest thanks.

We are also greatly indebted to the staff of the American Philosophical Society for cheerfully and effectively working on various aspects of the conference while carrying out their regular duties. Sandra Duffy, Secretary to the Librarian, and her assistant Karen Payano skillfully and tactfully handled all the day-to-day administrative and organizational details involved in putting on such a program. After Ms. Payano succeeded Ms. Duffy as Secretary to the Librarian she greatly facilitated the preparation of this volume, ably supported by Lois Fischbeck, Manuscripts and Printed Materials Assistant. Martin L. Levitt, Associate Librarian for Administration, spread the word of "Surveying the Record" through print and electronic announcements. Beth Carroll-Horrocks, Associate Librarian and Manuscripts Librarian, and Hedi Kyle, Head of Conservation, planned and mounted a beautiful and imaginative exhibit in the Reading Room featuring such Society treasures as the 1793 Michaux Expedition Subscription List and Instructions, the Journals of Lewis and Clark, the Titian Ramsay Peale expeditionary watercolors and sketches, and many other intriguing and significant items. Frank W. Margeson, Photographer, served as the conference projectionist and AV specialist and produced a number of the fine illustrations for this volume. The American Philosophical Society's President, Judge Arlin Adams, and the then Executive Officer, Herman H. Goldstine, lent their support to the enterprise.

Surveying the Record was expertly guided through publication by the Society's Editor Carole LeFaivre-Rochester. The book's extraordinarily beautiful design is the work of Adrianne Onderdonk Dudden, a nationally recognized practitioner of her craft. Both the conference and this volume were handsomely supported by the Andrew W. Mellon Foundation Library Endowment which has greatly benefited the scholarly and cultural life of the American Philosophical Society Library, its researchers, the academic community, and the general public for nearly three decades.

Over the years, the American Philosophical Society, which played an important role in mounting the Lewis and Clark Expedition of 1803–06 and other federal efforts, continued that tradition by making its extensive manuscript, printed, and graphic collections available for study in its Library, publishing modern monographs and articles in the field of exploration history and Native American linguistics and ethnohistory, awarding research grants in these areas, and serving as a co-sponsor of the modern edition of *The Journals of the Lewis and Clark Expedition*. Thus the "Surveying the Record" conference and this volume are the logical extensions of our history and traditional mission.

Philadelphia, June 1998

PART ONE
THE CARTOGRAPHIC RECORD

WHERE WE ARE AND HOW WE GOT THERE
Surveying the Record of Exploration Studies

For the past decade I served as the director and editor of a massive research project entitled *North American Exploration*. Funded by the National Endowment for the Humanities, this effort involved the cooperation of several dozen scholars of exploration, including over twenty who contributed to a three-volume collection of essays published in 1997.[1] During the years this project consumed, those of us involved in it struggled to bring some degree of coherence and continuity to a work that spans North American exploration from pre-Columbian times to the end of the 19th century. As we did so, it occurred to us on more than one occasion that an examination of the last century's worth of attempts by American scholars to develop a methodology for the study of one of humanity's most important endeavors— geographical exploration—was far overdue. The term "geographical exploration" is used to insure understanding that the concern of both the North American Exploration research project and this essay is not "exploration" in the general sense of the continuing quest for knowledge about all things but "exploration" in the very specific connotation of the quest for geograph-

---

1. John L. Allen, ed., *North American Exploration*, 3 vols., Vol. 1, "A New World Disclosed," Vol. 2, "A Continent Defined," Vol. 3, "A Continent Comprehended," (Lincoln, Nebraska and London: University of Nebraska Press, 1997).

ical knowledge—the knowledge about the nature and content of the various areas or regions of the earth's surface. The serendipitous opportunity to address a group of scholars collected at a conference on exploration at the American Philosophical Society in Philadelphia, a few weeks before the publication of the first volume of *North American Exploration*, seemed the perfect time and place to set in motion my and my fellow conspirators in the exploration project's desire to explore American exploration. At the Philosophical Society American exploration (meaning exploration undertaken by Americans) had its origins in the form of the Lewis and Clark Expedition. Here, under the watchful portraits of Washington, Jefferson, and Franklin, was surely the most logical place to begin surveying the record of exploration studies: where we are and how we got there.

Geographers refer to the study of geographical knowledge as "geosophy." And "historiography," to the historian, is the study of the methods of history. Our investigation here is into the study of the history of the development of geographical knowledge—since that is what studies in exploration really are. There is no proper term for this type of inquiry; "geosophical historiography" seems unnecessarily cumbersome and could be condensed to "geosophistry" far too readily for comfort. Perhaps it is best to leave us without a formal name for this inquiry and say simply that, in this essay, I will examine some of the ways in which geographers and historians have investigated the process of exploration and what their approaches mean for those of us who pursue the study of the exploratory process today.

Throughout most of the long history of humanity's efforts to make sense out of the apparent chaos that makes up the world's surface, a good portion of those efforts have been devoted to the study of geographical exploration. The ancient Greeks divided their studies of the world into two basic categories: geometry and geography.[2] The geometricians measured the earth, determined its size and shape, and puzzled over its place in the cosmos. The geographers wrote about the earth and described the varied

---

2. Still the most complete examination of the geographical thought of Greek and Roman scholars is the classic study by Edmund Bunbury, *A History of Ancient Geography* (London: Methuen, 1879).

character of its surface. And where the geometricians' tools were those of astronomer and mathematician, the tools of the geographer were the maps and accounts of explorers and travelers, those Greeks and others who had seen about and written about parts of the world, including the familiar locale of the Mediterranean basin but also areas beyond the general knowledge of classical scholarship, lands known perhaps only through rumor and folklore: the land of Kush, the kingdom of Punt, and the mountains of Zinj. "Geography" as opposed to "geometry" came to mean "description of the earth" and that is exactly what most practitioners of the art and science of geography from the time of the Greeks on did—they described the world. The bulk of the source materials for those descriptions came from exploration and travel—for whatever purpose: commercial, military, religious. For example, one of the greatest periods of expansion of geographical knowledge prior to the development of the Roman Empire was the period of Alexandrian conquest in which military "travel" contributed new lands and new peoples to the Greek world view. Nor did the post-classical decline and partial loss of ancient and classical geographical knowledge reduce the practice of using exploratory accounts in earth description. Throughout the medieval period in the western intellectual tradition, the writings of geographers and natural historians relied heavily upon the writing of explorers—both real and imaginary.[3] Thus the medieval European geographer could not describe the Atlantic Ocean without resorting to some reference to the actual-but-misunderstood voyages of the Irish cleric Brandan, or of the mythical archbishop of Spain who founded seven golden cities on the equally mythical island of Antillia; he could not describe Asia without borrowing heavily from the almost certainly apocryphal travel writings of Sir John Mandeville. During the classical revival of the Renaissance, geographers once again looked to the theoretical and speculative geographies of Strabo and Ptolemy, Pliny and Seneca, to inspire their descriptions of the then-known

3. There are two excellent studies of medieval geographical thought: the immense three-volume work by Clarence Beazley, *The Dawn of Modern Geography* (Oxford, England: Clarendon Press, 1906); and the more readable but equally erudite *Geographical Lore at the Time of the Crusades: A Study in the History of Medieval Science and Tradition in Western Europe* by John Kirtland Wright (New York: American Geographical Society, 1925; reprint edition by Dover Publications, 1963).

world or *ecumene*, that included the "world island" of Europe, Africa, and Asia, surrounded by the all-encompassing Ocean Sea; and they relied on the very real traveler Marco Polo for accounts of the lands on the farthest verge of the *ecumene*. As the Renaissance exploded outward into the Age of Exploration, a centuries-long process based initially on classical and medieval knowledge but soon responsible for developing its own fund of geographical lore, the disciplines of geography and natural history began to experience dramatic increases in subject material as the journals and accounts of voyagers to the heretofore-unknown New World, and to vaguely-known Africa and Asia became a part of European geographical lore.[4] But works of the imagination were still just as important as they had been, in spite of real explorers looking at real areas. Jonathan Swift said it best: "Geographers in Afric maps, with savage pictures fill their gaps, and o'er unhabited downs, place elephants in want of towns." What Swift was talking about was the tendency for geographers to expand what was known to fill the unknown—to continue to rely on whatever kind of information was available in describing the world as it was becoming known through expanding actual (or empirical), as opposed to invented, information. It was partially because of this expansion in information and partly because of the process of exploration itself that during the early stages of the Age of Exploration, the study of exploration began to change and became as much—if not more—the subject matter of the historian and political economist than the geographer and the natural historian. The study of exploration (and hence geography) began to change from a relatively simple cataloguing of the features of the earth's physical and human surface for purposes of understanding the character of the world to a romanticized, politicized, and commercialized justification of Europe's success at the expense of much of the remainder of the world. From the beginning of the sixteenth century through the end of the nineteenth and even into the early twentieth centuries, the study of exploration was largely involved with the compilation of collections of voyages on the basis of their romantic interests, commercial successes, and political or imperial aspects. Early on, the collections of the European scholars like Giovanni Ramusio, Theodor De Bry, and Rich-

---

4. The most authoritative source for this period of exploration is Boies Penrose, *Travel and Discovery in the Renaissance* (Cambridge, MA: Harvard University Press, 1955).

ard Hakluyt and his successor Samuel Purchase[5] provided the basis for the
territorial claims of European states to non-European chunks of the world;
the same collections also offered most of what passed for geographical
knowledge about that non-European world. From this early period, the
work of compiling, editing, annotating, and commenting on the narratives
of exploration has continued, and even became somewhat of an art form in
the hands of scholars like Reuben Gold Thwaites in the late 1800s and early
1900s.[6]

But fortunately for those of us who pursue the study of exploration, the
practice of simply compiling exploratory accounts and using them to describe portions of the earth's surface did not continue much beyond the first
decade of the present century, at least in the United States. By the time of
the First World War, most of the world was more-or-less known. There was
still considerable interest in "far-away places with strange sounding names"
and the Siren's song of exotic description fueled the success of fledgling geographical societies such as the National Geographic Society, the American
Geographical Society of New York, and the academically-oriented Association of American Geographers. And the prizes gathered by explorers stocked
the halls of the Smithsonian and the American Museum of Natural History.
But the accounts of exploration were being used more and more by students
of exploration for purposes other than simple description. We owe some of
the revision of the study of exploration to the changing character of exploration itself during the nineteenth century as the exploratory process shifted
from Enlightenment description to Humboldtean compilation to Darwin-
ian investigation. But we probably owe most of this new approach to the
study of exploration to the Columbian Quadricentennial. Like the present
decade and the Columbian Quincentennial, the decade of the 1890s was notable for its voluminous output of Columbian literature—some of it good,
much of it bad. The best of the good scholarship prompted more inquiry;
the worst of the bad helped scholars to know what to avoid as they began

5. The most representative—and the most influential in terms of public policy—of
this genre was Richard Hakluyt's *Principal navigations, voiages, traffiques, and discoueries of
the English nation* . . . , 3 vols. (London: 1598–1600).

6. *Cf.* Reuben Gold Thwaites, *The Jesuit Relations and Related Documents*, 22 vols.
(Cleveland: Burrows Brothers, 1896–1901); and *Early Western Travels 1748–1846*, 32 vols.
(Cleveland: A. H. Clark and Co., 1904–07).

reshaping the intellectual tradition of exploration studies. Among the best output of the 1890s was a remarkable piece of work by an American scholar named William H. Tillinghast, published in Justin Winsor's *Narrative and Critical History of America*.[7] Tillinghast's unusually profound study of the relationship between ancient geographical theories and Renaissance exploratory behavior was a watershed study since it elevated the study of exploration beyond the level of mere description to the level of interpretation and analysis. While most of his contemporaries were content to cast exploration and explorers in a heroic mold, and link exploration to the "white man's burden" of civilizing the world, Tillinghast was the first scholar to suggest that exploration was an intellectual process and that studying it was valuable because exploratory behavior could be generalized to other kinds of human behavior as well. Also spawned by the Quadricentennial, although published somewhat later, was George E. Nunn's study of the origins of the geographical conceptions of Columbus and how those conceptions, with their roots in ancient and classical theory, bore upon Columbus's objectives on his first and subsequent voyages.[8] Like Tillinghast, Nunn suggested that the behavior of explorers had its origin in things other than the traditional romantic, heroic, or imperialistic context in which exploration and explorers were being viewed by other scholars.

Since the pioneering work of Tillinghast and Nunn around the turn of the century, there have emerged three American scholars who, beginning in the 1920s, have revitalized and re-invented the study of exploration in the United States: the Harvard-trained Yankee geographer John Kirtland Wright whose works spanned the years from 1925 to 1965 but whose most seminal contributions came in the early 1940s; his fellow Harvard graduate, the iconoclastic essayist, novelist, and historian Bernard DeVoto, with his roots in Mormon Utah, whose exploratory trilogy capped by *Course of Empire* dominated the 1950s; and the Yale-educated Texan William H. Goetzmann, also the author of an exploratory trilogy that included the magiste-

---

7. William H. Tillinghast, "The Geographical Knowledge of the Ancients Considered in Relation to the Discovery of America," chapter one of volume one in Justin Winsor, ed., *A Narrative and Critical History of America*, 8 vols. (Boston and New York: Houghton-Mifflin, 1889–92).

8. George E. Nunn, *The Geographical Conceptions of Columbus* (New York: American Geographical Society, 1925).

rial *Exploration and Empire* of 1966 which not only garnered a Pulitzer prize but served as a foundation for much of the work in exploration studies since that time. Because these three scholars framed, in large measure, the kinds of questions we ask today about explorers and exploration, it seems that a good way to know where we are as scholars of exploration and how we got there is to examine their contributions briefly. It should be noted here that while most students of exploration will know the works of all these three, some will not. Indeed, some few of those who consider themselves exploration scholars may not really be conversant with the works of any of them. The literature of exploration is enormous and trying to determine which studies are the most important for our present understanding is individualistic and idiosyncratic. The three scholars whose works are offered up here are the ones I think the most important. Others who inquire into the exploratory process may come up with other names. But I am convinced that, through the nature of that mysterious process we call scholarship, each of the three have played an important role in the ways that we look at exploration today. All the more reason for us to pay some homage, as it were, to our intellectual underpinnings as we embark upon our collective scholarship of "surveying the record."

No discussion of exploration studies can begin without reference to John Kirtland Wright, a scholar whose unique perspectives on exploration and geographical knowledge framed most subsequent work in the field. Unfortunately Wright never held an academic post in a doctoral-granting institution and thus never trained graduate students. About his only contact with a subsequent generation of scholars came after his retirement from the directorship of the American Geographical Society. From his home in Lyme, New Hampshire, he periodically traveled south to Worcester, Massachusetts to give colloquia and seminars at Clark University. His contacts with Clark were particularly frequent while I was a doctoral student there and although he did not even hold a position as an adjunct member of the faculty of the Clark Graduate School of Geography, he was always available for consultation and more than willing to help those of us who were so inclined to sort out our own thinking on how best to approach the study of exploration. He served as an external member of my doctoral committee and one of the few disappointments of my professional life is that he died before my doctoral dissertation was finished—but not before he had made enormous contributions to it. Indeed, the topic of the dissertation itself and much of the work that has occupied me over the last thirty years came from a question Wright off-handedly tossed in my direction during the first year of my doctoral residence: "Wouldn't it be interesting," he asked, "if we knew something about the world view of Lewis and Clark in 1804?"[9] Unfortunately, Jack Wright never wrote books specifically about exploration although his massive *Geographical Lore at the Time of the Crusades* examined the role of exploratory literature in shaping the world view of late medieval Europe. But what Wright did do was to develop, through a series of remarkable articles, a methodology for studying the process of exploration. Wright's primary concern in studying exploration was its relevance for the history of geographical knowledge or what he called "geosophy . . . the study of geographical knowledge from any and all points of view."[10] It dealt with "the nature and expression of geographical knowledge both past and present." And it covered the "geographical ideas, true and false, of all manner of people—not only geographers but farmers and fishermen, business executives and poets, novelists and painters, Bedouins and Hottentots."[11] Geographical exploration was, for Wright, an exercise in both the implementation and development of geographical knowledge. Specific explorations, he noted, were primarily undertaken for commercial or political reasons and the acquisition of geographical knowledge was largely incidental. But adequately interpreted, the history of exploration must deal with geographical knowledge. This does not mean that exploratory studies should be dry catalogues of dates and names and routes, or romantic but unsubstantial (and unsubstantiated) chronicles of adventures in exotic lands. Rather, exploratory studies should "involve some examination of the complex factors that lie back of exploration in any given age or region" and, in turn, "should throw some light on the effects of the expansion of regional knowledge upon economic, political, social, spiritual, and intellectual con-

9. John L. Allen, *Passage Through the Garden: Lewis and Clark and the Geographical Images of the American Northwest* (Urbana, Illinois: University of Illinois Press, 1975).

10. John K. Wright, "*Terrae Incognitae*: The Place of the Imagination in Geography," presidential address to the Association of American Geographers, 1946; *Annals of the Association of American Geographers* 37 (1947):1–15; reprinted in John K. Wright, *Human Nature in Geography: Fourteen Papers 1925–1965* (Cambridge: Harvard University Press, 1966), pp. 68–88; citation, p. 83.

11. Wright, *Human Nature in Geography*, p. 83.

ditions." The process of exploration, for Wright, was "meaningless unless viewed against a wider historical setting."[12] What this boiled down to in methodological terms, was that studies of exploration should always seek to interpret three components of the process of exploration: "first, the influence of earlier geographical knowledge and belief upon the course of exploration; second, the actual relations between the course of exploration and the nature of the regions explored; and, third, the contributions made by exploration to subsequent geographical knowledge."[13] Wright was convinced that the systematic study of these three elements of exploration was of absorbing interest in itself: how did medieval and Renaissance geographical lore shape the exploratory goals of Christopher Columbus? Or, yes, what was the world view of Lewis and Clark in 1804 and how was it modified as they crossed a continent? Or what was the relationship between the explorations of the Rocky Mountain fur trade of the 1820s and 1830s and the subsequent agricultural migration and settlement of the American West? Wright was equally convinced that studying the three components of exploration was "absolutely essential to an adequate understanding of the enormously important part that exploration has played in human progress."[14]

We have no real way of knowing the full influence of the work of John K. Wright on Bernard DeVoto; both were Harvard-trained and their time there even over-lapped a bit. Beyond that the men were just about as different as it is possible to be in personality, background, style, habit, and approach to their work. After receiving his Harvard Ph.D., the quiet and self-effacing Wright went off to New York as librarian (and later director) of the American Geographical Society where his literary efforts were purely scholarly and contained within the community of professional geographers. Although barely known outside this small circle, he garnered great respect among his geographic peers and is the only member of the profession to have served as both Director of the American Geographical Society and President of the Association of American Geographers. The bombastic DeVoto, on the other

---

12. John K. Wright, "A Plea for the History of Geography," *Isis* 8 (1926): 477–491; reprinted in Wright, *Human Nature in Geography*, 11–23; citation, p. 18.

13. John K. Wright, "Where History and Geography Meet: Recent American Studies in the History of Exploration," *Proceedings of the Eighth American Scientific Congress*, IX (1943): 17–23; reprinted in Wright, *Human Nature in Geography*; citation, p. 27.

14. Wright, *Human Nature in Geography*, p. 27.

hand, became part of the Cambridge intellectual scene; he made his living as an essayist and novelist, was very much a member of the popular *literati*, and his column, "The Easy Chair" in *Harper's* was one of the most widely read in mid-century America. But as different as the two men were, they shared an intellectual interest in exploration and an on-and-off correspondence that lasted until DeVoto's death in 1955. While a graduate student at Clark I read—at Wright's urging—DeVoto's greatest book on exploration, *Course of Empire*, the capstone book of his magnificent trilogy that also included *Across the Wide Missouri*, one of the best books on the fur trade explorers of the Rocky Mountain fur trade, and *The Year of Decision, 1846* about (among other things) exploration and migration during the Mexican War.[15] *Course of Empire* began as a study of the Lewis and Clark Expedition but became something a great deal broader in scope. Shortly after my first reading of it, I wrote his widow, who still lived in Cambridge, to see if she could fill in the blanks regarding the source of DeVoto's ideas in *Course of Empire*, ideas that seemed so much like those Wright had written about in 1943, five years before DeVoto began work on *Course of Empire*. Avis DeVoto was a wonderful lady with a delightful sense of humor and an even more delightful willingness to humor a young scholar. We struck up a correspondence on how DeVoto dealt with geography and geographers during the research for *Course of Empire* and his other books. He was, she told me, an admirer of John K. Wright's ideas and was particularly intrigued by Wright's focus on geographical knowledge as the key element in exploration and his emphasis on the role of the regional environment in shaping expeditions in progress. "Benny always needed to know where he was in relation to where his explorers thought they were," she wrote me; "how high did they think the mountains were and how did they know that anyway, and where did they think the rivers ran and how did it all come together. . . we got lost many times trying to track down one of Benny's explorers."[16] DeVoto's biographer and friend, Wallace Stegner, also suggests that for DeVoto himself, a reliance on the geographical approach was troublesome because it

---

15. Bernard DeVoto, *Year of Decision 1846* (Boston: Houghton-Mifflin Co., 1942); *Across the Wide Missouri* (Boston: Houghton-Mifflin Co., 1947); and *Course of Empire* (Boston: Houghton-Mifflin Co., 1952).

16. Personal communication, John L. Allen from Avis DeVoto, April 13, 1964.

required so much of an author.[17] DeVoto began work on *Course of Empire* to focus tightly on the years from 1804 to 1806 and the trans-continental exploration of Lewis and Clark. But in tracking the influence of earlier geographical knowledge on the captains, DeVoto ended up reaching backward and backward and backward to Columbus and beyond and he didn't get to Lewis and Clark until chapter 11 of a 12-chapter book. "What do I do about geography?" he wrote a friend, trying to explain his methods in *Course of Empire*. "I mean what do I do about it? Have I got to go up the Saskatchewan? Or Lake Winnipeg? This guy Burpee appeared to know which peak was up but I got stalled when he had the Red River flowing both north and south in the same stretch. . . . I can't dig out the background of the background of the background. How the hell do I learn historical geography?"[18] Well, eventually learn it he did and when *Course of Empire* was completed, Wright's approach to exploration—an approach that Wright himself never applied to a book-length study—had undergone its first testing and was enormously successful. While DeVoto studied North American exploration before Lewis and Clark, he made his own exploration of the "boundaries and nature of his subject." As he did so, his own conception of exploratory studies changed, just as "the conception of the continent changed for the men who pushed into it" from south and east and north.[19] And what held the whole thing together was John K. Wright's conception of exploration as geosophy: the study of geographical knowledge. In referring to the knowledge upon which explorers based their exploratory objectives, DeVoto wrote: "We speak of the white light of knowledge but rainbows playing along the mist that hides the Islands of the Sea are there because the components of knowledge have different wave lengths. In the infinitely difficult act of thinking nothing is more difficult than to separate what is known from what is not known."[20] What DeVoto was referring to in this key passage was the crucial difference between that end of the spectrum of geographical knowledge that is based on experience and observation and that end of the spectrum where rumor and conjecture rule. The exploration of North

17. Wallace Stegner, *The Uneasy Chair* (Garden City, NY: Doubleday & Co., 1974).
18. Stegner, *The Uneasy Chair*, p. 329.
19. Stegner, *The Uneasy Chair*, p. 330.
20. DeVoto, *Course of Empire*, pp. 51–52.

America, he noted, involved enormous interaction between these two ends of the spectrum of knowledge and it was the task of the careful scholar of exploration to know the difference between them and to understand that often misconceptions were as important as realities in shaping the ideas that people had about portions of the earth's surface. DeVoto also adopted an important idea suggested by Wright as early as 1925 by postulating that geographical knowledge could be regionalized: that is, it was possible to think of some geographic areas as being characterized by geographical knowledge that was accurate and based on observation and experience, some areas where the existing geographical knowledge was purely conjectural, and some areas where fact and fancy mixed. In describing DeVoto's treatment of the Lewis and Clark Expedition, his biographer Wallace Stegner, recognized the Wright-DeVoto concept of "zones" of geographical knowledge of differential quality. Stegner noted that DeVoto described the transition of knowledge that Lewis and Clark made when, on their way up the Missouri River, they passed the Mandan villages of central North Dakota (a region visited by Canadian and St. Louis fur traders for decades). DeVoto moved Lewis and Clark "across the map . . . beyond the last cleanly drawn lines of knowledge" at the Mandans, through the twilight zone of hearsay" of the region of the upper Missouri, and into the Rocky Mountains "made of guess and wish and fable and the blankness of total ignorance." Lewis and Clark remained in the zone of what had been conjectural geography until they came out of the mountains and, eventually, into the Columbia—"a real river in a real and discovered geography." [21] For later scholars of exploration, this was an enormously important conceptual leap. [22]

Course of Empire did not meet with immediate favor with academic historians—for all that it won the National Book Award for history—but historical geographers, and particularly historical geographers who "did exploration," adopted the work quickly, viewing it as the book that could have (and perhaps should have) been written by John K. Wright, and from the mid-1950s onward, the bulk of the work done on exploration by historical

---

21. Stegner, *The Uneasy Chair*, p. 336.
22. The Wright-DeVoto regionalization of knowledge was refined and enlarged in John L. Allen, "An Analysis of the Exploratory Process," *Geographical Review*, 62 (1972): 13–39 and in Allen, *Passage through the Garden*.

geographers has been heavily flavored with the spice of Jack Wright and Benny DeVoto.

It took another decade and a massive work by a formal academic historian before many American historians would again begin to recognize that the study of exploration was a valid excursion for the historian to make. William H. Goetzmann came from a different historical tradition than Wright and DeVoto. He was, like DeVoto, a Westerner who came east to study. But unlike the cantabrigians Wright and DeVoto, Goetzmann was educated at Yale, a university with unique ties to the American West in a New England city with unique ties to the American West. The New Haven-Western connection came about partly through the William R. Coe Foundation that endowed a massive collection of Western Americana at Yale University (and also funded a library and a school of American Studies at the University of Wyoming) and partly through various other links such as the New Haven firearms industry for which the West and the Westerner were such a crucial market. The tradition of Western American studies was firmly fixed at Yale University when Goetzmann arrived there and in that tradition, studying western exploration was viewed as a valid and respectable academic exercise. Goetzmann prepared for his major work by doing his doctoral dissertation on one aspect of exploration in the American West. That work, published as *Army Exploration in the American West, 1803–1863*, was sound scholarship and conventional expeditionary history, chronicling the major explorers and explorations of the period.[23] It was such a solid piece of work that a major New York publisher asked for more and Goetzmann began thinking of a book with broader intellectual and geographic horizons. Goetzmann was stimulated by the collaborative work of American scholars R. A. Skelton and William Cumming and the British scholars David Beers Quinn and Glyndwr Williams, by the American western historian Dale Morgan and the cartographic historian Carl I. Wheat, and by Thomas Manning's fledgling history of the U.S. Geological Survey.[24] Common to all these works was a heavy dollop of imagery, whether it be reliance upon the graphic arts of

23. William H. Goetzmann, *Army Exploration in the American West 1803–1863* (New Haven: Yale University Press, 1959).

24. W. P. Cumming, R. A. Skelton, and D. B. Quinn, *The Discovery of North America* (London: Peter Elek, 1971); W. P. Cumming, S. E. Hillier, D. B. Quinn, and G. Williams, *The Exploration of North America* (London: Peter Elek, 1974); Dale Morgan, *Jedediah Smith and*

exploration or the repeated attempts to convey landscapes as maps that both hid and revealed geographical lore. Goetzmann's *Exploration and Empire: the Explorer and the Scientist in the Winning of the American West* was published in 1966 and garnered both the Parkman Award and the Pulitzer Prize for history.[25] Although he came to it independently, throughout *Exploration and Empire*, Goetzmann utilized the same tripartite methodology for studying exploration recommended by John K. Wright and attempted by DeVoto in *Course of Empire*—examining the influence of earlier geographical knowledge upon explorers, studying the relationship between exploration and the character of the region explored, and recording the subsequent influence of explorations on both geographical knowledge and broader historical processes.

Unlike DeVoto's sprawling, centuries-long examination of American exploration, Goetzmann's work focused tightly on the nineteenth century and the American confrontation with unknown geography during that century. Goetzmann's central thesis was that exploration had enormous impact upon American culture and therefore deserved greater attention than historians had been giving it. The American West provided an excellent case study to test this idea, to show how western exploration "helped to create in the centers of dominant culture a series of images which conditioned popular attitudes and public policy concerning the new lands."[26] "Out of the charts and travel literature," wrote Goetzmann, out of the "scientific reports, the collections of exotic specimens, the lithographs, the photographs, the adventure novels and popular biographies, the schoolboy geographies, the museums, and even the children's books emerged a series of impressions—often a series of first impressions unconsciously conditioned by the established culture of the time—which became a crucial factor in shaping the long-range destiny of the newly discovered places and their peoples, and which at the same time altered forever the established culture."[27] This was a theme to which Goetzmann returned in greatly expanded form in the

the *Opening of the West* (Indianapolis: Bobbs Merrill, 1953); Carl I. Wheat, *Mapping the Trans-Mississippi West*, 5 vols. (San Francisco: Institute of Historical Cartography, 1954).

25. William H. Goetzmann, *Exploration and Empire: the Explorer and the Scientist in the Winning of the American West* (New York: Alfred A. Knopf, 1966).

26. Goetzmann, *Exploration and Empire*, p. ix.

27. Goetzmann, *Exploration and Empire*, pp. ix–x.

third book of his trilogy *New Lands, New Men: America and the Second Great Age of Discovery*, published in 1986.[28] It also was a theme that evokes the powerful memory of John K. Wright's notion that understanding "the geographical ideas, true and false, of all manner of people—not only geographers but farmers and fishermen, business executives and poets, novelists and painters, Bedouins and Hottentots" is necessary in order to assess the impact of those ideas. But Goetzmann went beyond Wright in that rather than just suggesting the links between the informal geographical lore in art and literature, he devoted considerable space in *Exploration and Empire* to portrayals of maps and sketches and lithographs and paintings and photographs and to discussions of how these materials shaped the character of American geographical images of the West. DeVoto had, in *Across the Wide Missouri*, done somewhat the same kind of thing in presenting the works of Alfred Jacob Miller as an integral part of the geographical lore of the Rocky Mountain fur trade. But Goetzmann did it more coherently and with more intention, following it with such later works as the companion book to the PBS television series *The West of the Imagination*.[29] Partly as a result, today we have scholars who specialize in the study of expeditionary art and others who focus on visual imagery as a means of comprehending the geographical lore of a particular time and place.[30]

Again independently mirroring Wright, Goetzmann also departed dramatically from earlier historians in his approach to exploration as a process rather than as a series of "dramatic discoveries—isolated events, colorful and even interesting perhaps, but of little consequence to the basic sweep of civilization."[31] Exploration, before Goetzmann's *Exploration and Empire* was rarely "viewed as a continuous form of activity or mode of behavior" and the words "exploration" and "discovery" were often "linked in the popular imagination simply as interchangeable synonyms for 'adventure.'"[32] For Goetzmann, as for Wright and DeVoto, exploration was something a

28. William H. Goetzmann, *New Lands, New Men: America and the Second Great Age of Discovery* (New York: W. W. Norton & Co., 1986).

29. William H. and William N. Goetzmann, *The West of the Imagination* (New York: W. W. Norton & Co., 1986).

30. *Cf.* John L. Allen, "Horizons of Romance: Invention of the Romantic Tradition of the American West," *Journal of Historical Geography*, 18 (1992): 27–40.

31. Goetzmann, *Exploration and Empire*, p. xi.

32. Goetzmann, *Exploration and Empire*, p. xi.

great deal more than adventure: it was purposeful seeking, itself a branch of science, a process rather than an event. The importance of viewing exploration as process was further underscored by Goetzmann when he noted — again echoing Wright and DeVoto — that the process of exploration is conditioned by earlier geographical lore and centers of cultural activity. The "purposes, goals, and evaluation of new data" that are part of any exploratory experience "are to a great extent set by the previous experiences, the values, the kinds and categories of existing knowledge, and the current objectives of the civilized centers from which the explorer sets out on his quest."[33] Jack Wright could not have said it any more clearly.

There were other important scholars of the exploratory process whose work paralleled that of Wright and DeVoto and Goetzmann in both temporal and spatial terms. But there were, I think, no other scholars whose ideas were so crucial for the present generation of those who seek to understand the process of exploration. Let us not forget those who provided us with the instruments with which we have defined the landscapes of our imaginations.

33. Goetzmann, *Exploration and Empire*, p. xi.

A NEW MODE OF THINKING
Creating a National Geography
in the Early Republic [1]

Introduction

In an argument of great subtlety Benedict Anderson argued that nations were not so much facts of race or ethnicity.[2] Rather, they were imagined communities. Anderson paid particular attention to the role of print capitalism in creating a national discourse, giving theoretical substance to the remark of the playwright Arthur Miller that "a good newspaper, I suppose, is a nation talking to itself." In a later elaboration Anderson identified three institutions of power: the *census*, the *map* and the *museum* that together allowed the state to imagine the people under its dominance, the geographic territory under control and the nature of historical legitimacy.[3] In this paper I want to concentrate on the *map* and extend its definition to include geographic representation.

The construction of national identity has been an important subject of recent writings. Attention has focused on the narrative of the nation, the notion of national environmental ideologies, the connection with gender and race, as well as developing Anderson's perspective in asking such basic

---

1. This paper was based on work undertaken at the American Philosophical Society Library under the generous support of an Andrew W. Mellon Resident Fellowship.
2. Benedict Anderson, *Imagined Communities* (London: Verso, 1983).
3. Benedict Anderson, *Imagined Communities*, revised ed. (London: Verso, 1991).

questions about imagined community and who imagines what and when.[4] In this paper I want to look at the connections between the elaboration of a national geography and the construction of national identity in a place and at a time of great plasticity, when neither "nationals" were firmly fixed. The basic premise of this paper is that the construction of national identity involves the creation of a national geography. I illustrate this argument with reference to the creation of a national geography in the early years of the United States. This geography was created through the reworking of "imported" geographies as well as the development of distinctly "American" geographies. The works of Jedidiah Morse and John Melish are examined in some detail, both their geographical as well as their more obviously "national" writings. The paper shows how the construction of a national identity and a national geography were embodied in notions of national exceptionalism, national expansion and continental dominance. The *national* in the national geography is revealed in the other writings of these early geography writers. The moralized, racialized and gendered nature of this discourse is also noted.

Geographical Concerns

In many editions of his *Geography Made Easy*, first published in 1784, Jedidiah Morse, geographer and Congregational minister, wrote of the United States of America,

> Till the year 1784 . . . the geography of this part of the world was unwritten, and indeed very imperfectly known to any one. Previously to this period we seldom pretended to write, and hardly to think for ourselves. We humbly received from Great-Britain our laws, our manners, our books, and our modes of thinking; and our youth were educated as British subjects, not as they have since been, as citizens of a free and independent na-

4. H. Bhabha, ed., *Nation and Narration* (London: Routledge, 1990); P. Chatterjee, "Whose Imagined Community?" in G. Balakrishna, ed., *Mapping the Nation* (London: Verso, 1996), pp. 214–25; P. Duara, "Historicizing National Identity, or Who Imagines What and When?" in G. Eley and R. Suny, eds., *Becoming National* (Oxford: Oxford University Press, 1996), pp. 151–77; J. R. Short, *Imagined Country* (London: Routledge, 1991).

tion. The Revolution has proved favorable to science in general among us; particularly to that of the Geography of our own country.[5]

The American Revolution constituted a break with the past, a break with Britain, a break with London. The rupture was both political and intellectual. The colonial connection was one of economic ties and of political power but, as Morse noted, also one of "modes of thinking." Britain had not only economic and political power over its New World colony, it maintained cultural hegemony. Books were imported from Britain, ideas were diffused out from the imperial center and the manners and mores of elite colonial society had their origin in Britain. Whereas the Revolution created political independence, cultural independence was more difficult to achieve. The North American colonials had forged a distinctive culture from the stream of diverse migrants making their way in the New World. But until the Revolution a distinct culture was the result of pragmatic adjustment, not a conscious endeavor.

The search for national identity in the new Republic involved experiments in fine arts, architecture, fiction, science and philosophy and linguistics. Shortly after the Revolution Noah Webster demanded that, "Every engine should be employed to render the people of the country national, to call their attachment home to their country; and to inspire them with the pride of national character."[6] Some of the experiments are better known than others and their legacy continues. Webster himself published his *American Spelling Book* in 1783 and distinguished distinct American forms of spelling (the u was dropped from *colour* and *labour*, the re was reversed in *theatre* and *centre*) and new words were introduced such as *tomahawk* and *prairies* not used by the English lexicographers.

In 1743 when he established the American Philosophical Society Benjamin Franklin proposed that there be seven members: a physician, a botanist, a mathematician, a chemist, a mechanician, a natural philosopher and a geographer. Most of the categories would still be appropriate for a similar venture planned today, albeit with engineer for mechanician and physicist

---

5. J. Morse, *Geography Made Easy*, 20th edition (Utica: Williams, 1819), p. iii.
6. R. M. Rollins, *The Long Journey of Noah Webster* (Philadelphia: University of Pennsylvannia Press, 1980), p. 37.

for natural philosopher. One category stands out today: that of geographer. It was, however, not surprising at the time. There was an intense interest in geographical issues and concerns. A look again at Franklin's seven categories shows that there was no historian or political scientist, no economist, or social scientist. The list was dominated by the natural sciences with geography as the sole representative of what we now call the social sciences. Geography had a much broader definition then than now; it encompassed history, government, economics and public affairs. To be interested in geography was to be interested in the broad sweep of social affairs. Geography, with its wide definition, was an important part of the discourse of informed public opinion. A geographical discourse was an essential ingredient of literate public opinion and broader general knowledge.

But the geographical concern was not simply a result of the broad sweep of Geography. The narrower concerns of cartographic representation, map-making and geographic description were also important. The need to write a national geography was part of the broader attempt at cultural independence and the deeper search for a national identity. Jefferson's *Notes on Virginia* (1784–85) was both a geographic description of his state and a counterblast to those Old World writers and scientists who derided the New World. Geographical representation was an important element in the presentation of the country; a national geography was a portrait in words and maps, a collection of narratives that gave a picture and told the story of an emerging nation.

The Reworking of Imported Geography

Even after political independence the intellectual life in the new Republic was dependent on the importation of books and ideas from Britain. Books and the ideas in books were eagerly consumed in the colonial society. Much of colonial trade was in books and texts. Even after the Revolution books written and published in Britain were sold in the major cities of the new republic. The reprinting of books first published in Britain was the bread and butter trade of the early American printing industry. In order to create national identity, the imports from Britain had to be transformed and ultimately superseded. This was a conscious, pre-determined act of nationalism.

GUTHRIE'S GEOGRAPHY

One of the most popular geography texts before and even after the Revolution was known simply as *Guthrie's Geography*. William Guthrie (1708–1770) was born in Brechin in Scotland. He was an eager educator who wrote general histories and translated Cicero. His most famous work was his geography text. His first geography book was entitled *General View of geography . . . or an attempt to impress on the mind of a school-boy a general idea*. It first came out in 1769 and proved very popular. A second edition entitled *A new geographical, historical, and commercial grammar; and present state of the several kingdoms of the world . . . Illustrated with large maps* soon followed. The title soon became known as *Guthrie's Geography* and numerous editions appeared. The third in 1771, the twenty fourth in 1827 and even as late as 1842 new and revised editions were sold. *Guthrie's Geography* survived long after William Guthrie died. The name recognition assured publishers of a steady market for updated versions. It grew to a massive text, the 1795 (fifteenth edition) had 956 pages and twenty-five maps and contained chapters on planets, the earth, empires, climate, and the history of nations. The largest section was a description of the different countries of the world. To keep up with the expanding geographical knowledge, subsequent editions lead off with the latest discoveries. The 1795 edition, for example, had 164 pages of "New Discoveries."

In the later editions, there is an explicit acknowledgment of an interconnected world and a global economy: "In considering the present state of nations, few circumstances are more important than their mutual intercourse. This is chiefly brought about by commerce, the prime mover in the economy of modern states."[7] The global connections are still described from a particular place. The writing is centered in Britain in two ways. First, Britain is roundly praised: "the people are opulent, have great influence, and claim, of course, a proper share of attention."[8] The reference to proper share of attention is to head off any ideas that the country is suitable or ripe for revolution; social stability is assured by the "proper share of attention." Second, the world is centered on London by the establishment of the prime

---

7. W. Guthrie, *A New System of Geography* 11th ed. (London: Dilley, 1788), p. 7.
8. Ibid., p. 6.

888   A NEW GEOGRAPHICAL TABLE.

Names of Places.	Provinces.	Countries.	Quarter.	Lat. D. M.	Long. D. M.
Kiow,	Ukraine,	Ruffia,	Europe	50-30N.	31-12 E.
Kola,	Lapland,	Ruffia,	Europe	68-52N.	33-13 E.
Koningfberg,	Pruffia,	Poland,	Europe	54-43N.	21-35 E.
Lancafter,	Lancafhire,	England,	Europe	54-05N.	02-55 E.
Levantfea	Coaft of	Syria,	Afia	Mediterranean fea.	
Laguna,	Teneriffe,	Canaries,	A, Ocean	28-28N.	16-13W.
Landau,	Alface,	France,	Europe	49-11N.	08-02 E.
Landfcroon,	Schonen,	Sweden,	Europe	55-52N.	12-51 E.
Laufanne,	Cant. of Vaud.	Switzerland,	Europe	46-31N.	06-50 E.
Leeds,	Yorkfhire,	England,	Europe	53-48N.	01-29W.
Leicefter,	Leicefterfhire,	England,	Europe	52-38N.	01-03W.
Leipfic,	Saxony,	Germany,	Europe	51-19N.	12-25 E.
Leper's Ifland,	S. Pacific	Ocean,	Afia	15-23 S.	168-03 E.
Lefkard,	Cornwall,	England,	Europe	50-26N.	04-36W.
Lefparre,	Guienne,	France,	Europe	45-18N.	00-52W.
Leyden,	Holland,	Netherlands,	Europe	52-10N.	04-32 E.
Leith,	Edinburghfh.	Scotland,	Europe	55-58N.	03-00W.
Lahor,	Lahor,	Eaft India,	Afia	32-40N.	75-30 E.
Linlithgow,	Linlithgowfh.	Scotland,	Europe	55-56N.	03-30W.
Lincoln,	Lincolnfhire,	England,	Europe	53-15N.	00-27W.
Lima,	Peru,	South	America	12-01 S.	76-44W.
Liege,	Bifh. of Liege,	Netherlands,	Europe	50-37N.	05-40 E.
Limoges,	Limoges,	France,	Europe	45-49N.	01-20 E.
Lintz,	Auftria,	Germany,	Europe	48-16N.	13-57 E.
Lifle,	Fren. Flanders	Netherlands,	Europe	50-37N.	03-09 E.
Lifbon,	Eftremadura,	Portugal,	Europe	38-42N.	09-04W.
Lizard Point,	Cornwall,	England,	Europe	49-57N.	05-10W.
Louifburg,	C. Breton Ifle,	North	America	45-53N.	59-48W.
Limerick,	Limerickfhire,	Ireland,	Europe	52-35N.	08-18W.
Litchfield,	Staffordfhire,	England,	Europe	52-43N.	01-04W.
Loretto,	Pope's Territ.	Italy,	Europe	43-15N.	14-15 E.
Loxpon,	Middlefex,	England,	Europe	51-31N.	1ft Merid.
Londonderry,	Londonderry,	Ireland,	Europe	50-00N.	07-40W.
Louveau,	Siam,	Eaft India,	Afia	12-42N.	100-56 E.
Louvain,	Auftr. Brabant	Netherlands,	Europe	50-53N.	04-49 E.
Lubec,	Holftein,	Germany,	Europe	54-00N.	11-40 E.
St. Lucia Ifle,	Windward Ifles	Weft Indies,	N. Amer.	13-24N.	60-46W.
Lunden,	Gothland,	Sweden,	Europe	55-41N.	13-26 E.
Luneville,	Lorrain,	France,	Europe	48-35N.	06-35 E.
Luxemburg,	Luxemburg,	Netherlands,	Europe	49-37N.	06-16 E.
Lyons,	Lyons,	France,	Europe	45-45N.	04-54 E.
Macao,	Canton,	China,	Afia	22-12N.	113-51 E.
Macaffar,	Celebes Ifle,	Eaft India,	Afia	05-09 S.	119-53 E.
Madeira, Funchal,	Atlantic	Ocean,	Africa	32-37N.	17-01W.
Madras,	Coromandel,	Eaft India,	Afia	13-04N.	80-33 E.
MADRID,	New Caftile,	Spain,	Europe	40-25N.	03-20 E.
Magdalena Ifle	South	Pacific Ocean,	Afia	10-25 S.	138-44W.
Mahon Port,	Minorca,	Mediterr. fea,	Europe	39-50N.	03-53 E.
Majorca,	Ifle,	Mediterr. fea,	Europe	39-35N.	02-34 E.
Malacca,	Malacca,	Eaft India,	Afia	02-12N.	102-10 E.

8

Figure 1. Excerpt from gazetteer in Guthrie's Geography *1788.*

meridian in London. At the end of almost all of the editions of the book there is "A new Geographical Table," an early gazetteer giving the name of places and alongside their province, country, continent, latitude and longitude. London is the first meridian (Figure 1).

Guthrie's Geography contained a series of maps. The 1788 eleventh edition had twenty-one maps while the 1795 fifteenth edition had twenty-five maps. There is no map of the United States as such in either volume; it is included in a map of North America. In the 1788 map there is a general map of North America which includes present day Canada, United States and part of Mexico (Figure 2). While Canada is noted, there is no naming

Figure 2. *A map of North America in* Guthrie's Geography *1788.*

of the United States. It is pushed up against a clearly depicted Canada and a vast wilderness beyond the Mississippi. The individual states have indistinct boundaries with no obvious claims nor connections to the huge western lands which have Spanish or English names. The map depicts the United States as a ragtag group of small states clustering along the eastern seaboard. The map exaggerates the size of Canada and the west and 'shrinks' the new republic to minor prominence. For an empire that has just lost its colonies it is fitting that the new Republic is not given pride of place, its own name or continental significance. In the 1795 edition, there are two maps of North America; one of Canada and the Great Lakes, the other covers the United States but the names of the states are not given. The map is full of Indian names, especially in the west which is depicted as peopled, full of potential allies and trading partners. It is not an empty wilderness ripe for US expansion, but a populated land, a place already inhabited. In both maps the longitude is given from London.

The construction of an independent, national geography meant that these imports had to be given an "American" perspective. An important figure in the development of an American perspective was Mathew Carey (1760 – 1839) whose life and work spanned the full flowering of book publishing in the United States.[9] He was born in Dublin on January 28, 1760 to the family of a hard-working baker who ensured a good education for all of his five sons. From an early age Carey was fascinated by printing and publishing. Against his father's wishes he apprenticed himself to Thomas Mc-Donnel, bookseller and publisher of the *Hibernian Journal* an anti-English, pro-American publication. Throughout his life Carey expressed the political sentiments espoused in this Journal. He was consistently anti-English.

On the first day of November, 1784, Carey arrived in Philadelphia, then the largest city in the country and the center of printing and publication. Philadelphia had one of the most sophisticated and cosmopolitan populations in the country. It was the leading city of scientific and medical knowledge as well as commerce. There was a relatively large population of readers and potential bookbuyers. The center of political debate, it was soon to become the temporary capital of the new Republic, a position it held for

---

9. J. Green, *Mathew Carey: Publisher and Patriot* (Philadelphia: Library Company of Philadelphia, 1985).

the final decade of the eighteenth century. Carey began his career in the city
by publishing a newspaper, the *Pennsylvania Evening Herald*, and later a
magazine, *The American Museum*. Carey also began to publish books. In
1794 he published *Guthrie's Geography*,[10] one of the largest undertakings in
American publishing. He produced 2,500 copies of the book, a large number for the time. Only Carey could take such a risk because of his reputation and distribution network. He hoped to use his national reputation and
the national network of agents he had used in distributing his magazine to
sell so many copies. He borrowed heavily to pay for the printing. It was a
gamble to publish so many copies of such an expensive book; it sold for
$16, a hefty price tag.

Some changes were made between the British version and the American version of *Guthrie's Geography*. The biggest change was the written section on the United States and the maps. Carey got Jedidiah Morse to write
a section on the United States. When the 1795 British *Guthrie's* noted "No
country in Europe equals England in the beauty of its prospects, or the opu-
lence of its inhabitants"; Carey's edition noted that "England swarms with
beggars." The change in orientation, the writing from a different place is
encapsulated in the change in the gazetteer, now longitude was given from
Philadelphia rather than London (Figure 3). There was no fixed prime
meridian at the time. There was no international agreement, which was to
come much later, at the International Meridian Conference of 1884. There
is no natural prime meridian of longitude. Unlike the equator which fixes
the latitude with a natural phenomenon, the first line of longitude is entirely a social construct, a construct which reflects nationalism as well as
science. By putting Philadelphia as the prime meridian, Carey was making
a statement—the new Republic was going to have its own measuring of
longitude.

Carey's edition of *Guthrie's Geography* also involved changes in cartographic representation. Not only did Carey get new maps drawn but they
formed the basis for some of the first atlases produced in the Republic. In the
second volume of *Guthrie's,* published by Carey in 1795, there were forty-
seven maps and these maps formed the basis for Carey's 1795 *American*

---

    10. W. Guthrie, *A New System of Geography*, 1st American ed. (Philadelphia: Mathew
Carey, 1794).

(10)   A NEW GEOGRAPHICAL TABLE.

Names of Places.	Provinces.	Countries.	Quarter.	Latitude. D. M.	Longitude. D. M.
Patrixfiord	Iceland	N. Atlan. Ocean	Europe	65-35 N.	60-55 E.
Pau	Bearn	France	Europe	43-15 N.	74-56 E.
St. Paul's Ifle	South	Indian Ocean	Africa	37-51 S.	152-53 E.
Pegu	Pegu	Eaft-Indies	Afia	17-00 N.	172-00 E.
Peking	Petchi-li	China	Afia	39-54 N.	168-31 W.
Pelew	Iflands	Pacific	Ocean	7-00 N.	150-00 W.
Pembroke	Pembrokefhire	Wales	Europe	51-45 N.	70-10 E.
PENSACOLA	Weft Florida	North	America	30-22 N.	12-20 W.
Penzance	Cornwall	England	Europe	50-08 N.	69-00 E.
Perigueux	Guienne	France	Europe	45-11 N.	75-48 E.
Perinaldi	Genoa	Italy	Europe	43-53 N.	82-45 E.
Perth	Perthfhire	Scotland	Europe	56-22 N.	71-48 E.
Perth-Amboy	New-Jerfey	North	America	40-30 N.	00-40 E.
Perfepolis	Irac Agem	Perfia	Afia	30-30 N.	129-00 E.
St. Peters' Fort	Martinico	Weft-Indies	N. America	14-44 N.	13-44 E.
St. Peter's Ifle	North	Atlantic Ocean	America	46-46 N.	18-48 E.
PETERSBURG	Ingria	Ruffia	Europe	59-56 N.	105-24 E.
Petropawlofkoi	Kamtfchatka	Ruffia	Afia	53-01 N.	126-20 W.
PHILADELPHIA	Pennfylvania	North	America	39-56 N.	Firft merid.
St. Philip's Fort	Minorca	Mediterr. Sea	Europe	39-50 N.	78-53 E.
Pickerfgill Ifle	South	Atlantic Ocean	America	54-42 S.	38-07 E.
Pico	Azores	Atlantic Ocean	Europe	38-28 N.	46-39 E.
Pines, Ifle of	N. Caledonia	Pacific Ocean	Afia	22-38 S.	117-17 W.
Pifa	Tufcany	Italy	Europe	43-43 N.	85-17 E.
Placentia	Newfoundland Ifle	North	America	47-26 N.	20-00 E.
Plymouth	Devonfhire	England	Europe	50-22 N.	70-50 E.
Plymouth	Maffachufetts	New-England	North America	41-48 N.	71-35 E.
Pollingen	Swabia	Germany	Europe	47-48 N.	85-48 E.
Pondicherry	Coromandel	Eaft-Indies	Afia	11-41 N.	154-57 E.
Ponoi	Lapland	Ruffia	Europe	67-06 N.	111-28 E.
Porto Bello	Terra Firma	South	America	9-33 N.	4-45 W.
Porto Sancto Ifle	Madeira	Atlantic Ocean	Africa	32-58 N.	58-40 E.
Port Royal	Jamaica	Weft-Indies	America	18-00 N.	1-40 E.
Port Royal	Martinico	Weft-Indies	America	14-35 N.	13-56 E.
Portland Ifle	South	Pacific Ocean	Afia	39-25 S.	106-43 W.
Portland Ifle	North	Atlantic Ocean	Europe	63-22 N.	56-11 E.
Portfmouth	Hampfhire	England	Europe	50-47 N.	73-59 E.
Portfmouth	New-England	North	America	43-10 N.	4-40 E.
Potofi	Peru	South	America	21-00 S.	2-00 W.
Prague	Bohemia	Europe	50-04 N.	89-50 E.	
Prefburg	Upper	Hungary	Europe	48-20 N.	57-30 E.
Prefton	Lancafhire	England	Europe	53-45 N.	72-10 E.
Prince of Wales' Fort	New N. Wales,	North	America	58-47 N.	18-58 W.
Providence	New-England	North	America	41-50 N.	3-39 E.
Pulo Candor Ifle	Indian Ocean	Eaft Indies	Afia	8-40 N.	177-35 W.
Pulo Timor Ifle	Gulf of Siam,	Eaft Indies	Afia	3-00 N.	179-30 E.
Pyleftaart Ifle	South	Pacific Ocean	Afia	22-23 S.	99-24 W.
Quebec	Canada	North	America	46-55 N.	5-12 E.
Queen Charlotte's Ifle	South	Pacific Ocean	Afia	10-11 S.	88-35 W.
St. Quintin	Picardy	France	Europe	49-50 N.	78-22 E.
Quito	Peru	South	America	0-13 S.	2-55 W.
Ragufa	Dalmatia	Venice	Europe	42-45 N.	93-25 E.
Ramhead	Cornwall	England	Europe	50-18 N.	70-45 E.
Ratifbon	Bavaria	Germany	Europe	48-56 N.	87-05 E.

Figure 3. Excerpt from gazetteer in first American edition of Guthrie's Geography *(1794).*

Atlas (twenty-one maps) and his 1796 *General Atlas* (forty-seven maps). All the maps are marked "*Engraved for Carey's American edition of Guthrie's Geography improved.*" Many of the engravings were done by Samuel Lewis, a writing and drawing master of Philadelphia who exhibited landscapes, still lifes, watercolor drawings and trompe l'oeil from 1795 to 1817. Although most of the maps of the world and countries outside the United States remained the same, the maps produced by Carey for his edition of *Guthrie* and for his *General* and *American* atlases constitute a major change in geographic representation. Philadelphia was used as the prime meridian of longitude in addtion to London. Many of the maps used a dual system with Philadelphia at the top and London at the bottom. Philadelphia was cited as an act of nationalism while the cultural and scientific dominance of London meant that it was also used in a uniquely parallel system that reflected national aspirations as well as an awareness of the power center in international scientific discourse.

Both the *General Atlas* and the *American Atlas* contained only maps; there was no text. It was a collection of maps with little consistency in scale or key. The atlases were collections of maps taken from a variety of sources, however, the *American Atlas* represents a significant departure as a cartographic collection. It contains maps of all of the states as well as the United States. The atlases helped the states to become united by representing them together in a shared text.

Carey was a publisher and a patriot. His geography texts were not incidental to his life and work. They were published because there was a market, Carey was a businessman; but he was also a patriot, eager to represent his adopted country in a vigorous and independent manner. He could also read a market and knew there was a demand for "American" material. *Guthrie's Geography* and the atlases were not only publishing ventures, they were acts of nationalism. The book and the atlases were widely distributed to the cultural and political elite. Among the subscribers were George Washington, Benjamin Rush and David Rittenhouse. It was an important element in the library of the political and intellectual elite of Philadelphia and the wider nation.

Jedidiah Morse: "Father of American Geography"

MAKING GEOGRAPHY EASY

Jedidiah Morse was a Congregational clergyman and writer of geography books. Recent biographers have repeated the assertion that he was the Father of American Geography although they have all tended to concentrate on his role in religious debates rather than his geographical work.[11]

Morse was born in Woodstock, Connecticut on August 23, 1761. He attended Yale College and on his graduation in 1783, he decided to enter the ministry. He remained in New Haven for two more years studying theology, and to support himself he wrote a school textbook on geography. It was entitled *Geography Made Easy*. It was first published in 1784 with the subtitle *Being a short but comprehensive system of that very useful and agreeable science*. It proved immensely popular. It was aimed at an American audience; it was decidedly patriotic both in its praise of the United States and persuasive in its argument that a distinctly American geography should be written and read. There were few competitors; it was one of the first national textbooks produced in the new Republic written by a native-born which sought to both describe and praise the new country. It was the first geography book written and printed in the United States. The book went through many editions and for the rest of the century was reissued on a regular basis; the second edition came out in 1790, the third in 1791, the fourth in 1794, the fifth in 1790 and a sixth in 1798. In the preface to a later edition Morse notes:

> No national government holds out to its subjects so many alluring motives to obtain an accurate knowledge of their own country , and of its various interests as that of the UNITED STATES OF AMERICA. . . . To discharge the duties of public office with honor and applause, the history, policy, commerce, productions, particular advantages and interests of the several states ought to be thoroughly understood. It is obviously wise and prudent, then, to initiate our youth into the knowledge of these things, and thus to form their minds upon correct principles, and prepare them for future

11. R. J. Moss, *The Life of Jedidiah Morse: A Station of Peculiar Exposure* (Knoxville: University of Tennessee Press, 1995); J. W. Phillips, *Jedidiah Morse and New England Congregationalism* (New Brunswick: Rutgers University Press, 1983).

usefulness. There is no science better adapted to the capacities of youth, or more likely to engage their attention than Geography . . . This part of ed-ucation was long neglected in America. Our young men, formerly, were much better acquainted with the Geography of Europe and Asia than with that of their own country. . . .[12]

The book is in two parts. The first includes general remarks on the solar sys-tem, globes and maps, volcanoes and political divisions of the world. The second part of the book is a regional geography which describes the differ-ent parts of the world. The emphasis is firmly on North America which in the 1819 edition takes up pages 53–246, while Europe is considered in pages 247–312, Asia 315–38, and Africa 340–58.

The historic description of the United States follows the conventional view of a land of darkness awaiting the light of European presence:

When North-America was first visited by Europeans, it might be regarded, except Mexico, as one immense forest, inhabited by wild animals, and by a great number of savage tribes, who subsisted by hunting and fishing.[13]

The largest section is devoted to the United States (pp 88–213), which is by far the largest entry; it is entitled *Independent America or, The United States*, and is full of nationalist praise for the people, a "free and vigorous yeo-manry" and their political institutions. The later editions of the book also contain maps. Figure 4 is a map of the United States taken from the 1819 edition. Compare this with Figure 2 and note how the country is now repre-sented on its own and how the individual states are enumerated. There are still traces of British influence. The longitude is given from Greenwich as well as Washington and the New Albion notation in present day California is a distant echo of an English presence reproduced by a lazy cartographer.

The bulk of the entry on the United States is taken up with separate sec-tions devoted to each state. Each state is given detailed description including situation and extent, boundaries, population of counties according to 1810 census, the face (physical geography) of the country, bays, lakes and rivers, soil and productions, minerals and fossils, manufactures and commerce,

12. J. Morse, *Geography Made Easy*, 20th edition (Utica: Williams, 1819), p. iii.
13. Ibid., p. 66.

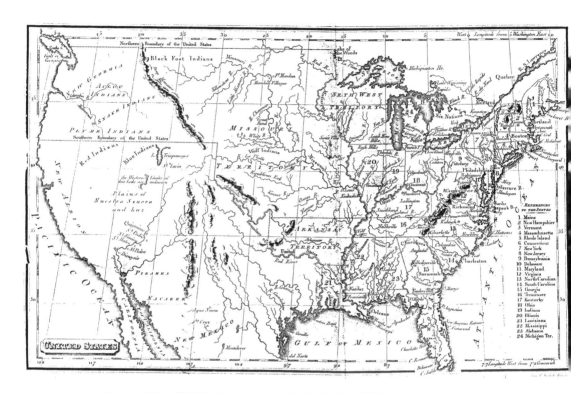

Figure 4. Map of USA in Morse's Geography Made Easy *1819.*

education, cities and towns. Some mention is also made of Indians. For example in the New York entry he writes of "the remains of the Six Confederated Nations . . . their whole number is supposed to be about 6000 souls" (out of nearly 1 million). Under Georgia he has a longer description of the native-Americans and he notes that the Creek Indians are "a hardy, sagacious, polite people, extremely jealous of their rights."

Morse's descriptions were not separate from his religious beliefs and moral standards. Under cities and towns he noted "New-orleans in the licentiousness of its morals, rivals the corruption of the old world." Morse saw New England as the source of American democracy and the container of solid enduring values of Christian worship and hard-work. He praised the yeoman farmer of New England and took a more jaundiced view of the slave owners in the south. The south, in the moral geography that underpinned his regional geography, was a place of feckless, indolent people lax in morals and and ripe with sin. His moralizing was a constant in his descriptions of southern regions and cities. Morse was only partially concerned with the scientific principles of a general geography. He wanted to create a national geography that was not a socially neutral depiction of abstract principles, but a body of knowledge that would provide an ideological cement for civic education and national cohesion, and inculcate moral virtues and values. His geography text was not just an academic book, it was part of a wider, deeper attempt to create a morally correct American citizenry.

The year after *Geography Made Easy* first came out Morse was licensed to preach. His working life then followed a dual track, sometimes overlapping, sometimes in conflict. On the one hand he became a Congregational minister. After preaching in Georgia and New York he accepted a position at Charleston in Massachusetts, a position he held for over thirty years. Morse took an active role in the religious debates of the day. He was a profoundly orthodox Calvinist who organized against the liberal Christians, the Unitarians. He opposed the election of Henry Ware to a professorship at Harvard in 1805, he launched and edited a magazine the *Panoplist* which preached the orthodox position, and he helped to found the Andover Theological Seminary in 1808. He was unremitting in his attack against what he saw as the inroads of the liberals and was instrumental in forcing out the Unitarian churches from the Congregationalists. He was also involved in evangelical missions. He helped to found the New England Tract Society in

1814 and the American Bible Society in 1816. He was secretary of the Society for Propagating the Gospel among the Indians in North America. His geographic writings are suffused with his religious convictions and his moral concerns. His was a moralized geography.

Geography Made Easy was so popular and successful that Morse earned a place as the preeminent geographical commentator of the new Republic. Other books were to follow. His next book was his *American Geography*, published to coincide with Washington's inauguration. In the Preface Morse noted:

> Europeans have been the sole writers of American Geography, and have too often suffered fancy to supply the place of fact, and thus have led their readers to errors, while they have professed to aim at removing their ignorance. But since the United States have become an independent nation, and have risen into Empire, it would be reproachful for them to suffer this ignorance to continue; and the rest of the world have a right to expect authentic information. To furnish this has been the design of the author of the following work.[14]

Having distanced himself from the Europeans and asserted the intellectual independence of the United States, Morse goes on to reinforce the civic virtue of the book:

> Every citizen of the United States ought to be thoroughly acquainted with the Geography of his own country, and to have some idea, at least, of the other parts of the world . . . this book offers them such information as their situation in life may require; and while it is calculated early to impress the minds of American Youth with an idea of the superior importance of their own country, as well as to attach them to its interests, it furnishes a simplified account of other countries, calculated for their juvenile capacities, and to serve as an introduction to their future improvement in Geography.[15]

A majority of the book is a description of the states. Each is described in standard terms noting such features as boundaries and rivers; then a range of topics varying by state are covered. Massachusetts has sections on

---

14. J. Morse, *American Geography* (Elizabeth Town: Kollock, 1789), p. v.
15. Ibid., p. vii.

Witchcraft Infatuation and Quaker Persecution while Connecticut has a section on the war between Mohegans and Narragansetts. A long description of the states may seem commonplace to us now, but Morse was writing when only the first President of the United States had been inaugurated. Federal power was new, untried and distrusted by many. To write a book with all the states grouped together was to join them in a narrative of national cohesion; it was a conscious political act that readers of the day could understand.

A consistent theme in Morse's writings, and particularly evident in his *American Geography*, is his distaste for the South. He attacks slavery especially for its corruption of the work ethic of the slaveowners. A dissipated, slave-owning south is continually counterpoised against an idealization of his home state of Connecticut, which has the largest single entry. Connecticut, and New England in general, with its family farms and hard working people is seen as a perfect model for American democracy. In contrast, the south is a pit of iniquity where indolence, gambling and drunkenness predominate. Morse did not so much describe America but passed moral judgment on the different regions and peoples of America.

The book was enormously popular. It was distributed throughout the country giving Morse a national and indeed international reputation. The book became the standard geography text at a time when there were very few other school textbooks of any kind. Geography texts were the miniencyclopaedias of their day; they covered the range of physical and social sciences, history and government, politics and biology. Morse's text was a vital element in the school socialization of generations of American schoolchildren.

The success of Morse's text assured him a pivotal position in the world of ideas in the fledgling republic. He was hired by Thomas Dobson, on the strength of *American Geography*, to rewrite the entry on America for a new encyclopaedia. Morse's article was later sold as a separate volume. His entry on America took a more anti-British line and espoused his moralizing condemnation of southern manners and lifestyles.

American Geography went through numerous changes and editions. It was first published in 1789 with 534 pages. In 1793 the work was enlarged to 1,250 pages and published in 2 volumes as *The American Universal Geography*. The book expanded to almost 1,500 pages in later editions. It was a massive book that also became an important part of the publishing industry then emerging in the United States. At this point, Morse crossed paths with Mathew Carey. Just as Carey had invested heavily on publishing *Guthrie's Geography*, a second edition of Morse's *American Universal Geography* was being published by Isaiah Thomas in Boston. At that time most publishers only sold in their own regions. However, Morse's book was capable of selling nationally and Thomas looked around for co-publishers. It was a huge, two-volume edition with twenty-eight maps and charts, much bigger than *Guthries'* but much less expensive; moreover, Morse's book was better suited to an American audience. So despite his interest in *Guthrie's Geography* Carey took a third of the entire second edition, publishing it in 1795/96 and sold it throughout Pennsylvania and the South.

The *American Universal Geography* was always poorly illustrated with maps. However, the book was so successful that maps could be sold using its name. The fifth edition was accompanied by *A New And Elegant Atlas* consisting of sixty-three maps drawn by Arrowsmith and Lewis. This is a beautiful atlas with pleasing uniformity of style, and marks the beginning of the convention of American atlases of similar style, yet differing scale so that each state is depicted on one page.

CRITICISMS

Morse's work did not go unchallenged. The most sustained attack came in 1793 in a sixty page pamphlet. The author was James Freeman and he entitled his critique, *Remarks on The American Universal Geography*. Freeman's main objections were the lack of uniformity in method and plan, inconsistencies and contradictions, inaccurate maps, poor judgement and obvious prejudices, appearance of haste and carelessness, mistakes and omissions. Freeman criticized Morse's use of Philadelphia as the first meridian.

> It is to be regretted that Mr. M. should reject the Royal Observatory at Greenwich, with which most men of science in America are familiar. His intention may be to compliment the capital of the United States, But whilst Philadelphia continues the first city in America for populousness and wealth, it can derive little honour from being the beginning of longitude. A

first meridian ought to be a precise point. But Philadelphia is an extensive city; and Mr M. has not informed us, from what part of it he reckons.[16]

Freeman makes an important point. Placing Philadelphia as the prime meridian makes the nationalist point; however, since there is no precise point identified in Philadelphia it is less than accurate. Morse does not say where exactly in Philadelphia the measurement is taken. Freeman takes much time correcting the errors because as he writes, Morse's book will "probably circulate through every part of the United States. It will be read in families and taught in schools." Freeman is the voice of rational objectivity and he is criticizing Morse for his cavalier use of figures, his sloppiness and his moralizing. "To listen to every exaggerated account of the faults of a town or state, and then to publish it in a system of geography, may demonstrate his hatred of vice, but it affords no proof of his judgment or candour." This pamphlet takes issue with both the empirical errors and the sanctimonious moralizing and sweeping generalizations used by Morse. What the debate highlights is the distinction between a religious moralizing and the beginnings of an apparent and self-conscious objectivity.

Morse also wrote a range of pamphlets. On the 19 February 1795, he published a thirty-seven page pamphlet entitled *The present situation of other nations of the world, contrasted with our own*. This was his most nationalistic tract. After this survey of a world in chaos and collapse he paints a rosy picture of the United States, a country blessed with peace both in the international stage and the domestic peace that comes with "internal tranquility." This peace is achieved through

the possession of constitutions of government which unite—and by their union establish liberty with order and wise and salutary laws which flow from and correspond with free government, free election, patronage and encouragement given to publick and school education, religious and civil liberties, prosperity of all classes of citizens.[17]

16. J. F[reeman] and Hall, *Remarks on The American Universal Geography* (Boston: Belknap, 1793), p. 56.

17. J. Morse, *The present situation of other nations of the world, contrasted with our own* (Boston: Samuel Hall, 1795), p. 32, 33.

The Republic is different from the rest of the world. Other countries measure unfavorably against the new republic. This is an early stating of American exceptionalism; this country is not just another country in the world, but different, better, designated for a special place. And given Morse's theology this can only have come from God. America's position is the blessing of God who is the source of this wealth and prosperity.

But there was another side to Morse's nationalism. An identification of the United States as a special place had as a corollary, in his nationalist theology, a place beset by danger, a place under attack from the forces of chaos and disorder. In 1799 he published a fifty page pamphlet entitled *A Sermon exhibiting the Present Dangers and consequent Duties of the Citizens of the United States*. It is a rambling discourse. In language that is eerily reminiscent of Senator Joseph McCarthy, at his xenophobic worst, Morse claimed,

> I have, my brethren, an official, authenticated list of the names, ages, places of nativity, professions etc of the officers and the members of a Society of Illuminati . . . consisting of one hundred members.[18]

The Illuminati were the late eighteenth–century equivalent of the Elders of Zion, more a product of fear than analysis, a secret group supposedly dedicated to world domination. In the politics of the time they were associated with Freemasons, free thinkers and the anticlerics of the French Revolution. Even in its earliest decades then, the new republic had conspiracy theories and a demonology of evildoers dedicated to creating chaos and confusion in the promised land. Morse continues, again in language that is disturbingly familiar:

> we have in truth secret enemies, not a few scattered through our country . . . enemies whose professed design is to subvert and overturn our holy religion and our free and excellent government. And the pernicious fruits of their insidious and secret efforts (include) the unceasing abuse of our wise and faithful rulers, the virulent opposition to some of the laws of our country . . . the industrious circulation of baneful and corrupting books

18. J. Morse, *A Sermon exhibiting the Present Dangers and consequent Duties of the Citizens of the United States* (Charlestown: Samuel Etheridge, 1799), p. 15.

and the consequent wonderful spread of infidelity, impiety and immoral-
ity . . . and lastly, the apparent systematic endeavours made to destroy, not
only the influence and support but the official existence of the Clergy.[19]

Morse called for an end of political connections with France and a strict ad-
herence to the Christian religion to bind together all members of the society. Throughout the latter half of the 1790s he believed that Jefferson was
an agent of France, a dangerous radical detrimental to the health of the new
nation. Morse's "national" geography was part of a broader nationalism, a
xenophobic nationalism, that saw the United States as a special place, but a
place under attack, beset by conspiracies and internal enemies, whose only
salvation lay in establishing a national coherence bound by the ties of the
Protestant religion.

Jedidiah Morse died on June 9, 1826. He grew up at a time when colonial resistance to British rule increased; only fifteen when the Declaration
of Independence was signed, he came into maturity as the new country was
establishing political forms of government, civil society and an intellectual
independence. He was involved in religious controversy and wrote some of
the first geography texts. He is a distant figure, rarely quoted or examined.
He is distant in a number of ways; he wrote centuries ago and his books lie
unread in research libraries. For those who make the effort to read him, his
style can grate modern readers and his religious and political beliefs have a
harsh moralizing quality that does not fit in well with current concerns of
pluralism and cultural diversity. And yet Morse is an authentic voice, opinionated and idiosyncratic, but with echoes for the modern reader. He
writes in a time when objectivity was not the focus of academic devotion,
in an era of religious dispute, when the country was identifying its heart and
soul, when conspiracy theories were accepted by many and when political
disputes were mean and fractious. Sound familiar? And yet a disservice
would be done if we were to try to make him too modern, to see his concerns merely as forerunners of our own. He wrote his geography about and
from a particular place. He wrote in his own time of current concerns.

And it is his position at the heart of these concerns that makes Morse
so important. His geography texts were some of the most widely read and

19. Ibid., pp. 16–17.

published books, of any kind of their time. He wrote best-selling books, widely-read pamphlets; he was a figure of some import at a time when the United States was more states than united and when a distinct intellectual tradition was emerging in the new republic. Indeed, Morse was a major figure in the conscious attempt by intellectuals to create and foster a uniquely "American" identity. He was the most important figure in the construction of a "national" geography at the turning of the eighteenth into the nineteenth century.

John Melish: Geographer, Mapmaker, Nationalist

John Melish was born in Methven Scotland on June 13, 1771. He was proud of his Scots heritage and continued to praise the Scots educational system. Like many Scots, before and since, his early anti-English feelings remained, yet metamorphosed easily into a later pro-American stance. As a young man he was apprenticed to a cotton merchant in Glasgow who traded with the West Indies and United States. Melish was personally involved in the Atlantic trade. He made numerous business journeys across the ocean. He crossed it four times from 1798 to 1809.

As an able, ambitious man, he ventured to establish his own business dealings and in 1806 he sailed to Savannah, Georgia to create an import-export business in which raw cotton from the South was exported to Britain and manufactured goods were imported. He traveled through the country taking extensive notes with a mind to writing a book. He visited Georgia, North and South Carolina, New York, Rhode Island, Massachusetts, Delaware, Maryland, Washington DC and Virginia. In 1807 he returned to Scotland. His business was badly affected by the deterioration in relations between the United States and Britain that resulted in the trade embargo of 1807, which lasted for fourteen months. In 1809 Melish returned to the United States to wind up his existing business interests. He stayed in New York for a while, traveled the interior of the country and in 1811 he settled in Philadelphia and there he remained for the rest of his life, an important figure in the city's vigorous book and map publishing business. Despite his importance, very little is written about him.[20]

20. But see W. W. Ristow, *American Maps and Mapmakers* (Detroit: Wayne State University Press, 1985), pp. 179–90; M. E. Wolfgang, "John Melish: An Early American Demographer," *Pennsylvania Magazine* 82 (1958): pp. 65–81.

"A SENSIBLE FOREIGNER"

Before coming to America Melish had read some travel books of the new republic but was very disappointed. They were, he thought, neither accurate
nor fair. As he traveled through the country he took extensive notes with the
idea of writing a book. It was published in 1812 with the accurate, if pro-
saic, title *Travels in the United States of America in the Years 1806 & 1807, and
1809, 1810 and 1811*. He wrote that the work might embody a complete geography of the United States. The two–volume work is a fascinating piece of
travel writing. Melish had an observant eye and an easy writing style. The
narrative takes the form of his journey with telling insights and observations. In the preface he writes that, when judiciously compiled, a travel journal should present a *living picture* and in this he succeeds. The book contains rich descriptions of people, places, topography, society and economy;
recurring themes are trade and commerce, geographic description, an assessment of good and bad in the society, and accounts of meetings with
important figures such as Thomas Jefferson and Tom Paine. Melish met
Jefferson while he was still President, who remained an important influence
in Melish's professional life. They communicated through the years; Melish
continued to send him his maps and books, and took Jefferson's *Notes on
Virginia* as the model for much of his own geographical writing.

Melish writes in a clear, crisp and direct manner. He is much closer to
us in style and disposition than Morse. Compared to the heavy moralizing
and baroque style of Morse, Melish's is lighter, based more on direct observation. Running through Melish's *Travels* is a supportive attitude to the
United States. Unlike many British, and especially English, travel writers of
the time, Melish does not use his book as a vehicle to attack the manners,
institutions and customs of America. Quite the opposite. He is critical of
much in the society but celebrates the positive. He does not vent his spleen
on the U.S. and is very supportive of the American character. Not surprisingly, the book was well received in the United States; one reviewer called
him "a sensible foreigner." Melish sent a copy of his book to Thomas Jefferson whom he had met earlier in his travels. In a letter written at Monticello
January 13, 1813 the former President thanked him for the book:

> The book I have read with extreme satisfaction and information. As to the
> Western States, particularly, it has greatly edified me. . . . The candor with

which you have viewed the manners and condition of our citizens, is so unlike the narrow prejudices of the French and English travellers . . . your work will be read here extensively, and operate great good . . . I consider it as so lively a picture of the real state of our country, that if I can possibly obtain opportunities of conveyance, I propose to send a copy to a friend in France, and another to one in Italy, who, I know, will translate and circulate it as an antidote to the misrepresentations of former travellers.[21]

A NATIONAL GEOGRAPHY

The success of his *Travels* secured an important place for Melish in the crowded and competitive book trade of the day. In volume 2, in a small footnote he noted:

Indeed it would very easy to procure materials for a *national geography*, which might be published every 10 years, under the auspices of the United States. The profits on the sale of such a work would do much more than defray the expence of a national geographical establishment.[22]

The note shows Melish's concern with a national geography and although the scheme was never established, Melish undertook in the rest of his writings to create such a national geography.

Melish published a number of diverse geographical works. There were small, gazetteer-like works such as *A Description of The Roads in The United States* which was published in 1814, with the usual subtitle *Compiled from the most authentic materials*. The title page described the author as John Melish, Geographer and Map Seller, 209 Chesnut Street. This was a small pamphlet, no more than eighty pages, which gave the road distances between major cities. Concerned with accuracy, Melish gave the distance in two columns, one for distance from one town to another and the other distance from the starting point. A pamphlet on road distances may not seem out of the ordinary, however, the work involved extensive research and a political agenda. At a time when the road network was rudimentary, the

21. A. E. Bergh, ed.*The Writings of Thomas Jefferson* (Washington: Memorial Association, 1907), vol. 13, p. 206.
22. J. Melish, *Travels in The United States of America* (Philadelphia: Melish, 1812), p. 439.

work not only created an important data base but gave a sense of national geography. A country linked together by roads was a connected one, a country pulled together by the strands of communication. A good transport network was part of the economic national agenda of the day that would help create an integrated national economy. A small pamphlet on roads was more than just a small pamphlet on roads; it was a statement on national coherence, national economic integration and economic nationalism.

In 1816 Melish published *The Traveller's Directory*. This was a small pocketbook, 8 inches by 3 inches and 134 pages meant for the amusement of the general reader and and the enlightenment of the traveler. It was not only a geographic description but a gazetteer, road map descriptions and a general promoter of the new territories. The *Directory* gave information on each state including situation, boundaries, extent, area, face of country (ie physical geography), rivers, minerals (described as commodities rather than geological features), soil (with special reference to fertility), produce, climate and for each county, the number of townships and the population of principal towns. The model that Melish worked from was Thomas Jefferson's *Notes on Virginia*. Melish follows a similar classification and order to Jefferson. Where Jefferson recorded the state of his state, Melish, by bringing all the states together, attempted to show how they were part of a larger national whole. The *Directory* was not simply providing a geographic description; it was suggesting a geopolitical order.

The *Directory* also contained information on the new territories: Indiana, Mississippi, Illinois, Michigan, North-west and Missouri. Here the tone was less scientific classification and more raw enthusiasm. Some examples:

> *Indiana* This interesting country, lately dominated the Indiana territory, may now be considered as a nineteenth state, and such is the fertility of the soil, the salubrity of the climate, and its commanding situation, that it will unquestionably become a very bright star in the galaxy of the republic.

> *North-West Territory* This extensive territory has not yet been organised into a regular government; but it is rising fast into importance. Colonel Hamilton's Rifle regiment stationed at the village of Prarie de Chiens, will check and control the Indians in that quarter.[23]

23. J. Melish, *Travellers Directory Through The United States of America* (Philadelphia: Palmer, 1816), p. 38.

The *Directory* was more than just an academic exercise. It gave very practical help to the traveler and settler. Melish included a list of land offices where public lands were sold. The *Directory* contained a large section on roads with directions for finding them, and distance in miles from Washington, Philadelphia and other main cities. These data, as we have noted before, were more than information on mileages; they pointed to the connection of the urban system and thus the connection of the country, the cohesion of the national economy, and embodied a sense of a national space.

MELISH'S MAPS

Melish also published maps. His 1812 *Travels* contained eight maps, all drawn by Melish in a fine, elegantly understated style. This was the beginning of his career as a mapmaker and map seller. By the end of the decade he had an establishment that employed over thirty people. Melish produced a variety of maps. They are marked by a understated elegance and refined style. He made and published maps at a variety of scales. His catalogue of maps runs to over sixty items including maps of states, cities, the United States and the world.

He published his first large–scale map of the the United States in 1813 at a scale of 1 inch to 100 miles. It sold for one dollar. And it sold well. In 1816 Melish produced another large scale map of the United States (Figure 5). At 1 inch to 50 miles the map was massive, a map meant for public display. The new Republic had found its epic representation. Its position in an imperial struggle is hinted at in the title of the map: *Map of the United States with the contiguous British and Spanish Possessions*. The title had the usual claim *Compiled from the latest and best authorities By John Melish*. The map gave longitude from Washington and London and included Lewis and Clark's wintering places on the west coast and among the Mandans, 1804–05. In a letter from Monticello, dated December 31, Thomas Jefferson thanked Melish for the map, "It is handsomely executed, and on a well-chosen scale; giving a luminous view of the comparative possessions of different powers in our America."[24]

24. Bergh, *The Writings of Thomas Jefferson* vol. 14, pp. 219–20.

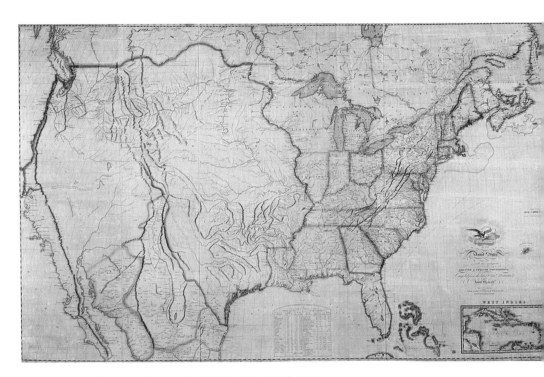

Figure 5. A map of the USA by John Melish 1816.

When he planned the map Melish intended to draw the map no farther west than the Rockies. He added two western sheets to take the map to
the Pacific Ocean. In a flourish that predates the doctrine of Manifest Destiny, Melish notes:

> Part of this territory unquestionably belongs to the United States. To pre-
> sent a picture of it was desirable in every point of view. The map so con-
> structed, shows at a glance the whole extent of the United States territory
> from sea to sea; and in tracing the probable expansion of the human race
> from east to west, the mind finds an agreeable resting place on its western
> limits. The view is complete, and leaves nothing to be wished for. It also
> adds to the beauty and symmetry of the map; which will, it is confidently
> believed, be found one of the most useful and ornamental works ever ex-
> ecuted in this country.[25]

From "sea to sea" was a confident act of cartographic appropriation that
foreshadowed the act of geopolitical dominance to come.

In 1820 Melish produced his largest map of the United States. It was
large-scale, at 1 inch to 50 miles. It is a beautiful, finely engraved map. The
engravers were John Vallance and H. S. Tanner. The map was meant to be
hung, in a public display that represented the country. The map contains a
picture of the American eagle and the national motto *e pluribus unum*.
Longitude is given from London on the bottom of the map, and from
Washington on the top.

This map is not only a geographical description, it is national celebra-
tion. The general Statistical Table, located in the bottom left of the map, gives
area and population and inhabitants per square mile. The current population of the national territory is given as 18,629,903 yet Melish asserts that it
is capable of supporting 500 million. This is a continental map full of the
promise of the new west—vacant, inviting, capable of taking more population—a map reflective of continental exploration and indicative of continental expansion.

---

25. J. Melish, *Geographic Description of the United States: with the contiguous British
and Spanish possessions intended as an accompaniment to his map of these countries* (Philadelphia: Melish, 1816), p. 4.

AN AMERICAN NATIONALIST

Throughout all his works from 1812 until his death Melish was an American nationalist. He not only described the United States, but celebrated it, praised it, compared it favorably with every country in the world. From his first writing to his last he praised and promoted the growth of the nation through a constant boosterist rhetoric. In his earlier *Travels in The United States* he described it as "an immense territory, a great part of it is still unoccupied, or very thinly inhabited, so that there is room for the industry of thousands of generations yet unborn."[26] This notion of almost limitless expansion was a constant theme in all of Melish's writings. He was keen to see the growth and enlargement of the republic. He was not a narrow nationalist like Morse; Melish wanted to encourage immigration and westward expansion. In 1819 he wrote and published *Information and Advice to Emigrants to the United States: And from The Eastern to The Western States Illustrated by A Map of The United States*. The book promotes the United States as "an independent nation of great political importance, possessing the best system of government in the world, and holding out advantages to mankind of very great importance."[27] In the book Melish identifies those groups most likely to succeed in America: industrious farmers, mechanics (tradesmen such as masons, shoemakers) manufacturers (spinners, weavers hatters etc), laborers of every description and gentlemen of republican principles and manners. Those who will have more trouble include merchants, learned professions (lawyers and doctors), noblemen and gentlemen of high birth and aristocratic principles. The "emigrants" Melish wants to encourage are male; women are neither noted nor encouraged.

Melish's nationalism was most vividly expressed in his evolving advocacy of economic protection of domestic industry and manufacturing. Even his mentor Jefferson shifted his position on this critical issue after 1800. In his 1812 *Travels* he included in the appendix of volume 1 an essay on the trade between Britain and America that argued that the United States should import manufactured goods and devote most attention to clearing and cul-

26. J. Melish, *Travels in The United States of America* (Philadelphia: Melish, 1812), p. iii.
27. J. Melish, *Information and Advice to Emigrants to the United States* (Philadelphia: Melish, 1819), p. 3.

tivating the land. But by the 1819 *Guide to Emigrants* he argues that economic growth will come from protecting national manufactures, especially cotton and woollen goods. Melish was keen for Congress to enact legislation that would protect local manufactures. To this end, on January 1, 1820 he printed an open letter to President James Monroe. It was in the form of a thirty-two page pamphlet entitled *On the state of the country with a plan for improving the condition of society*. In this pamphlet he refers to the depressed state of agriculture, commerce nearly annihilated, the unfavorable balance of payments amounting to $120 million and the fiscal deficiency of $5 million dollars. The reason for all of this economic distress, claims Melish, is the neglect in protecting the manufacturing industry. He argues that there was a pressing need to raise tariffs. Doubling tariffs for most items such as wine, spirits, molasses, teas, coffee, sugar, salt, hemp, beer, soap, cheese, shoes, iron and steel, and prohibiting the import entirely of tobacco and cotton goods would solve the fiscal crisis and give net revenue, after expenses of collection, of $24 million. These measures would make room for domestic articles, give farmers a market, bolster employment and increase government revenue without increasing taxes. He ends the pamphlet with the detailed case of the cotton trade, something of which he had personal experience. He argued that if the US manufactured rather than exported cotton there would be national gain of $100 million and the employment of 94,000 men and 94,000 women and children. Efficient protection would ensure economic independence.

Melish returned to this theme in a twenty-seven page pamphlet, published on the 4th of July 1822. It was addressed like an open letter to fellow *Citizens, the People of the United States* and entitled *Views On Political Economy*, and was one of the last things he wrote or published. Although small, the pamphlet is packed with information; it gives detailed tables of each state, with data drawn from the 1820 Census, giving population and numbers in agriculture, manufacturing and commerce. Melish argued that too few citizens of the United States were employed in active industry. The only answer lay in increasing manufacturing industry:

> it would be judicious policy, and correct national justice, *to exclude the manufactures of all nations who will not indiscriminately receive the produce of our soil* and as the manufactures of the country would thereby be mate-

rially promoted, a tax could be raised from them to support the revenue; but perhaps the most simple process, for the present, would be to augment the present rate of duties.[28]

John Melish died in 1822. He had established a national reputation as one of the foremost American geographers and mapmakers of his day. He provided descriptions and maps of the United States and the world. He wrote in a style that was clear and crisp and his maps were marked by a simplicity and elegance. With his use of statistics he also prefigured the more empirical turn in both geographical analysis and policy analysis. Melish was a geographer, a map maker and a nationalist. All these elements were part of his work. He described the territory of the United States, but this description was also used to boost emigration and national economic self-sufficiency. By his maps and writings Melish both described and promoted the territorial expansion of his adopted country.

Conclusions

At the dawn of the American Republic national identity was not a given. The Revolutionary rupture had created a break with the past. In geographical writings and cartographic constructions an emphasis was placed on the construction of a national geography, a description and representation of the territory of the fledgling nation. In the last two decades of the eighteenth and the first two of the nineteenth century some of the most important and best–selling books were geography texts and maps that created, advanced and codified a national geography. This project had a number of elements. Nationalist concerns were wrapped around more purely "scientific" endeavors, such as accurate location and description of unknown territory. The shift in identification of the prime meridian from London to Philadelphia and later Washington and in some maps to a dual system reflected the tensions of the project. The mapping of the national territory, especially at a time of geopolitical flux in the Far West, was also loaded with political significance as well as geographical science. There were a variety of strands to this discourse. Early forms of American exceptionalism and

28. J. Melish, *Views on Political Economy* (Philadelphia: Melish, 1822), p. 27.

Manifest Destiny can be discerned. The geographies and maps both described and celebrated the extension of the national territory towards the Pacific, the intensification of settlement and the westward movement of the frontier.

The discourse of national geography/identity was racialized, gendered and moralized. Native Americans rarely figure as little more than blocks to westward progress. Criticisms of slavery were raised by Morse in his description of the South but this was lacking in Melish whose audience of emigrants were all assumed to be male. Morse, because of his religious convictions also moralized the debate; his writings were value-laden and highly critical of moral backsliding, the South and liberal interpretations of Biblical injunctions.

There were also conflicts within the nationalist discourse. This was exemplified by the two most important writers of the time. Jedidiah Morse was the Protestant zealot, disdainful of the South and able to see conspiracy everywhere. His nationalism differed from Melish whose emphasis was on promoting immigration and fostering economic independence. While Morse saw a moral geography Melish was more concerned with an economic geography. While Morse relies on an opinionated text and outdated maps, Melish uses a gentler style and drew a large number of beautiful maps. Despite the differences, Morse and Melish shared a common concern to represent the new Republic. They differed in their scope, style and execution but they both wanted to represent the new Republic in the best possible light.

The project of a national geography was a major discourse of the new Republic. This national geography, like the nation itself, was paradoxical, ambiguous, richly varied, argumentative, and full of conflict.

And like the nation it represents the project is unfinished, continuous and ongoing.

TOWARD A RELIABLE GEOLOGIC MAP OF THE UNITED STATES, 1803–1893

Prologue

Reports of geological explorations, reconnaissances, and surveys in nineteenth-century North America used images and texts to fix and diffuse knowledge gained. Synthesizers compiled geologic maps, principal components of geology's visual language, on topographic bases whose hachures, shading, or contours depicted the shape of that part of the earth's surface. The geologic overprints displayed the strata, structure, and history of the mapped areas in the unifying four dimensions of space and time.

Surviving manuscript geologic maps long predate the development of printed geologic cartography.[1] The modern geologic map, however, evolved in several overlapping phases from a combination of scientific ideas and artistic techniques developed and applied in western Europe and North America between the late seventeenth and the late nineteenth centuries. Before 1840 geologic maps passed through four successive, but overlapping, cognitive intervals and cartographies—"distributional" (mineralogic

1. James A. Harrell and V. Max Brown, "The World's Oldest Surviving Geological Map: The 1150 B.C. Turin Papyrus from Egypt," *Journal of Geology* 100, no. 1 (1992): pp. 3–18.

maps), "structural" (geognostic maps), "temporal" (geologic maps), and "causal" (paleogeographic and other theoretical maps).[2] On mineralogic maps, iconographic symbols added to the topographic base showed the sites of minerals, rocks, soils, mines, and quarries, and areal bands (sometimes in color washes or tints) indicated the lateral extent of strata based on rock type (lithology).

Geognostic Maps of the Antebellum United States, 1803–1832

To the information on mineralogic maps, compilers of geognostic cartography added the series of colored boxes that identified the bands or belts shown on some mineralogic maps. They arranged these rock units (formations) in the order of their original vertical sequence (superposition) in columnar sections (keys) to the maps to indicate relative age. During the last third of the eighteenth century, geognosists increasingly grouped formations within a time scale of international classes or orders named for rock type and (or) sequential position. From oldest to youngest, these classes comprised Primitive or Primary (crystalline igneous and metamorphic rocks with metallic minerals) upwards through Transition (highly tilted sedimentary rocks with fossils), Secondary (fossiliferous and flatter-lying sedimentary rocks), Tertiary (fossiliferous consolidated debris of the older rocks), and Alluvial (unconsolidated stream and shoreline sediments). Developing conventions assigned specific colors for some of these classes — red for Primitive, blue for Secondary, and yellow for Alluvial.

Between 1803 and 1832 Constantin-François Chasseboeuf (later the Comte de Volney), William Maclure, Edwin James, and John Hinton compiled, on hachured-topographic bases at various scales, eight geognostic

2. Martin J. S. Rudwick, "The Emergence of a Visual Language for Geological Science," *History of Science* 14, pt. 3 (1976): 177–81. See also François Ellenberger, "Recherches et réflexions sur la naissance de la cartographie géologique, en Europe et particulièrement en France," *Histoire et Nature* no. 22/23 (1983 [1985]): 3–54; Kenneth L. Taylor, "Early Geoscience Mapping, 1700–1830," *Proceedings of the Geoscience Information Society* 15 (1984): 15–49; and Ralph E. Ehrenberg, *The Earth Revealed: Aspects of Geologic Mapping: Catalog of the Exhibition* (Washington: Library of Congress, 1989), pp. 9–16.

maps of the United States. Using their own observations and those of their predecessors, they extended the graphic portrayal of the young nation's strata and structure from the Atlantic littoral to the Rocky Mountains.

Volney, in discussing in 1803 the nation's human and inanimate geography, described three distinct physiographic entities—a coastal Atlantic, a western Mississippi valley, and an intervening mountainous district. He also depicted five lithologic regions of interior structure: (1) the mostly crystalline Granitic of the Adirondacks, areas east of the Hudson River, and the fall-line Piedmont (Bande d'Isinglass); (2) the tilted Grit or Sand Stone of the Catskills, Alleghenies, and Blue Ridge; (3) the Calcareous or Lime Stone of the Mississippi and Shenandoah valleys; (4) the maritime Sea Sand; and (5) the Alluvial or River-Formed Soil. A few copies of Volney's accompanying "Carte des États-Unis d'Amérique-Nord" (1:6,800,000),[3] colored by hand, highlighted three of these rock regions—Granitic (red), Sand Stone (brown), and Calcareous (green). Volney expanded his map's data past the Mississippi River by suggesting that his calcareous region, according to Alexander Mackenzie, extended from the Appalachians northwestward to the Rockies.

Maclure, inspired by Volney's three years in the United States, continued his older friend's geological explorations east of the Mississippi. Like Volney, the independently wealthy Maclure studied the relationships between the nation's bedrock, minerals, soils, topography, climate, agriculture, and public health, intending his reports to serve societal as well as scientific purposes. Maclure used European geognostic methods based on superposition, lithology, and mineralogy to distinguish the content, arrangement, and history of American strata. He adopted the European stratigraphic sequence of the rock classes, and those of its thirty-eight formations

---

3. The colored version of Volney's map accompanied some copies of his *Tableau du climat et du sol des États Unis d'Amérique: Suivi d'éclaircissement sur la Floride, sur la colonie française au Scioto, sur quelques colonies canadiennes et sur les sauvages*, (Paris: Courcier, 1803), 2:534, but not *A View of the Soil and Climate of the United States of America*, trans. Charles B. Brown (London: J. Johnson, and Philadelphia: J. Conrad, 1804). See George W. White's introduction to the reprint of the London edition (New York and London: Hafner, 1968), pp. xi, xv. John W. Wells, "Notes on the Earliest Geological Maps of the United States, 1756–1832," *Journal of the Washington Academy of Sciences* 49, no. 7 (1959): 200, reproduced as a halftone the central part of Volney's colored map.

he himself observed, as best expressed by Abraham Werner at the Berg-akademie Freiberg.[4]

In five geognostic maps imprinted and hand colored on copperplate-engraved bases (from 1:4,700,000 to 1:7,600,000) in Philadelphia and Paris before and after the War of 1812, Maclure extended what he also considered universal formations hundreds of miles beyond the Mississippi River. Maclure's maps and his accompanying five east-west transverse sections displayed four of the rock classes, keyed vertically in the *inverse* order of their age: (1) Primitive, in light orange or "siena brown," for the intrusive igneous and metamorphic rocks of the Appalachians and separate Adirondacks; (2) Transition, in pink or carmine, for a narrow band of steeply dipping sedimentary and metamorphic rocks within and west of the Appalachians; (3) Flœtz or Secondary, in light blue, for most of the gently dipping sedimentary rocks of the trans-Appalachian central interior; and (4) Alluvial, in yellow, for the poorly consolidated or unconsolidated and youngest coastal and valley sediments. He also showed on his maps two of the twelve formations in Werner's Secondary: the basal "Old Red Sand Stone" (today's Triassic), in dark blue; and "A [green] Line to the westward of which has been found the greatest part of the [overlying] Salt & Gypsum." Maclure considered placing his "Old Red" and its accompanying strata in the Transition, but that assignment would have destroyed the structural distinction between his Secondary and Transition rocks and limited expectations for discovering coal beds equivalent to those in Britain between its Old (later Devonian) and New (later Triassic) Red Sandstones, which Maclure's unit also encompassed. On the last of these maps, Maclure restricted his Secondary color to the western boundaries of Louisiana, Arkansas, and Missouri.

4. William Maclure, "Observations on the Geology of the United States, explanatory of a Geological Map." *Transactions of the American Philosophical Society* 6 (1809): 412, and map [on Samuel Lewis's base]. Reduced-scale color reproductions of the 1809 map are in George P. Merrill, "Contributions to the History of American Geology," in *Report of the U.S. National Museum, Under the Direction of the Smithsonian Institution, for the Year Ending June 30, 1904*, ed. Richard Rathbun (Washington: Government Printing Office, 1906), plate 1; George P. Merrill, *The First One Hundred Years of Geology in America* (New Haven, Conn.: Yale University Press, 1924), plate 1 [frontispiece]; and John C. Greene, *American Science in the Age of Jefferson* (Ames: Iowa State University Press, 1984), plate facing p. 230. Hubbard Scientific Company, of Northbrook, Illinois, reprinted in 1972 the geognostic "Carte des Etats-Unis de l'Amérique-nord" (on Volney's base) that accompanied the translation of Maclure's 1809 article in *Journal de Physique, de Chimie, d'Histoire Naturelle et des Arts* 72 (1811): 137–65.

After the American-British war ended in 1815, the United States, protected principally by the new balance of power in Europe, resumed its economic growth, maritime trade, and westward expansion across North America. While traveling in Europe between 1805 and 1814, Maclure had seen firsthand some of the economic, political, and social effects of the Revolutionary-Napoleonic global wars that began in 1793. He now hoped that his "attempt to apply Geology to agriculture" in his expanded text would help to make the Mississippi basin a wet-land democracy and "a place of refuge to oppressed humanity."[5]

The Adams-Onís treaty of 1819 reduced American hegemony in the western part of the Mississippi basin, but expanded the national domain to the Pacific north of the forty-second parallel. A year later, the Army Topographic Bureau, created by Congress in 1818 to improve mapping for national defense, continued the series of multi-purpose reconnaissances of transportation routes and natural resources west of the Mississippi that the seventh U.S. Congress began with funding in 1803 for what became Lewis and Clark's Corps of Discovery. As a member of Major Stephen Long's equally Humboldtian expedition, Edwin James (trained in natural history by John Torrey and Amos Eaton) examined the country west from Council Bluffs along the Platte River, passed south along the new mountain boundary, and then turned east down the Canadian and Arkansas rivers to Fort Smith. James's report included a black-line geognostic map of the "Country drained by the Mississippi: Western Section" (1:4,700,000) that denoted

5. William Maclure, *Observations on the Geology of the United States of America; With Some Remarks on the Effect Produced on the Nature and Fertility of Soils, by the Decomposition of the Different Classes of Rocks; and an Application to the Fertility of Every State in the Union, in Reference to the Accompanying Geological Map* (Philadelphia: Abraham Small, 1817), pp. ix, 127, and "Observations on the Geology of the United States of North America . . . Map," *Transactions of the American Philosophical Society*, n.s., 1 (1818): 6, 90, and map [on John Melish's base]. George W. White, "William Maclure's Maps of the Geology of the United States," *Journal of the Society for the Bibliography of Natural History* [*Annals of Natural History* since 1981] 8, pt. 3 (1977): 266–269, analyzed Maclure's maps of 1809, 1811 (Paris, on Volney's 1803 base), and 1817 (States 1817-A, -B, and -C). Later printings of Maclure's book contain a revised geologic map (State 1817-B, on Melish's revised base and printed during or after 1821). The 1817-A map is reproduced in color in Cecil J. Schneer, "William Maclure's Geological Map of the United States," *Journal of Geological Education* 29, no. 5 (1981): following p. 242. Full-size color reproductions of the 1817-B map (Ulm/Do.: W. Fritsch, 1962) accompany the reprint (New York: Hafner, 1964) of Merrill, *One Hundred Years of Geology in America*, and the reprint (München: Werner Fritsch, 1966) of Maclure's *Geology of the United States*.

the eastern or western boundaries of seven formations on the southern plains or in the eastern Rocky Mountains. A key reconstructed from his map, text, and east-west transverse sections that extended two by Maclure, would contain Primitive Granite, five Secondary units (basal Red Sandstone, Argillaceous or Gray Sandstone, Rock-Salt, Limestone and Coal Strata, and Newest Flœtz Trap), and Alluvial Sand and Gravel. James, struggling with superpositional relations, wondered at the absence of Transition rocks, nearly all the Primitive stratified rocks, and the more recent calcareous formations.

James labeled as "Deep Sandy Alluvion" much of the southern plains. The area occupied by the red rocks, he warned his readers, would be perpetually desolate, but the immense grasslands on its southern and eastern borders would support cattle and sheep as well as present bison and wild horses. The region's coal, salt, iron, and other mineral resources, James admitted, would lose much of their value so far from navigable streams, but he hoped that the Mississippi valley's geological and political settings would make it "the seat of a powerful, and agricultural empire," supporting a cultivational and pastoral population "limited only by the immense internal resources of the country."[6]

In 1832 John Hinton, assisted by several unnamed "literary gentlemen in America and England," merged the contents of Maclure's and James's geognostic cartography in "A Geologic Map of the United States."[7] Compiled on a 1:16,000,000 base of North America between the twenty-fifth and fifty-fifth parallels, Hinton's map extended the geognostic limit of James's

6. Edwin James, compiler, *Account of an Expedition from Pittsburgh to the Rocky Mountains, Performed in the Years 1819 and '20, by Order of the Hon. J. C. Calhoun, Sec'y of War: Under the Command of Major Stephen H. Long . . . From the Notes . . . of the Exploring Party* (Philadelphia: H. C. Carey and I. Lea, 1823), 2:441, and atlas (1822). James's map appeared in vol. 1 of the London edition (Longman, Hurst, Rees, Orme, and Brown, 3 vols., 1823). The best reproduction of the several replicas (1905–1988), of James's map from the Philadelphia edition is Carl I. Wheat, *Mapping the Transmississippi West 1540–1861. Volume Two: From Lewis and Clark to Fremont 1804–1845* (San Francisco: Institute of Historical Cartography, 1958), map (353) facing p. 80.

7. John H. Hinton, ed., *The History and Topography of the United States of America* (London: Simpkin & Marshall, 1832), 2: map facing p. 45. The map is not in the American edition (Philadelphia: T. Wardle, 1832), but it appears in *An Atlas of the United States of North America* (London, 1832), an abridgment of Hinton's two-volume *History.* Black-and-white, reduced-scale reproductions of Hinton's map are in Wells, "Earliest Geological Maps," 202, and in Peter Lessing, "Early Geological Maps of West Virginia," *Earth Sciences History* 8, no. 1 (1989): 19.

map north by more than five degrees of latitude. Of the nine colors in Hinton's key's, however, only the two for Primitive and Alluvial rocks are displayed throughout the mapped area; the others remain regionally separated. Hinton modified James's Alluvion to Alluvial Formations with Tertiary Beds. This change reflected the growing use of mollusks and other fossils by native and expatriate naturalists in the 1820s to identify American equivalents to the newer Secondary (or Cretaceous) and Tertiary units of Europe within Maclure's Alluvial of the coastal plain and James's units in the western interior. Maclure decried "the inventions of all this shell geology,"[8] developed in Britain and France, when younger colleagues used the new fossil-based stratigraphic methods to correlate American strata with the European standard and to promote theories of rock origin.

Geologic Maps of the Antebellum United States, 1834–1858

The compilers of geologic maps used fossil-based stratigraphic methods to determine the relative age of rock units and to correlate and extrapolate between widely separated rock sequences. Between 1822 and 1841 the development of a fossil-based time scale provided a more reliable framework of chronologic and stratigraphic units independent of regional and local variations within and between formations and their biotas. By 1840 geologic maps had replaced mineralogic and geognostic maps as the means of showing the distribution of these units and their natural resources. Geologic maps presented the lithology, areal coverage, and structural arrangement of formations ordered temporally by a key based on superposition *and* the nonrepetitive sequence of their contained and characteristic fossils. The relative-age sequence based on fossils enabled geologists to determine if the original depositional sequences of formations had been disturbed by subsequent folding or faulting.

In 1834 the twenty-third U.S. Congress appropriated the funds that Lt. Colonel John Abert, Chief of the Topographical Bureau, sought to aid

8. William Maclure, Journal No. 20, Paris, 18 September 1824, *The European Journals [1805–1825] of William Maclure*, ed. John Doskey, *Memoirs of the American Philosophical Society* 171 (1988): 738.

the development of the nation's mineral wealth, inland trade, and scientific prosperity by conducting "systematic geological investigations" and constructing "a geological map of the United States."[9] As his "U.S. Geologist," Abert hired George Featherstonhaugh. Unlike Edwin James, Featherstonhaugh lacked a college education, but he had studied informally with eminent geologists in Britain and France in 1826 and 1827 and was made a Fellow of the Geological Society of London. Featherstonhaugh's short-lived *Monthly American Journal of Geology and Natural Science* (1831–1832) promoted the new fossil-based stratigraphy and advocated the public value of geology and his own employment.

Between 1834 and 1836 Featherstonhaugh examined, for Abert, the geology and mineral deposits in the Midwest, including those in his assigned areas in Arkansas and Wisconsin Territories and the Cherokee lands. The nine color boxes of the transverse section between New Jersey and Mexico's Texas province that Featherstonhaugh published in his initial report showed a youngest-to-oldest stratigraphic sequence derived from the British-Continental standard: Superficial Sand and Soil, Tertiary, Ferruginous Sand, Subcretaceous beds, Sandstone with bituminous coal, Carboniferous limestone (intruded by granites and greenstone), Old Red Sandstone, Grauwacke, Transition Limestone, and Primary rocks.[10]

Featherstonhaugh's reconnaissances for Abert ended when he failed to produce the promised practical results, an omission that David Dale Owen did not repeat in his survey of the mineral lands in Illinois and Wisconsin in 1839 for the Treasury Department's General Land Office. Perhaps Featherstonhaugh served science best when he aided Charles Lyell, his younger colleague in the Geological Society of London. Like Yale's Benjamin Silliman, Featherstonhaugh shared data with Lyell and recommended sites to visit in the United States and British Canada.

9. *U.S. Statutes at Large* 4 (28 June 1834), p. 704, provided the $5,000 for these "geological and mineralogical survey and researches," requested in John J. Abert, "Report of the Chief of the Topographical Bureau," in *Report of the Secretary of War*: 23d Congr., 1st sess., 1833, H. Exec. Doc. 1, serial 254, p. 121.

10. George W. Featherstonhaugh, *Geological Report of an Examination Made in 1834, of the Elevated Country Between the Missouri and the Red Rivers* (Washington: Gales and Seaton, 1835) [23d Congr., 2d sess., H. Exec. Doc. 151, serial 274]. Featherstonhaugh changed Grauwacke to Silurian and Transition Limestone to Cambrian in his second report (1836), one year after these new units had been defined in Britain.

Lyell spent twelve months in eastern North America during 1841 and 1842, lecturing and extending his geological observations and explanations to the continent's fossil and rock record, especially its coal deposits. Lyell, and his wife Mary (Horner), who aided his work, traveled widely in New England, New York, the Atlantic littoral, the upper Ohio Valley, the eastern Great Lakes region, the St. Lawrence River valley, and Nova Scotia. James Hall and other eminent American and Canadian geologists often guided the Lyells in the field. Lyell drew data from their collections and maps, especially the draft of Hall's 23-unit "Geologic Map of the Middle and Western States" (1:1,900,000, 1843), but Lyell clearly distinguished between locales he visited and those he had not seen. Lyell's careful citation of all sources on his "Geologic Map of the United States, Canada &c." (on a 1:8,200,000 lithographic base) and in the accompanying text,[11] diminished the concerns of Hall and other Americans that their assistance during and after his visit would be insufficiently credited.[12]

On Lyell's geologic map, twenty numbered or lettered and hand-tinted colors (some with patterns) showed the distribution (west to about the one hundredth meridian) of seventeen sedimentary, one metamorphic, and two igneous units. Lyell used his own Alluvium and Post-Pliocene, Miocene, and Eocene to divide the Tertiary and Quaternary coastal and riverine units from Cape Cod to the Rio Grande. The map displayed three Mesozoic units: Cretaceous, in parts of the lower Mississippi, Red, and Missouri River valleys; "Coal (Oolite?)" in Virginia; and "New Red Sandstone & Trap," in a narrow band from Virginia through part of Connecticut. Lyell showed ten Paleozoic units. His "Coal Measures" and "Carboniferous Limestone" defined major basins between the Appalachians and the Mississippi. Lyell's "Old Red Sandstone or Devonian" surrounded these basins and outlined, as did Hall's map, a ridge-valley province of Upper Silurian and Lower Silu-

11. Charles Lyell, *Travels in North America; With Geological Observations on the United States, Canada, and Nova Scotia* (London: John Murray, 1845), 2:238–59, and plate 2 [frontispiece] (reprint, New York: Arno Press, 1978, halftone), and (New York: Wiley and Putnam, 1845) 2:200–19, and plate 2 [frontispiece]. Additional reduced-scale reproductions of Lyell's map are in Philip B. King and Helen M. Beikman, "Explanatory Text to Accompany the Geologic Map of the United States," *U.S. Geological Survey Professional Paper* no. 901 (1974): 4 [line drawing], and Lessing, "Early Geological Maps," p. 23 [halftone].

12. Robert H. Silliman, "The Hamlet Affair: Charles Lyell and the North Americans," *Isis* 86, no. 4 (1995): 556, and Robert H. Dott, Jr., "Lyell in America—His Lectures, Field Work, and Mutual Influences, 1841–1853," *Earth Sciences History* 15, no. 2 (1996): 115.

rian rocks (divided into seven of the groups recognized by the New York Survey) west and south of the "Hypogene" granites and gneisses of the eastern Appalachians. He extended the Silurian rocks into New York south and west of the Hypogene Adirondacks and New England. On Lyell's map, Hypogene rocks also formed most of Upper and Lower Canada, beginning the definition of the Canadian Shield, and the core of the Ozarks.

Information from the mostly civilian scientists who participated in linear and areal reconnaissances for the Army topographical unit (reorganized in 1838 as the Corps of Topographical Engineers), the General Land Office (transferred to the new Interior Department in 1849), and the state geological surveys (begun in 1823) contributed to additional regional or national geologic maps published before the Civil War. James Hall, Edward Hitchcock, Jules Marcou, and Henry Rogers compiled national geologic maps, on which twelve to twenty-three units increasingly were represented by chromolithographic tints, patterns, and numbers. In 1853, Hitchcock and Marcou published geologic maps that drew heavily on Lyell's geocartography. Hitchcock, professor and president of Amherst College, and the former state geologist of Massachusetts, whom Lyell visited in 1841, compiled a 15-unit "Geological Map of the United States and Canada," at the same scale as Lyell's, to accompany a global analysis published as a sequel to his *Elementary Geology*. Hitchcock extended "this map across the whole continent," using Ami Boué's maps and other extranational sources, yet he wished "it to be understood that west of Missouri and Iowa the coloring is intended to give only a general view of the geology, and probably in many parts may be greatly erroneous."[13] Hitchcock showed nearly all of the lands west of the one hundred and fifth meridian as "Hypozoic and metamorphic rocks, with granite, syenite, and porphyry"; small and widely separated ellipsoids of Tertiary-Alluvial igneous rocks denoted the mountain ranges that defined the Great Basin.

Also in 1853 Louis Agassiz saw into print his *protégé* Jules Marcou's

13. Edward Hitchcock, *Outline of the Geology of the Globe, and of the United States in Particular: With Two Geological Maps, and Sketches of Characteristic American Fossils* (Boston: Phillips, Sampson, 1853), pp. 71–72 [microfiche edition, Woodbridge, Conn.: Research Publications, 1994], and (London: Sampson, Low, 1853). King and Beikman, "Explanatory Text," p. 6, reproduced Hitchcock's map as a line drawing.

hand-tinted, twelve-color "Geological Map of the United States and the British Provinces of North America" (1:5,700,000; State 1853-A, herein). The map appeared after Marcou had left Harvard to accompany the Topographical Engineers's survey of the thirty-fifth-parallel route for the Pacific railroad. On Marcou's map, Modern deposits stood separate from the Tertiary and Quaternary; Secondary strata linked Cretaceous, Lias or Jurassic, and New Red Sandstone or Keuper, and Paleozoic rocks joined Coal Measures, Lower Carboniferous, Devonian, Upper Silurian, and Lower Silurian. His basal Eruptive and Metamorphic Rocks comprised Copper Trap and a unit of six types of crystalline igneous and metamorphic rocks. Marcou intended his map "chiefly to synchronize the sedimentary rocks of America with those of Europe,"[14] but it extended knowledge only to the one hundred and tenth meridian. Hall anonymously savaged Marcou's map and text in the *American Journal of Science (AJS)* in 1854. Although Hall had never traveled beyond Iowa, in the 1840s and 1850s he reported as a federal contractee on the geology revealed by the observations and collections from explorations of the Rocky Mountains, the Great Basin, Oregon, and California. While Owen mapped and assessed for the General Land Office the geology and mineral resources of its Chippewa Land District in Minnesota and Wisconsin, Hall helped Josiah Whitney and John Foster to examine the adjacent Lake Superior district in Michigan. Hall also guided field studies associated with the survey (1849–1855) of the United States's new boundary with the Republic of Mexico and accepted Major William Emory's request as U.S. Commissioner to summarize from notes and specimens the area's geology and paleontology. In 1853 Hall advised William Blake about Blake's work for the southernmost of the Pacific Railroad surveys; Hall also sent his assistant Fielding Meek and his collector Ferdinand Hayden to study the geology and fossils of the middle Missouri country.

Marcou's "Carte géologique des États-Unis et provinces anglaises de l'Amérique du Nord" (1:11,400,000), published twice in 1855 in Paris

---

14. Jules Marcou, *A Geological Map of the United States, and the British Provinces of North America, With an Explanatory Text, Geological Sections, and Plates of the Fossils Which Characterize the Formations* (Boston: Gould and Lincoln, 1853), p. 58, and map. State 1853-B is "Carte géologique des États-Unis et des provinces britanniques de l'Amérique du Nord," in Guillaume Lambert, *Voyage dans l'Amérique du Nord, en 1853 et 1854, avec notes sur les expositions universelles de Dublin et New-York: Atlas* (Liège: E. Noblet, 1855).

(1855-A1 and 1855-A2, herein),[15] extended his understanding of national geology to the Pacific. Marcou's twelve-unit key duplicated much of his stratigraphic column of 1853, but combinations of printed solid, dotted, and ruled-line chromolithographic colors replaced the single-color washes of the earlier map. Marcou added letter symbols to help define map units, placed the Quaternary in "Moderne," fixed the "Limite méridionale du Terrain Erratique du Nord" as the dashed-line boundary of continental-glacier deposits of Pleistocene age, joined the Lower and Upper Silurian rocks as a single "Silurien," and separated "Trapp Cuprifére" and "Volcans" from the "Eruptives & métamorphiques." Marcou resigned his federal appointment in 1854 and returned to France. Blake, using materials left by Marcou, prepared the report. Two years later, Blake, as principal geologist in the Topographical Engineers's Office of Pacific Railroad Explorations and Surveys, led by Captain Andrew Humphreys, presented preliminary versions of his geologic and orographic maps of the Trans-Mississippi West, and damned Marcou's 1855 maps in the *AJS*. Although Blake and Hall thought much of Marcou's geocartography of dubious value, they clashed over Blake's report of Marcou's federal work, which included Hall's evaluation of Marcou's fossils, but without Hall's review or approval. Hall then cast such doubt on Blake's competence that Humphreys considered giving all of Blake's material to Hall for revision and decided not to publish Blake's maps, including his geologic compilation on the master hachured-topographic map of the Trans-Mississippi West (1:3,000,000) prepared by Lieutenant Gouverneur Warren of Humphreys's office. Henry Rogers's national geologic map

15. Jules Marcou, "Résumé explicatif d'une carte géologique des États-Unis et des provinces anglaises de l'Amérique du Nord, avec un profil géologique allant de la vallée du Mississippi aux côtes du Pacifique, et une planche de fossiles," *Bulletin de la Société Géologique de France*, 2d ser., 12 (1855): 813–936, and plate 20 (Paris: Avril) [State 1855-A1]. The same map (inside the neatlines) is in Marcou, "Esquisse d'une classification des chaînes de montagnes d'une partie de l'Amérique du Nord," *Annales des Mines*, 5th ser., 7 (1855): 329–350, and plate 9 (Paris: Avril) [State 1855A2: "GÉOLOGIE" added above the outside neatline]. Marcou's "Geologische Karte der Vereinigten Staaten und Britischen Provinzen von Nord-Amerika" (1:14,000,000) is in "Über die Geologie der Vereinigten Staaten und der Englischen Provinzen von Nord-Amerika," *Mittheilungen aus Justus Perthes' Geographischer Anstalt über Wichtige Neue Erforschungen auf dem Gesammtgebiete der Geographie von Dr. A. Petermann* 1 (1855): 149–159, and plate 15 (Gotha: Justus Perthes) [State 1855-B, herein]. The Spanish version (not seen) is in *Revista Minera* (Madrid) 6 (1855): 288–313. Seymour I. Schwartz and Ralph E. Ehrenberg, *The Mapping of America* (New York: Henry N. Abrams, 1980), p. 282, reproduced Marcou 1855-A2 in color at a reduced scale.

(1:10,800,000) of 1855,[16] displayed seventeen units (including Lyell's Plio-
cene, Miocene, and Eocene) and gave Hall additional, if less objectionable,
competition.

Emory convinced Hall in 1856 to prepare, with Rogers's former assistant Peter Lesley, a new geologic synthesis of the Trans-Mississippi West on
Emory's master hachured-topographic map, to supplement Hall's summary
of the boundary survey's geology. Their compilation was still in-press when
Marcou published in 1858 a same-scale revision[17] of his 1855-A1 map. Although Marcou considered the new map "little improved," he changed colors and patterns for the map units and modified or removed some of the
questioned geology, principally by blanking out a large area between the
Cascade Range and the Missouri River and south from the international
boundary to the Wind River Mountains. In the accompanying text, Marcou asked that his map be judged as an approximate ensemble and not on
its details. Agassiz and Yale's James Dana, the *AJS*'s editor, centered their
part of the paper war on the identity of the 500,000 square miles in the West
that Marcou delineated as Triassic and Jurassic, but which American geologists, who suspected Marcou had mixed data and collections from both
continents, thought mostly Cretaceous and Tertiary.

Hall and Lesley's "Map illustrating the General Geologic features of the
Country West of the Mississippi River,"[18] hand-tinted on prints from a
1:6,100,000 lithographic version of Emory's steel-engraved "1:6,000,000"
base of "1857–8," appeared in 1858. Their twelve-unit map displayed "Des-

16. Henry D. Rogers, "Geological Map of the United States and British North America, Constructed From the Most Recent Documents and Unpublished Materials . . . Boston
U.S. 1855," in *The Physical Atlas of Natural Phenomena: A New and Enlarged Edition*, ed.
A. Keith Johnston [the elder] (Edinburgh: William Blackwood and Sons, 1856), pp. 29–32,
and plate 8.

17. Jules Marcou, *Geology of North America; With Two Reports on the Prairies of Arkansas and Texas, the Rocky Mountains of New Mexico, and the Sierra Nevada of California,
Originally Made for the United States Government* (Zurich: Zürcher and Furrer, 1858), map
[frontispiece] (Paris: Avril). Marcou's volume also was sold by publishers in Leipzig, London, New York (Wiley and Halsted) and Paris. King and Beikman, "Explanatory Text," 5,
reproduced Marcou 1858 as a reduced-scale line drawing.

18. Hall and J. Peter Lesley's map [New York: Sarony, Major & Knapp, 1858] accompanied some copies of James Hall, "Palœontology and Geology of the Boundary," in William H.
Emory, *Report on the United States and Mexican Boundary Survey, Made Under the Direction
of the Secretary of the Interior* (Washington: Cornelius Wendell, 1857), 1, pt. 2: 101–40 [34th
Congr., 1st sess., H. Exec. Doc. 135, serial 861; reprint, Austin: Texas State Historical Association, 1987], and (Washington: A. O. P. Nicholson, 1857) [S. Exec. Doc. 108, serial 832].

ert Quaternary," Tertiary, Upper and Middle Cretaceous, Lower Cretaceous, Upper Carboniferous, Coal Measures, Lower Carboniferous, Devonian, Upper Silurian, and Metamorphic as its stratigraphic sequence, but
its key distinguished "Lava & other igneous rocks" as a multiage unit. The
War and Interior Departments had kept Hall and Lesley from adding to the
key of their in-press map some unpublished information about the Permian through Jurassic rocks of the upper and middle Missouri country
that they took from but did not credit to Meek and Hayden. The title blocks
of some copies bore a slant-printed "1857," added as another ploy for priority. All title blocks cited only the surveys of the U.S.-Mexican boundary,
those for a Pacific railroad, "& other sources," showing that Hall had learned
nothing from Lyell's ethics. Hall's refusal to publish in the *AJS*, or elsewhere,
the clarifying article that Meek and Hayden requested to credit *all* uncited
sources led Meek to depart for the Smithsonian Institution.

The geologic maps of part or all of the American West published in the
1850s made known significant contributions to knowledge when based on
data from locales actually examined. In refusing to extrapolate geological
units over large areas where little or no information was available, however,
Hall and Lesley clearly showed the areas that needed study. Their map began the process of showing accurately the nature and history of the geology
underpinning the entire region's physiography. Hall and Lesley's map also
provided a framework for those western territories and states without geologic surveys or for those, like Texas, just beginning their work.[19]

Geologic Maps of the Postbellum United States, 1867–1879

In postbellum years, federal geologic mapping increasingly became a function of civilian rather than military agencies as areal reconnaissances replaced linear explorations. Spurred by the continuing industrialization of
the United States, the increasing settlement of the nation's western lands,

19. Hall also compiled the U.S. portion of Sir William Logan and others, *Geological
Map of Canada and the Adjacent Regions, Including Parts of Other British Provinces and of the
United States* (Paris: Jacobs and Ramboz, 1866); 1:1,600,000; 33 units.

and the development of their natural resources, federal funds financed four principal multiyear reconnaissances. These surveys, sponsored by the War and Interior Departments, mapped and assessed in greater detail huge areas of the Trans-Mississippi West in the first two decades after the Civil War. Their geologists no longer were "dragged in the dust of rapid exploration," but "took a commanding position in the professional work of the country." [20] In 1863 the Corps of Engineers had absorbed the Topographic Engineers, who had employed Ferdinand Hayden in the late 1850s. The Engineers, now led by Brigadier General Humphreys, sponsored civilian geologist Clarence King's U.S. Geological Exploration of the Fortieth Parallel (field work, 1867–1872; publications, 1870–1880) and First Lieutenant George Wheeler's U.S. Geographical Surveys West of the One Hundredth Meridian (field work, 1871–1879; publications, 1872–1889). The Department of the Interior directed Hayden's U.S. Geological and Geographical Survey of the Territories (field work, 1867–1878; publications, 1867–1890) and John Powell's U.S. Geographical and Geological Survey of the Rocky Mountain Region (field work, 1871–1878; publications, 1872–1893).

King's well-planned, multiyear-funded, and civilian-staffed exploration served as the model and standard for the field and laboratory methods and products of the three other surveys and supplied them with trained personnel. In 1867, King's survey began triangulation mapping, from astronomically determined and then ground-measured baselines, and resource-assessments of the lands that flanked the route of the proposed transcontinental railroad between the Sierra Nevada and the Great Plains. King and James Gardiner, Yale alumni, learned additional mapping skills from German expatriate Charles Hoffmann and Yale's William Brewer during their mutual service earlier in the 1860s with Josiah Whitney's state-sponsored Geological Survey of California. King's staff mapped geology and topography simultaneously at 1:126,720, and at larger scales in the mining districts, but they photographically reduced the field sheets for publication. Julius Bien's New York firm printed King's two atlases of chromolithographic geo-

20. Clarence King, *First Annual Report of the United States Geological Survey to the Hon. Carl Schurz, Secretary of the Interior* (Washington, Government Printing Office, 1880), p. 4.

logic maps compiled on contour-topographic bases, which located more accurately the contact lines between units. In 1870, the initial volume displayed the geology of the Austin, Comstock, and White Pine districts;[21] the summary atlas of 1876 contained pairs of geologic and topographic maps (at 1:253,440) for each of the five 165-by 100-mile quadrangles that covered most of the 87,000 square miles examined.[22] Wheeler's survey, principally a military reconnaissance conducted by soldiers and civilians, proposed in 1872 to map all the lands west of the one hundredth meridian to yield an atlas of ninety-five sheets. Wheeler and his staff examined about 360,000 square miles, mostly in the Southwest. Using some of King's data, they published geologic and land-classification maps, on mostly hachured-topographic bases (1:506,880 or 1:253,440), as separate sheets for some fifty of the quadrangles.

The surveys sponsored by the Interior Department did not employ trained topographers before 1871 or publish their own geologic maps until 1873, the year Henry Gannett, James Gardiner, Allen Wilson (who also came from King's survey) and Hayden's other topographers and geologists began mapping the Colorado Territory.[23] In 1874, the Hayden and Powell surveys embarked on an Interior-sponsored program to map and evaluate the resources of the 147 quadrangles (1:253,440) into which the department divided the nation's public lands west of about the one hundredth meridian. After 1876, Hayden's organization mapped north of forty-two degrees north latitude. Powell's survey worked south of that parallel and mapped some 67,000 square miles, mostly in Utah. A third Interior-sponsored survey, led by Walter Jenney and Henry Newton, examined the geology and resources of some 9,000 square miles in the Black Hills of the Dakota Territory in 1875 and 1877; Powell published their atlas in 1879 and its text in 1880. A

21. Clarence King and others, "Atlas Accompanying Volume III on Mining Industry" (New York: Julius Bien, 1870), fourteen single-folio sheets [text: *Professional Papers of the Engineer Department, U.S. Army. No. 18. Report of the Geological Exploration of the Fortieth Parallel* (Washington: Government Printing Office, 1870)].

22. Clarence King and others, *Geological and Topographical Atlas Accompanying the Report of the Geological Exploration of the Fortieth Parallel* (New York: Julius Bien, 1876), one single and eleven double-folio sheets.

23. Ferdinand V. Hayden and others, *Geological and Geographical Atlas of Colorado and Portions of Adjacent Territory* (New York: Julius Bien, 1877), twenty double-folio sheets.

nine-color, "General Geological Map of the Area Explored and Mapped by Dr. F. V. Hayden and the Surveys Under His Charge" (1:2,600,000),[24] covering some 420,000 square miles in the West, summarized in 1880 both earlier reconnaissance mapping and the later 110,000 square miles of systematic surveys in Colorado, Wyoming, Idaho, and Montana. Hayden's map continued to show the "Post-Cretaceous or Laramie" rocks between those of definite Tertiary and Cretaceous age.

Only a little of the new geocartographic data from these western surveys appeared on the chromolithographic "Geological Map of the United States," compiled for Interior's Census Office by Charles Hitchcock (Edward's son, a professor at Dartmouth and state geologist of New Hampshire) and William Blake (then a professor at Berkeley), and published at 1:5,700,000 to 1:7,900,000 six times between 1872 and 1876. An *AJS* reviewer bemoaned the 1873 map's inferior lithography, omission of the geographic distribution of information on economic mineral deposits, miscoloring of areas better left blank, and the misidentification of other well-known areas. An improved "general U.S. geological chart," combining federal and state data and issued "in the best possible style" by the government "would be a great thing for the nation's industry as well as its science."[25] Hitchcock and Blake modified their map before the Census Office published in 1874 its official version (1:7,100,000),[26] the one preferred by the authors. The new map replaced solid colors with lined colors for two of

24. Ferdinand V. Hayden, *The Great West: Its Attractions and Resources. Containing a Popular Description of the Marvellous Scenery, Physical Geography, Fossils, and Glaciers of This Wonderful Region* (Philadelphia: Franklin and Bloomington, Ill.: C. R. Brodix, 1880).

25. Anonymous, "Geological Map of the United States," *American Journal of Science and Arts*, 3d ser., 6, no. 31 (1873): 64–66.

26. Francis A. Walker, superintendent, *Statistical Atlas of the United States Based on the Results of the Ninth Census 1870 With Contributions from Many Eminent Men of Science and Several Departments of the Government* (New York: J. Bien, 1874), [paired] plates 13 and 14. Hitchcock and Blake's maps appeared in Rossiter W. Raymond, *Statistics of Mines and Mining in the United States and Territories West of the Rocky Mountains* (Washington: Government Printing Office, 1873) [43d Congr., 1st sess., H. Exec. Doc. 141], at 1:7,900,000 in 1876 in the Smithsonian's special report for Philadelphia's Centennial Exposition, and at 1:20,700,000 in Friedrich Ratzel, *Die Vereinigten Staaten von Nord-Amerika: Erster Band. Physikalische Geographie und Naturcharakter* (München: R. Oldenbourg, 1878), plate 1 [Leipzig: Wagner & Debes]. Hitchcock published modified versions of these maps in *The National Atlas* (Philadelphia: O. W. Gray and Son, 1872, 1876, 1879). Lessing, "Early Geological Maps," p. 24, reproduces as a halftone the eastern half of the 1872 federal map.

its nine units. Hitchcock and Blake continued to display all pre-Cambrian stratified and crystalline rocks and some younger metamorphic rocks as "Eozoic"; Paleozoic now linked Cambrian-Silurian, Devonian, and Carboniferous-Permian units; Mesozoic included the Triassic-Jurassic and Cretaceous sequences; and Cenozoic comprised Tertiary, Alluvium, and Volcanic rocks. They retained the Paleozoic and Cenozoic rocks as one unit west of the one hundredth meridian, but they emphasized the great distribution of volcanic rocks in the West and the occurrence of Triassic strata in Texas and the Indian Territory.

Geologic Maps of the United States by the U.S. Geological Survey, 1884–1893

In March 1879, the Forty-fifth U.S. Congress and President Rutherford Hayes ended the feudal age of federally sponsored geology by enacting legislation that established the U.S. Geological Survey (USGS)[27] to aid the mineral industry in advancing the nation's economy, to improve the civil service, and to reduce expenditures. The USGS assumed some of the functions of the competing surveys led by Hayden, Powell, and Wheeler, and the departmental atlases, all discontinued by the same statute. As USGS Director, King set high standards for appointments to and work by the staff toward fulfilling the congressionally mandated assessment of the national domain. King planned a scientific classification and mapping of the nation's lands, a comprehensive assessment of the extent, nature, and geologic relations of its mineral resources, and other wide-ranging but supportive practical and general studies. He chose Raphael Pumpelly to lead the USGS's investigations in economic geology and its co-funded, cooperative statistical studies of minerals and mining for the Tenth Census of 1880. Allen Wilson, as King's Chief Topographic Engineer, directed the USGS's large-scale mapping of mining districts in the public lands, to which area the agency's work initially was confined, and the completion of Powell's smaller-scale cartography of the Colorado Plateau. King aimed the latter mapping and

27. *U.S. Statutes at Large* 20 (3 March 1879), pp. 394–95.

the USGS's general investigations in geology primarily toward finishing a reliable national geologic map. Such a map awaited new topographic coverage for the portions of the West that lacked base maps adequate for geologic compilation. To avoid dissipating the USGS's limited resources for an in-house national program of large- and medium-scale topographic mapping, King supported the ultimately unsuccessful efforts in Congress to revive Wheeler's organization (which had planned to produce a national atlas of 210 sheets) or to establish elsewhere in the War Department a new geographical agency like the British Ordnance Survey.

Seven months after King's resignation in March 1881, Pumpelly also left the USGS to lead for the Northern Pacific Railroad a survey of the resources in the more than 400,000 square miles of the company's land grant between Lake Superior and the Pacific. Wilson also resigned from the USGS to serve as Pumpelly's chief topographer. While Pumpelly and his men conducted their census-survey of railroad lands and resources as a guide to their development, Powell, whom King recommended as his successor, began the needed national mapping program by default and design. During August 1882, King's and Powell's friends in Congress convinced their legislative colleagues and President Chester Arthur to extend and fund USGS operations nationwide "to continue the preparation of a geologic map of the United States."[28] Under this rubric, Gannett, the Tenth Census's geographer since 1879, joined the USGS as its Chief Geographer to direct Powell's national topographic-mapping program, and Powell hired William McGee and asked him to compile the national geological map. Powell also initiated co-funded topographic mapping with several eastern states and expanded the USGS's efforts in general geology, but at the expense of the congressionally mandated studies of mineral resources.

Powell used the new national geologic map for scientific and institutional entrepreneurship, both domestically and internationally. The International Geological Congress (IGC), at its initial meeting at Paris in 1878, had decided to compile a geologic map of Europe and established committees to standardize geologic colors, symbols, names, and classification. In 1881, Powell had alerted the United States and Canadian members of the

---

28. *U.S. Statutes at Large* 22 (7 August 1882), p. 329.

IGC's American committee and attendees at the second IGC in Bologna that the USGS would use a common system of general stratigraphic names, uniform colors (tones and tints) and overprinted color-patterns (lines or dots) most easily distinguished and economically printed, conventional characters (letters and numbers), and a single map form for geologic and topographic charts and atlases.[29] Charles Hitchcock, who also served on the American committee, completed that year as a teaching tool a 1:1,300,000 national map printed by Bien. Hitchcock's twenty-one-unit map, displaying many colors he used in the 1870s rather than those proposed by Powell, showed the transcontinental distribution of rocks from the Quaternary to the Archean, including a separate "Laramie or Lignite Tertiary." Hitchcock then aided McGee in compiling the USGS's eleven-color "Map of the United States Exhibiting the Present Status of Knowledge Relating to the Areal Distribution of Geologic Groups (Preliminary Compilation)" on Gannett's new drainage-only base (1:7,100,000).[30] McGee's 1884 map, also printed by Bien, used most of Powell's colors and letter symbols (shown here in boldface), but omitted his proposed Permian and divided Archean. McGee's units included the **Q**uaternary (gray), **N**eocene (light yellow), and **E**ocene (dark yellow) of the Cenozoic, the Mesozoic's Cretaceous (**K**, light green), and Jurasso-**T**riassic (dark green), the Paleozoic's Carboniferous (**P**, blue), **D**evonian (dark purple), **S**ilurian (light purple), and **C**ambrian (deep purple), and the **A**rchean (brown) and **V**olcanic (red) of the Azoic. Pleading a dearth of available or reliable data from nonfederal sources, McGee left blank large areas in the Far West to justify the continued appropriations the USGS needed for field work to complete the map. McGee's map, the *AJS* suggested, would be of "great value to the geological student" and praised its careful preparation and coloration "in the best style of the art."[31]

29. John W. Powell, "Plan of Publication," in Powell, *Second Annual Report of the United States Geological Survey to the Secretary of the Interior, 1880–'81* (Washington: Government Printing Office, 1882), pp. xlviii–xlix, and plates 1–7 (Philadelphia: T. Sinclair & Son).

30. W[illiam] J[ohn] McGee, "Preliminary Geologic Map of the United States and Thesaurus of American Formations," in John W. Powell, *Fifth Annual Report of the United States Geological Survey to the Secretary of the Interior 1883–'84* (Washington: Government Printing Office, 1885), pp. xxvii–xxx, and plate 2 (New York: Julius Bien, 1884).

31. Anonymous, "Geological Map of the United States," *American Journal of Science*, 3d ser., 30, no. 177 (1885): 244.

Powell used McGee's map to induce the IGC at its third meeting at Berlin in 1885 to adopt the USGS's geocartographic standards for the planned "Carte Géologique International de l'Europe" (1:1,500,000). In 1886, to support the American committee's recommendation that all geologists use the IGC's standards, Hitchcock modified McGee's map as a "Geological Map of the United States and Parts of Canada . . . to Illustrate the [IGC's] Schemes of Coloration and Nomenclature."[32] Hitchock accepted the IGC's five-level hierarchy of stratigraphic (group, system, stage, rocks, beds) and chronologic (era, period, epoch, age, phase) names, emphasizing that "formation," signifying origin rather than time, was not used in a stratigraphic sense. Hitchcock's all-but-filled-in map also displayed thirteen principal units, but different colors for the Jurassic (blue), Triassic (violet), Permo-Carboniferous (gray), Devonian (brown), Silurian (bluish-green), Cambrian (greenish-gray), and Volcanic (vermillion). He continued to use the Canadian divisions of the Archean, Huronian (A^2, pale rose) and Laurentian (A^1, rose), distinguished Cretaceous and Jurassic metamorphic rocks, and sacrificed details in places to show the narrowness of some mountain ranges. Powell, claiming that USGS cartographic products could not wait for international unity, fixed the agency's usage independently of the IGC in 1889. He decided on a sequence of prismatic and chromatic colors (and patterns) different from those on the McGee's 1884 map and replaced its Archean with Algonkian.[33]

Powell organized sessions on geocartographic standards at the fifth IGC held at Washington in 1891. There, Britain's Thomas Hughes, who had helped to host the fourth IGC at London in 1888, reluctantly echoed Powell's views on the natural selection of usage, but Hughes also called for international monitoring of maps, nomenclature, and classification. Jules Marcou, who had returned to Harvard in 1859, and served with Wheeler in 1875, severely criticized the compilation, content, and scale of McGee's maps in

32. Charles H. Hitchcock, "The Geological Map of the United States," *Transactions of the American Institute of Mining Engineers* 15 (1887): pp. 465–88, and map (New York: Julius Bien, 1886). Hitchcock evaluated Maclure's and subsequent regional and national maps.

33. John W. Powell, "Conference on Map Publication," in Powell, *Tenth Annual Report of the United States Geological Survey to the Secretary of the Interior, 1888–'89: Part I— Geology* (Washington: Government Printing Office, 1890), p. 71, and plate 2.

1892 as part of his general condemnation of Powell's USGS.[34] McGee re-vised his 1884 map as "Reconnoissance Map of the United States Showing the Distribution of the Geologic Systems So Far as Known" (1:7,100,000; State 1893-A, herein).[35] Bien printed the revised, but still significantly in-complete, thirteen-unit map on Gannett's new contour-topographic base. On McGee's new map, ice- or water-deposited Pleistocene units replaced the Quaternary, Powell's revised colors (but not his symbols) depicted the Neocene (orange), Cretaceous (yellow-green), "JuraTrias" (blue-green), Devonian (violet), and Cambrian (pink), and Archean and Igneous units reappeared to bracket the Algonkian. Hitchcock's 1886 map, and McGee's partial refinement of 1893, used unit contacts to define nearly all of the nation's major structural-stratigraphic features. Hitchcock's and McGee's maps summarized nine decades of sometimes commensal efforts by pri-vate individuals, commercial firms, academic institutions, scientific soci-eties, and the state and federal governments to produce a reliable national geocartography as part of fostering the nation's defense, economy, expan-sion, and health, and the compilers' more personal goals.

Epilogue

McGee's cartographic products did not end efforts by the USGS to com-plete and improve its national geologic map, but this work continued un-der new compilers and directors. In 1893, just before the Secretary of the Interior appointed Charles Walcott (whom King hired in 1879) to lead and reform the USGS's geologic unit, McGee resigned and retreated to Powell's

34. Jules Marcou, *The Geological Map of the United States and the United States Geological Survey* and *A Little More Light on the United States Geological Survey* (Cambridge, Mass.: William H. Wheeler, 1892).

35. W J McGee, "Report of Mr. W J McGee," in John W. Powell, *Fourteenth Annual Report of the United States Geological Survey to the Secretary of the Interior 1892–'93: Part I— Report of the Director* (Washington: Government Printing Office, 1893), pp. 212–13, 226, and plate 2 [New York: Julius Bien, 1893, in *Part II—Accompanying Papers* (1894); State 1893-A]. Powell repeated the new colors in "The Geologic Map of the United States," *Transactions of the American Institute of Mining Engineers* 21 (1893): 883. King and Beikman, "Explanatory Text," 8, showed the evolution of McGee's 1893-A map. McGee and the USGS's John B. Torbert produced two 1:15,000,000 maps (State 1893-B, herein), showing separately the two Pleistocene units and the eleven Neocene to Igneous units, for Charles K. Adams, ed., *Johnson's Universal Cyclopædia: A New Edition* (New York: A. J. Johnson, 1893–1897).

Bureau of Ethnology at the Smithsonian. In 1894, Congress voted to cut Powell's USGS salary and he resigned, ending his policies that had contributed heavily to the requirement of line-item appropriations for USGS publications (1887) and programs (1888), the demise of the agency's "Irrigation Survey" (1890), and a USGS-wide reduction-in-force (1892) that decimated its funds and staff.[36] King recommended Walcott as Powell's successor. As USGS director, Walcott revived King's mission orientation, but broadened its scope and rebalanced applied and basic studies. Walcott also professionalized and revitalized, respectively, the agency's topographic and geologic mapping programs, and began co-funded, cooperative geologic mapping with the states. Walcott also served as a consultant to a new international committee and contributed to the standards for map usage adopted at the eighth IGC at Paris in 1900. Walcott's revisions of USGS usage also aided the agency's "Geologic Atlas of the United States," a topographic-geologic project founded by Powell, renewed by Walcott, and maintained actively by the USGS through the 1920s. Using data from the geologic atlas's folio sheets (1:62,500 or 1:125,000), USGS geologists Bailey Willis, George Stose, and Olaf Ljungstedt published new national geologic maps between 1903 (1:18,000,000) and 1932 (1:2,500,000), the latter completed for use at the sixteenth IGC at Washington in 1933. From the 1940s, acceptance spread internationally for the present tripartite distinction of chronologic (era, period, epoch, subepoch), chronostratigraphic (erathem, system, series, subseries), and time-independent lithostratigraphic (supergroup, group, formation, member) units, and standardized names and colors for the major time and time-stratigraphic divisions. In the 1960s and 1970s, the USGS published two new national geologic maps based on data from the agency's 1:24,000 mapping program and from other federal and state agencies, academic institutions, and commercial firms. Douglas Kinney's fourteen-color "Geology" (1:7,500,000) of 1966 appeared four years later in a one-volume national atlas,[37] and Philip King and Helen Beikman pub-

---

36. Mary C. Rabbitt, *Minerals, Lands, and Geology for the Common Defence and General Welfare: Volume 2, 1879–1904* (Washington: U.S. Government Printing Office, 1980), pp. 132–214.

37. Arch C. Gerlach, ed., *The National Atlas of the United States of America* (Washington, D.C.: Department of the Interior/Geological Survey, 1970), pp. 74–75 [Alaska, at 1:17,000,000, and Hawaii, at 1:7,500,000, appear as inserts].

lished in 1974 a separate, multisheet, 1:2,500,000 map using 196 colors and patterns.[38] The USGS reprinted the King-Beikman map in 1982 and reissued it in 1994 on a CD-ROM.[39] The new digital technology also is being used in preparing the geocartography for the USGS's forthcoming "Electronic National Atlas."[40]

38. Two map sheets and one legend sheet accompany King and Beikman, "Explanatory Text."

39. Paul G. Schruben, Raymond E. Arndt, and Walter J. Bawiec, "Geology of the Conterminous United States at 1:2,500,000 Scale—A Digital Representation of the 1974 P. B. King and H. M. Beikman Map," *U.S. Geological Survey Digital Data Series* DDS-11 (1994).

40. Critical and constructive reviews by Barbara M. Christy, Robert H. Dott, Jr., Peter Lessing, Robert C. McDowell, John C. Reed, Jr., Eugene C. Robertson, Cecil J. Schneer, and Arthur P. Schultz, my colleagues within or outside the USGS, significantly improved the manuscript versions of this article.

PART TWO
OCEANIC EXPLORATION

SCIENCE AS A LANDED ACTIVITY
Scientifics and Seamen Aboard the U.S. Exploring Expedition[1]

At its core the Western process of modernization has meant both the transgression of existing boundaries and the creation of new ones. Imperial interests have taken Europeans outside their premodern domain, and into "New World" lands—lands that often were almost literally unbounded until their geographic carving by Western settlers. Analogously, as European states and the United States continued to divide geographic space, the economy followed suit. The rewards of empire necessitated a division of labor and the subsequent rise of the professions.

In the past two decades, historians have placed science within the context of professionalization and imperialism. The products of empire filled neatly divided cabinets of curiosities, and natural historians and philosophers became more specialized, in part because of the exponential leap in phenomena the New World offered. Scientists frequently insinuated them-

1. I am very grateful to Jane Camerini, Tom Gieryn, Brad Hume, Craig McConnell, Jack Green Musselman, Lynn Nyhart, Richard Sorrenson, and my fall 1994 sociology of science classmates for encouragement and valuable comments on earlier drafts. This material is based partly on work supported under a National Science Foundation Graduate Fellowship.

selves aboard naval expeditions to the New World, and sometimes (as with Joseph Banks) even funded their own voyages. Museums, zoos, libraries, and traveling exhibitions sprang up all over the Western world in an attempt to contain and display the natural wonders of empire.

This has become a commonplace story to historians of exploration and of science. However, a major historical shift that occurred around mid-nineteenth-century deserves more attention. Namely, as both the American scientific community and navy attempted to professionalize, they fought heated skirmishes over scientific spaces and tasks. Hugh Slotten and Thomas Manning have accounted for the institutional battles between civilian and naval science. Helen Rozwadowski has exposed recently the abrasive relationships in the 1850s–70s between scientists and crew members aboard sea-dredging expeditions.[2] In this paper I will examine the U.S. Exploring Expedition (1838–1842) to show that prior to the mid-nineteenth century, work space on voyages of discovery was clearly if uneasily divided: the navy had a standing claim on sea science (navigation, cartography, astronomy, etc.), while civilian scientists generally did land science when the ship docked.

I want to emphasize that paying attention to physical space can inform our understanding of the history of exploration, examining literally a figurative suggestion made by E. L. Towle in his dissertation thirty years ago: "the seafaring frontier competed with the continental frontier as a formative zone of conflict between civilian and military scientist, between pure and applied science and between emerging scientific institutions."[3] Maritime voyages faced issues of limited space not encountered by land expeditions. Intense limitations of space aggravated social tensions between navigation-oriented naval officers and the academic scientists who occasionally accompanied these expeditions. In the confined and contentious spaces of naval vessels and of the pre-professionalized scientific landscape, *discipline* (in both senses of that word) was a crucial tool for gaining control.

---

2. H. Rozwadowski, "Small World: Forging a Scientific Maritime Culture for Oceanography," *Isis* 3 (1996): 409–429.

3. E. L. Towle, "Science, Commerce, and the Navy of the Seafaring Frontier (1842–1861): The Role of Lieutenant M. F. Maury and the U.S. Naval Hydrographic Office in Naval Exploration, Commercial Expansion and Oceanography before the Civil War," (Ph.D. diss., University of Rochester, 1996), p. xvi.

Recent sociological literature suggests that the very interaction of different social groups leads them to redefine themselves in relation to each other. As the professions have proliferated they have engaged in a Malthusian struggle for the resources of space and prestige. Science—or any other seemingly well-defined pursuit—is "[n]othing but a *space*, one that acquires its authority precisely from and through episodic negotiations of its flexible and contextually contingent borders and territories."[4] Rather than seek an essential definition of science, the sociological approach historicizes the boundaries drawn around science. In this way, science is understood not as a transcendental entity but as a historically changing territory. The cartographic metaphors pervading these sociological studies take on particular resonance for the U.S. Exploring Expedition, for which mapping was a primary mission. The scientific and naval crew members may have laid implicit claims to professional territory, but claiming *physical* territory was also part of the voyage's explicit mission. Moreover, within the voyage's limited ship space and personnel, boundary issues proved quite tangible.[5]

One critical boundary in this episode is that between land and sea. Although scientists had been integral to voyages long before the U.S. Exploring Expedition, their role on ship still was mainly that of the passenger. Natural history—the specialty of the civilian scientists on this voyage— was done on land, and sea travel for these men was largely a necessary evil in *getting to* exotic locales. The type of science generally practiced by naval officers was, not surprisingly, done at sea: cartography, navigation, hydrography, oceanography, meteorology, astronomy, and the like all could be per-

4. T. F. Gieryn, "Boundaries of Science," in *Handbook of Science and Technology Studies*, (ed. S. Jasanoff, et al., Thousand Oaks, CA, 1995), p. 405. An incomplete but good sample of this literature would also include: M. Lamont and M. Fournier, eds., *Cultivating Differences: Symbolic Boundaries and the Making of Inequality* (Chicago, 1992); A. Abbott, *The System of the Professions: An Essay on the Division of Expert Labor* (Chicago, 1988); D. Wood, *The Power of Maps* (New York, 1992). Theoretical roots for much of this work can be found in Mary Douglas's anthropology, which she retrospectively outlined in *How Institutions Think* (Syracuse, NY, 1986).

5. For intriguing analyses of ship spaces, see G. Dening, *Mr. Bligh's Bad Language: Passion, Power and Theater on the Bounty* (Cambridge, 1992), pp. 19–33 and passim; D. Outram, "New Spaces in Natural History," in *Cultures of Natural History*, ed. N. Jardine, J. A. Secord, and E. C. Spary (Cambridge, 1996).

6. One striking indicator of this workplace division is that the scientists' journals became very prolific at sea, while officers found the idle time to write while on shore. See

formed within the confines of the ship.[6] This kind of work required years of on-board training that no armchair or university could provide.[7] Naturalists on the U.S. Exploring Expedition often were derided for their "land-lubberliness," while some of the officers were noticeably incompetent in over-land expeditions.[8] In conflicts between landlubbers and salts, class and physical occupational boundaries reinforced each other. Civilian science was a landed activity.[9]

In light of this strained shore-line boundary, we might wish to reconsider the extent to which Humboldtian science worked as a well-orchestrated program. Susan Faye Cannon argued dramatically and convincingly that Alexander von Humboldt's geophysical and geonaturalist pursuits served as a model for much science (especially state-supported science) in the nineteenth century.[10] I would amend this admirable thesis with a note of physical reality: in practice, the various pursuits that constituted Humboldtian science were often at odds, as they were on the U.S. Exploring Expedition. One could easily forget the importance of global relationships when one was aboard a cramped ship.

The constraints of ship size and of naval discipline created another boundary that is central to this paper: that between idleness and usefulness. Expedition commander Charles Wilkes would write of the voyage that "[i]n all our explorations the constant aim has been to obtain *useful* results."[11] Limits of space, money, and time all required the expedition's participants

---

D. B. Tyler, *The Wilkes Expedition: The First United States Exploring Expedition, 1838–1842* (Philadelphia, 1968), p. 30.

7. For an example of this position, see Anonymous, "Character and Duties of the Naval Profession," *Naval Magazine* 3 (May 1837): 228–245, especially p. 235.

8. On a trip through the Cascades led by Lt. Johnson, it became clear that "Johnson had no previous experience as an overland leader and Pickering and Brackenridge, at home in the woods, found it irritating to be under this youngster's command." Tyler, *Wilkes Expedition*, p. 244.

9. For figures on the class backgrounds of nineteenth-century civilian scientists, see R. V. Bruce, *The Launching of Modern American Science 1846–1876* (Ithaca, NY, 1987), p. 216.

10. S. F. Cannon, *Science in Culture: The Early Victorian Period* (New York, 1978), pp. 73–110; also see a lengthy discussion of this thesis in H. Slotten, *Patronage, Practice, and the Culture of American Science: Alexander Dallas Bache and the U.S. Coast Survey* (Cambridge, 1994), pp. 113–146.

11. C. Wilkes, *Synopsis of the Cruise of the U.S. Exploring Expedition during the Years 1838, '39, '40, '41, & '42; Delivered before the National Institute by its Commander . . .* (Washington, 1842), p. 42.

to be efficient. Any breach of this code of productivity, especially in the commander's eyes, constituted a subversion of the mission, and a potential loss to the glory of the country. This expedition's commander in particular performed some fascinating boundary work in his attempts to decide which individuals and functions would most efficiently fulfill the expedition's ultimate aim—the expansion of American commercial, naval, and scientific influence.

Uncertain Boundaries

After over a decade of delay and controversy, the U.S. Exploring Expedition finally set sail from Hampton Roads, Virginia, on 18 August 1838. This was America's first peacetime navy–science endeavor, and its mission was suitably grandiose: to chart the South Pacific for commercial traders, determine the existence or non-existence of a Great Southern Continent, establish the United States as a global contender in science, and spy on the coveted British Hudson's Bay Company in Northwest America. The expedition's success can in some sense be measured in sheer volume: the crew drew more than 200 charts, explored 1,500 miles of Antarctica's coast, and deposited tens of thousands of biological and geological specimens into what would become the Smithsonian museums. More intangibly, the voyage established not only the United States' position on the global stage, but also much of the framework for future navy–science interaction in America.[12]

Six ships, Lieutenant Charles Wilkes, a squadron of naval officers and seamen, and nine "scientifics" (scientists and artists of various specialties) embodied the final outcome of prolonged debates among the Congress and navy over the expedition's organization.[13] The selection of Wilkes, based on his scientific skill rather than naval experience, and the downsizing of the scientific staff from the original thirty two, indicate that much of the boundary work occurred before the voyage even began.

Proficient in many sciences and a fierce promoter of the navy, Wilkes

12. G. S. Smith, "The Navy before Darwinism: Science, Exploration and Diplomacy in Antebellum America," *American Quarterly* 28 (Spring 1976): 41–55.

13. H. J. Viola and C. Margolis (eds.), *Magnificent Voyagers: The U.S. Exploring Expedition, 1838–1842* (Washington, DC, 1985), p. 10.

insisted that his crew were not to be designated simply "hewers of wood and drawers of water."[14] As the expedition commander, he claimed—and rather easily won—jurisdiction over virtually every scientific function on the voyage; he regulated the scientifics' activities and often assigned himself or other seamen to scientific tasks. Upon the voyage's completion, he was placed in charge of the specimen collections and (less unusually) of publishing the authoritative first account of the expedition—much to the chagrin of the expedition's scientifics. Despite some private grumblings, however, the American scientific community launched no protest against Wilkes's dominion over the voyage's scientific functions and products. Such objections seemed trivial in the face of the status boost and specimens the expedition gave to American science.

The expedition began as the brain child of one Jeremiah N. Reynolds, a well-connected young proselytizer with a great interest in John Cleve Symmes' theory that the earth was made of concentric spheres, and that one could travel to the center of the earth through openings in the poles. Reynolds soon realized, however, that far more marketable than such scientific esoterica was the prospect of improving America's commercial trade status. After drumming up support among merchants—especially fishers and whalers—Reynolds successfully lobbied Congress to organize an expedition, and on May 21, 1828, the House of Representatives passed a resolution requesting a ship to use in charting the South Pacific more accurately.[15]

In peacetime, commerce had become a primary concern for the navy, which had established the U.S. Coast Survey (1807) and the Depot of Charts and Instruments (1830) to support and protect American merchants in poorly-charted seas.[16] These joint ventures with civilian scientists had not

14. Ibid., p. 14. For biographical material on Wilkes, see his *Autobiography of Rear Admiral Charles Wilkes, U.S. Navy, 1798–1877* (Washington, DC, 1978); D. Henderson, *The Hidden Coasts: A Biography of Charles Wilkes* (New York, 1966).

15. For an excellent account of these events, see W. Stanton, *the Great United States Exploring Expedition of 1838–1842* (Berkeley, CA, 1975). A more popularized portrayal of the expedition can be found in W. Bixby, *The Forgotten Voyage of Charles Wilkes* (New York, 1996).

16. S. Schlee, *The Edge of an Unfamiliar World: A History of Oceanography* (New York, 1973), p. 23; J. H. Schroeder, *Shaping a Maritime Empire: The Commercial and Diplomatic Role of the American Navy, 1829–1861* (Westport, CT, 1985); H. L. Burstyn, "Seafaring and the Emergence of American Science," in *The Atlantic World of Robert G. Albion*, ed. B. W. Labaree (Middletown, CT, 1975). The history of oceanography is also discussed in M. Deacon, *Scientists and the Sea 1650–1900; a Study of Marine Science* (London, 1971).

always been successful; for instance, navy engineers took over the work of
the U.S. Coast Survey from civilian Ferdinand Hassler, and the results were
so disastrous that the navy had to admit the charts were unsafe and in some
cases useless.[17] Regardless, the $300,000 that Congress finally appropriated
in 1836 to the U.S. Exploring Expedition appeared to be a wise investment.[18]

In part because of these same tensions, the U.S. Exploring Expedition
came very near extinction several times during its thirteen years of bureaucratic planning. Congressional disagreements concerning appropriations,
squabbles over distribution of authority, and other delays caused many original participants to resign in frustration long before the voyage began. Most
important for our story was one of these sources of delay: the extensive debates between scientists and the Navy Department about the nature and
composition of the "scientific corps."[19] Navy Secretary Mahlon Dickerson
spent at least three years soliciting opinions on this very subject from scientific societies (which had begun to flourish at the beginning of the century), although he did not always heed their advice. Himself an amateur botanist, president of the Columbian Institute for the Promotion of Arts and
Sciences, and member of the American Philosophical Society,[20] Dickerson
had sought to give the navy exclusive control over the expedition, but while
some well-trained navigators and astronomers entered the service, the navy
would not have an equivalent of West Point for training scientists until 1845.
Seemingly endless negotiations ensued as Dickerson avoided officially appointing or acknowledging any civilian scientists.[21]

In 1836, physician-naturalist James Dekay recommended to Dickerson

17. F. Cajori, *The Chequered Career of Ferdinand Rudolph Hassler: First Superintendent of the United States Coast Survey* (Boston, 1929), p. 124; in Slotten, *Patronage*, pp. 50–51.

18. See, for example, J. A. Pearce, Senate Joint Committee of the Library Report, June 1846; in D. C. Gilman, *The Life of James Dwight Dana: Scientific Explorer, Mineralogist, Geologist, Zoologist, Professor in Yale University* (New York, 1899), p. 49.

19. The designation of the scientists and artists as a "scientific corps" signifies imme-diately that the Navy Department did not consider these naturalists outside the purview of naval authority.

20. Stanton, *Great . . . Expedition*, p. 33; A. H. Dupree, *Science in the Federal Govern-ment: A History of Policies and Activities*, reprint, 1957 (Baltimore and London, 1986), p. 34.

21. Some interesting notes are appropriate here: The original Congressional alloca-tion had almost been spent in 1838, when Dickerson became ill. The expedition was hastily assembled and put to sea before the Secretary could cause further delay. Also, Nathaniel Hawthorne submitted an unsuccessful application to be ship historiographer. See Tyler, *Wilkes Expedition*, p. 12.

a substantial $3,500 salary for each of the expedition's scientists. When Dickerson balked, naturalist Asa Gray responded that the "labors of the two classes [scientists and officers] are as distinct as their professions, and can have no more bearing upon each other, as regards their respective remunerations in this Expedition, than has the pay of a naval commander on the salary of a professor in one of our universities." Furthermore, Gray argued, naval officers' pay would continue past the end of the voyage; the scientists, on the other hand, would have to return to the still-meager market for full-time scientific work.[22] Scientific appointee Horatio Hale similarly was peeved when Dickerson refused his request for due pay—but responded quite differently. Hale, like the other scientifics, had been refusing other work for the seven months since his appointment to the expedition, but had yet to receive any pay. "I ask, then, only the rights of a common sailor."[23] From these and other letters, it seems evident that, especially when it came to finances, the boundary between science and the navy was a flexible one.

Some of the scientifics were wary of naval control of the voyage. Joseph Couthouy, who eventually would be the expedition's conchologist, wrote in 1836 to President Andrew Jackson to request that conchology be added to the sciences represented on the voyage. Jackson recommended that Couthouy deal directly with the expedition commander, but the naturalist replied, "I have preferred addressing myself directly to Your Excellency, as the fountain head, rather than to any of those Gentlemen at the head of the [navy] department presuming that you would be best qualified to judge of the importance of the measure."[24] Physical anthropologist Samuel Morton, on the other hand, seemingly did not feel such territorial proclivities. One month after Couthouy's exchange with Jackson, Morton implied in a letter to Dickerson that for all he cared, geology could be subsumed under the expedition's hydrography department, which was under the navy's direct control.[25] The very next day, Morton and Reynell Coates wrote Dickerson on behalf of the Academy of Natural Sciences, urging that "the duties and rel-

22. The salary was eventually set at a still-considerable $2,500. A. Gray to M. Dickerson, Nov. 8, 1836; *Records of the U.S. Exploring Expedition under the Command of Lt. Charles Wilkes, 1838–1842*, 25 vols. (Washington, DC, 1978). Hereafter, I will refer to this collection as *Records of the U.S. Ex.Ex.*

23. H. Hale to M. Dickerson, July 16, 1837; *Records of the U.S.Ex.Ex.*

24. J. Couthouy to A. Jackson, Aug. 10, 1836; *Records of the U.S.Ex.Ex.*

25. S. G. Morton to M. Dickerson (?), Sept. 26, 1836; *Records of the U.S.Ex.Ex.*

ative positions of members of the scientific corps, should be clearly and explicitly laid down by the proper authorities,"[26] namely, the navy.

Six months later, as the voyage's departure date neared, the scientifics still had not once met the expedition's original commander, Thomas ap Catesby Jones, to discuss division of expedition duties.[27] Asa Gray, Charles Pickering, and Reynell Coates—all original scientific appointees—wrote a nervous joint letter to Dickerson: disciplinary boundaries in science, they wrote, were "often vague—and sometimes arbitrary."[28] Several months later, another exchange centered on the perceived arbitrariness of scientific specialization: since two of the expedition's naturalists (Peale and Pickering) wanted to be appointed mammalogist, the naturalists as a whole decided that the department was simply too encompassing to be assigned to only one person. Coates wrote to the naval committee which had been appointed to deal with the scientifics that "it is to be feared that by the assignment of this branch exclusively to either of the two persons desirous of it . . . feelings might be engendered, which may result in a serious detriment, both to the harmony of the corps and the interests of Science."[29] The committee responded tersely that only an "exact and definite division of labor" would "prevent collision or carelessness" among the scientifics. Peale was assigned mammalogy and the case was closed.[30]

In the face of such infighting over the division of scientific disciplines, many scientists yearned for *naval* discipline to settle these issues quickly and

26. S. G. Morton and R. L. Coates to M. Dickerson, Sept. 27, 1836; *Records of the U.S.Ex.Ex.*

27. Jones had made a name for himself as a hero in the Battle of New Orleans in 1814, and by establishing formal trade relations between the United States and the Society Islands. See Schroeder, *Shaping*, p. 18. For more of Jones, see U. T. Bradley, "The Contentious Commodore: Thomas ap Catesby Jones of the Old Navy 1788–1858," (Ph.D. Diss., Cornell University, 1933).

28. C. Pickering, A. Gray, and R. Coates to M. Dickerson, March 7, 1837; *Records of the U.S.Ex.Ex.*

29. R. Coates to the Committee of Conference with the Scientific Corps, Aug. 17, 1837, *Records of the U.S.Ex.Ex.*

30. P. M. Patterson to M. Dickerson, Aug. 24, 1837, *Records of the U.S.Ex.Ex.* The committee's official reason for giving Peale mammalogy was equally arbitrary according to "purely" scientific standards: Patterson argued that Pickering (already head of ichthyology and herpetology) would be responsible for about 10,000 species, while Peale (as head of ornithology) would only have 3,000 bird species. The 800 then-known species of mammals should therefore go to Peale. Unofficially, the committee thought Pickering was incompetent (Patterson to Dickerson, September 12, 1837, *Records of the U.S.Ex.Ex.*).

efficiently. As Hugh Slotten has argued, "discipline" meant more than a sub-set of scientific endeavor to 1830s scientists; the imposition of discipline (in its punitive or didactic sense) on American scientists would also mean that they could eventually achieve (and surpass) the morally sound, charlatan-free reputations of their European colleagues. Pushing a Whiggish concep-tion of science, the Lazzaroni especially would seek to emphasize discipli-nary control and moral standards. Far from inevitable, scientific progress had to be "guided and directed, ideally by managers and administrators." Even Hassler, when he regained control of the Coast Survey in 1832, con-tinued to insist on employing navy and army staff because he admired their discipline.[31] In this process, if academic science could define itself against other professions like the navy, it might avoid internal territory disputes. At a time when science was rapidly professionalizing and specializing, many scientists were willing to allow an outside arbiter to assign convenient boundaries and moral duties.

Science at Sea—Naval Discipline and the Definition of Boundaries

Lieutenant Charles Wilkes was all too happy to oblige. From the time he re-placed Jones as expedition commander in 1838,[32] Wilkes intended to keep the scientifics on a short leash. The navy had discipline problems of its own to face, since the post–War of 1812 military was notorious for its disorder-liness.[33] Furthermore, the official naval order for the expedition stated that Wilkes had been chosen for his scientific expertise and that he was to lead a strictly scientific mission:

> The armament of the Exploring Expedition being adapted merely for its necessary defense, while engaged in the examination and survey of the

31. Slotten, *Patronage*, pp. 16, 27–28, 51, and *passim*. Also see D. W. Howe, *The Political Culture of the American Whigs* (Chicago, 1979), pp. 51–54.
32. Like many other appointees to the expedition, the original commander, Jones, grew tired of the bureaucratic delay and resigned from the expedition on 1838. After his elec-tion, Martin van Buren took the expedition's organization from Dickerson and turned it over to Secretary of War Joel Poinsett, who assigned Wilkes to the commanding post.
33. J. D. Kazar, Jr., "The United States Navy and Scientific Exploration, 1837–1860," (Ph.D. diss., University of Massachusetts, 1973), pp. 4–5.

Southern Ocean, against any attempts to disturb its operations by the savage and warlike inhabitants of those islands; and the objects which it is destined to promote being altogether scientific and useful, intended for the benefit equally of the United States and of all commercial nations of the world; it is considered to be entirely divested of all military character.[34]

Of course, much of the cautious rhetoric of this order was an outright diplomatic white lie intended to placate the Europeans. However, the fact remained that Wilkes was a commander with unusual qualifications and jurisdiction. As former superintendent of the navy's Depot of Charts and Instruments he had significant training in navigation, surveying,[35] mathematics, and art. His original association with the expedition was as the procurer of instruments and books: while in Europe selecting the finest instruments, Wilkes had consorted with some of the foremost natural philosophers and instrument-makers. Rather than the "Banksian Learned Empire" whose main interests lay in natural history, medicine and antiquaries, the American lieutenant's acquaintances more naturally derived from the Cambridge and London mathematical practitioners who sought to loosen Banks's virtual monopoly on publicly supported science.[36] Likewise, in the United States, Wilkes, Maury and others stood in stark contrast to an older generation of officers, like former Navy Secretary Samuel L. Southard, who did not deem naval personnel as competent to perform geophysical, let alone natural historical, tasks.[37] When Wilkes returned from his overseas trip, Charles Pickering complained about the disproportionate number of physical science texts purchased, but then demurred that Wilkes "could not have been expected to know the tools of a Zoologist."[38]

34. This order was signed by Dickerson on June 22, 1838; in Gilman, *Life*, p. 64.

35. In fact, Wilkes had a reputation as the finest surveyor in the Navy (Tyler, *Wilkes Expedition*, p. 10). He had been trained by Coast Survey superintendent Ferdinand Hassler.

36. The rivalry between these two groups instigated the infamous decline-of-science debates and Royal Society reforms in British science. This is argued in D. P. Miller, "Between Hostile Camps: Sir Humphry Davy's Presidency of the Royal Society of London, 1820–1827," *British Journal for the History of Science* 16 (1983): 1–47.

37. Kazar, "U.S. Navy," p. 30. Also see the entry on Dickerson in P. E. Coletta (ed.), *American Secretaries of the Navy*, 2 vols. (Annapolis, MD, 1980), vol. 1, p. 156.

38. C. Pickering to M. Dickerson, Feb. 15, 1837; *Records of the U.S.Ex.Ex.* On Wilkes's European tour, see S. J. Dick, "Centralizing Navigational Technology in America: The U.S. Navy's Depot of Charts and Instruments, 1830–1842," *Technology and Culture* 33 (1992): 467–509; D. E. Borthwick, "Outfitting the United States Exploring Expedition: Lieuten-

For his own part, Wilkes sympathized with the expedition's former commander, Jones, who had anticipated having to "preserv[e] harmony and . . . reconcil[e] any discordance which may arise between the scientific and naval members of the Expedition."[39] Wilkes had written to Dickerson earlier that year that science would hardly suffer, and command structure would greatly benefit, if naval officers were to perform all scientific duties.[40] In August 1838, he even suggested that the medical officers could do the natural history in their spare time, thus ridding the voyage of any civilians.[41] He was denied by Secretary of War Joel Poinsett only because dismissing the scientific corps at such a late date would have "creat[ed] a clamour." This did not prevent Wilkes from reducing the scientific corps from thirty two to nine members or from dismissing civilian Walter R. Johnson, who originally had been assigned to handle magnetism, electricity, and astronomy. Instead, Wilkes made himself surveyor, astronomer, physicist, meteorologist, and historiographer.[42] This was no honorary self-appointment: during the voyage, when geologist James Dwight Dana attempted to aid an officer with meteorological measurements, Wilkes sharply reprimanded him for encroaching on naval (read: natural philosophical) functions.[43]

But if Wilkes was no scientific ignoramus, then neither were all the scientifics landlubbers. Couthouy had seventeen years of naval experience, and Dana had traveled on naval expeditions in the Mediterranean. In fact, out of necessity Wilkes came to rely on the scientifics for non-scientific functions. On one island, Couthouy tried to negotiate with hostile natives, and expedition naturalist Titian Peale then was asked to draw his gun to frighten

---

ant Charles Wilkes's European Assignment, August-November, 1836," *Proceedings of the American Philosophical Society* 109 (1965): 159–172.

39. T. ap Catesby Jones to M. Dickerson, Aug. 11, 1837; *Records of the U.S.Ex.Ex.*

40. C. Wilkes to M. Dickerson, March 18, 1837; *Records of the U.S.Ex.Ex.*

41. It was not unusual for the ship's surgeon to serve double duty as naturalist. See, for instance, the disastrous relationship between Darwin and the Beagle's surgeon, described in J. W. Gruber, "Who Was the *Beagle's* Naturalist?" *British Journal for the History of Science* 4 (1969): 266–282.

42. Memorandum by C. Wilkes and reply from J. Poinsett, Aug., 1838 (?); *Records of the U.S.Ex.Ex.* The first memo is unsigned, but is in Wilkes's handwriting. Also see C. Bordwell, "Delay and Wreck of the *Peacock*: An Episode in the Wilkes Expedition," *Oregon Historical Quarterly* 92 (1991): 119.

43. J. D. Dana to Redfield, 1843, Yale University Rare Book Library, New Haven; in Tyler, *Wilkes Expedition*, p. 37.

them.[44] New Navy Secretary J. K. Paulding's final instructions to Wilkes might be seen as encouraging such fluid relationships between the scientifics and crew:

> [n]o special directions are thought necessary in regard to the mode of conducting the scientific researches and experiments which you are enjoined to prosecute, nor is it intended to limit the members of the corps each to his own particular service. All are expected to co-operate harmoniously in those kindred pursuits, whose equal dignity and usefulness should insure equal ardor and industry in extending their bounds and verifying their principles.[45]

Accordingly, over the course of the voyage, Wilkes continually made temporary assignments of scientific tasks not only among the scientists, but also among himself and other officers. For example, he wrote in his journal that "[o]n our arrival at Valparaiso, the officers and scientific gentlemen were assigned to such duties as were deemed most desirable to insure the results in the different departments."[46] Wilkes considered the expedition's scientific aims to be very important—too important, in fact, to leave entirely to the scientifics. He voraciously drove *both* crew members and scientists to collect specimens and map territory. In Rio, Wilkes chastised two junior officers for climbing Sugar Loaf Mountain without taking instruments to record elevation. He sent a memo to their superior (Hudson) regretting that their jaunt had resulted only in the "idle and boastful saying that its summit had been reached, instead of an excursion which might have been useful to the expedition." The officers made the climb again with the proper instruments.[47] Even the scientifics occasionally forgot Wilkes's devotion to data collection. In Tierra del Fuego only a few months later, the

---

44. C. Wilkes, *Voyage Round the World, Embracing the Principal Events of the Narrative of the United States Exploring Expedition* (New York, 1851), p. 126.

45. Ibid., p. ix. Paulding is best known for his pro-slavery tract, *Slavery in the United States*, 1836, reprint (New York, 1968).

46. Wilkes, *Voyage*, pp. 67–68.

47. Dec. 15, 1838 memo, in Jessie Poesch, ed., *Titian Ramsay Peale 1799–1885 and His Journal of the Wilkes Expedition* (Philadelphia, 1961), p. 73; D. D. Jackson, "Around the World in 1,392 Days with the Navy's Wilkes—and His 'Scientifics,'" *Smithsonian* 16 (1985): 51.

scientifics embarked on two different excursions into the mountains, both times neglecting to bring along instruments for measuring altitude.[48]

When it came to assigning tasks, Wilkes often saw those under his command—including the scientifics—as interchangeable parts in a machine that never quite lived up to his hopes for efficiency. As it was expedient, Wilkes would assign tasks to anyone he deemed competent to complete them, regardless of rank or pre-assigned duties. Not surprisingly, this attitude annoyed many of his subordinates. Peale in particular began to feel that he and his colleagues were just so much scientific equipment. Once, he noticed that a first lieutenant had ordered the following cargo onto the boats being sent ashore: "2d cutter, Lt. Emmons, will take 10 water bags, 2 buckets, 1 shovel, & Mess[rs] Hale & Peale." Even worse, another officer once ordered, "bring off the yams, hogs & scientifics."[49]

In addition, Wilkes often would move officers and scientifics around from ship to ship. At almost all times, however, the scientifics were divided between different ships. From what information is available, the divisions appear arbitrary, since there are no obvious similarities between the scientists assigned to any particular ship. It also does not seem that Wilkes consistently kept his favorites (or the troublemakers for that matter) on board the *Vincennes* with him.[50]

In fact, what seems more likely is that Wilkes occasionally forgot about the scientifics. As was clear from his instructions, Wilkes's first priority was charting land; any natural history work performed was simply a pleasant bonus—priorities which echoed those of the U.S. Coast Survey.[51] During the first two years of the expedition, in fact, the ships rarely landed, and the scientifics subsequently had little opportunity to collect. To the scientifics, time spent on board ship was practically wasted. To Wilkes, the opposite was true: coming to port sometimes enabled him to set up astronomical observatories or the occasional land survey, but it also meant the crew was collecting diseases and hangovers rather than cartographic data. Peale com-

48. Stanton, *Great . . . Expedition*, p. 109.
49. Journal entry, April 24, 1841; in Poesch, *Peale*, p. 186.
50. Only once did Wilkes indicate any reason for dividing up the scientifics: "The scientific gentlemen, previous to departure, were distributed between the *Vincennes, Peacock,* and *Relief,* in order to produce the best chance for results." Wilkes, *Synopsis*, p. 9. This still does not explain why he continually shuffled the scientifics between ships.
51. Slotten, *Patronage*, p. 44.

plained bitterly about his idleness; in a final fit of frustration off the island of Raraka, he wrote in his journal:

> *No Naturalist* [sic] *were permitted to land . . .* It is our misfortune, not our fault, that both England and France are doing this kind of service in a much superior manner. We have been close to this Island all day, could see it abounded in Scientific riches, & boats were swinging idly to their davits, men were looking as to a paradise, but no, a survey is made, *nothing more* is requisite, and time flies. WHAT WAS A SCIENTIFIC CORPS SENT FOR?[52]

Peale must have confronted Wilkes soon thereafter, for the captain soon developed a routine that was more palatable to both him and the scientifics: he would deposit them on shore to collect, the ships would make their surveys, collect the scientifics again, and move on to the next island. In this way, Wilkes fully acknowledged the division of workplace between the two groups: his work was done at sea; their work was done on land. For the sake of maximum efficiency, he was willing to accommodate that difference. In the most dramatic manifestation of this decision, Wilkes left the scientifics behind to collect specimens on land while the naval crew traveled south for several months to establish the presence of a Great Southern Continent (Antarctica). With little hope of finding biological or geological specimens—in fact, with no guarantee of finding any land at all—he and the scientifics agreed that their presence would be pointless and burdensome.[53]

---

52. Journal entry, Aug. 29, 1839; in Poesch, *Peale*, pp. 153–154. Helen Maria Williams, the English translator of Humboldt's *Personal Narrative*, complained of this phenomenon earlier in the century: "[I]t must be admitted, that in general sea-expeditions have a certain monotony, which arises from the necessity of continually speaking of navigation in technical language. The mariner also, while he braves the element on which he steers his perilous course, is chiefly occupied by it's [sic] dangers. The outlines and the bearings of coasts are leading objects of his researches; he visits only the shores of the countries where he disembarks, and holds but slight communications with the natives by whom they are peopled." See Humboldt, *Personal Narrative of Travels to the Equinoctial Regions of the New Continent* (London, 1818), p. vi.

53. See for example, Dana's Jan. 28, 1840 letter to Herrick: "The scientific corps were detached soon after as a worse than useless appendage to an expedition cruising among the ice; for we should find little or nothing in natural history in those frigid regions, and would only add to the number of mouths that must be filled from the stock of provisions on board." In Gilman, *Life*, p. 114. The exception was Peale, who did accompany the first Antarctic trip. Peale found it impossible to do much work in the midst of the Antarctic's violent, icy storms.

This episode more than any other highlights that the two kinds of work had been clearly divided: the very locales that were (ostensibly) of no interest to the naturalists were a top priority for the crew.

Any guidance from Wilkes concerning the division of scientific labor (except that the scientifics were not to encroach on "naval science") was generally ad hoc, and the scientifics were left to their own devices to parse up their work. Presumably this would have been a dicey business, since many of the scientifics rightly felt they were not all equally qualified. For example, Dana reflected midway through the expedition on the progress thus far: "Rich has done so-so. Peale has got some fine birds and butterflies. . . . Agate is very busy, sketching and taking portraits. Drayton has made an immense collection of zoological drawings. . . . Brackenridge, in the botanical department is invaluable."[54] Dana's mild contempt for Rich probably stems from Rich's status as a political appointee—he had only token qualifications as a botanist, but had the supreme fortune to be one of Mahlon Dickerson's collecting buddies.[55] However, there is no evidence of any territorial disputes between the scientifics during the voyage, even though several encroached on others' duties. For example, Dana and Peale chose to do their own drawings, even though Drayton and Agate were the expedition's official artists.[56] Also, usually only a few scientifics were allowed ashore at once, so they often collected for each other.[57]

Such collegial interest in science was harder to obtain from the crew members. Wilkes had promised the scientifics they would receive any required aid from the crew—for which the crew was to receive extra pay[58]— but the promise was fulfilled more and more grudgingly as the voyage wore on. At first many of the men were amused by the scientifics' curious habits. A paradigmatic case is that of Lt. William Reynolds, who gushed at the voyage's outset,

54. Gilman, *Life*, pp. 121–123.
55. Stanton, *Great . . . Expedition*, p. 47.
56. Poesch, *Peale*, pp. 68–69.
57. J. D. Dana to his brother, June 1839; collection of Marie T. Dana, New Haven, CT; in Tyler, *Wilkes Expedition*, p. 72.
58. Wilkes promised this extra compensation to the crew for their participation in scientific duties (implying, of course, that such work was outside the *normal* bounds of naval duty). However, when the expedition returned, Secretary of War Poinsett informed Wilkes that such compensation was illegal.

I like the associates we shall have during the cruise—these enthusiastic Art-ists, and those headlong, indefatigable pursures [sic] and slayers of birds, beasts, and fishes, and the gatherers of shells, rocks, insects, etc., etc. They are leaving their comfortable homes, to follow the strong bent of their minds, to garner up the strange things of strange lands, which fact proves that the ruling passion is strong in life. . . . We, the ignoramuses, will no doubt take great interest in learning the origin, nature and history of many things, which we have before regarded with curious and admiring eyes.[59]

But the repetitious gathering and storing of specimens soon lost its charm. The crew resented the scientifics for the "additional workload they represented, such as the need to ferry them from ship to shore so they could collect specimens from the islands the squadron surveyed."[60] Several months into the voyage, Dana wrote a friend that the naval personnel (Wilkes and second-in-command Hudson excluded) were notably apa-thetic to scientific pursuits. He remarked, for example, that when taking reg-ular temperature readings, officers would often hold the thermometer half in the sun and half in the shade.[61]

Peale thought of the sailors as children,[62] and this attitude, needless to say, did not make him popular with the crew. In particular, he had trouble with one junior officer, who capriciously challenged Peale's right to take a crew member ashore for specimen collecting, even though the naturalist had received permission from Wilkes. Peale indignantly reported the incident to Lt. Hudson, claiming that "the duty on which I have been sent by the government is my first obligation, the wounded dignity of a subaltern shall not change my course while I can retain the support of higher authority."[63]

Peale invoked the right "higher authority," for few dared question Wilkes's martinet-like authority over the expedition's resources—those

59. W. Reynolds to sister Lydia, Aug. 12, 1838; in A. H. Cleaver and E. J. Stann (eds.), *Voyage to the Southern Ocean: The Letters of Lieutenant William Reynolds from the United States Exploring Expedition, 1838–1842* (Annapolis, MD, 1988), pp. 2–3.

60. Ibid., p. xxxvi.

61. J. D. Dana to E. Herrick, Jan. 2, 1839, MS Dana-Herrick Letters, Yale University Library, New Haven, CT; in Poesch, *Peale*, p. 69.

62. "Sailors are perfect children, and have to be governed by the same rules, if you rea-son with them it must be after their own fashion." Journal entry, Oct. 16, 1838; in ibid., p. 131.

63. Ibid., p. 176.

who did challenge it were rapidly dismissed. When Couthouy and Wilkes's relationship deteriorated midway through the voyage, the conchologist was dismissed and returned to Washington.[64] Couthouy's duties were promptly and unceremoniously reassigned to Pickering and Peale,[65] although Dana eventually performed most of the work on crustaceans. This signified once again that to Wilkes the scientifics were so many interchangeable parts. He cared little who performed which tasks, so long as they were done efficiently and did not disturb other work.

On a long sea voyage, control over resources was real power, and one that many captains guarded cautiously. Space was a particularly scarce commodity, and it was assigned carefully. Although the scientists and officers had larger berths, Peale complained in a letter to his two daughters that

> [t]he little stateroom in which I live is just about as large as your mother's bedstead; in it I have a little bed over and under which is packed clothes, furs, guns, Books and boxes without number, all of which have to be tied to keep them from rolling and tumbling about, and kept off the floor as it is sometimes covered with water.[66]

Dana also felt cramped, but based on his previous experience on the *Macedonia*'s expedition to the Mediterranean, noted that their accommodations were spacious by navy standards.

> I am now very snugly stowed away on board the *Peacock* in a small stateroom six feet by seven and a half, where I am required to keep, in addition to my own private stores, which are not a little bulky, all the public stores pertaining to my department. . . . Yet I feel that our prospects are fine, that our accommodations are better than they would have been aboard the *Macedonia*.[67]

Dana was willing to concede that on a naval expedition, ownership of space had to be defined relatively rather than absolutely.

---

64. Viola and Margolis, *Magnificent*, p. 74. Interestingly, Wilkes reported in his synopsis of the cruise that Couthouy departed because of illness rather then impudence. Wilkes, *Synopsis*, p. 48

65. Poesch, *Peale*, p. 168.

66. Poesch, *Peale*, p. 67.

67. J. D. Dana to E. Herrick, Aug. 14, 1838; in Gilman, *Life*, p. 96.

Regardless of the quantity of space available, quality of space was also an issue. Wilkes confined scientific work to one cabin, and any organic specimens had to be kept on deck because of the smell. Not satisfied with this arrangement, Peale complained in his journal that the captain's cabin was the only place suitable for their labor and that the *Relief* (the most recently built vessel) was the only one in the fleet fitted for scientific work.[68] In the next section I will argue that since the ships' spaces were so small and were required for many diverse purposes, Wilkes carefully controlled allotment of that space.

Boundary Objects

If we can say that the U.S. Exploring Expedition participants shared a common goal, it was the re-declaration of American independence. As we have seen, however, even raw patriotism could not reconcile the differences between naval officers and scientists. How can we make sense, then, of such diverse practitioners still producing such a vast collection of specimens and publications?

Susan Leigh Star and James R. Griesemer's concept of "boundary objects" will help to answer this question. They write that "[c]onsensus is not necessary for cooperation nor for the successful conduct of work."[69] Heterogeneous actors at work on one problem may define their common terms and instruments differently, but as long as these boundary objects continue to serve some useful function for everyone, cooperation can be maintained.[70] Boundary objects serve to align a diverse group of actors such that they can work together while still maintaining their profession's distinct attitudes and work habits.

Boundary objects can be concrete and/or abstract,[71] so the list of such objects for the U.S. Exploring Expedition might include the following: spec-

---

68. Journal entry, Sept. 2, 1838; in Poesch, *Peale*, p. 126. Ironically, the *Relief* was also a poor vessel for sailing; in a symbolic sense, anyway, this reinforces the incompatibility between natural historic and naval purposes on this voyage.

69. S. L. Star and J. R. Griesemer. "Institutional Ecology, 'Translations' and Boundary-Objects: Amateurs and Professionals in Berkeley's Museum of Vertebrate Zoology, 1907–39," *Social Studies of Science* 19 (1989): 388.

70. Ibid., p. 393.

71. Ibid., p. 408.

imens, maps, journals, sketches, American prestige, ships. To examine one of these: the expedition's ships were viewed by all as the necessary means of transportation, but the scientists also viewed them as receptacles for specimens; Wilkes and the officers needed to think of their vessels rather as cartographic instruments[72] and as weapons. Despite the scientists' and crew members' different needs from the ship, their common recognition of its importance for their mission(s) required cooperation and downplayed differences. The naval officers could not chart territory fully without supplementary biological and geological information, and the scientists could not jeopardize the ship's integrity by overloading it with their specimens. In their need to reach "generalizable findings" that would increase American prestige, the expedition members had to overcome at least partially their "divergent viewpoints."[73]

One lesson we learn from the U.S. Exploring Expedition is that the more limited the space and resources, the more the available tools become shared boundary objects. On a naval voyage, for the sake of space and efficiency, very few objects or people could serve only one function. For example, when Wilkes and his crew wanted to celebrate Independence Day while exploring the Oregon territory, they had to improvise: "The 'Hall of Science' [the temporary astronomical observatory the crew had constructed] was converted into a banquet hall by decorating it with flags and using a large drafting table as a table and covering it with a fine Sandwich Islands mat."[74]

Tension rose when a boundary object could not serve all ends simultaneously. When Jones, the expedition's original commander, tried to select the *Macedonia* as his flagship because it was large enough to house the scientifics, their instruments, and the heavy armaments required for intimidating natives, he was criticized; if the ship crashed, the press argued, it would be difficult to save the crew from such a large vessel, and they would never fit onto the smaller ships in the fleet.[75] In another example of the struggles to stretch boundary objects to their maximum potential, specimens had to be sent home periodically to preserve space aboard ship. An

---

72. R. J. Sorrenson, "The Ship as a Scientific Instrument on the Eighteenth Century," *Osiris* 2nd series, 11 (1996): 221–236

73. Star and Griesemer, "Institutional," p. 387.

74. Tyler, *Wilkes Expedition*, p. 243.

75. Bradley, "Contentious," pp. 116–117.

anonymous crew member recorded in his journal that his ship could not fire a salute to Emperor Don Pedro in Rio de Janeiro because of the delicate scientific instruments on board.[76] Another sailor tossed some of Couthouy's specimens overboard because he was tired of the smell of invertebrates.[77] Wilkes, also offended by the smell of the shell specimens, ordered Couthouy not to collect more than one specimen of each species and not to store them anywhere but above deck. The conchologist

> maintained that they could not be properly examined in the noise and bustle of the spar deck and that foreign scientists habitually made large-sized collections. Wilkes's reply was that he didn't give a damn what other expeditions did and that "he would take responsibility of deciding all matters relative to our collections relative to his own views."[78]

Couthouy was fully aware of the expedition's nationalistic purpose, and tried to use this to his advantage, but for Wilkes the only means to success was the management of boundary objects.

All compromises had to be made on Wilkes's terms. As lord of the ship's space, Wilkes controlled the professional domains in every sense. I do not mean to suggest that he ruled the ship like a despot; rather, I mean to indicate that when one party has such dominance over the "agonistic field,"[79] this dramatically changes the boundary problem. In this case, professional boundaries ultimately were managed by one individual rather than evenly negotiated by all involved. If the scientifics and crew members were not always able to cooperate fully in their use of ship resources, at least Wilkes could ensure that *some* element of their patriotic mission was accomplished.

Science on Land—The Expedition Returns

A great deal changed in the four years the Wilkes expedition spent at sea. Two administrations came and went, and the new president—John Tyler—

76. Anonymous journal kept aboard the *Vincennes*, entry for Nov. 11, 1838; *Records of the U.S.Ex.Ex.*
77. Couthouy journal, Feb. 18, March 11, 17, 18, 20, 26, April 16, 1839; in Tyler, *Wilkes Expedition*, p. 66.
78. Couthouy journal, Aug. 31, 1839; in Tyler, *Wilkes Expedition*, pp. 89–90.
79. See Gieryn, "Boundaries." The agonistic field represents the area (money, prestige, etc.) that different people, professions, etc. battle over in their boundary work.

had more pressing concerns than six boatloads of charts and shells. The expedition's progress had received little coverage in the popular press, and, in considering all the money they had spent, many members of Congress (Senator Pearce notwithstanding) began to feel that this endless project needed to be contained financially. The naval cartographers had fulfilled their lucrative mission of charting the seas for America's commercial profit, but the civilian scientists' mounds of rotting specimens and continuing requests for money to publish scientific texts led Senator Simon Cameron to remark that he was "tired of all this thing called Science here."[80]

Wilkes had more immediate concerns, however. After an embarrassing court-martial and reprimand from the Navy Department for being unnecessarily harsh in his discipline, Wilkes faced a massive amount of information to compile for his narrative. Not only did he have the official logs and his own journals to draw from, but he also had informed the crew and scientifics from the outset that their journals and specimens would become public property upon the voyage's completion.[81]

Wilkes was very clear on another point—regardless of whether the expedition's *own* scientifics were to write up the reports on the specimens (and in some cases they did not), the reports were under *no* circumstances to be written by Europeans. In his nationalistic zeal, Wilkes almost forbade Dana to use the standard European names when classifying his specimens.[82] To the end, the U.S. Exploring Expedition was to remain a full-blooded American endeavor.

In all, the expedition produced twenty-four volumes, eight written by Wilkes. What remained of the poorly handled specimens became a foundation for the Smithsonian Institution's Museum of Natural History collections. One lesson the commander and others would draw was that the real work of the civilian natural historian began on shore after the expedition was over. Once returned to land, Wilkes began to appreciate the need

---

80. In Schlee, *Edge*, p. 32.

81. Poesch, *Peale*, p. 121. Wilkes made it clear that none of their private affairs would become part of the public record. Further exploration of this private-public boundary would yield interesting insights into the nature of experience, duty, and property. One salient issue is that the crew's openness was bounded by the realization that these thoughts would pass under the scrutiny of their superior.

82. Gilman, *Life*, p. 144.

for expert analysis of the voyage's natural specimens. His scientifics were "necessary now and even more so than at any other period of the cruize nor can their services be dispensed with or the work concentrated without great loss to the Expedition and the reputation of the country."[83] Coast Survey superintendent Alexander Dallas Bache similarly supported natural history by returning specimens to academic scientists like Louis Agassiz on shore, rather than crowding his vessels with scientifics.[84] In subsequent voyages like the North Pacific Surveying and Exploring Expedition and Lynch Dead Sea expedition, the civilians' only presence on board was their instructions on what to collect.[85]

Conclusion

In a setting such as the U.S. Exploring Expedition, disciplinary boundary work took place under discipline of a different sort. The scattered assignment of scientific tasks allowed Wilkes to ensure that no other expedition member became an authority in anything but a narrowly defined space (e.g., conchology). The expedition's scientifics appeared willing to accept such narrow circumscription of their territory. Dana simply wrote upon the voyage's return of his gratification that the knowledge they had collected would be distributed to the American public (as taxpayers, the rightful owners of the information). Despite this communal emphasis, however, each scientific would "prepare his own reports, reap his own honors, and be held responsible for his own facts."[86]

While the older Philadelphia scientific elite had been concerned with divisions between the sciences, the younger, more eager scientifics actually on the expedition had little pressing concern for such professional boundary work. Before the voyage, there had been some dispute between the zoologists about how they would divide the labor,[87] but as I have argued, there

---

83. C. Wilkes to A. P. Upshur, 16 July 1982, reprinted in N. Reingold (ed.), *Science in Nineteenth-Century America: A Documentary History* (Chicago and London, 1964), pp. 123–126.

84. Slotten, *Patronage*, pp. 132–139.

85. Smith, "Navy," pp. 41–55; Towle, "Science," pp. 91, 196, 218, 484–486.

86. J. D. Dana, "The U.S. Exploring Expedition," *American Journal of Science and Arts* 44 (1843): 394.

87. J. D. Dana to E. Herrick, Aug. 1837; in Gilman, *Life*, p. 56.

is no evidence that these intra-scientific disputes resurfaced during the cruise. Most of the officers and crew, and all of the scientifics, were under forty years old — boundaries could be redrawn later.

Ultimately, Wilkes did not subvert the scientific aims of the expedition. In fact, when the voyage ended, he relentlessly drove the scientifics to publish their findings, and he recalled that his relationships with the scientifics were harmonious, "with but one exception" (presumably, Couthouy).[88] I see this as a recognition that the United States' struggle for international prestige depended both on scientific and military might. Naval voyages taken in the next two decades did not, however, have the strong natural history presence of the U.S. Exploring Expedition.[89] The experience had taught civilian scientists and naval officers alike that whether or not their aims were similar, they did not enjoy working together. Lt. Matthew F. Maury commented as he was organizing the Depot of Charts and Instruments' scientific program: "I was determined to ask no advice or instruction from the savants, but to let it be out and out a Navy work."[90]

As for the civilian scientists, many still hoped to reconcile differences with the navy while making territorial claims on the geophysical sciences. In the 1840s when Cyrus Field initiated the transatlantic cable project, scientists and naval officers once again cooperated uneasily. Chandra Mukerji has argued that this uneasy relationship still served the young scientific community: despite disagreements, the military's mounting resources provided a welcome site for theory-testing and collecting.[91] Slotten has shown that when Bache became Coast Survey superintendent in 1843, many hoped his combined military and Philadelphia high-society background would smooth over fragile relations between civilian and naval scientists.[92] While Slotten isolated Hassler's disastrous leadership of the Coast Survey as the major rift in that relationship, I would argue that Hassler exacerbated a wound already opened by the Wilkes expedition. In fact, one of Bache's bold political strokes was putting down rumors in 1844–45 that Wilkes might

88. Wilkes, *Synopsis*, p. 49.

89. Schlee, *Edge*, p. 35.

90. M. F. Maury to W. Blackford, 1847, Maury MSS., *Letter Books*, vol. 3; Library of Congress MS Division; in Schlee, *Edge*, p. 36.

91. C. Mukerji, *A Fragile Power: Scientists and the State* (Princeton, 1989), pp. 25–26.

92. Slotten, *Patronage*, pp. 20, 49–53, 74, 148–149.

take over the Coast Survey.[93] The navy's post-bellum attempts to assume the survey's functions also were ultimately unsuccessful.[94]

With the increase of philanthropic support for science during the nineteenth and early twentieth century, funding for science became increasingly privatized. Regardless, science and military power have become more—not less—inseparable in the United States' attempt to gain and maintain international prestige. However, beginning with the Lazzaroni in the 1840s and '50s civilian science has managed since then to define its functions and subspecialties more clearly—making it a formidable contender in agonistic games rather than a poorly organized (and thus easily controlled) resource for the military.

93. Ibid., pp. 83–84.

94. T. G. Manning, *U.S. Coast Survey vs. Naval Hydrographic Office: A Nineteenth Century Rivalry in Science and Politics* (Tuscaloosa, 1988).

ELISHA KENT KANE
AND THE ESKIMO OF ETAH
1853, 1854, 1855

Few nineteenth-century American exploring expeditions came close to capturing the imagination and sympathies of the American public as did the Arctic adventures in the 1850s of a diminutive and frail Philadelphia medical officer, Elisha Kent Kane. He was just one of scores of naval officers and private citizens from both sides of the Atlantic who set off by foot, sledge, sail and steam in search of the fabled and elusive Northwest Passage that supposedly existed through the ice floes of the Canadian Arctic. Kane joined the field just as the search entered its most quixotic stage, as explorers and nations responded to the entreaties of Lady Jane Franklin, the elderly damsel in distress whose husband, the intrepid Sir John, had disappeared in the Arctic with his ship and crew in 1845.

Elisha Kane participated in two Arctic voyages in search of the missing Franklin party, the first as medical officer assigned to Lt. Edwin DeHaven's 1850–51 expedition and the second under his own command from 1853–55. Both voyages failed to achieve either their humanitarian or, in the case of the second expedition, their scientific goals. In the course of the second expedition, Kane and his crew were forced to spend two winters clinging to life aboard their ice-imprisoned vessel, unable to either search for Franklin or an "open polar sea" that Kane believed existed at the top of the world. Yet despite such meager results, Americans embraced their voyagers as heroes upon their return. Kane in particular was accorded celebrity status and became the darling of the American public as well as the scientific community. His two-volume narrative, *Arctic Explorations: The Second Grinnell Expedition in Search of Sir John Franklin, 1853, '54, '55* became one of America's best-selling books of the nineteenth century. It was said that Kane's narrative "lay for a decade with the Bible on almost literally every parlor table in America."[1]

The popularity of Elisha Kent Kane and his work owed much to the romantic tastes of the American public in an era where the "quest," no matter the outcome, was revered. Tragedy only enhanced its nobleness. A second factor contributing to Kane's popularity was his talent as a writer of eloquent narrative prose. His powers of description vividly brought to life for his readers the totally alien environment of the polar regions. Still, it is hard to ignore the fact that very little of philosophical substance was generated by his efforts. Indeed, Kane's voyages were no doubt among the least successful of the various American land and sea expeditions from the 1830s through the 1850s. It is only in the field of ethnology, in his description of the Eskimos of Etah—"the northernmost people known to man"—that Kane is considered to have made any lasting contribution.

In this paper I will discuss Elisha Kent Kane's attitudes towards and relationship with the Etah Eskimos during the Second Grinnell Expedition of 1853, 1854, and 1855. In doing so, I will propose another explanation for the young doctor's heroic standing among the American public and the "civilized world." Readers of Kane's narrative were intrigued not so much by his enumerated successes (which were negligible) but by the expedition's survival. Americans saw in Kane's adventures a confirmation of their own ability to prevail over the forces of nature in the nineteenth century. Kane excited a sympathetic and agreeable chord with his readers through his unremitting efforts to survive by asserting the almost metaphysical powers of dominance supposedly possessed by "civilized" man over the "savage." The party's survival and self-rescue seemed to confirm these powers of superiority inherent in all Americans, powers that were seemingly manifest in the political and military events of the period. This accomplishment outweighed the mere temporal failures of the voyage. The expedition was thus

---

1. *Dictionary of American Biography* (New York: Charles Scribner's Sons, 1932), 5:257.

a triumph in the eyes of both Kane and his adoring public. According to Professor Charles W. Shields, a Kane eulogist in the 1850s, these were indeed the real "lessons he has left to the world":

> In that slight physical frame, suggestive only of refined culture and intellectual grace, there dwelt a sturdy force of will, which no combination of material terrors seemed to appall, and, by a sort of magnetic impulse, subjected all inferior spirits to its control. It was the calm power of reason and duty asserting their superiority over mere brute courage, and compelling the instinctive homage of Herculean strength and prowess. . . . Immured in a dreadful seclusion, where the combined terrors of Nature forced him into all the closer contact with the passions of man, he not only rose, by his energy, superior to them both, but . . . converted each to his ministry. Even the wild inmates of that icy world, from the mere stupid wonder with which at first they regarded his imported marvels of civilization, were, at length, forced to descend to a genuine respect and love, as they saw him compete with them.[2]

In the course of this paper I will show that this confrontation between "civilization" and "savagery" permeated Kane's thoughts as expressed in his field journal and eventually in his published narrative. However, while Kane and his crew indeed exhibited considerable fortitude and courage, they in fact owed their survival not to any conquest of nature, nor to their Anglo-Saxonism—of whom Kane referred to as the "dominant tribe." They survived two ill-prepared years in the upper polar regions, where no explorer had ever dared to reside, due to the intervention of the residents of the area, the Eskimos of Etah.

Elisha Kent Kane was born into a prominent and learned Philadelphia family in 1820. His father, John Kane, once served as President of the American Philosophical Society. The younger Kane was graduated from the University of Pennsylvania Medical School in 1843, and for the next seven years embarked on a succession of adventures in such far-flung spots as China, Southeast Asia, India, Egypt, Africa, and Mexico. All the while, he was burdened with a physical handicap—rheumatic heart disease contracted in his late teens.

---

2. Elisha Kent Kane, *Arctic Explorations; The Second and Last United States Grinnell Expedition in Search of Sir John Franklin* (Hartford, Conn.: R. W. Bliss, 1868), pp. 763–64.

In January 1850, President Zachary Taylor called upon the United States to participate in the search for British explorer Sir John Franklin, whose party had been missing in the Arctic for four years. Kane, inspired by accounts of the search for the Northwest Passage and moved by the ongoing efforts to locate Franklin, volunteered for an American expedition commanded by Lt. Edwin De Haven and cosponsored by the Navy and newspaper magnate Henry Grinnell. In May, mere days before the voyage was to begin, the Navy assigned Kane to the Expedition as senior surgeon and naturalist. Eventually De Haven led his two small sailing vessels—*Advance* and *Rescue*—across Baffin Bay and into Davis Strait, following in the wake of numerous British vessels already searching for Franklin. Several months later, a combination of bad luck and poor judgment led to both vessels being frozen fast in the offshore ice pack. They remained prisoners within an ice floe that held them captive for 267 days, the Arctic currents eventually carrying the two ships northward, then south and east to safety after drifting over 1000 miles.[3]

Despite the ignominious performance and negligible results of what came to be known as the First Grinnell Expedition, Americans enthusiastically greeted the party upon its return in October of 1851. Requests immediately came forth for lectures and written accounts of the exploits of the Grinnell Expedition. De Haven, however, was not up to such tasks. Instead it was Kane who moved to satisfy and capitalize on America's passion for stories of Arctic adventure. Upon their return, it was the young surgeon and not De Haven who was besieged with requests for a lecture tour and lucrative offers to pen a popular narrative.

On 29 December 1851, Kane presented the first of three lectures at the Smithsonian Institution. He not only related his adventures among the ice floes, but also used this opportunity to call for a second American expedition to the Arctic. He believed that the British were searching for Franklin in the wrong area. Instead of making their way southward towards known settlements, Kane felt that the explorers had instead turned northward up Wellington Channel towards the legendary *polynya*, or open polar sea, where the weather was supposed to be milder and the flora and fauna plentiful. Many scientists had acknowledged the possibility of the existence of an

---

3. Elisha Kent Kane, *The U.S. Grinnell Expedition* (New York: Harper & Bros., 1854).

open polar sea, the most prominent in America being Matthew Maury. In his study of hydrography, Maury determined that, owing to Arctic river drainage, ocean currents, and the topography of the sea bottom, the North Pole had to be ice-free.[4] This theory also harked back to John Cleves Symmes's idea of "Holes in the Poles," which had helped to inaugurate American overseas exploration in the 1830s.[5] Having determined to conduct his search northward, Kane proposed to go there by the shortest route possible: not by way of Wellington Channel, through which Franklin would have to have traveled, but through Smith Sound, hundreds of miles to the east of where the British were searching.

With this proposition, which was enthusiastically received not only among the learned heads at the Smithsonian, but by nearly every other scientific institution in America, Kane had artfully merged his desire to reach the heretofore unattainable polar sea with the heroic and gallant search for the lost Englishmen. He accomplished this despite the fact that there was virtually no evidence to indicate that Franklin's party would have headed north instead of toward the inhabited settlements in the south. No matter. Kane was eager to join the latter-day quest for the grail. An inspired Kane testified to author Francis Hawkes that "the Crusade is not yet ended. Those who have gone out before have failed, but they have left the prize for others to win."[6] His lobbying met with success; Kane secured a commission from the Navy, seventeen crewmen and Grinnell's loan of *Advance*. On 31 May, 1853, the expedition left New York Harbor for the Arctic with the intent of sailing as far as possible up Smith Sound, then sledging northward until reaching the open polar sea, where small boats would be launched and the search for Franklin prosecuted around the shores of the *polynya*.

The general story of the second Expedition is as follows: By August 1853, less than three months after its departure from New York, *Advance* was frozen fast above Smith Sound at 78 degrees 41′ north latitude, never to be freed again. The first, harrowing winter resulted in the deaths of two of the crew. In April of the following year, Eskimos from neighboring Etah, a tiny settle-

4. Matthew Maury, *The Physical Geography of the Sea* (New York: Harper & Bros., 1855).

5. John Cleves Symmes Jr. to Elisha Kent Kane, (1851?) Elisha Kent Kane Papers, American Philosophical Society, Philadelphia.

6. Elisha Kent Kane to Francis Hawks, 19 July 1853, Elisha Kent Kane Papers, American Philosophical Society, Philadelphia.

ment not heretofore known to exist in such northern climes, began to visit the ship. They maintained contact off and on through the spring and brief summer of 1854. By August, faced with the dreary prospect of a second winter trapped on the ice, eight of the exploring party voted to attempt an escape southward, only to return defeated in December. In May 1855, after a second winter of imprisonment, Kane abandoned his ship and led the remainder of the crew southward on a eighty-three day exodus to safety and rescue.

The Second Grinnell Expedition returned to America in October of 1855 aboard a rescue vessel minus three crew members, and bearing only "the furs on our backs, a little boat . . . documents, tow dogs, and our flag— a relic of the Wilkes Expedition."[7] Kane had failed in each of his objectives: he had not reached an open polar sea, nor had he found Franklin.[8] Despite these obvious failures, America greeted Kane's return with greater enthusiasm than before and were soon thrilling over the account of his adventures. Over and above the celebrity status accorded the young surgeon, the popularity of his two-volume narrative owed much to his artfully vivid depictions of the day-to-day survival of the party, which had spent two winters aboard the imprisoned *Advance* in latitudes higher than any other "civilized" people had resided before. Particularly gripping was Kane's account of the final desperate eighty-three-day exodus southward to "civilization." For readers of the 1850s (as well as for Kane himself), such adventures were further confirmation of the inherent capabilities of "civilized man," and in particular, Americans, to persevere and ultimately overcome the most abject adversity and danger set forth by man and nature. The great lesson of *Arctic Explorations* that Americans found so appealing was precisely this: the unrelenting assertion of American superiority over the people and elements encountered and the events that transpired during the "voyage" had been rewarded by the survival and ultimate salvation of the members of the Second Grin-

7. *Arctic Explorations*, p. 746.
8. Kane insisted that Thomas Morton, one of his crew members, had actually seen an open sea lying in the distance during a sledge journey northward. It is interesting to note that the Eskimo hunter Hans Hendrik, who accompanied Morton, never mentions this "discovery" in his published account. As for the search for Franklin, one of the first bits of information shared with Kane upon his return was the fact that in the interim, physical remains of the British party had been found by Englishman John Rae nearly one thousand miles to the south of Kane's location; *Arctic Explorations*, pp. 304–317, 742–43.

nell Expedition. Only in this light could they be considered heroes, given their paucity of results.

Unfortunately, a study of the facts as presented both in Kane's narrative and his journal, plus accounts given by other members of the Expedition, shows that, while their great courage and perseverance cannot be denied, their survival owed nothing to their perceived "superiority." Though it could be argued that such notions provided Kane, at least, with the psychological fortitude to face the travails of Arctic exploration, the insistence upon maintaining cultural dominance in a seemingly hostile environment only served to make a challenging situation more harrowing and life threatening. Missing from Kane's paean to the courage, ingenuity, intelligence and morality of white civilization is the basic fact that his Expedition survived for over two years in the Arctic because of the kindness and generosity of the Eskimo inhabitants of this most northward and isolated land. Thomas Kane, Elisha's brother, confirmed that "without the free intercourse which they enjoyed with the native Esquimaux of Smith Sound, the Americans of the Expedition would not have survived or succeeded in making their way home."[9]

Kane, like other explorers, spent a great deal of time acquiring ethnological data. But unlike other expeditions to other parts of the world, such scientific pursuits were by necessity subordinated scientific interests to those of basic survival. The Second Grinnell Expedition became dependent on the good graces of the natives as had no other American expedition of this period. It soon became obvious to Kane that his men would have to adopt many of the habits of their Eskimo neighbors, as well as depend upon them for sustenance if they were to survive. Without a doubt, the escaping party would never have survived the three month exodus to "civilization" without the constant intervention of inhabitants of the neighboring villages. Yet, both during and after the two year journey into the Arctic, Kane could give no more than grudging acknowledgment to the people to whom he and his party owed their lives. Throughout his journal and carrying over to *Arctic Explorations*, he clung fast to the notion that it was his personal physical, mental, and cultural superiority that had pulled the Expedition through.

What disturbed Kane was that, as the Expedition struggled to exist from

9. Knox to Hornsby, request for information on Elisha Kent Kane, 12 June 1943, Cruises and Voyages, National Archives.

day-to-day—or more accurately, from meal-to-meal—he and his men were consciously forced to become "savage" in order to survive, adopting Eskimo ways of living in the Arctic. The more they were forced to do so, the more Kane became obsessed with maintaining the barriers that he had constructed between "savagery" and "civilization." Indeed, he believed that the key to the survival of the Expedition was the degree to which he could assert his "civilized" dominance over his Eskimo neighbors.

Throughout the Expedition, Kane fought to establish and maintain this assumed superiority. That quest continued to dominate his thoughts and perceptions and is explicitly expressed in the composition of his two-volume narrative. Throughout this work, Kane misrepresented and otherwise misquoted his own journal entries, juxtaposed events, and otherwise contrived to place the Eskimos in an unfavorable light. He managed to transform even the most obvious acts of Eskimo humanity and kindness into mere animal-like reactions to the acknowledgment of what he insisted was innate white superiority. Kane held fast to these views with every encounter with the Eskimos. In each instance he exhibited an unsettling mixture of fear, distrust, envy, and condescension toward the people who represented his primary means of survival and rescue.

At every juncture, the men of the Expedition owed their survival to the Eskimos. Hans Hendrik, an Eskimo hunter hired in south Greenland, unceasingly strove to supplement the main party's inadequate provisions with life-sustaining fresh meat. Their Etah neighbors fed them at crucial periods of scarcity. Eskimo assistance was also extended to the seceding party of eight, in spite of the fact that these Americans had resorted to stealing from the natives—even drugging several with opium at one point. Even so, when the seceding party's failure was assured and they were too weak to continue in either direction, the party was escorted back to the ship by the concerned Eskimos. At every turn, and through each encounter, Kane strove to maintain the dominance he considered self-evident by virtue of his racial superiority. As a consequence, Kane attributed the assistance offered by the Eskimos as proportionate to his success in convincing them "that the whites are and of right ought to be everywhere the dominant tribe." [10]

For Kane, the dilemma early on was thus: Owing to his machinations,

10. *Arctic Explorations*, 374.

he and his men were trapped and isolated in the frozen Arctic, with no hope of immediate escape or rescue. Following the first devastating winter, in which the men had come perilously close to succumbing to the natural elements and scurvy, he found to his surprise that he had neighbors, and that they obviously had the ability his men lacked to survive in these high latitudes. But, despite the Eskimos' friendly demeanor and assurances by Hans Hendrik, Kane thoroughly distrusted these people—even feared them. While he considered them "like the North American Indian," to be "of ethnological interest," the Eskimos, like Indians, were never to be trusted. He eyed their offers of assistance cynically, as typical examples of savage "cunning, duplicity, [and] deceit," which were "matters of course" and an inherent "trait" with such people.[11] He concluded that such "traits" in "savages" were universal, and could in some ways be attributed to their various modes of existence around the globe. For Kane indolence bred savagery. In this view, all "savages" were essentially the same "whether in the high Arctic regions" or "in the Torrid Zone." He felt that this supposed "spontaneous life supplies its lazy natives with abundance—It is little matter whether it be a Banana or a walrus—the facility of obtaining it imparts the same improvidence."[12] By this reasoning, Kane was able to turn the Eskimo's ability to sustain life in the Arctic into evidence of their "savagery"; likewise, following this line of reasoning, the expedition's failures no doubt testified to the superiority of its members!

Kane claimed that, as a result of his travels, he spoke with the voice of experience and scientific observation. The Eskimos, he was convinced, were the most "inert" and "primal" beings of humankind:

> I have seen and travelled among the Negroitos of Luzon and the Papuans, the Andamans—the Arafuras—and some of our most rudimental of the North and South American aborigines—none of these men seems to me so inert and primal. . . . I have never met a people who less engaged my sympathies or more my interests than these. Pity and wonder are always uppermost in my mind.[13]

11. Elisha Kent Kane, journal kept on board *Advance*, 23 September 1854. Original at Stanford University Library.

12. Ibid., 1 August 1854.

13. Ibid., 23 September 1854.

The problem, of course, was that as much as Kane distrusted and disparaged the natives, he could not ignore the fact that the Etah Eskimos were existing in much better health and comfort than were he and his men on board his ship. Despite his mistakes and miscalculations, he was wise enough to realize that his party would not survive that harsh environment without cooperation from those people.[14] Therefore, it is not surprising that a fearful Kane recounted his "unexpressible mortification" whenever the Etah Eskimos "abandoned" the party, even if for a short time.[15]

Following their first winter of deprivation, Kane went further still, finally acknowledging that, not only did the party need to maintain positive relations with its Eskimo neighbors, but that it would be necessary for him and his crew to become "more than half Esquimaux,"[16] adopting "their form of habitations and their peculiarities of diet," without, of course, "their unthrift and filth."[17] "Borrowing a lesson from our Esquimaux neighbors," Kane converted *Advance* "into an iglöe" so as to conserve precious warmth during the upcoming winter.[18] He was forced to admit that "the experience of the natives is the surest guide" to survival in the Arctic.[19]

The psychological dilemma, however, still remained unsolved and was in fact intensified. How does one maintain a sense of superiority while in the midst of an alien environment that relentlessly imposes obstacles that one's culture or "civilization" is unprepared to meet? While most explorers experience such challenges on a relatively non-threatening level, Kane perceived that his ability to deal with this dilemma would dictate the eventual fate of the party. So, while Kane allowed for the utilitarian superiority of Eskimo ways in the Arctic, he persistently attempted to assert, through word and deed, his own and his culture's supposed dominance over the Eskimos. Both his journal and his narrative document his mania for asserting the superiority over the very people who made it possible for him and his beleaguered party to survive their ordeal in the Arctic. To this end, he methodically worked to instill fear and awe in the Eskimos by alternating acts of

14. Ibid., 30 September 1854.
15. Ibid., 30 August 1854.
16. *Arctic Explorations*, p. 548.
17. Ibid., p. 359.
18. Ibid., p. 360.
19. Kane journal, 13 December 1854.

"extreme kindness" with punishments of "excessive severity," always careful *never* to show any weakness of any sort to the Eskimos.[20] He felt impelled by "both policy and duty . . . to preserve with this people relations of fear and respect":[21]

> My faith in these people is very slender and my system of treatment that of extreme kindness qualified by excessive severity. I never lose an opportunity of doing a kindly act or propitiating a member of their tribe, but I always punish a misdeed and never lose a chance of inspiring fear.[22]

Kane was driven by a fear of exhibiting to the Eskimos any signs of "weakness." When the first visitors arrived from Etah in April of 1854, he hastened to conceal the "signs of our disabled condition which it was important they should not see." To this end, he hid the bodies of his recently deceased comrades in the forecastle.[23] Then, after exchanging a few items— "needles and beads and a treasure of old cask-staves"—with the Eskimos for precious food, Kane proceeded to dictate a "treaty," which required the natives to bring meat to the brig regularly in exchange for more presents and Kane's promise not to molest them. In doing so, he felt he had succeeded in maintaining his superiority, despite the dire straits of his party. In negotiating this treaty, Kane "tried to make them understand what a powerful Prospero they had had for a host, and how beneficent he would prove himself so long as they did his bidding."[24]

Throughout the remainder of the Expedition, Kane was true to his word, never missing a chance to reinforce his perceived superiority over the Eskimos. More than once he imprisoned natives within the bowels of the ship for disobeying him.[25] Always he strove to impress upon the Eskimos

---

20. Ibid., 8 December 1854.
21. Ibid., 13 December 1854.
22. Ibid., 8 December 1854. The "misdeeds" that Kane referred to most often involved violation of the expedition's sense of private property by the visiting Eskimos—a missing axe or bit of wood—that constituted crimes in Kane's eyes, but represented something quite else according to the people of Etah, whose culture stressed sharing and not hoarding.
23. *Arctic Explorations*, p. 214.
24. Ibid., p. 215.
25. Ibid., 215, 372–74; *Memoirs of Hans Hendrick*, translated by Dr. Henry Rink (London: Trübner & Co., 1878), pp. 24–25.

just who was the "dominant tribe." [26] Such a mind set led Kane to attribute
the repeated acts of Eskimo generosity not to any humanitarian traits of the
natives but to "fear" and "respect." Thus, according to Kane, the Eskimos
brought food to the brig because he had taught them to "act up to contract,"
and not out of kindness or even for the items they would secure in trade. [27]
By these actions, he was convinced that he had gained the respect of the natives—"respect," in his terms meaning "little else than a tribute to superiority either real or supposed,—and that among the rude [meaning Eskimos
or any other "savage" peoples] at least, one of its elements is fear." [28] Even
though the exploring party was increasingly forced to "become more than
half Esquimaux," [29] the barriers between the "superior" and the "inferior"
had to be maintained. To this end, while Kane was often a houseguest of the
Eskimos in their igloos at Etah, he was compelled to erect a physical barrier—a roped-off section on the deck of *Advance*—that would expressly
delineate what area the visiting Eskimos were allowed to inhabit within
the realm of civilization. He considered this barrier a necessary tangible
"dividing-line between us and the rest of mankind—'simplex munditis.'" [30]
Kane went so far as to remark that the eight men who had tried to leave the
Expedition had failed because "they had neglected to impress the Esquimaux with a sense of their superiority," and because their "familiarity as
equals had destroyed their influence." [31]

In April 1855, Kane decided that further attempts at locating Franklin
and the open polar sea were impossible. He and the entire party abandoned
the imprisoned *Advance* and began a long exodus southward. His justification for ending the search, contained in a "brief memorial," revealed a fear
that transcended his apprehensions of starvation and isolation:

A third winter would force us, as the only means of escaping starvation, to
resort to Esquimaux habits and give up all hope of remaining by the vessel and her resources. [32]

26. *Arctic Explorations*, p. 374.
27. Ibid., p. 382.
28. Ibid., p. 447.
29. Ibid., p. 548.
30. Ibid., p. 392.
31. Kane journal, 12 December 1854.
32. *Arctic Explorations*, p. 629.

Ironically, later Arctic explorers learned that resorting to "Esquimaux habits" was the only way to *succeed* in reaching their goals.[33]

The ensuing eighty-three day journey was punctuated by unfailing efforts on the part of various Eskimo villages to assist the escaping Americans. Over and over, Kane recorded that these people sacrificed their own provisions and precious hunting time to provide food, drink and labor for the explorers. They carried the sick from camp to camp and helped to transport the men and their supplies through the treacherous ice floes and finally onto open water:

> As we neared the settlements, the Esquimaux came in flocks to our assistance. They volunteered to aid us at the drag-ropes. They carried our sick upon hand-sledges. They relieved us of all care for our supplies of daily food. The quantity of little auks that they brought us was enormous. They fed us and our dogs at the rate of eight thousand birds a week, all of them caught in their little hand-nets. All anxiety left us for the time. The men broke out in their old forecastle-songs; the sledges began to move merrily ahead, and laugh and jest drove out the old moody silence.[34]

Kane brazenly chose to attribute such acts to the natives' acknowledgment of his superiority! Later, when an Eskimo family gave the commander its only dog team in exchange for Kane's worn out and sickly canines, he considered this merely a natural consequence of his ongoing efforts to inculcate his superiority. "Such had become our relations with these poor friends of ours," he concluded, "that such an act of authority [claiming the dogs] would have gone unquestioned if it had cost them a much graver sacrifice."[35]

Despite the overwhelming friendship and generosity shown by the Eskimos, Kane, to the end, could not bring himself to trust them or their motives. When Christian Ohlsen, a member of the party, had an accident on the final trek and subsequently died, Kane again feared for the impact this "weakness" may have upon the "savage" mind, particularly upon Kane's "superior" standing:

33. Joseph Everett Nourse, *American Explorations in the Ice Zones* (Boston: D. Lothrop and Co., 1884); Jeannette Mirsky, *To the Arctic! The Story of Northern Exploration from Earliest Times to the Present* (London: Allan Wingate, 1948).

34. *Arctic Explorations*, pp. 692–93.

35. Ibid., p. 655.

I had carefully concealed Mr. Ohlsen's sickness from the Esquimaux, with every thing else that could intimate our weakness; for, without reflecting at all upon their fidelity, I felt with them, as with the rest of the world, pity was a less active provocative to good deeds than the deference which is exacted by power. I had therefore represented our abandonment of the brig as merely the absence of a general hunting-party to the Far South, and I was willing now to keep up the impression.[36]

Somehow, he felt it necessary to deceive the natives into thinking that his party was merely going hunting—as if they could not discern the difference.

In the end, as the exploring party bid farewell to the Eskimos, Kane resorted to the same justification as that voiced by countless others to buttress his belief in native inferiority. He prophesied that the Eskimos—like all other "savages"—were doomed to extinction:

These poor wretches . . . are dying out; not lingeringly, like the American tribes, but so rapidly as to be able to mark within a generation their progress toward extinction.[37]

At the same time, Kane marveled that their "obvious" fate

seems to have no effect upon this remarkable people. Surrounded by graves of their dead, by huts untenanted yet still recent in their memory as homesteads . . . they show neither apprehension nor regret. Even ["chief"] Kalutunah . . . [when] I point out to him the certainty of their speedy extinction . . . will smile in his efforts to count the years which must obliterate his nation, [will] break in with a laugh as his children shout out their 'Amna Ayah' and dance to the tap of his drum.[38]

"How wonderful is all this!" Kane concluded. "Rude as are their ideas of numbers, there are those among this merry-hearted people who can reckon up to the fate of their last man."[39]

---

36. Ibid., p. 690.
37. Ibid., p. 559.
38. Ibid.
39. Ibid.

The above episode from *Arctic Explorations* came word for word from Kane's field journal, with the exception of the following lament, recorded only in his journal: "poor, poor devil, born to toil and *self-extinction*." [italics mine] [40]

Eventually Kane and the remaining expedition members found their way back to "civilization." They made contact with an American rescue party in southern Greenland, and shortly thereafter were back in New York. Despite the obvious failures of the Second Grinnell Expedition, Kane was again accorded celebrity status and a heroes' welcome. Newspaper accounts heralding his return mentioned little about the role of the Eskimos in preserving the party. Kane, though besieged by requests for lectures and plagued by poor health, immediately set to work on what became his triumphantly successful narrative—a project that he cryptically considered to be his "coffin." [41] In this work, Americans were enlightened as to the habits, traits, and impending extinction of the Etah Eskimos. [42] They were assured of the superiority and unstoppable conquest of civilized man over both nature and savagery.

Though he was convinced of the imminent demise of the Eskimo, it was Elisha Kent Kane, however, who succumbed first. Within two years of his return, at age thirty-seven, he died in Havana, Cuba. His funeral procession to Philadelphia rivaled that of presidents and kings. Charles Shield's eulogy reflected the hope that Kane, as a symbol of American expansion and the superiority of its civilization, had ushered in "that peaceful era when charity shall become heroic, and science be reconciled to religion." [43]

40. Kane journal, 13 April 1855. It is interesting to note that Hans Hendrik, the Eskimo hunter and companion of Kane, apparently did not share his commander's views on the imminent demise of the Etah Eskimos. Shortly before the party abandoned the brig, Hans left the party to live with these "doomed" people, eventually marrying, raising a family, and participating in several more expeditions led by white explorers. No doubt Hans Hendrik stands as one of the most persistent, brave, and experienced of all Arctic explorers in the nineteenth century.

41. *Arctic Explorations*, p. 759.

42. George W. Corner, *Dr. Kane of the Arctic Seas* (Philadelphia: Temple University Press, 1972), pp. 155–59; *Arctic Explorations*, pp. 762–66.

43. Ibid., p. 766.

A PIONEERING OCEANIC EXPLORATION
Spencer Baird in the Northeast Atlantic, 1871–1887

Thanks are due to the American Philosophical Society for including papers on oceanic exploration in this volume. Despite the existence of a sizeable body of scholarship on United States maritime activities,[1] Americans often seem to be firmly land-locked. It is good to stretch our imagination by including events occurring on the broad oceans that lap the shores of North America.

In examining Spencer Fullerton Baird's scientific exploration of the Northeast Atlantic ocean, at a conference organized by the American Philosophical Society, one might bear in mind the pioneering investigation of the Gulf Stream undertaken by Benjamin Franklin, the founder of this distinguished organization. It also should be pointed out that Baird, who became a member of the American Philosophical Society in 1855, was a native

---

1. See, for example, William H. Goetzmann, *New Lands, New Men: America and the Second Great Age of Discovery* (New York: Viking, 1986). General accounts of oceanography, with varying amounts of coverage on U.S. activities, include: R. E. Coker, *The Great and Wide Sea* (Chapel Hill, University of North Carolina Press, 1949); Mary Sears and Daniel Merriman, eds., *Oceanography: The Past* (New York: Springer-Verlag, 1980); and Susan Schlee, *The Edge of an Unfamiliar World: A History of Oceanography* (New York: E. P. Dutton, 1973).

of Pennsylvania, having been born at Reading in 1823. Although he grew up in modest financial circumstances, his mother, Lydia Biddle Baird, was connected with one of Pennsylvania's leading families. In the 1840s Spencer Baird received a bachelor's and master's degree at Dickinson College in Carlisle, and later joined that institution's faculty.

By mid-century, Baird was an established field naturalist with wide contacts in Philadelphia's scientific community. Among his correspondents were the anatomist and paleontologist Joseph Leidy, and the prolific ornithologist John Cassin. Baird's network of associates also included leaders in the New York, Boston, and New Haven scientific centers. In an era before formal advanced education was available in this country, Baird's graduate education in zoology consisted largely of the mentoring he received from these established scientists.[2]

In 1850, Spencer Baird moved from Carlisle to Washington, D.C. where he became an Assistant Secretary of the Smithsonian Institution under Joseph Henry. Twenty-eight years later, upon the death of Henry, Baird became the Smithsonian's Secretary, a post that he held until his own demise in 1887. Over the almost four decades that he lived in Washington, Baird distinguished himself as an editor, a Smithsonian administrator, a systematic zoologist, and as a leader in American science. In his scientific capacity, he is remembered for hundreds of papers on American birds, mammals, reptiles, amphibians, and fishes. Historians also recall the central role he played in organizing the intensive biological exploration of North America. In this work, Baird assured that competent field naturalists were selected to serve with the numerous American governmental and non-governmental exploring expeditions that were organized during the second half of the nineteenth century. The specimens gathered during those operations, together with materials provided by Baird's large network of volunteer natural historians, typically were sent to the Smithsonian where the Assistant Secretary was developing the National Museum. That organization cared for the scientific collections of the federal government and drew on appropriated funds, rather than the relatively limited Smithsonian endowment,

---

2. For accounts of Baird, see Dean C. Allard, *Spencer Fullerton Baird and the U.S. Fish Commission* (New York: Arno Press, 1978); William Healey Dall, *Spencer Fullerton Baird: A Biography* (Philadelphia: J. B. Lippincott, 1915); and E. F. Rivinus and E. M. Youssef, *Spencer Baird of the Smithsonian* (Washington: Smithsonian Press, 1992).

for its support. The enormous collections concentrated at the National Museum were essential for the type of systematic zoology that Baird championed. His approach featured detailed morphological and physiological descriptions of organisms, taxonomy, studies of geographic distribution, and the life histories of specific species.[3]

In addition to the National Museum, Baird created or influenced the establishment of a number of other governmental scientific institutions. One of these, the Fish Commission, is the focus of this paper. But he also was a key figure is establishing or expanding the Smithsonian's Bureau of Ethnology, the U.S. Geological Survey, and the zoological and botanical offices of the Department of Agriculture. The scientists of all these organizations were curators in the National Museum, which served as the repository for their collections. Obviously, the National Museum was at the center of a network of organizations that have considerable importance in the history of American science.[4]

After 1870 Baird became one of a number of mid-nineteenth century biologists who turned their attention to marine biology.[5] In his study of British naturalists, David Allen observes that one reason for this trend was the growing popularity of seashore vacations among the middle-class that led to a growing interest in coastal fauna and flora.[6] Spencer Baird reminds us of Allen's interpretation since he and his family typically escaped the oppressive Washington summers by fleeing to the Atlantic coast. Not surprisingly, the life forms abundant in that seashore soon commanded the attention of Spencer Baird.

Baird's establishment of a Fish Commission that would systematically

3. In addition to the citations in footnote 2, see: John Shaw Billings, "Memoir of Spencer Fullerton Baird, 1823–1887," *Biographical Memoirs of the National Academy of Sciences*, 3 (1895), pp. 141–60; and George Brown Goode, "The Three Secretaries," in *The Smithsonian Institution, 1846–1896*, ed. George Brown Goode (Washington: De Vinne Press, 1897). William H. Goetzmann, *Exploration and Empire* (New York: Alfred A. Knopf, 1966) refers to Baird's work with the western expeditions.

4. Allard, *Spencer Fullerton Baird*, pp. 242–46.

5. See, for example, Robert J. Bowler, *The Environmental Sciences* (New York: W. W. Norton, 1992), pp. 316–17; Jane Oppenheimer, "Some Historical Backgrounds for the Establishment of the Stazione Zoologica at Naples," in Sears and Merriman, eds., *Oceanography: The Past*, pp. 179–85; and Eric L. Mills, *Biological Oceanography: An Early History, 1870–1960* (Ithaca, NY: Cornell University Press, 1989), part I.

6. David Elliston Allen, *The Naturalists in Britain* (Princeton: Princeton University Press, 1994), pp. 111–14, 186–201.

explore the waters of the Northeast Atlantic originated during the summer of 1870 while he and his family summered at Woods Hole, Massachusetts. At Woods Hole, then an obscure and tiny Cape Cod village, Baird became aware of an angry public debate resulting from the growing use of fixed nets and barriers along the shores of Southern New England. Especially during the spring and early summer spawning seasons, these devices captured enormous quantities of fish. For that reason the nets and barriers were bitterly opposed by subsistence and sports fishermen, who used more traditional line fishing methods. Claiming that the new arrays were devastating local fish populations, the line fishermen demanded that they be outlawed or at least severely regulated.[7]

To evaluate the complaints of the line fishermen, Baird persuaded Congress to establish the U.S. Commission of Fish and Fisheries in the spring of 1871. An initial appropriation of $5,000 was provided. Soon thereafter, President Ulysses S. Grant appointed Baird to serve as the Commission's director. This position was in addition to Baird's duties as a Smithsonian official. He received no pay for his work with the Fish Commission.[8]

In the summer of 1871 the new Fish Commissioner returned to Woods Hole to investigate the reasons for the apparent decline of coastal fish stocks and to recommend necessary regulatory measures. From the outset Baird adopted a broad approach to solving these problems. Realizing that commercial species must be considered as part of their total environment, Baird studied the food of marine species, the migrations of fish, the impact of parasites and diseases, the influence of water temperature, salinity, and ocean currents, and the role played by man through pollution or fishing.[9] The Fish Commissioner's holistic, ecological agenda is praised by modern biologists who point out that it is as valid today as it was in the 19th century.[10]

In directing this new agency, Baird revealed his notable skills as a sci-

7. For the origins and legislative history of the Fish Commission see Allard, *Spencer Fullerton Baird*, pp. 69–86.

8. U.S. Commission of Fish and Fisheries, *Report, 1871–72* (Washington: Government Printing Office, 1873), pp. xiii, xvii (hereafter these annual reports are cited as *USFC Rpt.* plus year). Baird also investigated the Great Lakes and other regions outside the New England area. But the Northeast Atlantic was the focus of his interest.

9. Allard, *Spencer Fullerton Baird*, pp. 87–110.

10. Paul S. Galtsoff, *The Story of the Bureau of Commercial Fisheries Biological Laboratory, Woods Hole, Massachusetts*, Circular 145, U.S. Department of the Interior (Washington: the Department, 1962), pp. 11, 16; Marine Biological Laboratory, Woods Hole, Notice

entific organizer. Taking advantage of a clause in the Commission's enabling legislation that authorized other governmental agencies to provide assistance, Baird obtained the loan of Naval and Revenue Service vessels and in later years U.S. Coast Survey ships to make the large scientific collections needed for his investigations. The most important of these materials were earmarked for deposit in Baird's National Museum. Another government agency, the Light House Board, provided a vacant building at Woods Hole's Little Harbor for Baird's laboratory.

In addition to these physical resources, it was essential to appoint an able scientific corps. In 1871 Baird recruited a group of approximately ten investigators, whose senior member was Addison E. Verrill of Yale University. Verrill, a specialist in marine invertebrates, was joined by a number of his associates and students. Several other scientists served as volunteers with the Commission. Baird paid the expenses of these investigators and in some cases offered them a small salary. But, more fundamentally, these individuals were attracted by the Fish Commission's unmatched oceanic collecting opportunities and the stimulation offered by a collaborative scientific organization. In an era when few scientific journals were available, Baird's offer to publish their papers in the Fish Commission's annual reports also appealed to many naturalists.[11]

At the end of the Fish Commission's first summer, Spencer Baird concluded that the fixed coastal nets and barriers had, in fact, diminished the fisheries off southern New England. Baird recommended that the New England states pass laws to partially close these arrays during the spawning season. But before any regulations were enacted, Baird had to admit—with chagrin—that a marked natural increase in coastal fish populations had occurred in 1871. In the future, Baird was very cautious in making judgments about fish stock dynamics. Nevertheless, this setback did not end the Fish Commission. Instead, the Commission became a permanent agency that expanded as it pursued its original as well as additional programs. The largest new effort was a major fish hatching program begun in 1872 that sought to increase the supply of commercial and sports species. Originating as a sum-

---

for Centennial Evening Lecture, August 5, 1988 (John Hobbie, "Ecology at Woods Hole: Baird, Bigelow, and Redfield").

11. Allard, *Spencer Fullerton Baird*, pp. 87–110.

mer activity, the Fish Commission now operated throughout the year. While he was in Washington, Baird typically devoted at least half of his time to Fish Commission business. In 1887, by the standards of its day, the Fish Commission was a sizeable governmental organization. It had a staff of 105 civilians plus the naval crews that manned the organization's two major ships. Baird's annual budget totaled $268,000. In the last decade of his life, Spencer Baird carried a heavy work load due to his simultaneous direction of three major institutions: the Fish Commission, the National Museum, and the Smithsonian.[12]

While pursuing the Fish Commission's utilitarian objectives, Baird continued to undertake a broad scientific exploration of the oceans since he was convinced that basic knowledge was essential for the solution of practical fishery problems. Between 1872 and 1880 he pursued his research agenda primarily at summer laboratories established along the Northeastern Atlantic seaboard between Noank, Connecticut and Eastport, Maine. From these locations, Baird's scientists surveyed virtually all of New England's coastal waters during the 1870s.[13]

During this era, Baird's summer scientific staff continued to number about ten individuals. The exceptional opportunities they enjoyed was illustrated by the fact that no fewer than 1,500 species of fauna and flora were collected during one season.[14] Many of these species were believed to be new to science. A notable example of the results of Spencer Baird's historic exploration of the Northeastern Atlantic was Addison Verrill's 500-page monograph on the invertebrates of Vineyard Sound. In addition to describing numerous species, Verrill demonstrated the Commission's ecological agenda by relating these organisms to their physical and biological environment.[15]

Scores of additional scientific contributions were made by other Fish Commission investigators. Among these individuals were Alpheus Hyatt, who worked on marine sponges, the marine botanist William G. Farlow, and

---

12. Ibid., pp. 87–132, 262.

13. Ibid., pp. 164–79. In addition, the Fish Commission maintained a Canadian station at Halifax, Nova Scotia during the summer of 1877.

14. *USFC Rpt. 1873–75*, p. viii.

15. Addison E. Verrill, "Report Upon the Invertebrate Animals of Vineyard Sound and the Adjacent Waters With an Account of the Physical Characters of the Region," *USFC Rpt. 1871–72*, pp. 295–778.

the ichthyologist George Brown Goode. Verrill and the other established scientists also brought with them a number of students who were destined for scientific fame, including David Starr Jordan, Edmund B. Wilson, and C. Hart Merriam. Some of the most exciting discoveries made by the Commission's scientific corps related to the region's biogeography. For example, Baird and his associates studied the cold current flowing south along the New England coast that contained examples of marine life heretofore found only in more northern waters. At the same time, previously unknown examples of southern fauna were discovered in the New England Gulf Stream.[16]

In 1881 Spencer Baird ended his roving summer stations and decided to establish a permanent laboratory at Woods Hole. That location also would be the site of the Commission's new hatchery for oceanic fish. The Fish Commission now operated its own small fleet of vessels and the deep harbor at Woods Hole was designated as the home port from which these craft could investigate East Coast commercial fishing grounds and continue the Commission's exploration of New England's coastal waters between Long Island Sound and the Bay of Fundy.[17]

Yet another reason for selecting Woods Hole as the Commission's field headquarters was its location near an exciting new area of investigation in the deep waters on the seaward flank of the Continental Shelf. Baird and his associates called this region of relatively warm water the Gulf Stream Slope. In 1877 USS *Speedwell*, a naval ship loaned to Spencer Baird, established the Fish Commission's first station in this area at a point about 40 miles east of Cape Ann, Massachusetts. Here the water was almost 160 fathoms (about 1,000 feet) deep. George Brown Goode later described the profound excitement as *Speedwell*'s dredge was hauled on board and its contents examined. He noted: "it seems incredible that American naturalists should not then have known that there was a fauna as unlike that of our coast as could be found in the Indian Ocean or the seas of China."[18]

Baird was able to return to the Gulf Stream Slope in 1880 when the

16. Allard, *Spencer Fullerton Baird*, pp. 174–75

17. *USFC Rpt. 1881*, pp. xxxviii–xxxix

18. Quoted in Henry Fairfield Osborn, "Goode As Naturalist," *A Memorial to George Brown Goode* (Washington: Government Printing Office, 1901), p. 22. See also Addison E. Verrill, "Physical Character of the Portion of the Continental Border Beneath the Gulf Stream," *USFC Rpt. 1882*, pp. 1045–52.

Commission's own steamer, *Fish Hawk*, was completed. *Fish Hawk* was built primarily as a floating fish hatchery. But she also was equipped for scientific dredging in waters as deep as 500 fathoms and her first station had nothing to do with the propagation of marine species. Instead, the ship explored the 100 fathom line at the outer limits of the Continental Shelf. Once again, the Fish Commission's investigators were astounded by the specimens taken from these deep waters, which Baird described as "vastly exceeding in richness and extent anything known to science." [19] The rich nature of these collections was suggested by Addison Verrill's claim that between 1880 and 1883 the *Fish Hawk* and other ships operated by the Fish Commission gathered no less than 1,600 invertebrate species, half of them new to the region's fauna. In one year alone (1881) Baird's organization obtained 117 species of fishes, mostly from the Gulf Stream Slope.[20]

Given his intense interest in exploring deep oceanic waters, it is not surprising that Spencer Baird began to lobby Congress for the famed *Albatross* in 1880. When completed two years later, that ship apparently was the world's first large, purpose-built research vessel. Baird assured Congressmen that he needed *Albatross* to locate prolific new fishing grounds that could be used by Americans. In fact, throughout her long career, the ship often gave direct support to the nation's commercial fisheries. But, as noted by Alexander Agassiz, another prominent ocean scientist of this period, *Albatross* was "the best equipped dredger for deep-sea work in existence." [21] Since prime commercial fishing areas are in relatively shoal waters, this capability revealed Baird's intense concern with basic scientific research. In fact, *Albatross*'s first exploratory station, in March 1883, was in waters 519 fathoms (more than 3,000 feet) deep. Later in the 1880s, the ship's dredges went much deeper in the Northeast Atlantic, including one 1883 station with a sounding of 2949 fathoms (almost 18,000 feet).[22]

19. Letter, Baird to George Perkins Marsh, 31 Oct. 1881, USFC Letters Sent, Record Group 22, U.S. National Archives.

20. Addison E. Verrill, "Notice on the Remarkable Marine Fauna Occupying the Outer Banks off the Southern Coast of New England," *USFC Rpt. 1882*, pp. 644, 650.

21. Alexander Agassiz, *Three Cruises of the United States Coast and Geodetic Survey Steamer "Blake"* (Boston: Houghton Mifflin, 1888), I, p. 51.

22. Sanderson Smith, "List of Dredging Stations of the U.S. Fish Commission, the U.S. Coast Survey, and the British Steamer Challenger . . . 1867–1887 . . . ," pp. 873–1017 in *USFC Rpt. 1886*. For the scientific work of *Albatross* in 1883, see Edwin Linton, "Remi-

During the 1880s, approximately fifteen investigators worked each summer at the Commission's laboratory in Woods Hole. Reflecting the organization's central role in the study of marine biology, students from four American universities and colleges (Johns Hopkins, Harvard, Princeton, and Williams), that had purchased research tables at the Fish Commission, also were present. According to Baird, the Fish Commission's essential mission continued to be the "advancement of science in general," including the ecological study of the "mutual relationships and dependencies" of all maritime life forms.[23]

Among the work pursued in this period was the continuing investigation of invertebrates by Addison Verrill and his associates. Verrill's group published numerous papers that concentrated on species taken from below 100 fathoms. The scope of the Fish Commission's work also was revealed by the interests of some of the other scientists recruited by Baird. Among them were the physical oceanographer William Libbey, Jr.; the brilliant theoretical embryologist John A. Ryder; and Edwin Linton, a specialist in marine parasites.[24]

The ichthyologists George Brown Goode and Tarleton H. Bean made other notable contributions in this period. They concentrated their study on fishes taken from deep waters, mostly by Fish Commission vessels. Although this work began in the early 1880s, the final report of Goode and Bean was not published until 1895. It was entitled *Oceanic Ichthyology* and discussed 49 genera and 147 species claimed to be new to science. The authors pointed out that *Oceanic Ichthyology* described more new deep sea fishes than *Challenger* had collected during her entire multi-year cruise around the world in 1872–1876.[25] Justifiably, *Challenger*'s operation is a legendary chapter in the history of oceanography. Sad to say, the work of the Fish Commission receives much less attention.[26]

---

niscences of the Woods Hole Laboratory of the Bureau of Fisheries, 1882–1889," *Science*, XLI (21 May 1915), p. 745.

    23. The quotes are from *USFC Rpt. 1883*, pp. xvii, lvi. For the sale of tables, see Allard, *Spencer Fullerton Baird*, pp. 322–23.

    24. Allard, *Spencer Fullerton Baird*, pp. 329–39.

    25. George Brown Goode and Tarleton H. Bean, *Oceanic Ichthyology* (Washington: Government Printing Office, 1895), I, pp. v–vi.

    26. For example, there is little or no reference to the scientific work of the Fish Commission in Sears and Merriman, eds., *Oceanography: The Past*; Robert C. Cowen, *Frontiers*

This relative neglect is unjustified. As Robert Cowen notes, European and American scientists of the nineteenth century typically organized a number of general or short-term expeditions whose "scattered soundings, samplings, and dredgings" revealed the "gross characteristics" of maritime areas.[27] That seems to be true in general. But in 1890 the Johns Hopkins University biologist William Keith Brooks pointed out that Baird's work in the Northeast Atlantic over the sixteen-year period after 1871 was an "exhaustive scientific exploration." In fact, Brooks claimed, it was the first intensive marine survey undertaken by any government in the world. The Johns Hopkins scientist added that the Fish Commission's approach and techniques were models for "most of the maritime nations of Europe."[28]

Brooks's observation is supported by the data presented in Table I, which demonstrate that Fish Commission vessels established more than 2300 dredging stations between 1871 and 1887. These investigations were initially concentrated in New England coastal waters, but after 1880 their focus shifted to the Gulf Stream Slope north of Cape Hatteras. The Fish Commission's statistics compare with the 638 stations recorded by Coast Survey ships working for Louis and Alexander Agassiz or their associates between 1867–1880. These primarily were located south of Cape Hatteras. Another comparison could be made with the achievements of *Challenger*, which established approximately 180 stations throughout the North and South Atlantic during its four-year cruise around the world in 1872–1876. In the Eastern Atlantic and Mediterranean the French ships *Le Travailleur* and *Talisman* did important deep-sea work during 1880–1883. But the combined total of the French vessels was only 354 research stations.[29]

William Goetzmann points out in his *Exploration and Empire* that the conquest of the American continent led to one of the "finest chapters in the

---

of the Sea: The Story of Oceanographic Exploration (Garden City, NY: Doubleday and Co., 1960); Margaret Deacon, *Scientists At Sea, 1650–1901: A Study of Marine Science* (New York: Academic Press, 1971); or William A. Herdman, *Founders of Oceanography and Their Work: An Introduction to the Science of the Sea* (London: Edward Arnold, 1923). On the other hand, Schlee, *The Edge of an Unfamiliar World*, and Coker, *The Great and Wide Sea*, do provide information on the programs of Baird's Fish Commission.

27. Cowen, *Frontiers of the Sea*, p. 46.

28. Letter, Brooks to Whom It May Concern, 30 June 1890, in *Report of the Investigation of the United States Fish Commission* (51st Cong., 2d sess., Senate Report 2361), pp. 544–45.

29. Smith, "List of Dredging Stations."

TABLE 1   DREDGING STATIONS

	North of Hatteras	South of Hatteras
U.S. FISH COMMISSION, 1871–87:		
Various ships assigned, 1871–79	1075	
Fish Hawk, 1880–1882	385	
Fish Hawk, 1883–1887	96	
Albatross, 1883–1887	518	230
Sub-total:	2074	230
AGASSIZ-ASSOCIATED COAST SURVEY SHIPS, 1867–72, 1877–80:		
L. F. Pourtales cruises, 1867–72		258
L. Agassiz in Blake, 1877–80	48	288
Sub-total:	48	546

OTHER OPERATIONS, 1867–83:

Lightning and Porcupine, 1867–70	194 stations north of U.K.
Challenger, 1872–1876	About 180 in N. and S. Atlantic
Swedish Arctic Expeditions, 1875–79	190 in Arctic Waters
Le Travailleur, 1880–83	198 in Eastern Atlantic and Mediterranean
Talisman, 1883	156 in Eastern Atlantic

Source: Sanderson Smith, "List of Dredging Stations of the U.S. Fish Commission . . . ,"
U.S. Commission of Fish and Fisheries, *Report, 1886*, pp. 873–1017.

history of science" featuring the establishment of permanent institutions "dedicated to the endless conquest of knowledge."[30] It seems to me that this fundamental observation can be applied to Baird's Fish Commission. That agency's work in the 1871–1887 era is continued today by its successor, the National Marine Fisheries Service. The Commission's research collections, held for the most part by the Smithsonian's National Museum, continue to be the basis for important biological investigations. In addition, as I have argued elsewhere, Spencer Baird exerted major posthumous influence on the establishment in 1888, one year after his death, of Woods Hole's famed Marine Biological Laboratory.[31]

As we have seen, Spencer Fullerton Baird met the challenge posed by a virtually un-explored ocean by establishing the Fish Commission in 1871. He then developed an imaginative ecological research agenda, recruited a talented group of scientists, and provided these investigators with essential institutional support. In the process, he created in the Fish Commission an organization that exemplified the distinction, freedom, and breadth of federal governmental science in the last half of the 19th century. The foundations laid by Spencer Baird and the other institution builders of the Gilded Age deserve to be remembered for their major influence on the development of science in modern America.[32]

30. Goetzmann, *Exploration and Empire*, p. 601. Goetzmann's later work, *New Lands, New Men*, provides excellent insight into the participation by the United States in maritime exploration.

31. See Dean C. Allard, "The Fish Commission Laboratory and its Influence on the Founding of the Marine Biological Laboratory," *Journal of the History of Biology*, XXIII, No. 2 (1990).

32. For the distinction of governmental science and the need to create scientific institutions, see A. Hunter Dupree, *Science in the Federal Government* (Cambridge: Harvard University Press, 1957), pp. 215–31; Francis C. Haber, "Sidelights on American Science as Revealed in the Hyatt Autograph Collection," *Maryland Historical Magazine*, 46 (Dec. 1951): 233–56; and Allard, *Spencer Fullerton Baird*, pp. 259–61. Robert V. Bruce discusses the demands of scientists for freedom ("support without strings," as Bruce phrases it) in *The Launching of Modern American Science, 1846–1876* (New York: Knopf, 1987), pp. 225–39.

PART THREE
EXPLORATORY ART—
SPREADING THE IMAGE

KATHERINE E. MANTHORNE

LEGIBLE LANDSCAPES
Text and Image in the Expeditionary Art of Frederic Church

Captain Meriwether Lewis and Lieutenant William Clark made yet another discovery upon returning from their overland exploration in 1806: written expeditionary texts alone proved insufficient to capture the public imagination. Thomas Jefferson attested to the fact that while even the most humble citizen excitedly anticipated their findings, their words alone failed to convey the character of the western scenery. Major Stephen H. Long's expedition to the Rockies in 1819–1820 was deemed more successful in that regard, a circumstance attributed to the visual images by Samuel Seymour contained in his report.[1] Topographical draftsmen, later replaced by photographers, greatly expanded the visual materials contained in subsequent field reports.

But what of the academic artist whose exploratory experiences result in a painted canvas, something he has created as an independent *work of art*? Take the celebrated example of the painter Thomas Moran (1837–1926), who is remembered today for being the last of the great documentary and visionary painters of the American West. His early Yellowstone watercolors and oil paintings that launched his career offer a variation on the interplay

---

1. For a useful overview of the need for images in the early literature of exploration, see Hans Huth, *Nature and the American. Three Centuries of Changing Attitudes* (Berkeley and Los Angeles: University of California Press, 1957), especially pp. 131–133.

between expeditionary text and image. Moran's interest in Yellowstone was initially aroused in 1870, when he was asked to illustrate—site unseen—Nathaniel P. Langford's article "The Wonders of the Yellowstone" for *Scribner's Monthly*. Vowing to see it for himself, he accompanied Ferdinand V. Hayden's Geological Survey of the Territories. Throughout the summer of 1871 Hayden's party carefully mapped and described the region while official artist Henry Elliott and official photographer William Henry Jackson recorded its appearance. Although Moran's presence was unofficial, it proved historically significant.[2] In 1871 the Yellowstone was largely unexplored territory; rumors of its canyons, thunderous geysers, and scalding mud craters were dismissed as tall tales. Even the government reports, carefully documenting its geological wonders, were unconvincing without pictorial evidence. Hayden himself observed: "To a person who has not visited the Yellowstone . . . it is simply impossible to conceive of the character of its scenery . . . unless accompanied by colored illustrations."[3] Moran obliged with sets of spectacular watercolors, which Prang & Company published as *chromolithographs*, and a third category: the large salon painting. Art served as the handmaiden of science, and the coloristic excesses of the western wonderland came to be accepted as "truth." All this *sounds* logical; obviously 'one picture *is* worth a thousand words' when it comes to the evocation of unknown lands. With "high art" as opposed to "documentary illustration," however, the situation is more complex. We are no longer talking about images which reside within the text, but independent works of art that exist in complex interaction with the written word.

Moran's predecessor Frederic Church (1826–1900) had been a pioneer in the visualizations of territorial exploration as fine art. While Moran traveled in the company of large-scale government expeditions to the American West, Church orchestrated his own private expeditions to South America, the Arctic, and elsewhere based on reading and study. His extensive library, which still exists intact at his former home *Olana* in Hudson, New York, helps us to establish the relationship between his travels in present-day Colombia and Ecuador (then known collectively as New Granada) and

2. For the latest and most complete account of the artist's life and work, see Nancy K. Anderson, *Thomas Moran* (Washington, DC: National Gallery of Art, 1997).

3. F. V. Hayden, *The Yellowstone National Park, and the Mountain Regions of Portions of Idaho, Nevada, Colorado, and Utah* (Boston, MA: 1876), p. III.

Alexander von Humboldt's *Personal Narrative of Travels to the Equinoctial Regions of America, During the Years 1799–1804* and *Cosmos*. But just as importantly, it fosters a profile of Church as a man who had a deep respect for books and the written word.[4] His art traffics back and forth between the visual and the verbal in a variety of ways, extending far beyond specific texts, that were central to his creative endeavor. This impulse toward the integration of text and image, however, was not only a personal predilection of the artist. Rather, the emphasis on the printed word was also deeply ingrained in the national culture. As John Gadsby Chapman advised generations of readers of his popular *American Drawing Book*: "Any one who can learn to write, can learn to draw."[5] On the surface, this statement is a curious initiation to the study of drawing; but it underscores the primacy of the word. Art historians (myself included) have tended to take for granted that the canvases of Church, Moran, and their compatriots bear witness to an explorer's empirical findings while the natural history exegesis provides a scientific basis for appreciating the pictures. We need now to focus our attention more specifically on this *interaction* between such landscapes of exploration that emerged in academic or salon art and the related texts. What follows are selected musings on one aspect of the problem: how expeditionary landscapes were looked at as both objects of art and patterns of information operating within a given set of constraining texts. We consider first, the artist's unpublished diaries and letters containing his own scripted responses to landscape; second, the critical discourse which identified the artist-explorer as a role for a painter; and third, the expository pamphlets prepared as viewing aids to his panoramic images.

Travel Diaries and Letters: The Artist as Author

Church made expeditions in 1853 and again in 1857 to the northwestern corner of South America, where he followed Humboldt's "Grand Tour" of

---

4. For background on Church's travels including his relation to Humbolt, library, and travel itinerary, see my *Tropical Renaissance. North American Artists Exploring Latin America, 1839–1879*. Washington, DC: Smithsonian Institution Press, 1989.

5. John Gadsby Chapman, *The American Drawing-Book, A Manual for the Amateur and Basis of Study for the Professional Artist* (1st ed. 1874; New York: J. S. Redfield, 1858), masthead for Contents (n.p.).

natural history. From the moment on 2 May 1853 when he disembarked at Barranquilla, on the coast of Colombia, he kept a written diary of his activities, supplemented by letters to family and friends. His writings reveal a search for linguistic equivalents for new experiences—ranging from the mundane (a new food he is served) to the magnificent (his first sight of the Cordillera).[6] In Church's case, this search is further complicated by his resolve to make all entries in Spanish, a language of which—by his own admission—he had had only a "very limited knowledge."[7] (He did keep his vow for the first several months.) Why, we wonder, did he persist in this literary exercise, when—as he himself phrased it—"it is not my province to handle the pen." Semantic confusion abounds. But like most of us when we travel, he obviously felt the obligation to document his movements, to keep track of details he would later forget; but as an artist who intended to forge major artistic productions from his experiences, there were other factors in play.

One of the first major sights he encountered on the reconnaissance of 1853 was Tequendama Falls (outside Bogotá, Colombia), later the subject of a full-scale painting (Figure 1). Here he supplemented his usual short, quotidian diary entries and slight, on-the-spot pencil sketches with several finished drawings as well as a carefully-crafted formal essay. Since his treatment of this site has received far less scholarly attention than his mountain scenery, it provides a useful point of departure for our analysis. He opens by casting the new—i.e., Tequendama—in terms of the familiar—i.e., Niagara:

> But there is another cataract as wonderful as Niagara and if not as imposing yet more beautiful and picturesque and presents a greater variety of interesting phenomena. I speak of the Falls of Tequendama near Bogota in the Republic of New Granada.[8]

6. The principle reference to Church's diaries from these travels still remains David C. Huntington, "Landscape and Diaries: The South American Trips of F. E. Church," *The Brooklyn Museum Annual* 5 (1963–64): 65–98. There are, however, a number of errors in the transcripts. My paper is part of a larger project to publish Church's South American letters and diaries.

7. Sangay diary, 9 July 1857; p. 2 of typed transcript. Olana State Historic Site Archives, Hudson, NY (hereafter referred to as Olana).

8. Tequendama Falls Manuscript, undated; Olana. The majority of Church's drawings belong to the Cooper Hewitt Museum, NYC, including the finished drawings of Tequendama Falls.

Figure 1. Frederic Church, Falls of the Tequendama near Bogotá, New Grenada, *1854.*
Cincinnati Art Museum.

This verbal introduction sets the stage for what is to follow. For just as his narrative recounts thwarted efforts to find the optimal viewing angle, so his prose gropes to convey the "very peculiar and striking view" of this "most wonderful cataract." His frustration is also carried over in his letters home to Hartford, where he continues his mission to convey its appearance:

> At the top of the fall you are in what is called cold country with the trees, plants and fruits of the temperate climate; at the bottom grow palms and oranges & c. The clouds formed by evaporation from the falls sometimes cover the mountains for miles and entirely prevent a view of the falls.[9]

In the end, it is more difficult for us to visualize "the Salto" (as the falls were known) from his written accounts than it was for him to glimpse them through the cloud covering.

Remember, however, that parallel to these efforts at verbalization was the process of visualization. He drew the falls from various perspectives and distances, presumably as he prepared to put paint to canvas. Already famed for his extraordinary visual powers, Church could recall minute details of a scene long after he had left it. Clearly, then, the essay was intended to serve as something other than an aide-de-mémoire. Begging the reader to "excuse the boldness" he will grasp his pen "no matter how awkwardly." He insists that he can only attempt "a simple description" of "a visit to one of the grandest and most lovely works of nature which I have been fortunate enough to witness." His choice of the term "witness" is here significant, suggesting the need for objective testimony.

As Church had already learned from the critical response to previous work, realism was the essential measure of his imagery. But given that almost no one who gazed upon the painting outside the artist and its owner (Cyrus Field, promoter of the Trans-Atlantic Cable and Church's friend and traveling companion) had any first-hand acquaintance with the site, its perceived realism could only be measured against textual sources. It should not be assumed, in other words, that these images subscribed to some absolute conception of the real; instead each should be understood as a production brought about by artistic action within a textual framework. Given

9. Frederic Church to his mother, 7 July 1853, Bogotá; Waldron Phoenix Belknap Jr. Collection, Henry Francis duPont Winterthur Museum, Winterthur, DE.

the paucity of accessible texts on the subject, the artist himself took up the pen to frame (intellectually, rather than physically) his own production. He intended, I believe, to author his own explanatory pamphlet on the Tequendama Falls to accompany its public exhibition; in the end the picture appeared at the National Academy of Design's annual exhibition without the advantage of written text, and stirred little public interest. But whether or not these expository writings reached the public directly, they provided a blueprint for the artist's own extended creative process that ultimately gave rise to the work of art.

Church's experiences of a second landscape wonder provides further insight. Continuing from Bogotá into Ecuador, Church reflected on the relative proximity of another landscape site: "Two days from here is the Splendid volcano of Sangai [sic], which I believe is the most active volcano in the world." He seems to have made no effort on that occasion to get any closer. But on his return reconnaissance of 1857, it had become the primary destination of a five-day trek from Riobamba to its remote location in the eastern Cordillera. The editing that occurs between the first and second trip is significant. For "in so far as the journey has to become a journal, a map or a drawing in order to enter spatial history," as Paul Carter observes, "going back is the traveler's opportunity to check his facts. It is analogous to the process of revision." [10] So we find Church already revising the record of his journey, covering over his previous omission of Sangay. But here a curious reversal occurs. For while the Sangay diary constitutes one of his most sustained literary efforts, his visual responses are scanty.

The diary tells of his first-hand encounter with the active volcano, complete with aural as well as visual effects:

> I commenced to sketch the effect as rapidly as possible, but constant changes took place and new beauties revealed themselves as the setting sun turned the black smoke into burnished copper, and the white steam into gold. At intervals of two or three minutes an explosion would take place; the first intimation was a fresh mass of smoke with sharply defined outline rolling among the mountains. I was so delighted with the changing effects

10. Paul Carter, *The Road to Botany Bay. An Exploration of Landscape and History* (Chicago: University of Chicago Press, 1987), p. 173.

that I continued making rapid sketches of the different effects until night overtook me and a chilly dampness warned me to retrace my steps.[11]

Strangely, the sketches he mentioned remain the sole visual documents to emerge from that trip; for although the Sangay encounter seems to have made a great impact on him, he never produced a full-scale painting of it. I and other art historians have tried to explain this omission, suggesting that his experiences of the active Sangay were incorporated into his renderings of its sister volcano Cotopaxi, which spanned a good two decades of his life. It's also possible that his inhibitions about painting Sangay may have been self-imposed, his pictorial imagination restricted by his own inadequate prose. In any case he took up the subject of Sangay again some forty-odd years after he left Ecuador. For along with the handwritten diary of 1857 there exists at Olana a typescript dating from the last years of Church's life and incorporating some alterations and additions, apparently in preparation for a never-realized compendium of his Memoirs. The fact remains, then, that the artist himself regarded his essay as a vital document. The journal page provides a laboratory in which slowly edged his thinking and working methods closer to the scientific, as can be detected in the progression from the language of the picturesque in the encounter with Tequendama in 1853 to the ascent of Sangay in 1857. In his writing, he prepared the ground for artistic discovery, both for himself and his public. His own authorial voice, however, was but one in the larger artistic-scientific discourse.

Critical Discourse: The Artist as Explorer

The artist has often stood outside mainstream American society. By the 1850s he was beginning to rise above "the butcher, the baker, and the

---

11. Frederic Church, Sangay Diary, July 11. This is the sole portion of the expedition of 1857 to survive in this format. The passage just preceding this one is also pictorially evocative:

> . . . I turned my back and lo! Sangay, with its lofty plume of smoke stood clear before me. I was startled with the beauty of the effect—above a serrated, black rugged pile of rocky mountain two columns arose, one creamy white against the blue sky melted itself away into thin vapor and was lost in the azure. The other, black and sombre, piled up in huge rounded forms cut sharply against the rich white of the first, and piling itself up higher and higher gradually diffused itself into a yellowish smoky vapor out of which occasionally would burst a mass of black smoke. . . .

candlestick maker," and one mechanism for effecting this elevated status
was by virtue of his association with the new, modern science. Aligning
with that tradition, Church's public identity was as carefully crafted as his
minutely painted canvases. The very language in which his accomplish-
ments were praised was borrowed from the literature of discovery:

> The indomitable explorative enterprise of the New England mind of
> Church has carried into landscape art, the infinite possibilities whereof, as
> accessory to and illustrative of natural science, were long ago foreseen by
> Humboldt, into whose views the young American painter entered with ar-
> dor and intelligence.[12]

The critic's emphasis on his "explorative enterprise" and art "illustrative of
natural science" remove the painter from what many regarded as the sub-
jective and even frivolous domain of art. He carefully traces his lines of descent directly to Humboldt, and postpones until later in his essay any discussion of his artistic predecessor Thomas Cole, father of the Hudson River
School.[13] In this re-telling, Church's possesses the heroic qualities of the
boldest explorer:

> Enterprise is, indeed, a prominent characteristic of Church; he has had the
> bravery to seek and the patience to delineate subjects heretofore scarcely
> recognized by art, one of whose benign missions it is to extend the enjoy-
> ment which time and space limit, and bring into mutual and congenial ac-
> quaintance the most widely separated glories of the universe.

In an age which revered "the cult of professionalism," the artist-explorer
could be appreciated as a 'specialist': the hero of his own drama, overcom-
ing all obstacles to achieve the peak of a mountain or the depth of a canyon,

---

12. Henry T. Tuckerman, *Book of the Artists. American Artist Life* (New York: G. P. Putnam, 1867), p. 370. Writing in 1867, Tuckerman was codifying an image of the artist that
had been in the making since the early 1850's.

13. Tuckerman further elaborated on the ties to Humboldt: "It seems to us a most
pleasing coincidence that, when Church sojourned in the vicinity of Quito, in order to study
tropical landscape, he lodged beneath the roof and shared the hospitality of the same family with whom Humboldt found a home fifty years before, while making his scientific researches in the same region"; ibid.

all the time maintaining an acuity of vision that allowed him to be the eyes of his countrymen. According to legend, the birds paid homage to the great realist painter of antiquity, Zeuxis, by flying down to eat from his painted vine. The grapes of Zeuxis represent a primary aim of western aesthetics: art as the supreme duplication of material objects, what Norman Bryson has termed the dream of the Essential Copy.[14] In mid-nineteenth century America, the Essential Copy re-emerged as a desired goal of landscape and Frederic Church its supreme practitioner, in works such as his over-sized *Niagara* of 1857 (Corcoran Gallery of Art, Washington, D.C.; 42½ × 90½"). And with it the trope of the painted image that fools the eye is handed down: legend had it that famed critic John Ruskin, upon viewing *Niagara* in a London gallery, was prompted to examine the window, so convinced was he that the refraction of an actual sunbeam was producing its painted rainbow at left.[15] Parallel tales, millennia apart.

Prior to painting *Niagara* Church had noted the challenge it presented: "Although it is a generally received opinion that Niagara can neither be described nor painted yet people will write about it and artists will copy it with different degrees of success according to their respective abilities."[16] He himself dispelled that generally received opinion by painting a canvas that convinced audiences he had duplicated everything but the roar.[17] Having proven his ability to produce the Essential Copy with the familiar and frequently rendered landscape icon of North America, Church was able to transfer that authority to the novel subjects encountered on his expeditions to distant locales. His canvases were "pictured with the fidelity of a naturalist"; they could be taken as truth.[18]

14. Norman Bryson, *Word and Image. French Painting of the Ancien Régime* (Cambridge University Press, 1981), pp. 1–8.

15. Tuckerman repeats this anecdote about Ruskin: "Ruskin, when he first saw Church's *Niagara*, pointed out an effect of light upon water which he declared he had often seen in nature, especially among the Swiss waterfalls, but never before on canvas; and so perfect is the optical illusion of the iris in the same marvellous picture, that the circumspect author of Modern Painters went to the window and examined the glass, evidently attributing the prismatic bow to the refraction of the sun." Tuckerman, p. 371.

16. Tequendama Falls Manuscript.

17. David C. Huntington, *The Landscapes of Frederic Edwin Church: Vision of an American Era* (New York: Braziller, 1966), p. 1ff analyzes the reception of *Niagara*.

18. Tuckerman, p. 372.

Expository Pamphlets

In 1859, two years after returning home, Church created *Heart of the Andes* (Figure 2) and displayed the 5 × 10 foot canvas in a frame that could double as a window casement. Thus, he announced his picture as a site where objects reappear in all their original presence, the armchair traveler's window into the Andean world. Yet for all his confident handling of pictorial detail and effect, doubts still lingered that the image itself could stand as the sole bearer of meaning. This time several close friends were prevailed upon to provide written exegesis: lengthy pamphlets by Theodore Winthrop and Louis Legrand Noble, sold along with admission to the solo exhibition of *The Heart of the Andes*. Sentence by sentence and paragraph by paragraph, Winthrop took the reader / viewer by the hand and guided him along its twisted pictorial pathways, explicating strange phenomena along the way.[19] Noble opened his commentary *not* with any mention of the picture, but with an explanation of the natural forces shaping the earth's crust:

> The origin of the broken surface of the earth, we learn, is the subterranean power of upheaval. In obedience to that power, inconceivable to the human mind, the outer crust of the globe is lifted into irregularities which we see. Around and upon these are the work and play and battles of the elements. The surf beats at the base, and the storm at the summit of the mountain; along its sides sweep the wind and rain; heat and frost dissolve, explode, and crumble. . . . Thus the elements and forces of the earth are forever busy in the apparently infinite task of reducing to a level the primeval erections.[20]

Winthrop and Noble presented an intellectual framework for understanding the great canvas, part science and part geography lesson. Here in fact the metaphor of "map-reading" offers a useful analogy, suggesting instruction in a requisite linguistic skill. Audiences were tutored in how to interpret these natural signs; a variety of authorial voices stepped forward, while the

---

19. Theodore Winthrop, *Companion to 'The Heart of the Andes'* (New York: D. Appleton, 1859).

20. Louis L. Noble, *Church's Painting: The Heart of the Andes* (New York: D. Appleton, 1859), p. 3.

Figure 2. Frederic Church, The Heart of the Andes, *1859. Metropolitan Museum of Art, NY. Bequest of Mrs. David Dows, 1909.*

artist himself stood aside (although undoubtedly whispering into the ears of his author-friends). Collectively the texts convert the image into a site of meaning, capable of being "read" by the thousands of visitors who paid the twenty-five cent admission. They helped transform *The Heart of the Andes* into a *legible landscape*: a synthesis of artistic practice and scientific thought. The myriad reviews and commentaries that appeared subsequently, echoing as they do these pamphlets, testify to the success of this strategy.

Conclusion

When word converts image into a site of meaning, as Bryson points out, it does so at a loss to the image:

> Only rarely has the image been granted full independence—allowed simply to exist, with all the plenary autonomy enjoyed by the objects of the world. Throughout its existence, painting has sought to circumscribe and delimit the autonomous image by subjecting it, as part of the overall impulse of renunciation, to the external control of discourse.[21]

Submerged beneath this textual layering, Church's images are reduced from a spatial to a linear narrative. Perhaps, as Goethe advised, "We ought to talk less and draw more. I personally should like to renounce speech altogether and, like organic nature, communicate everything I have to say in sketches." Goethe proceeded to fill his travel notebooks with wonderful object studies, although he fortunately never renounced speech. His remarks remind us, however, of the inherent tension between the visual and the verbal, between the part of our brain that thinks in images versus that which operates in words. Text is an artificial imposition on image, drawing the language of nature: a language in which the American landscape painters were fluent. In order to communicate in the dominant language, their pictures required anchoring in the written discourse of the day, even if it meant sacrificing something of their visual ambiguity. Text and image co-existed in a complex symbiosis, allowing landscapes of unknown terrain to be "read" as effectively as the contemporary genre scenes that took their subjects from everyday life. Embedded in this textual matrix, high or salon art entered the discourse of exploration.

21. Bryson, p. xvi.

ILLUSTRATED GOVERNMENT PUBLICATIONS RELATED TO THE AMERICAN WEST, 1843-1863

In an 1861 debate over distribution of duplicates of federally-published scientific studies, Senator John P. Hale of New Hampshire declared:

> I should like the country to know how much we have spent for printing pictures of bugs, reptiles, etc.... We [have] published eleven or twelve volumes ..., illustrated with pictures of bugs, snakes, and reptiles. It has cost us millions of dollars to print these pictures, and now we are going to spend $10,000 to distribute them.... The thing is all wrong, Sir.

Senator Simon Cameron agreed, complaining that, "I am tired of all this thing called science...."[1]

By the time Senators Hale and Cameron took the floor to object, the federal government had, in fact, published dozens of illustrated books containing thousands of pictures from various exploring expeditions. Some eighteen of them related to the American West, beginning with John C. Frémont's first report on the Rocky Mountains in 1843, and concluding with Lieutenant John Mullen's *Report on the Construction of a Military Road*

---

1. Daniel C. Haskell, *The United States Exploring Expedition, 1838–1842, and Its Publications, 1844–1874* (1942; reprint, New York: Greenwood Press, Publishers, 1968), p. 23.

from Fort Walla-Walla to Fort Benton in 1863, and including the reports of
the United States Exploring Expedition (a portion of which related to the
West), Frémont's subsequent explorations, the war with Mexico, the Bound-
ary Survey, the Pacific Railroad Surveys, and the Ives expedition to the
Grand Canyon. These reports contain a total of more than 1,600 unique illustrations, ranging from landscapes and portraits of individuals to genre
scenes and scientific drawings of flora, fauna, and geological specimens.
They were issued in editions of from 100 (the first printing of the Wilkes
Expedition) to 53,000 (Stevens's report, or volume twelve of the *Pacific
Railroad Surveys*), and the simple process of multiplying the number of il-
lustrations in each volume by the size of the edition shows that the government issued a total of more than 25,934,350 images related to the American
West during these years.[2] No wonder that Senator Hale compared the on-
going publications of the Wilkes Expedition to the "everlasting" lawsuit of
Jarndyce *vs*. Jarndyce in Charles Dickens's *Bleak House*.[3]

But even that does not tell the whole story of federally published pictures
of the West. This figure does not include the dozens of maps in theses volumes, subsequent printings of any of these books, other related government publications, or any of the substantial private publications that touch
on the West that were issued during these years.[4] The first five volumes of
the U.S. Exploring Expedition, for example, were reprinted fourteen times

2. See Appendix 1 for a list of the publications as well as my estimates of the number
of different illustrations produced as well as the total number printed. These figures cannot
be considered precise, because it is sometimes impossible to know exactly how many copies
of a book were actually published. Government publications usually indicate the printing
order in the preliminary information at the beginning of each volume; however, in the case
of Frémont's second report, for example, the government ordered 10,000 copies, but Baltimore lithographer Edward W. Weber initially delivered only 1,000 sets of lithographs because of some technical problem. Nor do the figures take into account the subsequent publication of government or private editions. See, for example, B. B. French, *Frémont's Report*
(29th Cong., 1st Sess., H.D. 118). See also Charles A. Seavey, "Government Graphics: The
Development of Illustration in U.S. Federal Publications, 1817–1861," in *Government
Publications Review*, 17 (1990): 121–142.

3. Haskell, *United States Exploring Expedition*, p. 15.

4. Nor does this figure include other significant government publications that relate to
the West, such as Alexander Dallas Bache's *Annual Reports of the Coast Survey* or Henry Rowe
Schoolcraft's *Historical and Statistical Information Respecting the History, Condition, and
Prospects of the Indian Tribes of the United States*; or important private publications such as
Prince Maximilian's *Travels in the Interior of North America, 1832–34* (1839–41), George
Catlin's *North American Indian Portfolio . . .* (1844), John James Audubon and John Bach-
man's *Viviparous Quadrupeds of North America* (1844–46), and John Russell Bartlett's *Per-*

by private publishers, Wilkes having taken the precaution of copyrighting it himself; Frémont's 1845 report was reprinted twenty-four times, once by the federal government and twenty-three times by private publishers; and William H. Emory's 1848 *Notes of a Military Reconnoissance . . .* was reprinted nine times, five times by the government and four by private publishers[5] (Figures 1, 2).

It is clear from these figures that during the two decades that we have come to know as the era of Manifest Destiny artist-explorers roamed over the trans-Mississippi West, contributing to an unprecedented spate of illustrated publications. An examination of the eighteen government-issued reports included in this study suggests that the federal government led the way in exploration of new territory through the Topographical Engineers and in dissemination of the findings in publications supervised by the newly-organized Smithsonian Institution, the Congressional Committee on Engraving, and, after 1852, the Superintendent of Public Printing.[6]

Yet these fascinating images have attracted the attention of few scholars over the years. While a number of scholars have studied the works of an individual artist, William H. Goetzmann is the only historian to incorporate a study of all the survey artists into the main body of his research in his trilogy on exploration.[7] David J. Weber and Robert V. Hine have dealt with the work of Richard and Edward Kern, who accompanied Frémont on several of his expeditions; Hine and J. Gray Sweeny have discussed the work of the artists of the U.S. and Mexican boundary survey; Ben W. Huseman has re-

sonal *Narrative of Explorations and Incidents in Texas, New Mexico, California, Sonora, and Chihuahua . . .* (1854), just to mention a few.

5. Haskell, *United States Exploring Expedition*, pp. 31–45; and Henry R. Wagner and Charles L. Camp, *The Plains & the Rockies: A Critical Bibliography of Exploration, Adventure and Travel in the American West,* Revised, Enlarged, and Edited by Robert H. Becker (4th ed.; San Francisco: John Howell—Books, 1982), entries 115 and 148.

6. William H. Goetzmann established the significance of the Topographical Engineers' work and their dedication to the cause of Manifest Destiny more than three decades ago in *Army Exploration in the American West, 1803–1863* (New Haven: Yale University Press, 1959).

7. Goetzmann's trilogy includes ibid. as well as *Exploration and Empire: The Explorer and the Scientist in the Winning of the American West* and *New Lands, New Men: America and the Second Great Age of Discovery* (New York: Viking, 1986). See also Goetzmann, "The Grand Reconnaissance," *American Heritage: The Magazine of History,* XXIII (Oct., 1972), 44-59-92-95. Brian W. Dippie has discussed the competition for federal money in *Catlin and His Contemporaries: The Politics of Patronage* (Lincoln: University of Nebraska Press, 1990).

Figure 1. Artist unknown, after A. T. Agate, Indian Burial Place, Oregon. *Wood engraving from Charles Wilkes,* Narrative of the United States Exploring Expedition, *Vol. 5. Courtesy St. Louis Mercantile Library at the University of Missouri—St. Louis. Wilkes visited the northwest coast of North America during the summer of 1841 as a part of the first American around-the-world expedition. The scientific and ethnographic materials that his crew gathered formed the basis of the new Smithsonian's collections.*

Figure 2. C. B. Graham after John Mix Stanley, Hyerogliphics, *from Emory,* Notes of a Military Reconnoissance. *Courtesy St. Louis Mercantile Library at the University of Missouri— St. Louis. Stanley accompanied Col. Stephen W. Kearney on his march from Fort Leavenworth to Sante Fe to California, bringing the ancient civilizations of the Southwest to the attention of Americans for the first time.*

cently studied Balduin Möllhausen's pictures from the Ives expedition; and Julie Schimmel discusses John Mix Stanley's pictures from the Kearny and Stevens expeditions in her unpublished dissertation.[8]

How much impact did these federally-produced pictures have on the exploration and settlement of the American West? I will attempt to answer four questions in this essay: Why did the government publish these pictures? How widely were they disseminated? And what was their impact?[9] We might also ask how they affected the fledgling lithographic industry, for it is also apparent that these expenditures stimulated the American printing industry at a crucial time when it was just beginning to grow and competent lithographers, usually British or European immigrants, were locating in most of the major coastal cities.

The Federal Government and Illustrated Books

Private publishers in Philadelphia issued the reports of early explorers Zebulon Pike, Lewis and Clark, and Stephen H. Long. Pike's and the Lewis and Clark volumes were to be published as soon as "a sufficient number of subscribers be obtained . . . ," and the federal government agreed to purchase

---

8. Katherine Karpenstein, "Illustrations of the West in Congressional Documents, 1843–1863" (M. A. Thesis, University of California, Berkeley, 1939), was one of the first to direct attention to these publications. See also David J. Weber, *Richard H. Kern: Expeditionary Artist in the Far Southwest, 1848–1853* (Albuquerque: University of New Mexico Press, 1985); Robert V. Hine, *Edward Kern and American Expansion* (New Haven: Yale University Press, 1962), reprinted as *In the Shadow of Frémont: Edward Kern and the Art of Exploration, 1845–1860* (Norman: University of Oklahoma Press, 1982); Hine, *Bartlett's West: Drawing the Mexican Boundary* (New Haven: Yale University Press, 1968); Gray Sweeny, "Drawing Borders: Art and the Cultural Politics of the U.S.-Mexico Boundary Survey, 1850–1853," in *Drawing the Borderline: Artist-Explorers of the U.S.-Mexico Boundary Survey* (Albuquerque: The Albuquerque Museum, 1996); Ben W. Huseman, *Wild River, Timeless Canyons: Balduin Möllhausen's Watercolors of the Colorado* (Fort Worth and Tucson: Amon Carter Museum and the University of Arizona Press, 1995); and Julia Ann Schimmel, "John Mix Stanley and Imagery of the West in Nineteenth-Century American Art" (Unpublished Ph.D. Dissertation, Institute of Fine Arts, New York University, 1983). I have dealt with the survey artists in *Prints of the West* (Golden, CO: Fulcrum Publishers, 1994), and Ann Shelby Blum examined the scientific prints in *Picturing Nature: American Nineteenth-Century Zoological Illustration* (Princeton: Princeton University Press, 1993).

9. Martha A. Sandweiss deals with these and other questions in "The Public Life of Western Art," in Jules David Prown et al., *Discovered Lands, Invented Pasts: Transforming Visions of the American West* (New Haven: Yale University Press, 1992), pp. 117–133.

only about a dozen copies of the Long report.[10] At the urging of the scientific elite, the federal government began publishing illustrated expeditionary accounts in 1843.[11] There were commercial and patriotic reasons as well, including the government's own desire for international respect and prestige. The legislation ordering publication of the Wilkes Expedition narrative, for example, specified that it be done "with illustrations and published in the form similar to the voyage of the *Astrolabe*, lately published by the Government of France."[12] Published reports furthered military careers and gave western congressmen something to show for their expansionist efforts. Diplomatic rivalries with European countries also probably hurried the decision along, for the American claim to the Pacific Northwest could only have been strengthened by Wilkes's visit and the information that he obtained.[13] No doubt, the improving technology of the printing industry, which could provide handsome lithographs at a relatively low cost, contributed to the decision as well.[14]

The huge amount of unexplored territory annexed into the Union in the first half of the nineteenth century further necessitated illustrated expedition reports. The United States had become a continental power with more than just a window on the Pacific. Along with a coastline of almost a thousand miles, the country assumed responsibility for the daunting prob-

10. Pike to John Conrad, Annapolis, Jan. 16, 1809, in Donald Jackson, ed., *The Journals of Zebulon Montgomery Pike, with Letters and Related Documents*, 2 vols. (Norman: University of Oklahoma Press, 1966), 2: 359; "The Conrad Prospectus," in Donald Jackson, ed., *Letters of the Lewis and Clark Expedition, with Related Documents, 1783–1854*, 2 vols. (Urbana: University of Illinois Press, 1978), 2: 396 (quote); and Roger L. Nichols and Patrick L. Halley, *Stephen Long and American Frontier Exploration* (Newark: University of Delaware Press, 1980), p. 161.

11. Publications were essential in establishing a naturalist's credibility, and illustrations were considered necessary because they often served as type specimens when preservation of the original was not possible. Charlotte M. Porter, *The Eagle's Nest: Natural History and Amerian Ideas, 1812–1842* (University: University of Alabama Press, 1986), p. 141; William Stanton, *The Great United States Exploring Expedition of 1838–1842* (Berkeley: University of California Press, 1975), pp. 24–30; and Blum, *Picturing Nature*, p. 119.

12. Haskell, *United States Exploring Expedition*, p. 9. The law authorizing publication of the Wilkes volumes passed on August 26, 1842.

13. Wilkes presented the Tyler administration with an enthusiastic special report on Oregon, urging that the U.S. claim of the entire territory as far north as 54°40'. David M. Pletcher, *The Diplomacy of Annexation: Texas, Oregon, and the Mexican War* (Columbia: University of Missouri Press, 1973), pp. 94, 107; Stanton, *Great United States Exploring Expedition*, 314 and note.

14. See Tyler, *Prints of the West*.

lems that had plagued Mexico's ownership of the region. The discovery of gold in California in 1848 solved the population problem, but exacerbated the formidable obstacles imposed by vast distances and difficult terrain, leading to thoughts of an independent California. Col. John J. Abert, commander of the Topographical Engineers, concluded that the "integrity of the Union" was at stake and sent his engineers into the field to establish our boundaries and search for transcontinental railroad routes.[15] They publicized their findings in handsome, calfskin-bound books that often contained eloquent descriptions of the new territory accompanied by "landscape views" calculated "to illustrate . . . ," as Lt. John W. Gunnison later explained, the "general character [of the country], and to exhibit on a small scale the character of its mountains and cañones [sic], and of its plains and valleys, . . . as seen in nature. . . ."[16]

The federally-supported artists and printers ultimately provided a virtual catalogue of the West's exotic scenery, from John Drayton's awesome Oregon pine trees to Charles Preuss's *Central Chain of the Wind River Mountains* (Figure 3). They documented the little-known ancient civilizations as well as the beautiful canyons of the Southwest; the deserts of California as well as the rugged north country along what became the railroad's northern route. Nor did they overlook the Indians, who populated every area that the explorers examined.

Such publishing projects made the government a major patron of artists and of the fledgling American lithographic industry. Congress shares the credit for establishing a policy that elevated art in the national agenda, for it appropriated the hundreds of thousands of dollars to pay for each of these expeditions and illustrated reports, but many who supported the surveys felt that art and scientific inquiry had shouldered aside commercial aspirations

15. Abert to Stephen Markoe, Washington, May 18, 1849, in Letters Sent by the Topographical Bureau of the War Department and by Successor Divisions in the Office of the Chief of Engineers, Vol. II, Oct. 16, 1848–Sept. 15, 1849 (Microcopy No. 66, Roll 13, National Archives). Abert had in mind the route described by William H. Emory in his *Notes of a Military Reconnoissance, from Fort Leavenworth, in Missouri, to San Diego, in California . . .* 30th Cong., 1st Sess, S.D. 7. See Goetzmann, *Army Exploration*, pp. 209–210.

16. J. W. Gunnison, *Report of Explorations for a Route for the Pacific Railroad . . . Near the 38th and 39th Parallels of North Latitude, from the Mouth of the Kansas River, Mo. to the Sevier Lake, in the Great Basin,* 33d Cong., 2d sess., Sen. Ex. Doc. 78 (s.s. 759), Appendix B, p. 126.

Figure 3. C. B. Graham after Charles Preuss, Central Chain of the Wind River Mountains, *from Frémont,* Report on an Exploration of the Country Lying Between the Missouri River and the Rocky Mountains. *Courtesy St. Louis Mercantile Library at the University of Missouri—St. Louis. Frémont's was the first illustrated government publication related to the American West. He carried daguerreotype equipment with him, but when he failed to successfully expose the plates, he had to rely on his cartographer's sketches for illustrations in his report.*

in the resulting publications. California Congressman John C. Burch, for example, complained that:

> The Government had expended hundreds of thousands of dollars in explorations, and elaborate reports thereof had been made and published in immense volumes, containing beautiful and expensive engravings showing the most picturesque and wonderful scenery in the world on the route of the exploration; highly colored pictures of the topography, accompanied by exact representations of the animals, birds, fishes, reptiles, shrubs and flowers found on the route . . . yet all this did not demonstrate the practicability of a route, nor show the surveys, elevations, profiles, grades or estimates of the cost of constructing the road over the route finally adopted.[17]

And the advice that George Gibbs, a thirty-one-year-old Harvard-educated attorney, gave Henry Rowe Schoolcraft, suggests that ulterior motives might have been involved in the decisions to publish these illustrations. As Schoolcraft sought government support for his *Indian Tribes of the United States*, Gibbs explained that, the "cupidity of the members" of Congress was the "grand secret." "The southwestern and western barbarians [in Congress] will not care a d—m for all the results of your labors if they find it only a Shawnee or Sioux dictionary," but they will vote "any amount of public money" to produce an expensive "picture book," which would be theirs for free to possess and give to their valued friends and supporters. Gibbs continued, "Make your reports to each Session upon the material & the tangible, and above all things have them full of plates. Congress will print them of course & pay for the engraving without writhing."[18]

A great deal of money was at stake. William H. Goetzmann estimated in *New Lands, New Men* that the government might have spent from one-fourth to one-third of its entire budget during certain years, which fluctuated between a low of $8,302,702 in 1843 to $74,056,699 in 1856, on lavishly printed scientific and exploration reports, many of which contain colored lithographs of the West[19] (Figure 4). *The United States & Mexican Boundary*

---

17. Quoted from Oscar Lewis, *The Big Four* (New York: Alfred A. Knopf, 1938), p. 11.
18. Brian W. Dippie, *Catlin and His Contemporaries: The Politics of Patronage* (Lincoln: University of Nebraska Press, 1990), p. 176.
19. Goetzmann, *New Lands, New Men*, p. 178. In addition to the sixty works dealing with the West, Goetzmann includes the reports of the Coast and Geodetic Survey, the Naval

Figure 4. After Charles Koppel, Los Angeles, *from* Reports of Explorations and Surveys,
*Vol. 5. Courtesy St. Louis Mercantile Library at the University of Missouri—St. Louis. This
first published view of Los Angeles was among the earliest illustrations of the new state of
California that Americans saw. It came from the survey of the Pacific Coast.*

Survey alone might have cost as much as $78,102 ($1,171,529 in 1991 dollars), while the Pacific Railroad Surveys probably cost a total of $1,655,000 ($455,000 for the surveys themselves, and $1,200,000 for the twelve-volume publication, with perhaps as much as $489,000 going for the 725 illustrations). The total spent on illustrations of the West during these years might have been as much as $650,000 (approximately $9,725,381 in 1991), a major federal subsidy for both artists and printers.[20]

This unprecedented government sponsorship was possible because the mechanism existed within the army, the topographical engineers, and the federal bureaucracy to bring artists and lithographers into the patronage system. By 1836 most of the officers had been educated at West Point, where figure, topographic, and landscape drawing were a part of the required curriculum, and they considered exploration and dissemination of the information an integral part of a democratic government.[21] Even those officers not educated there would have been more inclined toward the arts and culture than the average citizen, so artists regularly found staff positions with the exploring expeditions and were often included as guests when not a part of the official party.[22] When no artist was present on an expedition, the commander himself was usually capable by virtue of his West Point training of providing the maps and illustrations for his report. Capt. Randolph Marcy's 1852 search for the headwaters of the Red River may be a case in point.[23] The officer corps also wielded considerable political influence in Congress

---

Observatory, Schoolcraft's six volumes, the reports of the Great Lakes Survey, Humphreys and Abbott's studies of the Mississippi, and the *Annual Reports* of the Patent Office.

20. Estimates based on costs derived from records in the Settled Accounts and on assigning similar plates similar costs. John J. McCusker, "How Much Is That in Real Money? A Historical Price Index for Use as a Deflator of Money Values in the Economy of the United States," *Proceedings of the American Antiquarian Society* 101, Pt. 2 (1991): 328, 332.

21. Seth Eastman, a West Point graduate and an artist, produced the textbook that was used at West Point for years: *Treatise on Topographical Drawing* (New York: Wiley & Putnam, 1837).

22. Marilyn Anne Kindred, "The Army Officer Corps and the Arts: Artistic Patronage and Practice in America, 1820–85" (Ph.D. dissertation, University of Kansas, 1980); Patricia Trenton and Peter H. Hassrick, *The Rocky Mountains: A Vision for Artists in the Nineteenth Century* (Norman: University of Oklahoma Press, 1973); and Dippie, *Catlin and His Contemporaries*, p. 176.

23. No artist is listed for the twelve plates that appear in Marcy's book. See Randolph Barnes Marcy, *Exploration of the Red River of Louisiana, in the Year 1852* (32nd Cong., 2d Sess., S.D. 54), and Michael Tate, "Randolph B. Marcy: First Explorer of the Wichitas," *Great Plains Journal*, 15 (Spring, 1976): 80–113.

when it came time to appropriate funds to publish the findings of the most recent expedition, and they often had a hand in selecting the lithographer or engraver.[24]

It was not long before such a large expenditure of public funds attracted the graft so common to the era.[25] In an effort to get away from political patronage, Congress had returned in 1846 to a system of permitting the Senate and House clerks to take competitive bids.[26] The adoption of the new office of Superintendent of Public Printing in 1852 was a further attempt at reform, but the man selected for the job, A. G. Seaman, apparently was easily influenced himself. Seaman oversaw publication of some of the most important and lavishly illustrated reports before he left office in December 1857.[27]

In December 1858, the House of Representatives established a select committee to look into charges of corruption in Seaman's office. After questioning a number of witnesses, including many prominent lithographers and engravers, the committee concluded that Seaman was "guilty of improper and illegal practices in the discharge of his official duty," including the establishment of a "combination . . . for the purpose of compelling the paper contractors, and the lithographers and engravers, to pay . . . for the contracts awarded to them." The committee further found that the lithographers made up for the payments to Seaman by overcharging the government, sometimes two to four times the actual cost, for printing lithographs.[28] One example might be the chromolithographs that Sarony, Major & Knapp did for Emory's *United States & Mexican Boundary Survey*

24. Testimony of James Ackerman in "Accounts of the Late Superintendent of Public Printing," 35th Cong., 2nd Sess., House Report 189, p. 230. See also contracts between Lt. Nathaniel Michler and Maj. William H. Emory with engravers and lithographers Selmar Siebert (May 10 and Aug. 11, 1856), William H. Dougal (June 14, July 30, Sept. 22, Nov. 26, 1856, and Mar. 28, 1857), James D. Smillie (June 16, 1856), and Sarony & Company (June 22, 1854), all in the William H. Emory Papers (WA MSS S-1187, Box 12, Folder 136) in the Western Americana Collection, Beinecke Rare Book and Manuscript Library, Yale University, New Haven.

25. For example, see Mark W. Summers, *The Plundering Generation: Corruption and the Crisis of the Union, 1849–1861* (New York: Oxford University Press, 1987), esp. 46; and Culver H. Smith, *The Press, Politics, and Patronage: The American Government's Use of Newspapers, 1789–1875* (Athens: University of Georgia Press, 1977), p. 221.

26. From 1819 until 1846, each House of Congress selected its own printer, usually the publisher of the party newspaper. Leonard D. White, *The Jacksonians: A Study in Administrative History, 1829–1861* (New York: The Macmillan Company, 1954), pp. 290–293.

27. Summers, *The Plundering Generation*, p. 46.

28. "Report of the Select Committee," in "Accounts of the Late Superintendent of Public Printing," pp. 4, 5, 8, 9.

for $.088 each under Seaman vs. those that all the lithographers, including Sarony, Major & Knapp, printed for the Pacific Railroad Surveys at $.026 each after Seaman left office.[29] The committee finally determined that Seaman had charged from five to twenty percent of the contract and had gathered about $30,000 ($450,000 in 1991 dollars) in this manner over the four year period that he was in office.[30]

How Widely were the Books Disseminated?

As George Gibbs made clear in his cynical advice to Schoolcraft, the primary audience for government publications insofar as Congress was concerned was the legislators and their constituents, an important audience to be sure. But there were others. The legislation that authorized publication of one hundred copies of the Wilkes narrative, for example, also required that one copy go to each state in the Union, to the Naval Lyceum in Brooklyn, and to twenty-five designated countries; and two copies each to France, Great Britain, and Russia. The remaining copies were distributed to new states as they entered the Union and to other foreign countries as designated by Congress. Wilkes himself arranged for private publication of thousands of additional copies by commercial presses.[31]

Edition size of the other seventeen illustrated publications relating to the West ranged from 1,000 for Frémont's first report and the second volume of Emory's *Mexican Boundary Survey* to 22,000 of Abert's report on New Mexico to 53,000 of the Stevens survey (volume 12 of the Pacific Railroad Surveys). Furthermore, commercial publishers reprinted a number of

29. For the Pacific Railroad Surveys, see Account 127113 (Voucher 1614), Account 139226 (Voucher 4), Account 139907 (Vouchers 1274, 1339, and 1392), Account 139991 (Vouchers 853, 901, and 961), and Account 141294 (Vouchers 102, 253, and 302); for Emory, see Accounts 127338 (Voucher 817) and 131087 (Voucher 2334), all in Settled Records, Records of the Accounting Office of the Department of the Treasury, Office of the First Auditor, Miscellaneous Treasury Accounts, Record Group 217, National Archives. A slight difference in the coloring of the plates in the two projects may account for some of the discrepancy. The views in the Pacific Railroad Surveys appear to be printed in three colors, while those in the Emory survey might include an additional color, but that should not amount to a difference of $.062 per print.

30. "Report of the Select Committee," pp. 5, 9. McCusker, "How Much Is That in Real Money?" pp. 328, 332, provided data for the conversion to 1991 dollars.

31. Haskell, *United States Exploring Expedition*, pp. 9, 37–40.

them for sale to the public: Frémont's second report, Emory's, Simpson's, Stansbury's, and Sitgreaves's reports on the Southwest, Marcy's on the Red River, and the Stevens's survey of the 49th parallel.

The government distributed the first printings of these books just as it had the Wilkes expedition report—to members of Congress, their constituents, the states, certain libraries, and foreign countries. When commercial publishers picked them up, they distributed them, like other commercial publications, through bookstores, subscription, traveling agents, the mail, bookfairs, and auctions to the trade.[32] It seems safe to say, given the number of times some of these books were reprinted and the number of books printed, that some of these publications would have been on the bestseller list. These reports were also excerpted, reviewed, and reported in the national and international press.[33]

What was Their Impact?

It is evident that these publications acquainted thousands if not millions of Americans with the recently-acquired but largely unknown West and encouraged and endorsed American expansion into it.[34] Frémont's reports influenced Brigham Young to take the Mormons west and found Salt Lake City and Sarah Royce, the mother of philosopher Josiah Royce, to emigrate to California. Young read excerpts in the newspaper, while Mrs. Royce recalled in her memoirs that they were "guided only by the light of Frémont's

32. For example, see James Gilreath, "American Book Distribution," in David D. Hall and John B. Hench, eds., *Needs and Opportunities in the History of the Book: America, 1639– 1876* (Worcester: American Antiquarian Society, 1987), pp. 114, 145–161; and Michael Winship, "Getting the Books Out: Trade Sales, Parcel Sales, and Book Fairs in the Nineteenth-Century United States," in Michael Hackenberg, ed., *Getting the Books Out: Papers of the Chicago Conference on the Book in 19th-Century America* (Washington: The Center for the Book, Library of Congress, 1987), pp. 4–21.

33. Stanton, *Great United States Exploring Expedition*, pp. 308–310; Allan Nevins, *Frémont, the West's Greatest Adventurer*, 2 vols. (New York: Harper & Brothers Publishers, 1928), 229; and James H. Simpson, *Navaho Expedition: Journal of a Military Reconnaissance from Santa Fe, New Mexico to the Navaho Country, made in 1849*, ed. by Frank McNitt (Norman: University of Oklahoma Press, 1964), p. 218.

34. Part of the problem in assessing the significance of these government prints is the lack of a comprehensive history of the American printing industry. While it is clear that some, like John C. Frémont, encouraged western settlement, others, such as some of the desert images by Charles Koppel could hardly have caused anyone to want to live in the West.

Travels."[35] Frémont's map detailed the route that became known as the Oregon Trail, and he linked his cartographic studies with those of Wilkes in the Northwest, enabling the U.S. to produce a base map of the continent. The great Alexander von Humboldt praised him for "talent, courage, industry and enterprize," and he still occupies a place in the popular imagination as the great Romantic Pathfinder.[36]

Emory, Abert, Peck, Sitgreaves, Simpson and others charted the Southwest, opening it for new settlements. They discovered the ancient civilizations, established our southwestern boundary, made possible the Gadsden Purchase, and located a southern route for a transcontinental railroad, which initially proved impossible because of sectional strife. Their maps—along with those of Frémont's and Warren's—defined the West, and the pictures of Charles Preuss, James W. Abert, the Kern brothers, and John Mix Stanley helped Americans visualize and fill in the blanks on these great charts.

The Pacific Railroad Surveys identified not one but several transcontinental railroad routes, including the southern one that was eventually completed in 1882 (but not the first one that was completed in 1869). Secretary of War Jefferson Davis and the engineers favored the southern route that Whipple and Möllhausen documented.[37] Other images, such as Egloffstein's *Portion of the Main Mountain Passage* called attention to mountain barriers that would slow the railroad's progress, while others, such as Stanley's images of the northern route, encouraged the effort.

Taken together, these pictures present a largely positive image of the West—one calculated to popularize the territory and draw the country together.[38] The spectacular scenery that Richard Kern, Möllhausen, Egloffstein, and Stanley depicted, for example, could only have whetted the desire of thousands to see it for themselves, despite warnings of hardship issued by members of Congress and echoed by dozens of newspaper editors[39] (Figure 5). Stanley, Charles Koppel, and others documented what LaPérouse,

---

35. Leonard J. Arrington, *Brigham Young: American Moses* (New York: Alfred A. Knopf, 1985), p. 124; Goetzmann, *Army Exploration*, p. 108.

36. Goetzmann, *Army Exploration*, pp. 104, 108.

37. Ibid., pp. 303–304.

38. Stevens, as governor of Washington, gave a report on the northern railroad route that Secretary of War Jefferson Davis considered too positive. See Kent D. Richards, *Isaac I. Stevens, Young Man in a Hurry* (Provo: Brigham Young University Press, 1979), pp. 139–142.

Figure 5. After F. W. Egloffstein from a sketch by Lt. Ives, Black Cañon, *from Ives,* Report upon the Colorado River of the West. *Courtesy St. Louis Mercantile Library at the University of Missouri—St. Louis. Ives, leader of the first American expedition into the Grand Canyon of the Colorado, declared Black Canyon to be the head of navigation when his boat, the* Explorer, *struck a submerged rock.*

Vancouver, Wilkes, and others had told the world about the great Pacific ports of San Diego, Los Angeles, San Francisco, and Puget Sound.[40]

As a result, the question of accuracy naturally arises, and, while many of the pictures are faithful renderings of easily recognizable scenes,[41] accuracy seems to have escaped the artist on occasion, or perhaps the lithographer's tampering accomplished the same end.[42] One engineer, for example, took the time to point out that the published version of a drawing—Charles Koppel's *Valley of San Pasqual*—had been altered, apparently by the engraver, so as to make the ocean appear closer to the mountains than it actually is (Figure 6). As supervisor of many of the scientific reports, Spencer F. Baird, assistant secretary of the Smithsonian, was constantly on guard to obtain the best reproductions that the lithographers could produce, complaining on one occasion that there was "no perspective" in a landscape view, that "it looks more like an upright wall than a gently sloping bank."[43] Indians frequently suffered at the hands of the artists, who were either unwilling to give up their Romantic proclivities or unable to see beyond them. On the whole, they are shown to be no threat to would-be settlers.[44] Other accuracy problems might have been the result of a misunderstanding between the artist and the lithographer or, as Shady Creek appears to be virtually dry in one version of *Comanche Camp on Shady Creek*, but bank full in the other (Figures 7, 8).

39. John D. Unruh, Jr., *The Plains Across: The Overland Emigrants and the Trans-Mississippi West, 1840–60* (Urbana: University of Illinois Press, 1979), pp. 46–51.

40. Kevin Starr, *Americans and the California Dream, 1850–1915* (New York: Oxford University Press, 1973), pp. 3–12.

41. For Richard Kern, see Weber, *Richard H. Kern*, 271–281; for the art of the Mexican Boundary Survey, see Hine, *Bartlett's West* and *Drawing the Borderline*; 1996); for John Mix Stanley's northern railroad survey work, see Schimmel, "John Mix Stanley," pp. 265–268, and Richards, *Isaac I. Stevens*, pp. 143–145.

42. Although David J. Weber, "The Artist, the Lithographer, and the Desert Southwest," *Gateway Heritage* 5 (Winter, 1984–1985): 32–41, concludes that the lithographers usually copied Kern's work faithfully, he does point out several examples of substantial change.

43. Spencer's quote is in Blum, *Picturing Nature*, p. 194. Koppel's *Valley of San Pasqual* is in William Phipps Blake, "Geological Report," in *Reports of Explorations and Surveys, to Ascertain the Most Practicable and Economical Route for a Railroad from the Mississippi River to the Pacific Ocean . . .* , Vol. 5, 33rd Cong., 2d Sess., S.D. 78 (Serial 762) and 33rd Cong., 2d Sess, H.D. 91 (Serial 795).

44. Amiel W. Whipple was particularly upset with Heinrich B. Möllhausen's drawings of Navahos. See Goetzmann, *Army Exploration*, p. 332.

Figure 6. After Charles Koppel, Valley of San Pasqual, *from* Reports of Explorations and
Surveys, *Vol. 5. Courtesy St. Louis Mercantile Library at the University of Missouri—St. Louis.
One of the engineers criticized this engraving, saying that "the ocean is too fully represented
. . . and appears too near. The coast is about thirty miles from the valley," and, he concluded,
"according to recollection is scarcely visible from the hill" (p. 127.)*

Figure 7. Sarony, Major & Knapp after H. B. Möllhausen, Comanche Camp on Shady Creek, *from* Reports of Explorations and Surveys, *Vol. 3. Courtesy St. Louis Mercantile Library at the University of Missouri—St. Louis. Artist Möllhausen crossed the Texas Panhandle with the Whipple expedition in 1853, a part of the Pacific Railroad Surveys. Most of the published versions of this lithograph show Shady Creek virtually dry, but some few make it appear to be bank-full, as the other illustration (Fig. 8) shows.*

Figure 8. Sarony, Major & Knapp after H. B. Möllhausen, Comanche Camp on Shady Creek, *from* Reports of Explorations and Surveys, *Vol. 3. Courtesy Ron Tyler.*

It is true that the topographical artists did not depict many negative aspects of Western expansion, such as the havoc that it inflicted on Indians, Hispanics, and the thousands of immigrants who worked in the mines and on the railroad, but it is hard to blame the artists for this omission.[45] In many instances they did not witness the devastation, and they surely knew that such images would not be included in the reports that they had been commissioned to illustrate. They did call attention to the millions of acres that would be of no agricultural value, and Senator Daniel Webster *might have* based his belief that the Southwest was unsuited to slavery on Emory's 1848 *Report*, but even that concern vanished when many of those same areas proved to be rich in minerals. Nineteenth-century artistic conventions permitted what historians today recognize as inaccuracies. For example, Richard Kern might have argued that he was only following fellow artist John Gadsby Chapman's admonition to "distill the best from nature" in his *View of Santa Fe and Vicinity from the East*, in which he rearranged topographical features so as to bring the Sandía Mountains and Jémez close enough together that they might be included in the same scene. Had not Thomas Cole himself, the founder of the American landscape school of painting, warned that "if the imagination is shackled to what the eye sees, seldom will anything great be produced in painting"?[46] William H. Goetzmann concluded three and one-half decades ago that, "very often, realism in the sense of faithful reproduction of the scene is nowhere present. . . . At times what is unseen is more important than the objects depicted."[47]

These publications were but one way in which the federal government sought to hold the country together during the rapid expansion of the first half of the nineteenth century. Through them the government purpose-

45. Photographer Timothy O'Sullivan corrected part of this oversight in 1868 when, as a member of the Clarence King's Fortieth Parallel Survey, he documented the work of miners in Nevada, including some of the earliest underground photographs at the Comstock Mine in Virginia City. James D. Horan, *Timothy O'Sullivan, America's Forgotten Photographer* (New York: Bonanza Books, 1966), pp. 159–160, 196–210.

46. For Webster, see Goetzmann, *Army Exploration*, p. 138; Weber, *Richard H. Kern*, p. 276.

47. Goetzmann, *Army Exploration*, pp. 19, 138. William H. Truettner, *The West as America: Reinterpreting Images of the Frontier, 1820–1920* (Washington: Smithsonian Institution Press, 1991), p. 50, concluded that pictures "function as ideological statements" "so efficiently . . . that we grasp their import without evey realizing it, making them devastating as hidden persuaders. . . ."

fully began to create a constituency for expansion into and development of the West.

The Impact on Lithographers and Printers

The impact on lithographers and printers was more direct. At least thirty-one different printers and lithographers up and down the East Coast, from Washington to Baltimore, Philadelphia, New York, and Buffalo, shared in the production of these eighteen publications. This was important patronage in a time of financial uncertainty, when printers and lithographers were going broke. For example, Thomas McKenney had a great deal of trouble with his lithographers, who went broke one after the other, in publishing his *Indian History*. McKenney did not solve his problem until 1837 when he found John T. Bowen, who would also print Audubon's great *Birds of America* (1840–1844) and *The Viviparous Quadrupeds of North America* (1845–1846).[48] But, at least for those who worked with Superintendent Seaman the times were good. When asked why he did not ask that one of Seaman's agents pay back the "loan" of $2,576 over a nine-month period, New York lithographer Richard Major replied, "I knew it was during a time when he was short of money, and as we were in easy circumstances, I volunteered to give him the use of the money. . . ."[49]

Publication of the reports of Western expeditions continued following the Civil War, with photographers such as William Henry Jackson, Timothy O'Sullivan, and John K. Hillers replacing the topographic artist. But these eighteen illustrated publications had served their purpose. They had stimulated interest on the part of the public at a time when expansion into the West was a national goal and had provided patronage to artists and the lithographic industry during a crucial period of growth. Today they are an invaluable cultural, historical, and scientific document of the era of Manifest Destiny.

---

48. Herman J. Viola, *Thomas L. McKenney, Architect of America's Early Indian Policy: 1816–1830* (Chicago: The Swallow Press, Inc., 1974), pp. 257, 261–263, 266, 267, 272; Herman J. Viola, *The Indian Legacy of Charles Bird King* (Washington and New York: Smithsonian Institution Press and Doubleday & Company, Inc., 1976), pp. 80, 85. Bowen took over as lithographer in 1837 and as publisher in December 1841.

49. Testimony of Richard Major in "Accounts of the Late Superintendent of Public Printing," p. 76.

APPENDIX 1
GOVERNMENT PUBLICATIONS ON THE WEST BETWEEN 1843 AND 1863*

	Publication	Date	House	Senate	Plates	Edition	Total Plates	Printings	Printers
1	Frémont	1843		416	6	1,000	6,000		Weber
2	Wilkes	1844			25	100	2,500	15	Rawdon, Wright & Hatch, Tucker, Ellis, Steel
3	Frémont	1845	467		22	10,000	220,000	24	Weber
		1845		461	22	10,000	220,000	24	Weber
4	Abert	1846		438	11	2,100	23,100		Weber
5	Abert	1848	517		24	10,000	240,000		Graham
		1848		506	24	12,000	288,000		Graham
6	Emory	1848	517		40	10,000	400,000	9	Graham
		1848		505	40	2,100	84,000		Weber/Endicott
7	Johnston, A.R.	1848	517		1	10,000	10,000		
8	Johnston, J.E.	1850		562	72	3,000	216,000		Duval
9	Simpson	1850		554	72	0	0	2	Duval
		1850	577		2	2,500	5,000		Duval
10	Cross	1850		587	36	15,000	540,000		Ackerman/Weber
11	Stansbury	1852		608	59	10,000	590,000	5	Ackerman
12	Sitgreaves	1853		668	78	2,000	156,000	2	Ackerman
13	Marcy	1853	*		65	2,500	162,500		Lawrence
		1853		666	65	3,450	224,250	2	Ackerman
14	PRS 2	1855	792	759	27	21,000	567,000		Hoen, Sinclair, Sarony (Major & Knapp)
	PRS 3	1856	793	760	83	21,000	1,743,000		Sarony (Major & Knapp), Hoen, Lossing & Barritt, Sinclair, Orr, Roberts, Pinckney
	PRS 4	1856	794	761	49	21,000	1,029,000		Ackerman, Sullivant & Schrader

* This list does not include John N. Macomb, *Report of the Exploring Expedition from Santa Fe, New Mexico, to the Junction of the Grand and Green Rivers of the Great Colorado of the West in 1859* (Washington: U.S.Engineer Department, 1876), because it was not published until 1876.

	Publication	Date	House	Senate	Plates	Edition	Total Plates	Printings	Printers
	PRS 5	1856	795	762	188	21,000	3,948,000		Sinclair, Lossing & Barritt, Orr, Hoen, Richardson-Cox, Whitney & Joselyn, Robert, Bellman
	PRS 6	1857	796	763	29	21,000	609,000		Roberts
	PRS 7	1857	797	764	40	21,000	840,000		Hoen
	PRS 8	1857	798	765	43	21,000	903,000		Metzeroth
	PRS 10	1859	800	767	122	21,000	2,562,000		Artos, Metzeroth, Serz, Bowen
	PRS 11	1961	801	768	13	32,000	416,000		Siebert, Hinshelrood, Hunt
	PRS 12	1859		992	131	53,000	6,943,000	3	Sarony (Major & Knapp)/Bien
15	Warren	1856		822	2		0		Orr
16	Emory 1	1857	861		106	10,000	1,060,000		Sarony (Major & Knapp), Dougal,Smille
		1857		832	106	5,000	530,000		
	Emory 2.1	1859	862		139	1,000	139,000		Bowen
		1859		833	139	1,000	139,000		
	Emory 2.2	1859	863		134	1,000	134,000		
		1859		834	134	1,000	134,000		
17	Ives	1861	1058		76	0	0		Sarony (Major & Knapp)
		1861		*	76	11,000	836,000		
18	Mullen	1863		1149	10	1,500	15,000		Bowen

TOTAL UNIQUE PLATES   1,627

TOTAL PRINTS   25,934,350

LIST OF PRINTERS, LITHOGRAPHERS, AND ENGRAVERS

Ackerman

Artos

Bellman

Bien

Bowen

Connor/Mallard

Davesne

Dougal

Duval

Ellis

Endicott

Gavit

Graham

Hinshelrood

Hoen

Hunt

Lawrence

Lossing & Barritt

Metzeroth

Orr

Picart

Pinckney

Rawdon, Wright & Hatch,

Rebuffet

Richardson-Cox

Roberts

Sarony

Schmelz

Serz

Siebert

Sinclair

Smille

Steel

Sullivant & Schrader

Tucker

Weber

Whitney & Joselyn

SCIENCE AND ART MEET IN THE PARLOR
The Role of Popular Magazine Illustration in the Pictorial Record of the "Great Surveys"

When armchair travelers of the post-Civil War era pictured the American West, their vision was profoundly affected by the work of artists and photographers who were members of the four Geological and Geographical Surveys of the western United States territories conducted between 1867 and 1879. These are known collectively as the "Great Surveys," and individually by the names of their directors: King, Hayden, Powell, and Wheeler.[1] Originating at different times, beginning in 1867 with the King Survey, all were concluded when the U.S. Geological Survey was created as a federal agency in 1879. Adventurous tales about the scientists, engineers, artists, and photographers who traveled on these surveys and the exotic lands and peoples they encountered were featured in the new illustrated magazines, *The Aldine, Appleton's Journal, Harper's New Monthly Magazine, Harper's*

---

1. The standard history is Richard A. Barlett, *Great Surveys of the American West* (Norman: University of Oklahoma Press, 1962). See also William H. Goetzmann, *Exploration and Empire; The Explorer and the Scientist in the Winning of the American West* (New York: Knopf, 1966) and Mary Rabbitt, *Minerals, Lands, and Geology for the Common Defence and General Welfare, vol. 1: Before 1879* (Washington, DC: U.S. Geological Survey, 1979).

Weekly, and *Scribner's Monthly*. The vivid wood-engraved illustrations accompanying these dramatic stories interpreted paintings and photographs into linear black and white prints surrounded by text, providing thousands of American households access to contemporary art and new scientific discoveries on the same pages, to be enjoyed comfortably by the parlor fire. Susan Belasco Smith and Kenneth Price attribute the explosive expansion of the periodical market in mid-nineteenth century America to "technological developments in papermaking, the widespread use of the cylinder press, cheaper postal routes, rising literacy rates, and wide distribution by railroad."[2]

The Survey directors, always concerned about maintaining their funding, realized the need for public support. They depended on Congressional appropriations or the U.S. military for their funding. Congress was not always enthusiastic in its support, and funding levels varied from year to year. An 1874 investigation into suspected duplication of territories made Congress wary of automatic renewal of appropriations.[3] Though much of the information generated by the surveys was intended for science or defense, there was a popular audience the survey leaders targeted as well, especially to create public support for their continued research. Their efforts were not unlike the modern U.S. space agency NASA in the use of popular image and text media to generate widespread citizen support for government funding of scientific expeditions.

Like NASA's solicitation of television and the press, the survey directors turned to the most popular avenues to reach American homes in the nineteenth century, the periodicals. Smith and Price note: "By the 1870s the inexpensive weekly magazines, an estimated 4,295 of them, had a combined circulation of 10.5 million, a staggering figure given the fact that the population of the United States was only 30 million in 1870."[4] Newspapers, print-oriented magazines, and the new illustrated magazines ignited public interest in the surveys, allowing them to continue to gather information

2. Susan Belasco Smith and Kenneth M. Price," Introduction," *Periodical Literature in Nineteenth-Century America*, eds. Kenneth M. Price and Susan Belasco Smith (Charlottesville: University Press of Virginia, 1995), p. 3.

3. See Bartlett, pp. 310–311.

4. Susan Belasco Smith and Kenneth M. Price, "Introduction," *Periodical Literature in Nineteenth-Century America*, eds. Susan Belasco Smith and Kenneth M. Price (Charlottesville: University Press of Virginia, 1995), p. 5.

for mapping, defense strategies, mineral and agricultural prospects, and anthropological studies.

Newspaper editors saw these activities as fruitful sources for news items. Reporters attended summer expeditions as guests, and in turn produced valuable publicity. On the Hayden survey, for example, journalists kept the publicity machine well-oiled. Ernest Ingersoll of the *New York Tribune* worked as a naturalist during the 1873 season; J. E. Colburn of the *New York Times* traveled with artist Thomas Moran during the 1874 season; and E. A. Barber of the *Times* accompanied the survey in 1875.[5]

Print-oriented magazines such as the *American Journal of Science and Arts* featured articles on the surveys in almost every issue. Coverage was also prominent in magazines such as the *American Naturalist*, *The Atlantic Monthly*, *The Nation*, *North American Review*, *Overland Monthly*, and *The Republic*. Though photographic journals were not heavily illustrated at this time, they were nationally circulated. The *Philadelphia Photographer* and *Anthony's Photographic Bulletin* published a number of articles on survey photographers. The new illustrated magazines offered the greatest appeal, with a mix of news on art, culture, and science on visually stimulating pages that were digestible, entertaining, and edifying. *The Aldine*, which called itself "the art journal of America," began in 1868 with the intention to publish the highest quality illustrations. *Appleton's Journal of Science, Literature and Art* commenced in 1869 as a richly illustrated weekly to compete with the large pages of the well-established *Harper's Weekly*, founded in 1857. Two smaller-sized but immensely successful publications were *Scribner's Monthly*, which debuted in November of 1870, and *Harper's New Monthly Magazine*, created in 1850.

Scholars often point to the Congressional purchases of Thomas Moran's two enormous panoramic landscape paintings for the U. S. Capitol building in 1872 and 1874 (*Grand Canyon of the Yellowstone*, 1872, and *Chasm of the Colorado*, 1873–4 [both Department of the Interior, on loan

5. See William Henry Jackson, *Time Exposure*, (New York: G. P. Putnam's Sons, 1940), p. 223; Ingersoll's story on the cliff dwellings in Mesa Verde, published in the *New York Tribune*, 3 November 1874, is excerpted on pp. 232–4. See J. E. Colburn, "The Colorado Canon," *New York Times*, 4 September 1873, p. 2, cols. 1–3, and "The Land of Mormon," *New York Times*, 7 August 1873, p. 2, cols. 3–4. For information on Barber, see Jackson, *Time Exposure*, 237, and [E.A. Barber], "The Hayden Survey," *New York Times*, 27 April 1875, p. 1, cols. 5–6.

to the Smithsonian Institution, National Museum of American Art, Washington, D.C.]), to demonstrate the tremendous appeal of these scientific expeditions.[6] Less attention has been given to other forms of public information created by the survey leaders and the artists and photographers who accompanied them. The role of popular magazine illustration is an important factor in the powerful body of images and text that was generated for a public forum, including exhibitions of paintings and photographs, photographic albums and stereographs, illustrations in books, chromolithographs, and publicity about the artists and photographers, all of which escalated in production with the 1876 Centennial Exhibition in Philadelphia.[7]

Few publications exist on the American illustrated periodicals of the 1860s and 70s; only rarely do these consider the relationship between image and text, or examine the production of illustrations.[8] One is Joshua Brown's recent study of *Frank Leslie's Illustrated Newspaper*, in which he describes the process through which large wood-engravings were produced:

> After the art superintendent chose a sketch [or photograph] to be worked up into an engraving, a staff artist drew a new version on paper, rendered in outlines. The drawing was then rubbed down in reverse upon the white-

6. See Nancy K. Anderson, *Thomas Moran* (New Haven: Yale University Press with the National Gallery of Art, 1997); Joni L. Kinsey, *Thomas Moran and the Surveying of the American West* (Washington, DC: Smithsonian Institution Press, 1992); Anne Morand, Joni Louise Kinsey, and Mary Panzer, *Splendors of the American West: Thomas Moran's Art of the Grand Canyon and Yellowstone* (Birmingham, AL: Birmingham Museum of Art, 1990): Joni Louise Kinsey, "Creating a Sense of Place: The Art of Thomas Moran and the Surveying of the American West" (Ph.D. diss. Washington University, 1989); William Truettner, "'Scenes of Majesty and Enduring Interest': Thomas Moran Goes West," *Art Bulletin* 58 (June 1976): 241–259.

7. The visual representation of the surveys was the subject of my doctoral dissertation: Debora Anne Rindge, "The Painted Desert: Images of the American West from the geological and geographical surveys of the Western territories, 1867–1897" (Ph.D. diss. University of Maryland, 1993).

8. See Arthur John, *The Best Years of the Century: Richard Watson Gilder, Scribner's Monthly* and the *Century Magazine, 1870–1909* (Urbana: University of Illinois Press, 1981); John Tebbel and Mary Ellen Zuckerman, *The Magazine in America, 1741–1990* (New York: Oxford University Press, 1991); Thomas C. Leonard, *The Power of the Press: The Birth of American Political Reporting* (New York: Oxford University Press, 1986); JoAnn Early Levin, "The Golden Age of Illustration: Popular Art in American Magazines, 1850–1925" (Ph.D. diss. University of Pennsylvania, 1980); Robert E. Spiller et al., *Literary History of the United States*, 3d. ed. rev. (New York: Macmillan, 1963); Frank Luther Mott, *A History of American Magazines*, vol. III: 1865–85 (Cambridge: Harvard University Press, 1938). Susan Belasco Smith and Kenneth Price discuss the emerging interest in the history of the book and American literacy in the past decade, pp. 7–8.

washed surface of Turkish boxwood, itself composed of smaller sections of wood secured together by a system of nuts and bolts. Draughtsmen applied further detail in washes and pencil . . . , and then the composite block went to the engraving department where it was unbolted and distributed to a team of engravers. The engravers laboriously carved out the design (leaving the lines in relief to print black) on their individual pieces, after which the constituent blocks were rebolted together and a supervising engraver ensured that the incised lines met across the sections. The engraved block was then sent to the composing room where it was locked into place with handset type to create a *Frank Leslie's* page to be made into electrotyped copper plate.[9]

The first illustrated article on the surveys appeared in *Harper's New Monthly Magazine* in September of 1869.[10] The first story of the issue, entitled "Photographs from the High Rockies," describes a photographer's adventures beginning in 1867 on Clarence King's 40th Parallel Survey. The author's name is John Samson, a pen name for Timothy O'Sullivan, who was the official photographer for the King survey. The protagonist of the story is never referred to by name, but always as "our photographer friend." The thirteen wood engravings accompanying the article are based on O'Sullivan's photographs.[11]

The opening sentence of the article advises the reader that the photographer's concerns are aesthetic: "Places and people are made familiar to us by means of the camera in the hands of skillful operators, who, vying with each other in the artistic excellence of their productions. . . ."[12] Indeed, the photographer refers to himself as an "Artist" and a "photographing artist" when describing the company of "scientific gentlemen," civilians, and cavalry escort of which "the company [was] comprised."[13]

---

9. Joshua Brown, "Reconstructing Representation: Social Types, Readers, and the Pictorial Press, 1865–1877," *Radical History Review* 66 (Fall 1996): 8. See also Joshua Brown, "*Frank Leslie's Illustrated Newspaper*. The Pictorial Press and Representations of America, 1855–1889" (Ph.D. diss. Columbia University, 1993), forthcoming as a book from Cornell University Press.

10. John Samson, "Photographs from the High Rockies" *Harper's New Monthly Magazine* 34 (September 1869): 465–475.

11. Two engravers' names are decipherable among these illustrations: C. Parsons and H[arry] Fenn.

12. Samson, p. 465.

13. Samson, p. 466.

The narrative describes the photographer's adventures amid the grand scale and unusual geological formations encountered in the Rocky Mountain region. After passing by a salt lake, "peculiar" Humboldt and Carson sinks, and "strange" tufa, the article closes by comforting the armchair traveler with familiar landscape forms. On the last two pages, the illustrations (Figures 1, 2, 3) compare aspects of the western landscape with geological features the reader on the East Coast recognized. "Our photographer becoming tired of *too* much High Rocky" goes on to visit the "Shifting Sand-mounds" of Nevada, then moves northward to the Shoshone Falls on the Snake River in Idaho, then closes with a "picturesque little natural bridge."[14]

The engraving (Figure 1) of the photographer's developing wagon and mule team in the sand-mounds uses the same pictorial conventions as popular contemporary prints of New England winter sledding scenes by the Currier and Ives lithographic firm. The author calls such scenes to mind with this description of the landscape: "Arriving in the vicinity of the sand mounds, the first impression conveyed by them was that of immense snow-drifts, for in the sunlight the white sand sparkled like a hard frozen crust of snow."[15]

The Great Shoshone Falls (Figure 2) on the Snake River in Idaho is contrasted with the greater Niagara, but the comparison nevertheless makes visualization possible: "The volume of water pouring over the Shoshone Falls is small compared with the great flood which gives grandeur to the Niagara. Neither is the width of the river greater than that portion of Niagara known as the American Fall."[16]

The closing illustration (Figure 3) required no comparative reference: "Our photographic glimpses of Rocky mountain scenery end with the picturesque little natural bridge which serves for crossing over a deep gorge in the neighborhood of the falls."[17] Viewers would have immediately recognized the vignette as a reference to the famous Natural Bridge in Virginia, which earlier in the century had rivaled Niagara Falls as a tourist destination, and was still a popular geological attraction.[18]

---

14. Samson, pp. 474–5. For other publications on the King Survey at Shoshone Falls, see Rindge, pp. 75–76.
15. Samson, p. 474.
16. Samson, p. 474.
17. Samson, p. 475.
18. Rindge, pp. 103–108.

Figure 1. *"Shifting Sand-mounds," wood-engraved illustration from John Samson,* *"Photographs from the High Rockies,"* Harper's New Monthly Magazine *34 (September 1869): 474. Photo: From the author's collection.*

Figure 2. *"Above the Shoshone Falls," wood-engraved illustration from John Samson,* *"Photographs from the High Rockies,"* Harper's New Monthly Magazine *34 (September 1869): 474. Photo: From the author's collection.*

Figure 3. "Natural Bridge," wood-engraved illustration from John Samson, "Photographs from the High Rockies," Harper's New Monthly Magazine *34 (September 1869): 475. Photo: From the author's collection.*

After the King survey was completed in 1872, survey leaders Ferdinand V. Hayden and John Wesley Powell utilized the illustrated magazines as public venues utilized most effectively. The Hayden survey was the most lionized of the four, thanks to the publicity surrounding the creation of Yellowstone National Park in 1872, reports generated by the ambitious official survey photographer William Henry Jackson, and the prolific illustrations and paintings of artist Thomas Moran, which have been studied extensively by scholars.[19]

Scribner's Monthly, newly founded in 1870, had helped to sponsor Moran's first season with the Hayden survey and it published more articles on the Yellowstone than any other periodical of the era.[20] Moran's friendship with editor Richard Watson Gilder proved mutually beneficial as Moran provided the magazine with a wealth of illustrations throughout the decade. Hayden used *Scribner's* illustrations in his 1871 government report. The passage of the bill in May of 1872 which set aside the Yellowstone area as the first National Park also inspired articles in the illustrated magazines, *Appleton's Journal*, *The Aldine*, and *Harper's Weekly*.[21]

The Powell survey charted the Colorado River between 1869 and 1873. In 1873, for the first time, Powell failed to obtain the full appropriation he had requested from Congress.[22] He had been asking the artist Thomas

19. See Anderson, and Kinsey, *Thomas Moran and the Surveying of the American West*, pp. 80–87, 122–132.

20. Nathaniel P. Langford, "The Wonders of the Yellowstone," *Scribner's Monthly* 2 (May 1871), 1–17; June 1871): 113–128. Langford's articles include fourteen wood-engravings after wash paintings Moran created based on crude drawings brought back by the Langford party; see Anne Morand, "Thomas Moran and the Yellowstone," in Chris Bruce et al., *Myth of the West* (New York: Rizzoli, 1990), 69. Truman C. Everts, "Thirty-seven Days of Peril," *Scribner's Monthly* 2 (November 1871): 1–17, illustrated by "C. B." Ferdinand Hayden, "The Wonders of the West II. More about the Yellowstone," *Scribner's Monthly* 3 (February 1872): 388–396, with nine illustrations by Moran. Nathaniel P. Langford, "The Ascent of Mount Hayden," *Scribner's Monthly* 6 (June 1873): 129–157, with illustrations by Thomas Moran, William Henry Jackson, and engravings after Jackson's photographs, See Rindge, pp. 76–77, n. 55.

21. "Scenes in the Yellowstone Valley. With Illustrations." *Appleton's Journal* 7 (11 May 1872): 519–522, illustrated by Harry Fenn (after a William Henry Jackson photograph) and Thomas Moran. "The Yellowstone Region," *The Aldine* 6 (April 1873): 74–75, [70], illustrated by Thomas Moran. See Rindge, 75, n. 56. R. W. Raymond, "The Heart of the Continent. The Hot Springs and Geysers of the Yellowstone Region," *Harper's Weekly* 17 (5 April 1873): 272–274.

22. Elizabeth C. Childs, "Time's Profile: John Wesley Powell, Art, and Geology at the Grand Canyon," *American Art* 10 (Spring 1996): 22.

Moran to join his survey ever since the artist's successful sale of the *Grand Canyon of the Yellowstone* to Congress in 1872. Moran finally agreed to join Powell in the summer of 1873, bringing with him illustration commissions: "70 drawings for Powell, 40 for Appleton, 4 for Aldine, 20 for Scribner's. . . ."[23] The publicity angle and Congressional favor that Powell had hoped for in bringing Moran on his survey was ultimately achieved in July of 1874 when Congress purchased Moran's *Chasm of the Colorado* for the U. S. Capitol building.

After 1873, the illustrated magazines were rich with information on the Powell survey. *The Aldine* published several large illustrations by Moran accompanied by short articles in 1874 and 1875.[24] At the same time, Powell's ire was raised when a survey photographer who had departed his team in 1872 sold a series to *Appleton's Journal*. These articles, written by the photographer E. O. Beaman, appeared in April and May of that year, each accompanied by a single engraved illustration after one of his photographs.[25] The relation of the illustrations to the text is surprising. For, rather than echoing the text, the illustrations follow trends in contemporary American paintings, especially popular landscape subjects and picturesque conventions. "Carved Rock, Utah" (Figure 4), appeals to the audience with a large, craggy natural bridge. The popularity of these geological formations is attested to by the fact that this natural arch is prominently illustrated, although the site is never mentioned in the article.[26] The "Cañon of Lodore" (Figure 5) illustrates a heart-pounding adventure on the Colorado River approaching a cascade known as Disaster Falls. In the Cañon of Lodore, where the party is "shut in by vertical walls" and prepares for dangerous rapids, the illustration departs from the narrative in favor of picturesque

23. Thomas Moran, *Home Thoughts from Afar: Letters of Thomas Moran to Mary Nimmo Moran*, eds. Amy Bassford and Fritiof Fryxell (East Hampton, NY: East Hampton Free Library, 1967), pp. 41–42.

24. "Utah Scenery," *The Aldine* 7 (January 1874): 14–15, [10]; "A Storm in Utah," *The Aldine* 7 (September 1874): 175; "The Scenery of Southern Utah," *The Aldine* 7 (April 1875): 306–207, [302].

25. E. O. Beaman," The Cañon of the Colorado, and the Moquis Pueblos: A Wild Boat Ride through the Cañons—A Visit to the Seven Cities of the Desert—Glimpses of Mormon Life," *Appleton's Journal* 9 (nos. 265–271) (18 April 1874): 481–484; (25 April 1874): 513–516; (2 May 1874): 545–548; (9 May 1874): 591–3; (16 May 1874): 623–6; (23 May 187): 641–645; (30 May 1874): 686–689. See Rindge, p. 78, n. 59.

26. Beaman, (30 May 1874), p. 688.

Figure 4. "Carved Rock, Utah," wood-engraved illustration from E. O. Beaman, "The Cañon of the Colorado, and the Moquis Pueblos: A Wild Boat Ride through the Cañons—A Visit to the Seven Cities of the Desert—Glimpses of Mormon Life," Appleton's Journal *9 (no. 271) (30 May 1874), p. 688. Photo: From the author's collection.*

Figure 5. *"Cañon of Lodore," wood-engraved illustration from E. O. Beaman, "The Cañon of the Colorado, and the Moquis Pueblos: A Wild Boat Ride through the Cañons—A Visit to the Seven Cities of the Desert—Glimpses of Mormon Life,"* Appleton's Journal 9 *(no. 266), p. 513. Photo: From the author's collection.*

conventions, oddly including an innocuous figure placidly fishing in the right foreground.[27]

After Beaman's series appeared, Powell published his own articles at the request of *Scribner's* Editor Richard Watson Gilder. In July of 1874, Gilder contracted to pay Powell $500 to publish three articles and twelve wood-engravings. He also agreed to spend $2,000 on more engravings to which Powell would have the rights once the articles were published.[28] In 1874 and 1875, *Scribner's Monthly* featured a three-part series by Powell entitled "The Cañons of the Colorado" and an additional article on an overland trip to the Grand Canyon.[29] These were effectively a serialization of Powell's official report, which the Smithsonian Institution published in 1875 with *Scribner's* illustrations.[30]

The topographical survey conducted by George M. Wheeler was funded by the War Department, U.S. Army Corps of Engineers, and was publicized relatively late in the illustrated magazines. The first illustrated articles appeared in 1876–1877 in *Harper's New Monthly Magazine* and *Appleton's Journal*.[31] These resulted from two events: the 1875 publication of Wheeler's official government report, which was accompanied by a hand-assembled portfolio of photographs by survey photographers Timothy O'Sullivan and William Bell, and the presence of journalist William H. Rideing during the seasons of 1875 and 1876.[32] The photographs which served as the basis for the magazine illustrations were often modified and romanticized to com-

27. Beaman, (25 April 1874), p. 513.

28. Wallace Stegner, *Beyond the Hundredth Meridian: John Wesley Powell and the Second Opening of the West* (Boston: Houghton Mifflin Company, 1953), 151.

29. John Wesley Powell, "The Cañons of the Colorado," *Scribner's Monthly* 9 (December 1874): 293–310; (February 1875): 394–409; and (March 1875): 523–537. The illustrations are wood-engravings after drawings by Thomas Moran and photographs by Jack Hillers. See Rindge, 78, n. 59.

30. John Wesley Powell, *Exploration of the Colorado River of the West* (Washington, [DC]: Government Printing Office, 1875).

31. William H. Rideing, "The Wheeler Expedition in Southern Colorado," *Harper's New Monthly Magazine* 52 (June 1876): 15–24; William H. Rideing, "The Wheeler Survey in Nevada," *Harper's New Monthly Magazine* 55 (June 1877): 65–76; and William Rideing "With Wheeler in the Sierra," *Appleton's Journal* 3 (October 1877): 288–297, illustrated by Thomas Moran. See Rindge, 79, n. 64.

32. George M. Wheeler, *Annual Report Upon Geographical Explorations and Surveys West of the One Hundredth Meridian* (Washington, DC: Government Printing Office, 1875); *Photographs Showing Landscapes, Geological and Other Features, of Portions of the Western Territory of the United States, Obtained in Connection with the Geographical and Geological Explorations and Surveys West of the 100th Meridian (Seasons of 1871, 1872, and 1873)* (Wash-

plement a vague but poetically descriptive text. For example, in William Rideing's 1876 article for *Harper's New Monthly Magazine*, "A Trail in the Far Southwest," the illustration of "Cañon de Chelle" (Figure 6) alters the original Timothy O'Sullivan photograph (Figure 7) with the addition of figures around a campfire in the right foreground and a moon rising over the canyon wall at left. The one comparative reference to Cañon de Chelle appears at the end of the text, but is not served by the illustration. The only correlation for the illustration may be the tents on the canyon floor in the left foreground area: "[the traveler] pitches his tent . . . with the melody of sighing cotton-woods and snow fed brooks rippling in his ears, all his senses surfeited in a paradise of sweetness."[33]

Illustrations from the surveys proliferated widely to secondary publications. Travel and gift books republished many of these same images. Publishers encouraged the inclusion of illustrations previously printed in their stock because of the cost-saving benefits. *Picturesque America*, an enormously popular and profusely illustrated gift book edited by William Cullen Bryant was released in monthly installments in 1872 and 1874 and published as a two-volume edition by *Appleton's*, allowing the publishing firm to reap further profits from wood-engravings made originally for the magazine.[34]

Wider knowledge of the surveys was obtained through art criticism as well. Published commentary on photographs and exhibited paintings stimulated even greater public interest in the scientists' activities. The reviews of the paintings of Thomas Moran and Albert Bierstadt and the self-promotional writing of photographer William Henry Jackson in the photographic magazines generated a veritable flood of publicity for the surveys.

When Thomas Moran's *Grand Canyon of the Yellowstone* debuted in exhibition in 1872, the *Atlantic Monthly's* review went beyond a discussion of the merits of the painting to include this passage on the Hayden survey:

> It appeals a little to the pleasure we all have, and not be ashamed of it, in the fact that this wonderful place is not merely a bit of the continent, but is,

ington, DC: War Department, Corps of Engineers, U.S. Army, [1875]); William Rideing wrote on the Wheeler Survey for *Appleton's, Harper's,* and the *New York Times*, among other publications, see Bartlett, pp. 256–357.

33. Rideing, "A Trail in the Far Southwest," pp. 17–18.

34. *Picturesque America*, 2 vols., Ed. William Cullen Bryant (New York: D. Appleton and Co. 1872, 1874).

Figure 6. "Cañon de Chelle," wood-engraved illustration from William Rideing's "A Trail in the Far Southwest," Harper's New Monthly Magazine 52 (June 1876): 15–24. Photo: From the author's collection.

Figure 7. Timothy O'Sullivan, "Cañon de Chelle. Walls of the Grand Cañon about 1200 feet in height," albumen photograph. Photo: From the author's collection.

indeed, the private property of every man, woman, and child of us, being in the very middle of that generous tract of square miles which by the energy and persistence of Professor F. V. Hayden, backed by good men and true in both houses, Hon. S. C. Pomeroy in the Senate, and Hon. W. S. Claggett in the House, has been set apart forever as a public park for the people of the whole United States to walk abroad and recreate themselves.[35]

Others were inspired by Thomas Moran's success in selling this painting of survey imagery to Congress. Albert Bierstadt, the landscape painter who traveled with the King Survey in 1872 in the Sierra Nevada of northern California, changed the title of one of his paintings from *Autumn in the Sierras* to *Kings River Canyon* (1873, now known again as *Autumn in the Sierras*, City of Plainfield, New Jersey). With this new emphasis on his connection to the King survey, he submitted the painting to Congress for consideration for purchase in 1874–5. To the artist's regret, Congress declined.[36]

Reports by and about William Henry Jackson on the Hayden survey were featured in the *Philadelphia Photographer* and *Anthony's Photographic Bulletin* at least seven times between 1874 and 1876.[37] In 1875, the *Philadelphia Photographer* praised Jackson's survey photographs:

From Mr. William H. Jackson of Washington, the artist photographer . . . we have received a series of views. Each picture seems to have been admirably chosen, and would form a subject for a painter. As specimens of photography we think they excel anything in landscape work we have ever seen made in this country, . . . they are most excellent artistic studies, and we congratulate Mr. Jackson on his success. He has reached a standard of

35. "Art," *Atlantic Monthly* 30 (August 1872): 247.

36. Linda Ferber,"Albert Bierstadt: The History of a Reputation," in Nancy Anderson and Linda Ferber, *Albert Bierstadt: Art and Enterprise* (New York: Hudson Hills Press, 1990), pp. 42–52, n. 142. However, in 1875 Congress purchased Bierstadt's *Discovery of the Hudson River* (1875, U.S. Capitol, Washington, DC).

37. "Colorado Photographed," *Anthony's Photographic Bulletin* 5 (February 1874): 76; Editor's Table," *The Philadelphia Photographer* 113 (April 1876): 128; William Henry Jackson, "Correspondence," *Anthony's Photographic Bulletin* 7 (July 1876): 160; "Correspondence: Return of Mr. W. H. Jackson," *Anthony's Photographic Bulletin* 7 (January 1876): 31; "Interesting American Scenery," *The Philadelphia Photographer* 13 (April 1876): 120; and William Henry Jackson, "Field Work," *The Philadelphia Photographer* 12 (March 1875): 91–93.

excellence that we have often witnessed in some of the best European work, but have sighed for in vain in America until now.[38]

The pivotal moment in the "rise and fall" of visual representations of the surveys was the Philadelphia Centennial exhibition of 1876. In earlier World's Fairs of the 1870s, photographers were offered new opportunities to exhibit their work in gallery environs. The Vienna International Exhibition, for example, held from May to November of 1873, included the work of survey photographers in an exhibition of landscape photography organized by the American Geographical Society of New York.[39] But it was the International Centennial Exhibition, held in Philadelphia from May to November of 1876, that proved the most important public exhibition to feature the surveys. The Wheeler, Powell, and Hayden surveys were represented in exhibits shown in the United States Government Building in the sections devoted to the Department of the Interior and the U.S. Army. The Wheeler survey featured photographs by Timothy O'Sullivan and William Bell. The Powell Survey was represented by ethnological contributions in the section of the building devoted to the Smithsonian Institution, and by photographs; a writer for *The Nation* noted that some of the photographs had already been engraved to appear as illustrations for Powell's report.[40]

The Hayden Survey exhibit was the most comprehensive, as it included "models, maps . . . , publications, and pictures in water-colors," chromolithographs, and specimens.[41] Photographs were hung on the walls and displayed in albums. William Henry Jackson's survey photographs had become available by mail order in 1874.[42] Two editions of the catalogue were published in 1875; the second edition was revised to include wood-engraved il-

---

38. *The Philadelphia Photographer* 12 (1875): 30.

39. Joel Snyder, *American Frontiers: the Photographs of Timothy O'Sullivan, 1867–1874* (Millerton, NY: Aperture, 1981), p. 30, and Rindge, pp. 82–83.

40. L. N., "The International Exhibition—No. XVIII: The United States Exhibit," *The Nation* 23 (19 October 1876): 238.

41. Joseph Henry, "Report of the Secretary," *Annual Report of the Board of Regents of the Smithsonian Institution . . . for the Year 1876* (Washington [DC]: Government Printing Office, 1877), p. 57.

42. The first published was William Henry Jackson, *Descriptive Catalogue of the Photographs of the U.S. Geological and Geographical Survey of the Territories 1869 to 1873 Inclusive* (Washington [DC]: Government Printing Office, 1874).

lustrations, undoubtedly intended to attract orders from fair-goers.[43] One of the most marvelous elements of the display was placed appropriately at the far western end of the building. Here William Henry Jackson's photographs were printed as positives on panes of glass.[44] Contemporary responses, such as this passage from the *Atlantic Monthly*, convey the delighted astonishment of the audience:

> On reaching the end of the building, we confront a large window whose panes are beautiful photographs on glass of our wild, far western scenery. There are the tremendous heights, depths, flats, and contortions of Colorado and Arizona; the plains, ravines, ridges, and peaks amid which nature has indulged in so many Titanic freaks that the phenomena of all lands seems to meet together there. . . . The geological outlines are formidable, redoubtable, in their fantastic forms; there are horrible crags which look like fossil fungi or groups of petrified penguins of gigantic size. As we examine the photographs and plans in relief which give the natural features of these scarcely-explored tracts, we become conscious of a semi-mythical character which belong to them, and a sort of preternatural influence which breathes from them.[45]

Further attention was given to the Hayden and Powell surveys in the art exhibitions held in Memorial Hall and its Art Annex. Paintings exhibited by Thomas Moran featured three survey subjects and chromolithographs of his Yellowstone watercolors. In December 1873, publisher Louis Prang had approached the artist to paint a series of Yellowstone watercolors to be reproduced in a deluxe chromolithograph set.[46] Fifteen were chosen for a

43. William Henry Jackson, *Catalogue of the Photographs of the U.S. Geological and Geographical Survey of the Territories* (Washington [DC]: Government Printing Office, 1875). William Henry Jackson, *Descriptive Catalogue of the Photographs of the U.S. Geological Survey of the Territories 1869 to 1875 Inclusive* 2nd. ed. (Washington [DC]: Government Printing Office, 1875).

44. "Government Building," *The Philadelphia Photographer* 13 (October 1876): 294–295. Don Fowler believes half the photographs are by Jack Hillers. Conversation with the author, 15 March 1997. A photograph of this display, from the collection of the Smithsonian Institution Archives, is published in Julie K. Brown, *Contesting Images: Photography and the World's Columbian Exposition* (Tucson: University of Arizona Press, 1994), p. 9.

45. "Characteristics of the International Fair," *Atlantic Monthly* 38 (October 1976): 497.

46. See Carol Clark, *Thomas Moran: Watercolors of the American West* (Austin: University of Texas Press, 1980), 44–45. On Prang, see Peter Marzio, *The Democratic Art: Chromo-*

portfolio that was unveiled at the Centennial and issued in an edition of 1,000, sold by subscription at sixty dollars per set. Entitled *The Yellowstone National Park, and the Mountain Regions of Portions of Idaho, Nevada, Colorado, and Utah*, the portfolio featured an introduction by survey leader Ferdinand V. Hayden and was awarded a medal at the Centennial.[47] Even *The Nation*, which had reviled Moran's 1872 painting *Grand Canyon of the Yellowstone*, published an enthusiastic review: "Concerning Mr. Moran's artistic qualifications, we can cheerfully say that we think he is at his best when working on paper instead of on canvas . . . the boldness and facility of the drawing are really impressive."[48]

The Philadelphia Centennial was the last great exhibition in which the surveys figured. Severe financial setbacks to funding curtailed appropriations and activities in 1877 and 1878, virtually eliminating the raw material for the great publicity campaigns.

However, the wood-engraved illustrations in which publishers had made considerable investment continued to reappear in new publications. Later in the century these illustrations acquire a rich provenance. One charming book from 1883 is entitled, *Picturesque Journeys in America of the Junior United Tourist Club*.[49] It is an illustrated travelogue for the armchair traveling teenager of the late Victorian period. The book's premise is that its adolescent protagonists meet in one another's homes weekly to discuss interesting travel spots, using wood-engraved illustrations as visual aids. The narrative is written in the form of a dialogue. The illustration of Yellowstone Hot Springs (Figure 8) from the chapter on Yellowstone National Park was a variation of a wood-engraving produced by illustrator Harry Fenn after one of William Henry Jackson's photographs from 1871. The illustration was published twice in 1872, in *Picturesque America* as well as *Scribner's Monthly*.[50]

---

lithography 1840–1900. Pictures for Nineteenth Century America (Boston: David R. Godine, 1979), pp. 94–111.

47. James D. McCabe, *The Illustrated History of the Centennial Exhibition* (Cincinnati: Jones Brothers and Co., 1876), p. 817.

48. "Fine Arts," *The Nation* 24 (15 February 1877), p. 107.

49. Reverend Edward T. Bromfield, *Picturesque Journeys in America of the Junior United Tourist Club* (New York: R. Worthington, 1883).

50. O. B. Bunce, "Our Great National Park," *Picturesque America*, vol. 1, p. 310, and Hayden, p. 389.

Figure 8. "*Yellowstone Hot Springs,*" *wood-engraved illustration from Reverend Edward T. Bromfield,* Picturesque Journeys in America of the Junior United Tourist Club *(New York: R. Worthington, 1883), p. 84. Photo: From the author's collection.*

At the opening of Chapter 9, one of the adults speaks authoritatively about the image:

> Mrs. Victor: . . . And now . . . I will proceed to the Geyser districts of the Yellowstone. These are classified into two divisions, the calcareous hot springs of Gardiner's River at the north of the Park, and the upper and lower geyser basins of the Madison River, farther to the south and west of Madison Lake. Here is a view of the hot springs on Gardiner's River. The club will look at it while I tell them all I know about it.[51]

At this point, one of the teenage boys interjects: "Cyril: The artist has had the good sense to introduce two people—members of the J. U. T. C. [Junior United Tourist Club] I suppose—in the foreground. One has a large portfolio under his arm."[52]

The wood-engravings were the instrument for the meeting of Science and Art in the parlor. The activities of the fictional Junior United Tourist Club echo a favorite pastime in American homes, made more popular with the new illustrated magazines.[53] Even after the "Great Surveys" were concluded as independent projects in 1879, their wide appeal and tremendous public impact lived on through the reprinting and re-sale of these memorable illustrations.

---

51. Bromfield, p. 84.
52. Bromfield, p. 84.
53. See Joan D. Hedrick, *Harriet Beecher Stowe: A Life* (New York: Oxford University Press, 1994), viii. She calls this the tradition of "parlour literature" in the nineteenth century—the practice of reading for informal gatherings of friends and family.

PART FOUR
EXPLORATION AND ANTHROPOLOGY

DON D. FOWLER
DAVID R. WILCOX

FROM THOMAS JEFFERSON TO THE PECOS CONFERENCE
Changing Anthropological Agendas in the North American Southwest

Introduction

The purpose of this paper is to discuss the interrelated histories of Western American exploration and the development of anthropology, especially the sub-field of archaeology, with special emphasis on the North American Southwest. Our time frame is roughly 1780 to 1930. We focus on certain anthropological issues, and the research agendas developed to resolve them.

We broadly define "anthropology" as a concerted attempt to define and account for the range of human physical, social and cultural variability. By "North American Southwest" we recognize that the anthropological Southwest is defined in terms of indigenous cultural traditions, rather than political boundaries, and thus includes portions of present-day United States and Mexico. But, those of whom we write *saw the region from* the Eastern United States, that is, from the intellectual centers of Boston, New York, Philadelphia, and Washington, D.C., and labeled it as "the Southwest," a usage we follow.[1]

The Southwest is especially important in the history of American ex-

1. In Mexico, the region is *seen as* the "Northwest," and "American Southwest" is regarded as pejorative, a problem of which we are aware. However, our concern in this paper is with the "view from" the Eastern United States, hence we use the term "the Southwest."

ploration and research. Ethnographic and archaeological research therein from 1846 to the 1930s was principally done by exploring expeditions, at first military- and later civilian-led, which came into the region to collect information. Some broad anthropological and historical controversies, begun elsewhere, came to be focused on the Southwest, as will be seen.

Early Anthropology

Anthropology arose partly in the context of the encounter between Europeans and indigenous peoples in the New World (and later, other colonial areas), and attempts by the former to categorize, account for, and "manage" the latter. From the outset, European savants, administrators, explorers and settlers posed two broadly "anthropological" questions. One was the matter of *commensurability*: were "native" peoples as "fully human" as Europeans, or "natural slaves," or some lesser form of sub-humans? A variety of answers was provided to *justify* forced incorporation of indigenous populations into European economic or religious systems, or to eradicate them, or move them out of the way of colonial expansion. The answers given often determined how indigenous peoples were treated by their colonial overlords.[2]

There was also the related question of *origins*.[3] Given the Biblical framework for human history, where in the Old World had Indian peoples originated? When, how, and by what route(s) had they come to the New World? The questions were matters of intellectual curiosity, but also central to the issue of commensurability, since determining from whence Indians were derived might allow judgments as to their commensurability. Unfortunately, no clear answers were immediately forthcoming.

To politicians and administrators, both secular and clerical, the "otherness" of the Indians also generated certain "management needs," to use modern parlance. It seemed prudent to learn about the cultural and political practices of native populations, the better to deal with them diplomati-

---

2. Lewis Hanke, *Aristotle and the American Indians: a Study in Race Prejudice in the Modern World* (Bloomington: Indiana University Press, 1959); Anthony Pagden, *The Fall of Natural Man. The American Indian and the Origins of Comparative Ethnology* (New York: Cambridge University Press, 1982); Patricia Seed, "'Are These Not Also Men?': The Indians' Humanity and Capacity for Spanish Civilization," *Journal of Latin American Studies* 25, no. 3 (1993): 629–652.

3. Lee E. Huddleston, *Origins of the American Indians. European Concepts, 1492–1729* (Austin: University of Texas Press, 1967).

cally or militarily, as they were eradicated, subjugated, converted, or forced into dependency relationships with a government, or a church group.

North American Anthropology

In North America, scholars, government officials, and missionaries all studied Indian peoples, their cultures and languages. By the mid-1700s, there was a general assumption that Indian people were fully human, but benighted owing to their "low" level of development and lack of the Christian faith; hence they were not really commensurable with Europeans.

Origins continued to be a principal concern. To the inductive, naturalistic-oriented Enlightenment scholars of the late eighteenth century, the problem was one of "hard" evidence. Comparative studies of languages seemed to be an answer, rather than vague speculation. The idea of language "families," and of "mother" languages, with descendant "daughter" languages, had long been known.[4] By the 1770s, scholars in Europe were busily collecting word lists from various languages and comparing them for cognate words in attempts to arrive at family, or "genetic," classifications of world languages. Such classifications might provide hard evidence for migrations of peoples. The task was taken up by North American scholars in the 1780s, led by Thomas Jefferson. Their hope was to link one or more languages, or language families, to those in the Old World, thus resolving the origins issue.

A related origins issue was archaeological: Who had built the burial mounds and enormous earthen structures in the Ohio and Mississippi valleys? Were the ancestors of the current Indians the "Moundbuilders," or had there been some other group?[5]

The Jefferson/American Philosophical Society Research Agenda

Thomas Jefferson was deeply interested in the origins issue, both in its linguistic and archaeological aspects, but also in "applied" anthropology. He

4. Giuliano Bonfante, "Ideas on the Kinship of European Languages from 1200 to 1800," *Journal of World History* 1 (1954): 679–699.

5. Roger G. Kennedy, *Hidden Cities. The Discovery and Loss of Ancient North American Civilization* (New York: Penguin Books, 1994).

realized that the democratic governance of his envisioned "empire of liberty" in the West required collection of demographic and ethnographic information about the Indian tribes for diplomatic and management purposes. In his *Notes on the State of Virginia*, Jefferson[6] called for a systematic linguistic classification of Indian languages as the basis for approaching the origins issue, and the collection of vocabulary lists toward the classification.[7] He also called for a program to study the "mounds." In 1799, Jefferson and his colleagues in the American Philosophical Society (APS) distributed a circular[8] calling for systematic compilation of linguistic, ethnographic, historical, and archaeological data relating to the Indians. It became, in effect, a "charter" for American anthropology.[9]

Jefferson, Albert Gallatin, Stephen Peter Du Ponceau and others doggedly collected linguistic data, especially through an APS committee devoted to the task. The pursuit lasted more than three decades before Gallatin[10] produced his famous *Synopsis* of Indian languages. But it was only a partial classification, having few data from tribes beyond the Rocky Mountains or in the Southwest. Meanwhile, systematic study of the mounds had begun, especially in the works of Atwater,[11] and Squier and Davis.[12]

6. Thomas Jefferson, "Notes on Virginia [1784]," in *The Life and Selected Writings of Thomas Jefferson*, ed. by A. Koch and W. Peden (New York: Modern Library, 1944), pp. 220–227.

7. Don D. Fowler, "Notes on Inquiries in Anthropology: a Bibliographic Essay." In *Toward a Science of Man. Essays in the History of Anthropology*, edited by T. H. Thoresen (The Hague: Mouton, 1975), pp. 18–22.

8. Thomas Jefferson, et al., "Circular Letter," *American Philosophical Society Transactions* 4 (1799): xxxvii–xxxix. reprinted, *Transactions* 5 (1809).

9. Gilbert Chinard, "Thomas Jefferson and the American Philosophical Society," *American Philosophical Society Proceedings* 87, no. 1 (1943): 270; A. Irving Hallowell, "The Beginnings of Anthropology in America," in *Selected Papers from the American Anthropologist, 1888–1920*, ed. by F. DeLaguna (Evanston: Row, Peterson Co., 1960), pp. 16–18; ———, "Anthropology in Philadelphia," in *The Philadelphia Anthropological Society. Papers Presented on its Golden Anniversary*, ed. by Jacob W. Gruber (Philadelphia: Temple University Publications, 1967), p. 12.

10. Albert Gallatin, "A Synopsis of the Indian Tribes of North America," *Archaeologica Americana. Transactions and Collections of the American Antiquarian Society* 2 (1836): 1–422.

11. Caleb Atwater, "Description of the Antiquities Discovered in the State of Ohio and other Western States," *Archaeologica Americana. Transactions and Collections of the American Antiquarian Society* 1 (1820): 105–267.

12. E. G. Squier and W. D. Davis, *Ancient Monuments of the Mississippi Valley*. Smithsonian Contributions to Knowledge no. 1 (Washington, DC, 1848).

Anthropology & Western Exploration

Even before the acquisition of Louisiana Territory, Jefferson had planned an expedition to "stake a claim" there before the British could do so. With the territory in hand and the dispatching of Lewis and Clark to explore it, Jefferson saw an opportunity to collect information about the geography, natural history and Indians therein. He and his APS colleagues drew up detailed lists of questions for Lewis and Clark, who produced a remarkable amount of information in their journals[13] and their reports to Jefferson in answer to the questions. Providing detailed lists of questions set a precedent for all subsequent federally-sponsored parties of exploration. APS committees drew up instructions for the Long expedition to the Rocky Mountains in 1818[14] and the Wilkes Naval Expedition of 1838–42.[15]

A Synonymy / Encyclopedia

Another key figure was Lewis Cass who, as Governor of the Northwest Territory and Superintendent of Indian Affairs after 1818, saw the need to collect anthropological data for both scholarly and management purposes. He produced a detailed ethnographic and linguistic manual.[16] It also was Cass[17] who added an item to the research agenda. In an article in the *North American Review*, he noted that most historically-known and extant Indian tribes were known by a wide variety of names. A *Synonymy* of tribal names was

13. Reuben G. Thwaites, ed., *Original Journals of the Lewis and Clark Expedition, 1804–06*, 8 vols. (New York: Dodd, Mead, 1904–05).

14. Peter Stephen Du Ponceau, et al., "Heads of Enquiry and Observation Among each of the Indian Tribes of the Missouri," (1819) [Original manuscript in] American Philosophical Library, Philadelphia; Richard H. Dillon, "Stephen Long's Great American Desert," *American Philosophical Society Proceedings* 111, no. 2 (1967): 93–108.

15. Edwin G. Conklin, "Connection of the American Philosophical Society with our First National Exploring Expedition." *American Philosophical Society Proceedings* 82 (1940): 519–541.

16. Lewis Cass, *Inquiries Respecting the History, Traditions, Languages, Manners, Customs, Religions, etc. of the Indians, Living within the United States* (Detroit: Sheldon & Reed, 1823).

17. ———, "Review of J.D. Hunter's 'Manners and Customs of Several Indian Tribes . . . ,'" *North American Review* 22 (1826): 37–90.

required, he thought, if ever a linguistic classification was to be properly developed, or a comprehensive history of the tribes written.

The idea of a synonymy was expanded into that of an encyclopedia by Cass's protégé, Henry Rowe Schoolcraft. In 1847 Schoolcraft convinced Congress to appropriate $1,200 to begin to compile a "digest" of statistics and "other materials," on North American Indians. He sent out a census and ethnographic inquiry,[18] based on Cass's model, to Indian agents, traders, Army officers and missionaries. Ten years and nearly $130,000 later, Schoolcraft[19] completed the pell-mell compilation of answers received into six massive and largely unusable volumes.[20] The need for a useful Indian synonymy or encyclopedia of Indians remained on the agenda.

Anthropology in the Southwest

Prior to 1821, scholars in the United States had little first-hand information about the Southwest. The opening of the Santa Fe Trail began to change that. But scholars already were aware that the Southwest figured in the origins controversy. The British historian William Robertson had used Mexican codices and Spanish documents to call attention to pre-Hispanic Mexican history in his *History of America*, first published in 1777.[21] In 1787, the Jesuit historian Joseph Xavier Clavigero's[22] *History of Mexico* was published in English. It contained an extensive review of materials relating to pre-

18. Henry R. Schoolcraft, *Inquiries Respecting the History, Present Condition and Future Prospects of the Indian Tribes of the United States* (Washington, DC: Bureau of Indian Affairs, 1847, reprinted in Henry R. Schoolcraft, ed., *Historical and Statistical Information Respecting the History, Condition and Prospects of the Indian Tribes of the United States*, I (Philadelphia: Lippincott, Grambo Co., 1851–57), pp. 523–568.

19. ———, ed., *Historical and Statistical Information Respecting the History, Condition and Prospects of the Indian Tribes of the United States.*

20. Richard G. Bremer, *Indian Agent and Wilderness Scholar: the Life of Henry Rowe Schoolcraft* (Mt. Pleasant, MI: Clarke Historical Library, Central Michigan University, 1987).

21. William Robertson, *History of America.* In *The Works of William Robertson, D.D. to which is prefixed an Account of His Life and Writings by Dugald Stewart*, Book IV (London: William Ball, 1840), pp. 715–716, 800–851. [orig. pub. in 1777, at least 15 additional editions by 1851.]

22. Francisco Javier Clavigero, *The History of Mexico. Collected from Spanish and Mexican Historians, from Manuscripts, and Ancient Paintings of the Indians . . .* , 2 vols. (London: G.G.J. and J. Robinson, 1787), (New York and London: Garland Publishing, 1979).

Conquest Mexican history. These and other sources were used by Alexander von Humboldt in his studies of Spanish America.[23]

From these sources, American scholars learned of purportedly indigenous Aztec and Toltec histories claiming that both groups originated "north" of the Valley of Mexico. Clavigero gave a detailed "history" and chronology of pre-Conquest Mexico. Therein, he said that various known and named Southwestern ruins were "stopping places" for Aztecs or Toltecs during their southward migrations. Humboldt repeated Clavigero's history.

Here, then, was a derivative controversy within the more general origins debate: How far to the "north" did the Aztec and Toltec migrations originate? All the way to Asia? In the Southwest? In between? Were the mounds of the Mississippi drainage involved in those migrations, as points of origin or stopping places?

The American Ethnological Society

Albert Gallatin settled in New York City in 1840 after a long, illustrious career of public service.[24] He became the doyen of a group interested in American Indian archaeology and ethnology (as anthropology was then called). Gallatin and his colleagues founded the American Ethnological Society in 1842, and started a publication series. By the 1840s there was a rekindled interest in Spanish America. William Hickling Prescott[25] published his best-selling *Conquest of Mexico* in 1843. In an appendix he presented information on pre-Conquest Mexican history based on Humboldt, Clavigero and

23. Alexander von Humboldt, *Political Essay on the Kingdom of New Spain*, ed. by Mary M. Dunn (New York: A.A. Knopf, 1972), [abridged from the 1811 John Black translation, 4 vols., London]; ———, *Researches Concerning the Institutions and Monuments of the Ancient Inhabitants of America . . .*, Trans. by Helen M. Williams, 2 vols. (London: Longman, Hurst, Rees, . . . 1814 [1810]).

24. Henry Adams, *The Life of Albert Gallatin*. (New York: J.B. Lippincott, 1879); Raymond Walters, Jr., *Albert Gallatin, Jefferson Financier and Diplomat*. (New York: Macmillan, 1957).

25. William H. Prescott, *History of the Conquest of Mexico, with a Preliminary View of the Ancient Mexican Civilization, and the Life of the Conqueror, Hernando Cortes*, 3 vols. (New York: Harper Bros.; London: Richard Bentley, 1843).

manuscript sources, e.g., Ternaux-Compans.[26] Gallatin became interested in Mexico. Drawing on Prescott and many others, Gallatin[27] produced a lengthy paper on the "Semi-Civilizations" of Mexico and adjacent regions (see below).

Topographical Engineers in the Southwest

In 1846, the United States invaded the provinces of New Mexico and Alta California of the sovereign nation of Mexico. With the "Army of the West" were four Army Topographical Engineers assigned to explore the new region. Two of their reports on New Mexico, by Lt. James Abert[28] and Lt. William Emory[29], were published by the U.S. Congress and provided those in the East with accurate first hand information about the geography, topography, natural history, Indian peoples, and the ruins. As the U.S. Army and some civilians expanded their explorations in the Southwest, much data about the ruins and the various Indian tribes was presented in their reports.[30] Thus, by the eve of the Civil War there was a corpus of new anthro-

26. Henri Ternaux-Compans, comp. and ed., *Voyages, relations et mémoires originaux pour servir à l'histoire de la découverte de l'Amérique, publiés pour la première fois en français.* (Paris: A. Bertrand, 1837–41).

27. Albert Gallatin, "Note on the Semi-Civilized Nations of Mexico, Yucatan, and Central-America," *American Ethnological Society Transactions* 1 (1845): 1–352.

28. James W. Abert, *Report and Map of the Examination of New Mexico; made by Lt. J. W. Abert, of the Topographical Corps, in Answer to a Resolution of the U.S. Senate* [1848] (Washington, DC: 30th Congress, 1st Session, Senate Executive Document no. 23, 1848).

29. W. H. Emory, *Notes of a Military Reconnaissance from Fort Leavenworth in Missouri to San Diego in California . . . Made in 1846–47* (Washington, DC: 30th Congress, 1st Session, Senate Executive Document no. 41, 1848).

30. John Russell Bartlett, *Personal Narrative of Explorations and Incidents in Texas, New Mexico, California, Sonora and Chihuahua . . . in 1850–53*, 2 vols. (New York: D. Appleton Co., 1854); W. H. Emory, *Report on the United States and Mexican Boundary Survey made under the Direction of Secretary of the Interior*, vol. 1 (Washington, DC: 34th Congress, 1st Session, House Executive Document no. 135; Senate Executive Document no. 108, 1857.); Joseph C. Ives, *Report upon the Colorado River of the West, explored in 1857 and 1858.* (Washington, DC: 36th Congress 1st Session. House Executive Document no. 90, 1861); Jonathan Letterman, "Sketch of the Navajo Tribe of Indians, Territory of New Mexico," *Smithsonian Annual Report* (1855): 283–297; [Heinrich] Balduin Möllhausen, *Diary of a Journey from the Mississippi to the Coasts of the Pacific with a United States Government Expedition*, trans. by Mrs. Percy Sinnett, 2 vols. (London: Longman, Brown, Green, Longmans & Roberts, 1858, reprint New York: Johnson Reprint Corp., 1969); James H. Simpson, *Journal of a Military Reconnaissance from Santa Fe, New Mexico to the Navajo Country . . .* (Washington, DC: 31st Congress, 1st Session, Senate Executive Document no. 64, 1850); Lorenzo Sitgreaves, *Report of an Expedition Down the Zuni and Colorado Rivers on 1851*

pological data on the Southwest, based on first-hand observation and accompanied by numerous illustrations drawn in the field.

It was clear that there were literally thousands of ruins, from small piles of rubble to the great houses of Chaco Canyon. But with no way to date them, it was impossible to determine whether many people had lived there for a short time, or fewer for a longer time. It was clear that there had been more people than in the twenty-odd pueblos along the Rio Grande and those of Acoma, Zuñi and Hopi to the west. The connections between the Southwest and the ancient civilizations of Mexico continued to be of central concern, but there was no way to arrive at a consensus of what the connections might entail: north to south migrations, south to north migrations, ongoing trade, or other relationships.

Gallatin's Research Agenda

As we saw, a general research agenda for American anthropology was laid out by Thomas Jefferson and others. In the intervening four decades new publications and much new information appeared. In late 1847, Albert Gallatin received advanced information from Lt. Emory's[31] report. He combined this with his 1845 paper and other data in a forty four page essay, "Ancient Semi-Civilization of New Mexico."[32] Therein, he synthesized all the data and formulated a series of more sharply focused research questions, most of which are still under investigation 150 years later. Soon after the Abert and Emory reports appeared, E.G. Squier[33] published a summary

---

(Washington, DC: 32nd Congress, 2nd Session, Senate Executive Document no. 59, 1853, reprint Chicago: Rio Grand Press, 1962); P.G.S. Ten Broeck, "Manners and Customs of the Moqui and Navajo Tribes of New Mexico," *Historical and Statistical Information Respecting the History, Condition, and Prospects of the Indian Tribes of the United States*, ed. by H. R. Schoolcraft (Philadelphia: Lippincott, Grambo Co., 1854), pp. 72–98; A. W. Whipple, T. Ewbank, and W. W. Turner, "Report upon the Indian Tribes," in *The Report of Lieutenant A.W. Whipple, Corps of Topographical Engineers, upon the Route near the Thirty-Fifth Parallel. Reports of Explorations and Surveys to Ascertain the Most Practicable and Economical Route for a Railroad from the Mississippi River to the Pacific Ocean . . . in 1853–54* (Washington, DC: 33rd Congress, 2nd Session, Senate Executive Document no. 8, 1856), 3, pt. 3: 1–127.

    31. Emory, *Notes of a Military Reconnaissance.*

    32. Albert Gallatin, "Ancient Semi-Civilizations of New Mexico," *American Ethnological Society Transactions* 2 (1848): liii–xcvii.

    33. E. G. Squier, "New Mexico and California," *The American Review, Devoted to Politics and Literature* 2, no. 5 (1848): 503–528.

of them, together with a review of available Spanish documents, and proposed his own overview of Southwestern culture history. Squier had been active with Gallatin in the Ethnological Society and was co-author of a massive study of the Moundbuilders, the first publication of the Smithsonian Institution.[34]

The papers by Gallatin and Squier are extremely important in the history of Southwestern anthropology. They mark the beginning of systematic analysis of anthropological data on the region. Gallatin advanced a series of hypotheses concerning inter-tribal relationships, the origin and spread of agriculture, and the older question of Mexican-Southwest relationships, and Squier reacted to them. Both raised issues relating to Spanish-Indian acculturation, and acculturation between tribes. Squier challenged some of Gallatin's assertions. In short, modern analytical scholarship on the Southwest was underway. This was Gallatin's final contribution during a life of nearly nine decades; he died the following year.

The Mexican-Southwest historical connection was a sub-set of a larger origins issue, which might be termed the North-South Connection. How, and from whence, had Indians arrived? The early seafaring Europeans looked to other Old World seafarers, from Carthaginians to Chinese, but found no proof. But if not by sea, then perhaps by land? The Jesuit scholar Joseph de Acosta, in 1590, was the first to propose a land bridge between the two hemispheres, in either the extreme north or south.[35] In 1741, Vitus Bering demonstrated that the "bridge" was in the north by showing how close Asia and America actually are. Thus, by Jefferson's time, most scholars assumed that the Western Hemisphere was populated *from north to south*, either overland or by coasting along the shores of Asia, the Aleutians, and western North America. This brings us back once more to the question of acceptable evidence: Jefferson, Gallatin, and others agreed that linguistic affinity was the primary "hard" evidence through which connections between "races," "tribes," or "nations" could be scientifically established.

Gallatin steadfastly maintained that *all* American Indian languages have "a uniformity of character indicating a common origin" despite a great di-

34. Squier and Davis, *Ancient Monuments of the Mississippi Valley.*
35. Huddleston, *Origins of the American Indians.*

vergence into an estimated one hundred plus distinct languages.[36] He assumed that linguistic affinities would be demonstrated between Indian and Asian languages in due time. He asserted that Indians and East Asians share a "similarity of physical type," which would tend to "prove a general, though perhaps not universal, common origin."[37] If Indians derived from eastern Asia, there was the additional question of when? Gallatin[38] argued for a long, though indeterminate, length of time, given the great diversity of known Indian languages.

There was still an issue of commensurability: were the "semi-civilizations" of the New World indigenous developments, or derived from elsewhere? Commensurability, said Gallatin:

> Involves two most important questions in the history of man: that of the presumed inferiority of some races; and whether savage tribes can, of themselves, and without any foreign assistance, emerge from the rudest and lowest social state, and gradually attain even the highest degree of civilization known to us.[39]

He thought the answers lay in the abilities of peoples from differing cultures to independently develop astronomy, mathematics and a calendar system. Gallatin[40] examined Mesoamerican calendars and their underlying astronomy in detail and concluded that many cultures world-wide, including those of Mesoamerica, had independently figured out the "annual motion of the sun." Having achieved that, mathematics and calendars followed, and the path to civilization lay open. A related issue was the origins of agriculture. Gallatin[41] agreed with Humboldt that maize is of American tropical origin and its cultivation ultimately led to civilization. His conclusions were that since both New World agriculture and astronomy were indigenous, hence, so too were the "semi-civilizations" thereof.

36. Albert Gallatin, "A Synopsis of the Indian Tribes of North America," pp. 142, 160; "Note on the Semi-Civilized Nations of Mexico, Yucatan, and Central-America," pp. 2, 10, 177; "Ancient Semi-Civilization of New Mexico," p. 25.

37. Gallatin, "Note on the Semi-Civilized Nations of Mexico, Yucatan, and Central-America," pp. 10–11.

38. Ibid., pp. 177–78.

39. Ibid., p. 181.

40. Ibid., pp. 49–115.

41. Ibid., pp. 195–96.

Gallatin[42] then turned to the Southwest noting that the Pueblos plant the same crops, maize, beans and pumpkins, as the Mexicans, proof the Pueblos received agriculture from the latter. However, connections *beyond* food crops is another matter:

> Clavigero, who makes the Aztecs to come from the Rio Gila, appears to have embraced that opinion . . . on account of the ruins of buildings, on the banks of that river and others farther south, generally called "casa grandé," and which are supposed to have been built by the Aztecs.[43]

But then came the clincher: what is the "hard" evidence?

> No trace of the Mexican language has been discovered in any part of that region [present-day New Mexico and Sonora, hence,] it seems probable that the Indians of New Mexico and of the country south of it . . . were not of the same stock or family as the Mexicans or Toltecs, though they may have received their agriculture from those nations.[44]

Gallatin's final statement on the Mexican-Southwest Connection came in his 1848 paper in which he asserted that the Aztecs did not derive from the Southwest,

> but adjacent to Michoacan. . . . If an identity of languages should hereafter be ascertained, it appears . . . probable that the civilization of the river Gila, and of New Mexico, must be ascribed to an ancient Toltec colony. If the languages should prove different from the Mexican proper or any of the other spoken between the tropics, we may not be able ever to ascertain how this northern civilization originated.[45]

Gallatin's papers set forth hypotheses which helped shape Americanist anthropology, in some instances, to the present time. These are the salient elements:

42. Ibid., pp. 200–201.
43. Ibid., p. 200.
44. Ibid., p. 203.
45. Gallatin, "Ancient Semi-Civilization of New Mexico," pp. lxxxvi–lxxxvii.

1. That the Western Hemisphere was peopled from north to south, either by land across the Bering "bridge," or by coasting along the shores of Asia, Alaska and North America, at an undetermined but early time.

2. That the initial migrants were hunter gatherers who spread quickly southward, aided by a rapid increase in population.

3. That the "semi-civilizations" of Mexico and Peru were indigenous developments, with no appreciable influence from the Old World.

4. That agriculture, and possibly other elements of "semi-civiliza-tion," had diffused *from* the Mesoamerican core *into* the Southwest.

5. That the purported "northern" point of derivation of the Aztecs could *not be* the Southwest, because there was no hard evidence of linguistic connections between Southwestern and Northern Mexico tribes. The Toltec connection remained open, pending adequate linguistic data.

The "Great Surveys" and the Southwest

Following the Civil War there was a resurgence of Western exploration under the aegis of the so-called "Great Surveys" of the late 1860s – 1870s, led by Clarence King, Ferdinand Vandiveer Hayden, Lt. George Wheeler, and John Wesley Powell.[46] All the surveys, excepting King's, recorded anthropological data on the Southwest, e.g. William Henry Holmes[47] and William Henry Jackson.[48]

John Wesley Powell came to fame as the one-armed explorer of the Colorado River in 1869. In 1870, as he was preparing for his second river trip, Powell spent about a month in the Southwest, much of it at Hopi.[49] He was greatly taken with the Southwestern Indians and archaeology. Powell later became a central figure in the Washington intellectual community and

---

46. William H. Goetzmann, *Exploration and Empire. The Explorer and the Scientist in the Winning of the American West* (New York: Knopf, 1966), pp. 355 – 601.

47. William H. Holmes, "A Note on the Ancient Remains of Southwestern Colorado Examined during the Summer of 1875," *Bulletin of the Geological and Geographical Survey of the Territories* 2, no.1 (1876): 3 – 24.

48. William H. Jackson, "Ancient Ruins in Southwestern Colorado," *Bulletin of the United States Geological and Geographical Survey of the Territories* no. 1 (1875): 17 – 30; ———, "A Notice of Ancient Ruins in Arizona and Utah Lying about the Rio San Juan," *Bulletin of the United States Geological and Geographical Survey of the Territories* 2, no. 2 (1876): 25 – 45.

49. John W. Powell, "The Ancient Province of Tusayan," *Scribner's Monthly* 11 (1875): 193 – 213.

was able to greatly influence the growth of anthropological sciences and their application to the problems of government.[50] Powell and his staff took up two of the unfinished agenda items of American anthropology, the linguistic classification and an adequate and usable synonymy-dictionary-encyclopedia of Indian tribes. The linguistic classification appeared in 1891 and remains the basic source.[51] After numerous metamorphoses, the synonymy finally appeared in 1907–10 as the *Handbook of American Indians North of Mexico*.[52]

The Bureau of Ethnology and the Southwest

In 1879, Congress created the U.S. Geological Survey and the Bureau of Ethnology (after 1894, the Bureau of American Ethnology), the latter under the Smithsonian Institution, with John Wesley Powell in charge. Powell immediately sent a team to the Southwest: Jack Hillers, his photographer, James and Matilda Coxe Stevenson, assigned to collect artifacts for the Smithsonian, and Frank Hamilton Cushing, assigned to do two or three month's ethnography with a tribe of his choice, and report back. Cushing chose the Zuñi, and stayed five years.

In his first annual report, Powell[53] wrote, "It is the purpose of the Bureau of Ethnology to organize anthropological work in America." A major part of that work would take place in the American Southwest. From 1879 until Powell's death in 1902, one or more Bureau of Ethnology staff members was at work each year on some facet of anthropology in the Southwest.[54]

In 1881, Powell was forced by Congress to take up the "Mound Build-

50. J. Kirkpatrick Flack, *Desideratum in Washington. The Intellectual Community in the Capital City, 1870–1900*. (Cambridge: Schenkman Publishing, 1975), pp. 93, 97–98; Curtis M. Hinsley, *Savages and Scientists. The Smithsonian Institution and the Development of American Anthropology, 1846–1910* (Washington: Smithsonian Institution Press, 1981), pp. 81–189.

51. John. W. Powell, "Indians Linguistic Families of America North of Mexico," *Seventh Annual Report of the Bureau of Ethnology, 1885–86* (1891): 1–142, map.

52. Frederick W. Hodge, editor, *Handbook of American Indians North of Mexico* 2 vols, Smithsonian Institution Bureau of American Ethnology Bulletin 30 (Washington, DC: 1907–10.), pts. 1–2.

53. Powell, "Report of the Director," *First Annual Report of the Bureau of Ethnology, 1879–80* (1881): xii.

54. Don D. Fowler, *A Laboratory for Anthropology. Science and Romanticism in the Southwest, 1846–1930* (Washington, DC: Smithsonian Institution Press, n.d.), chaps. 4–5.

ers" problem. He reluctantly did so, appointing Cyrus Thomas to the task. After several years of intense field work, Thomas [55] produced his well-known *Report*, which effectively answered the Moundbuilders question—they were the ancestors of the Indian peoples found in eastern North America when Europeans arrived—thus completing another of the Jefferson/APS agenda items.

John Wesley Powell and Lewis Henry Morgan

The senior figure in American anthropology after 1870 was Lewis Henry Morgan,[56] whose *Ancient Society*[57] had a profound impact in both America and Europe. Powell and Morgan worked in tandem to develop anthropology in the U.S. As early as 1857, Morgan held that, "The institutions of all the aboriginal races of [North America] . . . bear internal evidence of a common paternity, and point to a common origin, but remote, both as to time and place."[58] Morgan remained puzzled by the evident diversity of Indian cultural institutions, as had Gallatin and others, but finally resolved matters by casting the institutions in an evolutionary framework.[59]

Morgan, Bandelier and the AIA

In 1879 a number of Harvard/Boston luminaries created the Archaeological Institute of America (AIA). Led by Charles Eliot Norton, their vision was toward the glories of the Classical Old World. But Morgan, Powell, Francis Parkman, and others argued that the Institute ought to have an American focus as well. As the pre-eminent Americanist of his time, the AIA turned to Morgan for advice.

In *Ancient Society*, Morgan [60] argued that all North American Indians lived in large joint family households for mutual support, which he called

---

55. Cyrus Thomas, "Report on the Mound Explorations of the Bureau of Ethnology," *Twelfth Annual Report of the Bureau of Ethnology, 1890–91* (1894): 3–730.

56. Carl Resek, *Lewis Henry Morgan, American Scholar*. (Chicago: University of Chicago Press, 1960).

57. Lewis H. Morgan, *Ancient Society, or, Researches in the lines of Human Progress from Savagery through Barbarism to Civilization*. (New York: Henry Holt & Co., 1877).

58. Frederic W. Putnam, "A Problem in American Anthropology," *Annual Report of the Smithsonian Institution*, (1895): 476.

59. Morgan, *Ancient Society*.

60. Ibid., pp. 366–367, 377.

"communism in living."[61] House architecture, thought Morgan, should reflect those family arrangements, and archaeology could provide a way to test his theory. In 1878 Morgan made a trip to the Southwest, visiting many archaeological sites, including Aztec ruins, as well as Taos Pueblo.[62] He was impressed by their potential for confirming his theory, and plunged into research that would lead to his *Houses and House Life of the American Aborigines*.[63] When the AIA asked for guidance, Morgan drew from sections of his manuscript and quickly prepared what today would be called a research design.[64] It was a seminal document, placing Southwestern studies within a larger Americanist whole. On method, Morgan reasoned as follows:

> There are reasons for assuming that all the tribes of the American aborigines were of one common stock; that their institutions, plan of life, usages and customs were similar; and that the houses in ruins in the various places named can be explained, by comparison with those now inhabited in New Mexico, as parts of a common system of house architecture. If this be so, *it follows that the facts of American archaeology must be studied ethnologically; i.e. from the institutions, usages, and mode of life of existing Indian tribes.*[65]

Morgan believed that a study of house ground plans should reveal the fact of communal living "from Zuñi to Cuzco:"

> All the facts relating to [the Pueblos'] ancient usages and mode of life should be ascertained, so far as it is possible to do so, from the present inhabitants of these Pueblos. The information thus gained will serve a useful purpose in explaining the Pueblos in ruins in Yucatan and Central

61. Ibid., pp. 350–351.

62. Leslie A. White, ed., "Lewis H. Morgan's Journal of a Trip to Southwestern Colorado and New Mexico, June 21 to August 7, 1878," *American Antiquity* 8, no. 1: 1–26; Resek, *Lewis Henry Morgan*, pp. 146–47.

63. Lewis H. Morgan, *Houses and House-life of the American Aborigines*. (Washington, DC: Contributions to North American Ethnology, vol. 4, 1881.) reprinted (Chicago: University of Chicago Press, 1965).

64. Lewis H. Morgan, "A Study of the Houses of the American Aborigines with a Scheme of Exploration of the Ruins in New Mexico and Elsewhere," *First Annual Report of the Executive Committee, with Accompanying Papers, Archaeological Institute of America, 1879–1880* (1880): 29–80.

65. Ibid., p. 30, emphasis added.

America, as well as on the San Juan, the Chaco, and the Gila. From Zuñi to Cuzco, at the time of the Spanish conquest, the mode of domestic life in all these joint tenement houses must have been substantially the same.[66]

In conclusion, Morgan[67] set forth a specific program of research, beginning in the Southwest:

It should ascertain by actual exploration and investigation:

1. The architectural style and extent of the ruins, and the ground plans of the principal structures;

2. The condition of the art of masonry and of house construction, as shown by the ruins;

3. The object and uses for which the houses were erected;

4. The social organization, usages, and customs of the native tribes in New Mexico, Yucatan, and Central America, and, so far as possible, those of their ancestors, who constructed the houses.

We also must note that in *Houses and House Life . . .* Morgan combined the stage theory of sociocultural development laid out in his *Ancient Society*, with the older "north to south connection," and "Southwest as point of origin" models, previously discussed:

These [San Juan Basin] ruins and those of similar character in the valley of the Chaco . . . suggest the possibility that the . . . [Basin] held a prominent place in the first and most ancient development of Village Indian Life in America. The evidence of Indian occupation and cultivation throughout the greater part of this area [the northern Southwest] is sufficient to suggest the hypothesis that the Indians here first attained to the condition of the Middle Status of barbarism, and sent forth the migrating bands who [sic] carried this advanced culture to the Mississippi Valley, to Mexico and Central America, and not unlikely to South America as well.[68]

Morgan[69] further argued that maize agriculture *originated in*, and was spread from the San Juan Basin by the "migrating bands" eastward and

66. Ibid., p. 46.
67. Ibid., p. 77.
68. Morgan, *Houses and House-life of the American Aborigines*, p. 210.
69. Ibid., pp. 218–220.

southward. He thus answered the questions of the origins of Moundbuilders, and the spread of agriculture across the New World.

The AIA commissioned Adolph Bandelier, a Swiss business man and
scholar from Illinois, and a disciple of Morgan's, to carry out Morgan's
plan.[70] Bandelier ranged broadly for several years in the Southwest under
various auspices, collecting archaeological, ethnographic and archival data.
The organization of his reports and the nature of his field inquiries reflect
Morgan's program.[71] He was nevertheless an erudite scholar in his own right,
and an astute observer.

Combining data from historic Pueblos and archaeological sites, Bandelier[72] made a basic distinction between many-storied "communal"
houses and one-storied "small houses," and saw that they were differentially
distributed. Glazeware pottery was associated with many late communal
houses; finer-quality non-glaze pottery and corrugated wares were associated with the small houses. In an arroyo south of Pecos Pueblo, Bandelier[73]
recorded a buried ruin eroding from the bank. Non-glaze and corrugated
pottery were associated with it. From the stratigraphy and ceramics Bandelier inferred that the small houses were earlier than the communal
houses.[74] In cases where small houses and communal houses occur in the
same region with the same pottery associations, he suggested that aggressive nomads probably forced the inhabitants of the former to build the
communal houses.[75] Here, then, is an archaeological theory built on stra-

70. Charles H. Lange and Carroll L. Riley, *Bandelier. The Life and Adventures of Adolph Bandelier. American Archaeologist and Scientist.* (Salt Lake City: University of Utah Press, 1996); Leslie A. White, ed., *Pioneers in American Anthropology: The Bandelier-Morgan Letters, 1873–1883* (Albuquerque: University of New Mexico Press, 1940).

71. Adolph F. Bandelier, "Report of the Ruins of the Pueblo of Pecos," *Papers of the Archaeological Institute of America, American Series* 1, no. 2 (1881); ———, "Report of A. F. Bandelier in His Investigations in New Mexico in the Spring and Summer of 1882," *Bulletin of the Archaeological Institute of America* 1 (1883): 13–33; ———, "Reports of A. F. Bandelier on His Investigations in New Mexico during the Years 1883–84," *Fifth Annual Report of the Archaeological Institute of America* 4 (1884): 55–98; ———, *Final Report of Investigations among the Indians of the Southwestern United States, Carried on Mainly in the Years from 1880 to 1885, Parts I and II.* (Cambridge: Papers of the Archaeological Institute of America, American Series, III and IV, 1890–92).

72. Bandelier, "An Outline of the Documentary History of the Zuni Tribe," *Journal of American Ethnology and Archaeology* 3, no. 4 (1892): 1–115.

73. Bandelier, "Report of the Ruins," pp. 92–97.

74. Ibid., pp. 104–107; ———, "Reports of A. F. Bandelier on His Investigations in New Mexico during the Years 1883–84," p. 62.

75. Ibid., pp. 78, 84.

tigraphy, classification and association—together with data from Pueblo traditions. It was the first anthropological model of how the Pueblos came to be as they are. It also just happened to parallel Morgan's theory of a progression from huts to small houses to tenement (communal) houses.

The Recognition of Stratigraphy

Bandelier's sequence was soon augmented from a surprising quarter. In 1888, ranchers named Wetherill discovered large "cliff dwellings" on the Mesa Verde and soon were hosting visiting scientists.[76] These included Gustaf Nordenskiöld, a Swedish engineer whose careful excavations of several cliff dwellings resulted in the first monograph on Southwestern archaeology, notable also for its careful descriptions of sites and their contents.[77] By the 1890s, the Wetherills were leading expeditions into various areas of the Southwest. Their work in Grand Gulch, in southeastern Utah in 1896–97, resulted in Richard Wetherill defining pre-pottery "Basketmaker" deposits stratigraphically beneath "Cliff Dweller" deposits.[78]

The sequence was first publicized by T. Mitchell Prudden, a prominent East Coast pathologist who spent his summers in the Southwest. Prudden became fascinated by its archaeology and began to publish enduring accounts of both the Wetherills' and his own findings. Prudden[79] gave the name "Basketmakers" to the pre-pottery cultural deposits *below* the "Cliff Dweller" levels (the latter term was later superseded by "Pueblo"). Prudden systematically surveyed the northern San Juan country, constructing a structural and situational typology of the sites he found and reported their distribution in relation to their physiographic settings.[80]

---

76. Maurine S. Fletcher, ed., *The Wetherills of the Mesa Verde. Autobiography of Benjamin Alfred Wetherill* (Rutherford, NJ: Fairleigh Dickinson University Press, 1977).

77. Gustaf Nordenskiöld, *The Cliff Dwellers of the Mesa Verde* (Stockholm: P.A. Nordstedt, 1893) reprinted (Mesa Verde, CO: Mesa Verde Museum Association, 1991).

78. Victoria Atkins, ed., *Anasazi Basketmaker. Papers from the 1990 Wetherill-Grand Gulch Symposium*. Cultural Resource Series no. 24 (Salt Lake City: Bureau of Land Management, 1993); Fred M. Blackburn and Ray A. Williamson, eds., *Cowboys & Cave Dwellers. Basketmaker Archaeology in Utah's Grand Gulch* (Santa Fe, NM: School of American Research Press, 1997).

79. T. Mitchell Prudden, "An Elder Brother to the Cliff-Dwellers," *Harper's New Monthly Magazine* 95 (June 1897): 56–62.

80. ———, "The Prehistoric Ruins of the San Juan Watershed in Utah, Arizona, Colorado, and New Mexico," *American Anthropologist* 5, no. 1 (1903): 224–288.

Prudden's "Unit Pueblos"

Out of this, Prudden[81] developed the concept of the "unit pueblo." Small sites contained a few rectangular rooms in linear arrays sharing common walls, like a modern motel, and usually with a small ceremonial chamber, a kiva, in front. The larger communal houses, such as the Great Houses in Chaco Canyon, or Taos Pueblo, were composed of many such "units" arranged in linear rows and multiple stories, with several kivas in a plaza at the front. Prudden[82] also understood that the small houses were the domains of social groups which had aggregated together in the "communal" houses. This aggregation concept became a central idea in Southwestern archaeology.[83]

The Hemenway Southwestern Archaeological Expedition

After five years of participant observation at Zuñi in the early 1880s,[84] Frank Hamilton Cushing chanced to meet Mary Hemenway, a wealthy Boston philanthropist. He persuaded Mrs. Hemenway to finance the first systematic archaeological expedition to the Southwest to do excavation, the Hemenway Southwestern Archaeological Expedition.[85] Searching for the "lost others" of Zuñi oral tradition, Cushing began work in the Salt River Valley, in Arizona, spending eighteen months excavating sites he thought fulfilled his quest. The expedition then redeployed to Zuñi. Ill health, mis-

81. Ibid., pp. 234–238.

82. ———, "The Circular Kivas of Small Ruins in the San Juan Watershed," *American Anthropologist* 16, no. 1 (1914): 33–58; ———, "A Further Study of Prehistoric Small House Ruins in the San Juan Watershed," *American Anthropological Association Memoirs* no. 5 (1918): 3–50.

83. Alfred V. Kidder, *An Introduction to the Study of Southwestern Archaeology*. Papers of the Southwestern Expedition No. 1 (Andover, MA: Department of Archaeology, Phillips Academy, 1924): 149.

84. Jesse Green, ed., *Zuñi: Selected Writings of Frank Hamilton Cushing* (Lincoln: University of Nebraska Press, 1979); ———, *Cushing at Zuñi. The Correspondence and Journals of Frank Hamilton Cushing* (Albuquerque: University of New Mexico Press, 1990).

85. Curtis M. Hinsley and David R. Wilcox, eds., "A Hemenway Portfolio," *Journal of the Southwest* 37, no. 4 (1995); ———, *The Southwest in the American Imagination: The Writings of Sylvester Baxter, 1881–1889* (Tucson: University of Arizona Press, 1996).

management, jealousy, and recrimination ended Cushing's directorship and no final report was completed.[86] What continues to fascinate us about the Hemenway Southwestern Archaeological Expedition is that Cushing the ethnographer acting as archaeologist employed Adolph Bandelier as historian and Herman Ten Kate and others as physical anthropologists, thus attempting to fulfill Morgan's vision of how anthropological archaeology should be conducted.

Scholar Entrepreneurs: Hewett, Cummings and Lummis

John Wesley Powell died in 1902. He and his staff had completed the Jefferson/Cass agenda, as previously noted. But his approach to anthropological fieldwork and Morgan's theory of social evolution were on the wane; new ideas were stirring. Franz Boas was on the scene, and his critique of the American evolutionist approach[87] soon resulted in a new anthropological concept of culture.[88] Research agendas became increasingly problem oriented and required a professional approach, training in new methods and intensive effort, arguments which Boas and his university-based colleagues advanced with vigor.[89]

In the Southwest, however, the pace of change was slower, and older humanistic ideals endured longer. The key figures were two educators, Edgar Lee Hewett in New Mexico, and Byron Cummings in Utah and later Arizona, and a newspaper man and publicist, Charles Lummis, in California. With support from local business and cultural elites, they founded anthro-

---

86. See Frank H. Cushing, "Preliminary Notes on the Origins, Working Hypothesis and Primary Researches of the Hemenway South-western Archaeological Exposition," [sic] *International Congress of Americanists* Berlin, 1888 (1890): 151–194.

87. Franz Boas, "Museums of Ethnology and Their Classification," *Science* 9 (1887): 587–589; ———, "The Limitations of the Comparative Method of Anthropology," *Science*, n.s. 4 (1896): 901–908.

88. George W. Stocking, Jr., *Race, Language, and Evolution: Essays in the History of Anthropology* (New York: Free Press, 1968); ———, *A Franz Boas Reader: The Shaping of American Anthropology, 1883–1911* (Chicago: University of Chicago Press, 1974).

89. ———, *A Franz Boas Reader: The Shaping of American Anthropology*; ———, *The Ethnographer's Magic and Other Essays in the History of Anthropology* (Madison: University of Wisconsin Press, 1992).

pological institutions that have endured to the present: the Arizona State Museum and the Department of Anthropology at the University of Arizona (Cummings), the Southwest Museum in Los Angeles (Lummis), and the Museum of New Mexico and School of American Research in Santa Fe, the Department of Anthropology at the University of New Mexico, as well as the San Diego Museum of Man and the anthropology program at San Diego State University (Hewett). Alike in many of their values, their ideas about the importance of archaeology contrasted sharply with those of many in the Eastern Establishment.[90] Even so, they, and especially Hewett, had important allies in the East, whose continuing support was critical to their activities in the Southwest.

Hewett came to archaeology in his forties by a circuitous route, after a career as an educator. In 1904, he prepared a memorandum of Southwestern ruins and their preservation for the General Land Office.[91] Therein, he outlined the scope and nature of ruins in the region and took the opportunity to do no less than formulate a national policy for the protection of archaeological sites. He was soon in the forefront of the battle to develop national legislation for the protection of antiquities on public lands, and became the principal author of the Antiquities Act of 1906.[92] The Act accorded federal protection to sites and laid the basis for many of the excavation programs in the Southwest in the following decades. In 1906 Hewett was appointed by the AIA to head the School of American Archaeology (later, the School of American Research), and he also succeeded in creating

90. ———, "The Santa Fe Style in American Archaeology: Regional Interest, Academic Initiative and Philanthropic Policy in the First Two Decades of the Laboratory of Anthropology," *Journal of the History of Behavioral Sciences* 18 (1982): 3–19; Curtis M. Hinsley, "Edgar Lee Hewett and the School of American Research in Santa Fe, 1906–1912." in *American Archaeology Past and Future*, ed. David J. Meltzer, Don D. Fowler, and Jeremy A. Sabloff (Washington, DC: Smithsonian Institution Press, 1986): 217–236; Don D. Fowler, "Harvard vs. Hewett: The Contest for Control of Southwestern Archaeology, 1904–1930" in *Mainstreams and Margins: Studies in the Professionalization of Archaeology*, ed. A. H. Kehoe and M. B. Emmrichs (Albuquerque: University of New Mexico, 1999[in press]).

91. Edgar L. Hewett, "Memorandum Concerning the Historic and Prehistoric Ruins of Arizona, New Mexico, Colorado and Utah, and Their Preservation," *General Land Office Circular relating to Historic and Prehistoric Ruins of the Southwest and Their Preservation* (Washington, DC: Government Printing Office, 1904) reprinted, "A General View of the Archaeology of the Pueblo Region," *Smithsonian Annual Report for 1904* (1905): 583–605.

92. Ronald F. Lee, *The Antiquities Act of 1906* (Washington, DC: National Park Service, 1970).

the Museum of New Mexico, housing and directing both organizations in the venerable Palace of the Governors in Santa Fe.[93]

Cummings and Hewett took both men and women into the field[94] and provided a humanistic experience designed to build character and appreciate a romanticized, and in some senses, timeless, past while camping out among the scenic wonders of the Southwest. By the 1910s, that tradition was under vigorous attack by a new generation of avant garde archaeology students, trained in the anthropology of Franz Boas at Columbia University.

The Time-Space Revolution

The "Boasians," students of Franz Boas, students of his students, and close collaborators, came onto the anthropological scene in the period 1900 to 1920. They included Alfred Kroeber, Robert Lowie, Pliny Earl Goddard, Nels Nelson, Edward Sapir, and Elsie Clews Parsons, and were centered at Columbia University and the American Museum of Natural History, in New York. By 1905, Boas was planning to train archaeologists in European methods of stratigraphic analysis.[95] In 1910–1911, he was Director of the AIA's International School of American Archaeology and Ethnology in Mexico City where stratigraphic methods were applied to local cultural sequences.[96] Berthold Laufer,[97] of the American Museum, pointing to Egyptian and Chinese studies, identified the principal drawback of Americanist archaeology as "the lack of a substantial chronology." Chronology became a central focus of Boasians working in the American Southwest.

93. Beatrice Chauvenet, *Hewett and Friends. A Biography of Santa Fe's Vibrant Era* (Santa Fe: Museum of New Mexico Press, 1983); Don D. Fowler, *A Laboratory for Anthropology*, chap. 6.

94. Frances J. Mathien, "Chaco Women," in *Recovering Our Past: Essays on the History of American Archaeology*, ed. Jonathan E. Reyman. (Aldershot, England: Averbury, 1992): 103–130.

95. Ricardo Godoy, "Franz Boas and his Plans for an International School of American Archaeology and Ethnography in Mexico," *International Journal of the History of the Behavioral Sciences* 13 (1977): 232.

96. Alfred Tozzer, "Report of the Director of the International School of Archaeology and Ethnology in Mexico for 1913–14." *American Anthropologist* 17, no. 2 (1915): 391–395; David L. Browman and Douglas R. Givens, "Stratigraphic Excavation: The First 'New Archaeology,'" *American Anthropologist* 98, no. 1 (1996): 80–95

97. Berthold Laufer, "Remarks by Berthold Laufer on Roland B. Dixon's 'Some Aspects of North American Archaeology,'" *American Anthropologist* 15, no. 4 (1913): 576–577.

In 1905 Clark Wissler became Curator of Ethnology at the American Museum.[98] In 1909, a trustee of the museum, Archer M. Huntington, agreed to fund a cultural survey of the American Southwest. Wissler[99] used the support to develop a long-term program focused on chronology, "the historical problem in the Southwest." In 1912 Nels Nelson was hired to begin work under the Huntington Survey. He trained briefly in stratigraphy with the Abbé Henri Breuil and Hugo Obermaier in Spain.[100] In 1913, Nelson began to excavate sites stratigraphically in the Galisteo Basin of New Mexico using arbitrary levels and subjecting the pottery sherds therefrom to a statistical analysis that revealed a succession of ceramic periods.[101]

In 1914, Alfred Vincent Kidder, who first came to the Southwest in 1907 as a student in Hewett's summer field school,[102] completed a dissertation at Harvard that also demonstrated the utility of potsherds in the reconstruction of culture history.[103] In 1915 he began a long-term program of research at Pecos Pueblo with much the same objectives as the Huntington Survey. He applied stratigraphic methods he had learned at Harvard from the Egyptologist George A. Reisner.[104]

In 1915, Wissler sent Alfred Kroeber to Zuñi to collect new ethnographic data. While there, Kroeber[105] amused himself by making a surface collection of potsherds, the statistical analysis of which suggested a cultural

98. Stanley A. Freed and Ruth S. Freed, "Clark Wissler and the Development of Anthropology in the United States," *American Anthropologist* 85, no. 4 (1983): 800–825.

99. Clark Wissler, "Explorations in the Southwest by the American Museum," *American Museum Journal* 15, no. 8 (1915): 395–398.

100. Browman and Givens, "Stratigraphic Excavation," p. 93; see also Richard B. Woodbury, "Nels C. Nelson and Chronological Archaeology," *American Antiquity* 25, no. 3 (1960): 400–401 and "Nelson's Stratigraphy" *American Antiquity* 26, no. 1 (1960): 98–99.

101. Nels C. Nelson, "Chronology of the Tano Ruins, New Mexico," *American Anthropologist* 18, no. 2 (1916): 159–180.

102. Alfred V. Kidder, "Reminiscences in Southwestern Archaeology, I," *The Kiva* 25, no. 1 (1960): 1–32.

103. ———, "Southwestern Ceramics: Their Value in Reconstructing the History of the Ancient Cliff Dwelling and Pueblo Tribes—An Exposition from the Point of View of Type Distinctions," (Ph.D. diss., Harvard University, 1914); ———, "Pottery of the Pajarito Plateau and of Some Adjacent Regions in New Mexico," *American Anthropological Association Memoirs* 13 (1915): 407–461.

104. Richard B. Woodbury, *Alfred V. Kidder* (New York: Columbia University Press, 1973).

105. Alfred L. Kroeber, "Zuñi Potsherds," *American Museum of Natural History Anthropological Papers* 18, pt. 1 (1919): 1–37.

sequence, a technique soon elaborated by Leslie Spier.[106] Confirming work by Nelson and others followed in Chaco Canyon and at Aztec Ruin.[107]

Meanwhile, A. E. Douglass had begun his tree-ring studies in the West.[108] Wissler encouraged Douglass to see if his method would work on wood from prehistoric ruins, and quickly found they could relatively date Pueblo Bonito in Chaco Canyon, and the Aztec Ruin. Excited by these results, Wissler[109] proclaimed "The New Archaeology" as a science that was successfully reconstructing cultural chronology through stratigraphic, statistical, and tree-ring methods. By 1921, "time-relations" were presented as the original objective of the Archer M. Huntington Survey.[110]

A. V. Kidder and the First Pecos Conference

In 1924, A. V. Kidder[111] [1964] published the first major Southwestern synthesis, *An Introduction to the Study of Southwestern Archaeology*. A masterful and beautifully written work, it drew from the earlier work of Edgar Lee Hewett,[112] Kidder's own work, and that of the American Museum. It soon became the touchstone for all subsequent students of the subject, and remains so today.

106. Leslie H. Spier, "An Outline for a Chronology of Zuñi Ruins," *American Museum of Natural History Anthropological Papers* 18, pt. 3 (1919): 205–311; ———, "Notes of Some Little Colorado Ruins," *American Museum of Natural History Anthropological Papers* 18, pt. 4 (1918): 332–362; ———, "Ruins in the White Mountains, Arizona," *American Museum of Natural History Anthropological Papers* 18, pt. 5 (1919): 363–387; see also Keith Kintigh, *Settlement, Substance, and Society in Late Zuñi Prehistory*, University of Arizona Anthropological Papers, no. 44 (1985).

107. Earl H. Morris, "Notes on Excavations in the Aztec Ruin," *American Museum of Natural History Anthropological Papers* 26, pt. 5 (1928): 259–420; Clark Wissler, "Unearthing the Secrets of the Aztec Ruin," *Harper's Magazine* no. 853 (1921): 46–56; ———, "Pueblo Bonito as Made Known by the Hyde Expedition," *Natural History* 22, no. 4 (1922): 343–354; ———, "The Aztec Ruin National Monument," *Natural History* 27, no. 3 (1927): 195–201.

108. Andrew E. Douglass, "A Method of Approximating Rainfall Over Long Periods and Some Results of the Application," *Science* n.s. 37 (1913): 33.

109. Clark Wissler, "The New Archaeology," *American Museum Journal* 17, no. 2 (1917): 100–101.

110. ———, "Dating Our Prehistoric Ruins," *Natural History* 21, no. 1 (1921): 13.

111. Alfred V. Kidder, *An Introduction to the Study of Southwestern Archaeology*.

112. Hewett, "Memorandum Concerning the Historic and Prehistoric Ruins"; ———, *Ancient Communities in the American Desert*, ed. Albert H. Schroeder. Archaeological Society of New Mexico Monograph Series: 1 (Santa Fe, 1993).

By 1927 Kidder felt the time was ripe to try to get all of those active in Southwestern archaeology together to see if they could form a consensus about what had been learned and to chart future research directions. Several versions of the newly formulated chronology, and different suggestions about terminology had already been published,[113] and there was a danger that confusion would reign unless something was done. Kidder sent informal invitations to a number of people, and in August, 1927, at his field camp at Pecos Pueblo, forty-six men and women, representing over fourteen institutions, gathered to talk things over.[114] The result[115] was the famous "Pecos Classification" which created a comprehensive scientific model of Puebloan prehistory that remains influential today. The conference set the modern agenda for Southwestern archaeology. Like Lewis Henry Morgan, the Pecos conferees saw the San Juan Basin as a cultural center. Unlike Morgan, however, they declared that maize and pottery were introduced from Mexico. After those "germs of culture" were introduced, they held that the Southwest's culture history was autochthonous, setting aside the nineteenth century preoccupation with Southwest / Mesoamerican connections in favor of reconstructing ever more detailed sequences of cultural phases. A compromise was struck between those who thought architecture should be the basis for classification and those who favored pottery typology. Although a year earlier Folsom points had been found *in situ* with extinct bison bones, a Paleoindian period was not included in the classification. These decisions all would become a focus for future criticism and refinement. But now the scientific study of Southwestern archaeology was firmly established as the joint enterprise of a community of scholars.

Charles Peirce[116] held that science necessarily involves a *community* of workers. Arguably, before the 1927 Pecos Conference, Southwestern archaeology was little more than a series of individualistic efforts of random importance. But consensus was achieved, a community of workers formed,

113. Nels C. Nelson, "Chronology of the Tano Ruins, New Mexico," pp. 159–180; Earl L. Morris, "The House of the Great Kiva at the Aztec Ruin," *American Museum of Natural History Anthropological Papers* 26, pt. 2 (1921): 109–138; Kidder, *An Introduction to the Study of Southwestern Archaeology*.

114. Richard B. Woodbury, *Sixty Years of Southwestern Archaeology: A History of the Pecos Conference* (Albuquerque: University of New Mexico Press, 1993), pp. 19–110.

115. Kidder, "Southwestern Archaeological Conference," *Science* 66 (1927): 489–491.

116. Justus Buchler, ed., *Philosophical Writings of Peirce* (New York: Dover, 1955).

and the science of Southwestern archaeology was launched. It began with observations of U.S. Army and civilian explorers in 1846 and after. It was informed by general anthropological research agendas put forth by Albert Gallatin in the 1840s, Lewis Henry Morgan in the 1870s, and Franz Boas and Clark Wissler in the 1910s. The 1927 Pecos Conference created a scholarly consensus and a new "culture history" research agenda which guided Southwestern archaeology until the 1960s and in some respects to the present day.

DOUGLAS COLE
ALEX LONG

THE BOASIAN ANTHROPOLOGICAL SURVEY TRADITION
The Role of Franz Boas in
North American Anthropological Surveys

The American anthropological survey tradition has been most often associated with the work of the Bureau of American Ethnology.[1] In this interpretation, one can trace a genealogy of government surveys from the Lewis and Clark expedition through the Pacific Railroad surveys, to the Western geographic and geological surveys, and the founding of the Bureau under J. W.

Dedication: In August of 1997, with this essay still in the early process of revision, Douglas Cole unexpectedly passed away. His integrity, generosity and friendship will be missed by those who knew him. This essay is dedicated to his memory.

1. Regardless of whether the anthropology of the Bureau of American Ethnology is defined as a "tradition" or "paradigm," it represents a baseline for nineteenth century American survey anthropology. See Regna Darnell, "The Development of American Anthropology 1879–1920: From the Bureau of American Ethnology to Franz Boas" (Ph.D. diss., University of Pennsylvania, 1969), pp. xxxvi–xxxxiii, 1–3, 13; Virginia Hull M. Noelke, "The Origin and Early History of the Bureau of American Ethnology, 1879–1910" (Ph.D. diss., University of Texas, Austin, 1974); Curtis M. Hinsley, Jr., *Savages and Scientists: The Smithsonian Institution and the Development of American Anthropology, 1846–1910* (Washington, D.C.: Smithsonian Institution Press, 1981); and Regna Darnell, "Theorizing Americanist Anthropology: Continuities from the BAE to the Boasians," eds. Lisa Valentine and R. Darnell, in *Theorizing the Americanist Tradition* (Toronto: University of Toronto Press, in press).

Powell in 1879.[2] While the Bureau played a significant role in American survey anthropology in the late nineteenth century, another distinct tradition exists, the continuities of which remain understated though not entirely unknown. This other tradition centers around Franz Boas, who instigated, defined, and organized its parameters, influencing a generation of anthropologists who came within his purview.

While Franz Boas's methodological assumptions are well-known and his influence on American anthropology is clearly understood, his role in anthropological surveys has not been examined.[3] Historians have occasionally mentioned Boas's relationship to anthropological surveys, but often in regard to his fieldwork and ethnography.[4] When they have specifically addressed his role, they have generally focused on either one survey in its institutional context or several surveys in their regional context.[5] Only

2. Darnell, "Development of American Anthropology," pp. 17–18, 22–33; Hinsley, *Savages and Scientists*, pp. 146–148; and William H. Goetzmann, *Exploration and Empire: The Explorer and the Scientist in the Winning of the American West* (New York: Vintage Books, 1966).

3. George W. Stocking, *Race, Culture, and Evolution: Essays in the History of Anthropology* (New York: The Free Press, 1968), pp. 195–233, 270–307; Darnell, "Development of American Anthropology," pp. 416–461; George W. Stocking, Jr., "The Basic Assumptions of Boasian Anthropology," in *The Shaping of American Anthropology, 1883–1911: A Franz Boas Reader*, ed. George W. Stocking, Jr. (New York: Basic Books, Inc., 1974), pp. 1–20; and George W. Stocking, Jr., "Ideas and Institutions" in *The Ethnographer's Magic and Other Essays in the History of Anthropology* (Madison: University of Wisconsin Press, 1992), pp. 114–177.

4. Ronald P. Rohner, comp. and ed., *The Ethnography of Franz Boas: Letters and Diaries of Franz Boas Written on the Northwest Coast from 1886 to 1931*, Trans. Hedy Parker (Chicago: University of Chicago Press, 1969), pp. xxvi–xxviii; Roger Sanjek, "The Secret Life of Fieldnotes," in *Fieldnotes: The Makings of Anthropology*, ed. Roger Sanjek (Ithaca: Cornell University Press, 1990), p. 196; Stocking, *Shaping of American Anthropology*, pp. 83–86; Ira Jacknis, "The Ethnographic Object and the Object of Ethnology," in *Volksgeist as Method and Ethic: Essays on Boasian Ethnography and the German Anthropological Tradition*, ed. George W. Stocking, Jr. (Wisconsin: University of Madison Press, 1996), pp. 187–194.

5. On institutional contexts, see Stanley A. Freed and Ruth S. Freed, "Clark Wissler and the Development of Anthropology in the United States," *American Anthropologist* 85 (1983): 804–809; Stanley A. Freed, Ruth S. Freed, and Laila Williamson, "Capitalist Philanthropy and Russian Revolutionaries: The Jesup North Pacific Expedition (1897–1902)," *American Anthropologist* 90 (1988): 7–24; Gale Avrith, "Science at the Margins: The British Association and the Foundations of Canadian Anthropology, 1884–1910" (Ph.D. diss., University of Pennsylvania, 1986), pp. 124–174, 224–250, 262–273; and Douglas Cole, "'The Greatest Thing Undertaken by Any Museum': Franz Boas, Morris Jesup and the Jesup North Pacific Expedition," in *Gateways to Jesup II: The Legacy of the Jesup North Pacific Expedition, 1897–1902*, ed. William W. Fitzhugh and Igor I. Krupnik (Seattle: University of Washington Press, forthcoming.) On regional contexts, see Douglas Cole, "Anthropological Exploration and the Great Northwest, 1778–1889 and After," in *Encounters with a Distant Land: Exploration and the Great Northwest*, ed. Carlos A. Schwantes (Moscow: University of Idaho Press, 1994), pp. 156–163.

in a few cases has a historian linked Boas's survey fieldwork to those of his students, situating them within the history of professionalization and Americanist linguistics.[6] In this essay, we briefly examine Boas's plans for anthropology and his neglected role in several anthropological surveys, delineating the similarities and differences among the fieldwork methods of Boas and his students Alfred Kroeber and Edward Sapir in relation to the shared tenets which constitute this tradition.[7]

During the late nineteenth century, North American anthropological surveys were often government-sponsored ventures. However, by the time Boas began to organize surveys, funding sources had shifted to include museum-based philanthropy. For Boas surveys functioned as a means of coordinating the research of his students and collaborators toward a common goal. They were part of his larger plans to establish "a well-organized school of anthropology" and to reconstruct the cultural history of Native North America.[8] He not only conceived the Jesup Expedition and the concurrent Vanishing Tribes surveys with these plans in mind, but later helped place Alfred Kroeber and Edward Sapir in institutions where extensive anthropological surveys were used to continue his historical project. While Boas did not have an administrative role in these later surveys, the fieldwork coordinated by Kroeber and Sapir was defined along Boasian lines. These surveys provided a basis for employment and field experience in anthropology, thereby helping establish the methods and practices of a generation of anthropologists.

The Bureau of American Ethnology as a Model of Survey Anthropology

When Franz Boas emigrated to the United States from Germany in the mid-1880s, he entered a pre-existing North American scientific scene. During the late nineteenth century, professional anthropology on the continent was

6. Darnell, "Development of American Anthropology," pp. 217–218, 252–254, 299–318, 424–444; and Regna Darnell, *Edward Sapir: Linguist, Anthropologist, Humanist* (Berkeley: University of California, 1990), pp. 24–29, 49–82.

7. This essay is part of ongoing research on the ethos, conditions and practices of Boasian anthropological fieldwork.

8. Franz Boas to Zelia Nuttall, 16 May 1901, Franz Boas Professional Papers, American Philosophical Society.

closely associated with geography and government-sponsored surveys. In the United States, the territorial surveys of Clarence King, F. V. Hayden, George M. Wheeler, and John Wesley Powell in the 1870s led to the consolidation and formation of the U.S. Geological Survey in 1879. The Bureau of American Ethnology, established by Powell under the same congressional bill, emerged from this context to become "a permanent anthropological survey."[9] In the same decade, the Geological Survey of Canada under Alfred R. C. Selwyn had its greatest period of expansion, coinciding with the attempts to determine the location of the Canadian Pacific Railway.

Government surveys tended to follow two patterns of organization. Field research was either organized around a corps of scientists in a single expedition, or around individual efforts merged under the banner of a regional or thematic survey. Both patterns in field research were designed for doing extensive mapping and reconnaissance work, not necessarily for intensive studies in one geographical area. The linked team efforts of the expedition, however difficult to manage, allowed for greater administrative control and coordination of research, while the individual-oriented surveys offered more flexibility for shorter seasonal trips, something ideal for the emerging university-based anthropology of Boas and his students.

At this time the Bureau of American Ethnology (hereafter BAE) dominated and defined North American anthropological practice. Powell created the BAE on the premise that ethnology was necessary to the effective administration of Indian Affairs. He was intimately aware of the devastating impact of the Indian wars of the 1870s, and argued that within a few years, "it will be impossible to study our North American Indians in their primitive condition, except from recorded history."[10] The structure and purpose of the Bureau followed that of the geological surveys and their tradition of mapping. Powell organized research through individual surveys and small expeditions, and encouraged a scattering of projects reflecting firsthand fieldwork. The initial projects included a history of treaty relations, a comparative synonymy of tribal groups, and a linguistic classification of the North American Indian Languages.[11]

9. Hinsley, *Savages and Scientists*, p. 147.

10. Noelke, "Bureau of American Ethnology," p. 30; Hinsley, *Savages and Scientists*, pp. 149, 147.

11. Hinsley, *Savages and Scientists*, p. 155.

During these early years, Powell attempted to systematize the linguistic work of the Bureau, which resulted in the publication of "Indian Linguistic Families of America North of Mexico" (1891).[12] He controlled Bureau linguistics and favored a genetic interpretation of American Indian language development. This interpretation was based more on lexical affinities than on grammatical ones. In other words, it relied more on an analysis of the similarities of vocabularies than grammar.[13] Powell also embedded his classification within contemporary theories of evolutionism, which dominated late nineteenth century British and North American anthropology. His classification of Indian languages would have a lasting impact on North American anthropology.

The institutional organization and field research of the BAE represented an important precursor and model for Canadian and American survey anthropology. In 1884, five years after the founding of the BAE, a number of prominent scientists, including Powell, gathered in Montreal for the meetings of the British Association for the Advancement of Science (hereafter BAAS). There eminent British anthropologist E. B. Tylor lobbied for the establishment of a Canadian Bureau of Ethnology, suggesting the BAE as an exemplar. Although his proposal was later turned down by the government, it led to the creation of the Committee to Investigate North-Western Tribes of the Dominion of Canada, which a few years later employed Boas.[14] The BAE provided an important model not only for Canadian anthropology, but also for Boas's later survey projects, which resulted from his plans for North American anthropology.

Boas's Plans for North American Anthropology

Franz Boas' plans for American anthropology can be traced to his emerging scientific ambitions in the mid-1880s.[15] His ambitions initially revolved

---

12. J. W. Powell, "Indian Linguistic Families of America North of Mexico," in *Seventh Annual Report of the Bureau of American Ethnology for 1885–1886* (Washington, DC: Government Printing Office, 1891), pp. 7–142.

13. Mary R. Haas, "Grammar or Lexicon?: The American Indian Side of the Question from Duponceau to Powell," *International Journal of American Linguistics* 35 (1969): 249–51.

14. Avrith, "Science at the Margins," pp. 47–50, 175.

15. In this section, I draw on Douglas Cole's Boas biography manuscript, which will be published in the summer of 1999. Douglas Cole, "A Certain Work Lies Before Me: The Early Years of Franz Boas, 1858–1906" (manuscript, Simon Fraser University, n.d.).

around creating organizations for the development of geography. Boas, it should be remembered, was trained in psychophysics and historical geography at the Universities of Bonn and Kiel in Germany, when contemporary debates in geography focused on whether it was a natural or historical discipline.[16] These debates would remain fundamental to his dualistic conception of "the study of geography."[17] As he later pursued ethnological fieldwork in British Columbia and cultivated his connections to scientific communities, his interests, experiences, and organizational impetus soon turned to anthropology. While Boas's plans cannot be easily spelled out— he articulated them only sporadically and they evolved to reflect his personal ideals, scientific training, professional connections, and developing methodologies—his general intentions and directions are clear.

By 1885 Boas began to articulate his professional ambitions of organizing geography in the United States. "If only I can create a geographical science and [the] places in which it can be nurtured," he wrote his parents, "I would consider myself happy. I consider that alone to be a worthy task."[18] The "places" to which Boas referred were the institutions and organizations needed for building a scientific community. At the time he believed geography in the United States was amateurish and did not follow the same rigorous standards as it did in Germany. He pursued a career in the United States partly because he thought he could better realize his plans there.[19]

While working as an assistant editor for the journal *Science* a few years later, he invested the journal with his high expectations, hoping it would provide "an opportunity to awaken here an interest in my field."[20] He likened it to an American version of the respected German journal, *Peter-*

---

16. Matti Bunzl, "Franz Boas and the Humboldtian Tradition: From Volksgeist to Nationalcharakter to an Anthropological Concept of Culture," in *Volksgeist as Method and Ethic*, ed. George W. Stocking, Jr. (Wisconsin: University of Madison Press, 1996), pp. 51–52; Klaus-Peter Koepping, *Adolph Bastian and the Psychic Unity of Mankind: The Foundations of Anthropology in Nineteenth Century Germany* (New York: University of Queensland Press, 1983), pp. 60–68.

17. Franz Boas, "The Study of Geography," *Science* 9 (1887): 137–141.

18. Boas to parents, 14 January 1885, Franz Boas Family Papers, American Philosophical Society.

19. Boas saw more opportunities in an American future than in a German one: "Everything in our science is in the raw," he told his uncle, Jacobi. "Here I see a possibility of success; at home in Germany, I see none at all." Boas to Jacobi, 13 January 1885, Boas Professional Papers.

20. Boas to parents, 10 January 1887, Boas Family Papers.

manns Geographische Mitteilungen, and believed it could provide a forum for scientific geography in the U.S. "If I can awaken interest in my science and make our paper a central place for geography, I will have accomplished something."[21] He not only thought of forming a "geographical institute" like the Perthes Institute in Gotha, Germany, but also cultivated plans for founding an ethnological society which might sponsor courses at the American Geographical Society and the American Museum of Natural History in New York. He even pondered the possibility of launching arctic and antarctic expeditions.[22] Turning *Science* into an American *Petermanns*, founding a geographical institute, and creating an American equivalent to the Berlin Anthropological Society—all reflected his high ambitions, which later took form in his plans for organizing American anthropology.

By the early 1890s, Boas had formed relationships with prominent scientists in Germany, Canada, and the United States. They included his mentors, employers and associates. Boas, though still very much on the periphery, had joined an elite professional community, comprised of men who either had organized geographical societies or administered and served on geological surveys. In Germany, the young Boas knew Johann Wilhelm Reiss and worked for Adolph Bastian. Reiss, vice president of the Berlin Geographical Society, introduced Boas to many luminaries in Berlin's geographical community. Bastian, who met Boas through Reiss and later employed him at the Royal Ethnographic Museum in Berlin, was an important theorist and organizer in German anthropology.[23] In the United States, Boas worked with J. W. Powell and F. W. Putnam. Powell, before founding the BAE, led the famous Colorado River expeditions. Putnam, who sponsored and mentored Boas during the 1890's, served on the Kentucky Geological Survey and later on Wheeler's survey in California.[24] In Canada, the Northwest Coast committee of the BAAS, which hired Boas from 1888 to 1897, included E. B. Tylor, George Dawson and Horatio Hale. Tylor, an Oxford-based anthropologist, chaired the committee from afar and inspired Boas to use statistical methods in his diffusionist studies of Northwest Coast

21. Boas to parents, 12 February 1887, Boas Family Papers.
22. Boas to parents, 28 June 1887, 25 November 1887, Boas Family Papers.
23. Bunzl, "Franz Boas and Humboldtian Tradition," pp. 47–49.
24. A. L. Kroeber, "Frederic Ward Putnam," *American Anthropologist* 17 (1915): 714, 717.

myths.[25] Dawson, a geologist (and later director) for the Geological Survey of Canada, compiled ethnological collections and published studies on the Haida, Kwakiutl, Interior Salish, and Yukon Indians.[26] Hale served on the Wilkes Expedition some fifty years earlier, where he collected anthropological and philological data in Polynesia and the Oregon territory.[27] As Boas's immediate superior, he directed his fieldwork toward comparative ends. Whether they taught, employed or mentored Boas, all were respected in their fields and experienced in conducting geographical and anthropological research. Significantly, Boas maintained relationships with these men throughout his career.

The early 1890s represented the nadir of Boas's professional career. The story is well-known. He wandered from job to job, never quite securing a permanent position. He worked as a docent at Clark University for a year, then as Putnam's assistant at the 1893 World's Columbian Exposition in Chicago. He continued doing fieldwork for the BAAS in British Columbia, but also made trips to Oregon to study the Chinook, to California to make somatological measurements of southern California tribes, and gathered casts, photographs, and collections for the American Museum. During these years, he spent much of his time doing fieldwork, an aggregation of experiences which proved useful to his future. His plans now shifted to converge on anthropology.

In 1895, with the help of Putnam and his uncle, Boas secured an associate curatorship at the American Museum, where Putnam worked as a part-time curator. Within a year Boas was also appointed as a lecturer in physical anthropology at Columbia University. With a secure institutional base, he finally was able to cultivate some of his long dreamt plans. But as his plans and experiences had moved closer to anthropology, he began to develop a specific historical approach to the study of North American Indians.

Boas's approach to ethnology was historical and based on diffusionist theories he had learned in geography. Boas was particularly interested in the histories of North American Indians, but with no written documents to

---

25. Stocking, *Shaping of American Anthropology*, pp. 129–130.

26. Douglas Cole and Bradley Lochner, eds., *The Journals of George M. Dawson: British Columbia, 1875–1878* (Vancouver: University of British Columbia Press, 1989), pp. 18–22.

27. Jacob W. Gruber, "Horatio Hale and the Development of American Anthropology," *Proceedings of the American Philosophical Society* 111 (1967): 9.

work from, he needed a reliable way to reconstruct their histories. Between 1891 and 1896, in an attempt to dispute the contemporary and doctrinaire "laws by which the culture of all mankind grew," he developed a method from which to infer the gradual diffusion of myths among neighboring tribes.[28] He described this method in his 1896 essay on "The Growth of Indian Mythologies," where he applied Bastian's notion of universal elementary ideas (*Elementargedanken*) and derivative folk ideas (*Völkergedanken*) to the mythology of the Northwest Coast tribes. According to Bastian, elementary ideas were transformed into local folk ideas in a "geographical province" or culture area.[29] "The forms which these [elementary] ideas take among primitive people of different parts of the world, 'die Völker-Gedanken,'" wrote Boas,

> are due partly to the geographical environment and partly to the peculiar character of the people, and to a large extent to their history. In order to understand the growth of the peculiar psychical life of the people, the historical growth of its customs must be investigated most closely, and the only method by which the history can be investigated is by means of a detailed comparison of the tribe with its neighbors.[30]

By examining the distribution of folktales and elementary ideas among tribes and their neighbors in a delineated cultural area, it was possible to better "understand the growth of the peculiar psychical life of the people."[31] Although this history had to be investigated before the psychological significance could be determined, the latter was another aspect of this method: to capture "the native point of view."

The best way Boas believed to understand "the native point of view" was through the careful study of language. Although his early linguistic fieldwork addressed classificatory problems, by 1894 he was committed to the intensive study of individual languages and their grammatical structures.[32]

---

28. Franz Boas, "The Growth of Indian Mythologies," *Journal of American Folklore* 9 (1896): 2, 11.

29. Alexander Goldenweiser, "Diffusionism and the American School of Historical Ethnology" *American Journal of Sociology* 31 (1925): 34.

30. Boas, "Growth of Indian Mythologies," p. 11.

31. Boas, "Growth of Indian Mythologies," p. 11.

32. George W. Stocking, Jr., "The Boas Plan for the Study of American Indian Languages," in *The Ethnographer's Magic* (Madison: University of Wisconsin Press, 1992), pp. 66–67.

As Regna Darnell and Joel Sherzer note, "Boas, in the tradition of von Humboldt and Steinthal, believed that a grammar should represent the way or ways in which a particular group of people viewed and verbalized the world around them. Because such a grammar was felt to reflect world view at a particular moment in time, it was necessarily synchronic and made no attempt to describe the origin of linguistic structure."[33] By this time Boas's approach to linguistics was descriptive and synchronic rather than comparative and diachronic. His methods in ethnology and linguistics, aimed at the reconstruction of the cultural history of Native North America, would form the basis for his teachings and a new anthropological survey tradition.

The Boasian Anthropological Survey Tradition

Franz Boas defined the initial parameters for the research methods and fieldwork practices of anthropologists, who participated in and helped constitute the Boasian anthropological survey tradition. This tradition, stretching across different regions and organized under a number of institutions, spanned nearly forty years: from Boas's fieldwork for the Northwest Coast committee, through his organization of the Jesup Expedition and the "Vanishing Tribes of North America" project, to his influence on the surveys of California and Canada, administered successively by his students Alfred Kroeber and Edward Sapir.

Despite individual idiosyncrasies and conflicting research strategies, this tradition was comprised of at least six shared tenets: first, a tendency toward anti-evolutionism; second, the use of diffusionist methods; third, the ethos of salvage ethnology; fourth, the collection of linguistic texts; fifth, the use of the traditional four fields of anthropology; and sixth, the employment of university-trained anthropologists.[34] These tenets were all aspects of Boas's project for reconstructing the cultural history of Native North America, which was the unifying rationale behind his early work and that of his students Kroeber and Sapir. However, neither Kroeber nor

---

33. Regna Darnell and Joel Sherzer, "Areal Linguistic Studies in North America: A Historical Perspective," *International Journal of American Linguistics* 37 (1971): 21

34. For comparable discussions on the philosophical and methodological assumptions of the "Boasian paradigm," see Darnell, "Development of American Anthropology," pp. 420–461; and Stocking, "Basic Assumptions," pp. 1–20.

Sapir equally followed all of the tenets; sometimes they emphasized one while de-emphasizing another, partly pursuing their own interests. Nevertheless, these tenets, which are briefly described below, constitute a single tradition, suggesting continuities in an inherited pattern of theories, methods and practices.

Boas instilled in many of his students a tendency toward anti-evolutionism. Evolutionism, in essence, assumed the uniformity of human nature and the progressive development of hierarchical "culture stages" from simple to complex forms.[35] Anthropologists like Tylor, Powell and the Philadelphia linguist Daniel Brinton extrapolated sequential stages of development for every aspect of language and culture, presupposing contemporary European and American societies as standards for comparison. Boas opposed this sort of cultural determinism and criticized its assumptions. Whether he directed his critique at "the limitations of the comparative method" (1896) or embedded it within his "history of anthropology" (1904), it was based on methodological and empirical concerns.[36] After all, Boas, in the words of George Stocking, "was not attacking evolutionism as a timeless abstraction but as an abstraction derived from a particular point in time."[37] What was needed, he argued, was an inductive historical approach. In a letter soliciting funding for his anthropological investigations, he described what he believed to be the fundamental differences between the evolutionary and historical points of view.

> Up to the present time there are two fundamentally distinct points of view among anthropologists. The one group of investigators consider the type of culture of any given tribe as representing a definite stage of human evolution and as an independent or almost entirely independent product of native thought: the other group of investigators is more inclined to consider the development of culture of each tribe as a complex historical growth, and favors the belief that the history of human evolution must be derived from a comparison of individual historical developments.[38]

35. George W. Stocking, Jr., *Victorian Anthropology* (New York: The Free Press, 1987), pp. 170–178, 286–289.

36. Franz Boas, "The Limitations of the Comparative Method," *Science* 4 (1896): 901–908; and Franz Boas, "The History of Anthropology" in Stocking, *Shaping of American Anthropology*, pp. 23–36.

37. Stocking, *Race, Culture, and Evolution*, p. 211.

38. Boas to R. S. Woodward, 13 January 1905, Boas Professional Papers.

The historical point of view, which compared the "individual historical developments" of the culture of each tribe, characterized the method of Boas
and his students.

Boas's historical method, as already noted, was based on the principles
of diffusion. Boas analyzed the distribution and dissemination of historical
phenomena across contiguous geographical areas to potentially multiple
sources, emphasizing geographical, psychological and historical causes.
Languages, myths, customs, and even patterns in art could then be interpreted as the historical products of migrations, accretions and borrowings.
Even though diffusionism and evolutionism were not mutually exclusive,
his students came to see it that way. They elaborated Boas's concern for the
geographical specificity of cultural relations (a la Bastian's "geographical
province) into the "culture area" concept, which dominated much of their
survey work.[39]

Boas and his students also shared what might be called the ethos of salvage ethnology. Salvage ethnology at the turn of the century stressed the
urgency of collecting the languages, cultures and material objects of "primitive" peoples, who were believed to be either rapidly dying out or losing
their culture through assimilation. Bolstered by the object-orientation of
the museum trade and the arts and crafts movement, it fueled the consumption of cultural objects, such as baskets and ceremonial regalia, to the
point of robbing some native communities of their cultural heritage.[40] Salvage ethnology emphasized the necessity of research in native communities threatened by centuries of colonial conflict, at a time when the myth of
the "vanishing Indian" dominated popular culture; it thus inspired a powerful sense of responsibility to history, science, and humanity. But this attitude often accompanied the assumption that cultural change in tribal societies brought degeneration, social disintegration, and the loss of authentic

39. Goldenweiser, "Diffusionism and the American School," 27–38; Darnell, "Development of American Anthropology," 436–41.
40. Jacknis, "Ethnographic Object," 188–189; Douglas Cole, *Captured Heritage: The
Scramble for Northwest Coast Artifacts* (Vancouver: UBC Press, 1985), 212–215; and Mela-
nie Herzog, "Aesthetics and Meanings: The Arts and Crafts Movement and the Revival of
American Indian Basketry," in *The Substance of Style: Perspectives on the American Arts
and Crafts Movement*, ed. Bert Denker (Hanover: University Press of New England, 1996),
pp. 69–70, 75–79.

traditions. Anthropology, in this context, became a moral pursuit geared toward the preservation of the past.[41] "If we do not collect this material," Boas wrote, "our failure to do so will be held up to our generation as a constant reproach."[42] Boas and his students used salvage rhetoric to propagate humanistic sympathies for the cultures of aboriginal peoples and engage philanthropic interests needed for the funding of survey fieldwork.[43]

Another tenet in this tradition involved the value placed on collecting linguistic texts. Boas encouraged his students and collaborators to work closely with native informants and transcribe their myths into linguistic texts and grammatical data. Sapir followed Boas's position on linguistic text collection more rigorously than Kroeber. Boas, in a testimony defending his jointly-sponsored expeditions, described what he required of his students:

> [I ask them] to collect certain things and to collect with everything they get information in the native language and to obtain grammatical information that is necessary to explain their texts. Consequently the results of their journeys are the following: They get specimens; they get explanations of specimens; they get connected texts that partly refer to the specimens and partly refer simply to abstract things concerning the people; and they get grammatical information.[44]

The mythological texts were not only needed for linguistic purposes, but also for contextualizing museum specimens, reconstructing cultural history, and documenting the native point of view. As Regna Darnell asserts, "Boas taught his students to argue that the data-base for both ethnography and linguistics ideally was to be texts in the words of native speakers of aboriginal languages, in those languages, presented with a translation which, whatever its literary merits (usually minimal), preserved as much as pos-

41. Jacob Gruber, "Ethnographic Salvage and the Shaping of Anthropology," *American Anthropologist* 72 (1970): 1297–1298. *Cf.* James Clifford, "Of Other Peoples: Beyond the 'Salvage' Paradigm," in *Discussions in Contemporary Culture*, No. 1, ed. Hal Foster (Seattle: Bay Press, 1987), pp. 121–130.

42. Boas to Archer M. Huntington, 18 May, 1904, Huntington file, Department of Anthropology Archives, American Museum of Natural History.

43. Regna Darnell, letter to Alex Long, 3 March 1998.

44. Hinsley, *Savages and Scientists*, p. 268.

sible of their original structure."[45] The value of the text was in representing the "original structure" of native thought—"the peculiar psychical life
of the people." The importance of this tenet was not simply methodological, but also humanist: it helped to create sources of literature comparable
to that of the Western literary tradition.[46]

Boasians also broadly defined anthropology to include the traditional
four fields: ethnology, linguistics, archaeology and physical anthropology.
Each field respectively had a different object of study (culture, language,
prehistory, and race) that required different methods. Boas worked and
trained students in ethnology, linguistics, and physical anthropology, but
often sent students who were interested in archaeology to Putnam at Harvard. Kroeber later continued to train students along these lines, sometimes
requiring they spend a year studying linguistics with Boas at Columbia.
Although Kroeber emphasized ethnology in his survey of California, and
Sapir, linguistics, in his survey of Canada, neither paid much attention to
physical anthropology. Nevertheless, they encouraged the use of all four
fields in their respective surveys.

Finally, Boasian surveys tended to employ university-trained anthropologists. Boas preferred to hire trained fieldworkers, and required of his
students rigorous study in linguistics and statistics. Kroeber sometimes
employed the university-trained students of Boas, Putnam or himself, but
also deviated from this ideal to include self-trained anthropologists. Sapir,
like Boas, preferred trained anthropologists, especially linguists, and frequently employed Boas-trained fieldworkers to the exclusion of others.[47]
The concern for employing university-trained anthropologists was part of
an attempt to promote professionalism in anthropology.

These six tenets gradually evolved out of Boas's expectations and experiences, and can be traced in his survey fieldwork and in that of his students. Boas's initial fieldwork with the Inuit on Baffin Island and a few years

45. Regna Darnell, "The Boasian Text Tradition and the History of Anthropology,"
Culture 12 (1992): 42.
46. George W. Stocking, Jr., "The Aims of Boasian Ethnography: Creating the Materials for Traditional Humanistic Scholarship," *History of Anthropology Newsletter* 4, no. 2
(1977): 5. See also Gruber, "Ethnographic Salvage," pp. 1297–1298; Darnell, "Boasian Text
Tradition," p. 45; and Jacknis, "Ethnographic Object," p. 193.
47. Darnell, "Canadian National Museum," pp. 163, 173.

later with the Kwakiutl and Salish of Vancouver Island served as precursors and exemplars. Beginning in the summer of 1883, Boas spent one year in Cumberland Sound and on Davis Strait off Baffin Island. He was interested in questions about the origin and history of Inuktitut migrations. Communicating in English and pidgin English, Boas transcribed myths, tales and songs, which he later asked Henrik Johannes Rink (an authority in Inuit languages) to translate. He used these texts to trace the history and migrations of the Inuktitut.[48] What is particularly significant here is Boas's use of diffusionism to explain the history of the population movements of Inuit peoples.

While his initial fieldwork had been among the Inuit, in 1886 Boas undertook, at his own initiative and expense, a field trip to British Columbia and Vancouver Island. He had been attracted to the problems of American Indian anthropology by the presence of a group of touring Bella Coolas in Berlin a year earlier. His report from this research attracted the attention of Horatio Hale, who had collaborated in the establishment of the Northwest Coast committee. Hale, who basically ran the committee, approached Boas to undertake the fieldwork in 1887.[49]

Over the next ten years, Boas made five trips to British Columbia under the sponsorship of the BAAS and the Canadian government (1888–1897). He was charged with securing "a general synopsis of the ethnology of the whole of British Columbia, according to linguistic stocks." Boas, however, preferred localized studies of single tribal or linguistic groups to the general comparative approach. He wanted to focus on the central and north coast, and challenged the restrictions imposed by Hale. Boas complained of the survey method to his wife, noting that he achieved only "one quarter of what I did last time [in 1886]. This is due to the fact that I had to travel back and forth so much and had to deal with so many different tribes."[50] Despite their differences, Boas complied with Hales demands, later noting the work was fragmentary, but "the opportunity which I have had to be-

---

48. Stocking, *Race, Culture, and Evolution*, p. 146; Douglas Cole and Ludger Muller-Wille, "Franz Boas' Expedition to Baffin Island, 1883–1884," *Etudes Inuit Studies* 8 (1984): 51, 53–54.

49. George W. Stocking, Jr., *After Tylor: British Social Anthropology, 1888–1951* (Madison: University of Wisconsin Press, 1995), p. 85.

50. From diary dated, 24 June 1888, in Rohner, "Ethnography of Franz Boas," p. 103.

come acquainted with so many different tribes was very welcome."[51] These short reconnaissance trips became by default exemplars for later anthropological research.

During his BAAS research, Boas began modifying his methods and learning new ones. After his first field trip in 1888, Hale directed Boas to take anthropometric measurements of the native physiognomy. That same year, under the stimulation of Tylor's work, Boas began to apply Tylor's methods in studying folk ideas.[52] Tylor furnished him with a way to statistically tabulate and map out the folktale and elementary ideas. By studying and mapping these folktales, Boas was able to learn about the process of myth construction, which suggested according to Stocking, "a model of the development of culture in general."[53]

Boas's work for the BAAS, which continued until 1897, overlapped with the first season of the Jesup North Pacific Expedition (1897–1902).[54] Sponsored by Morris K. Jesup of the American Museum, the expedition was organized to investigate the long-standing question of the historical relations between the races of America and Asia. Although Putnam assisted in planning it, Boas was in charge. The expedition was essentially a continuation of Boas's BAAS fieldwork: "A systematic investigation of the tribes of British Columbia was inaugurated by the British Association for the Advancement of Science. . . . The Jesup Expedition continues the systematic work of this committee over a wider area, and expands it on lines that were not touched upon before."[55] Boas had been pondering the question of relations for some time. By 1895 he had been certain that Northwest Coast mythology shared similarities with widespread "Old World" myths, and that a cultural connection between Asia and America was "very probable."[56] Many points of resemblance suggested an importation of ideas from Asia, and contact between the Pacific coasts of the two continents must have ex-

---

51. Horatio Hale to Boas, 21 May 1888, Boas Professional Papers; Boas to parents, 15 January 1891, Boas Family Papers.

52. Stocking, *Race, Culture, and Evolution*, p. 207.

53. Stocking, *Shaping of American Anthropology*, p. 130.

54. See Cole, "'Greatest Thing Undertaken,'" and Freed, Freed, and Williamson, "Capitalist Philanthropy," pp. 7–24.

55. Franz Boas, "The Jesup North Pacific Expedition," in Stocking, *Shaping of American Anthropology*, p. 112.

56. Franz Boas, "Zur Ethnologie von British-Columbien," *Verhandlungen der Gesellschaft für Erdkunde zur Berlin* 22 (1895): 270.

isted for long periods.[57] These assumptions would form the scientific premise for the research.

The expedition was a grandiose plan, designed to demonstrate the effi-
cacy of Boas's historical methodology. Over a five-year period, he sent parties into the field on both sides of the North Pacific to conduct work on the
American Northwest Coast, along the Okhotsk Sea, and in the Bering Sea.
Boas supervised a corps of anthropologists, including Livingston Farrand,
Harlan Smith, John Swanton, James Teit and George Hunt on the American side, and German sinologist Berthold Laufer and the Siberian special-
ists Waldemar Bogoras, Leo Sternberg, and Waldemar Jochelson on the
Siberian side. While the impact of the Jesup Expedition was more significant on Siberian scholarship than it was on North American, the expedition nevertheless represented Boas's first attempt at organizing and coordinating the fieldwork of others along diffusionist lines.[58]

Simultaneous with the Jesup Expedition, Boas initiated the "Vanishing
Tribes of North America" project (1899–1906), attempting to secure funds
to investigate the imperiled knowledge of the western American Indians.
The Vanishing Tribes project was not an expeditionary enterprise, but a
loosely-organized series of individual surveys, codifying the salvage ethos
in its title. "[O]ur generation," Boas wrote to Jesup, "is the last that will be
able to collect the data which will form the basis of the early history of America."[59] His plan had been to "call into life a thorough investigation of the
dying tribes and to build up ethnology to a recognized discipline in the university."[60] With philanthropic donations from Mrs. Jesup, Henry Villard,
and C.P. Huntington, Boas sent anthropologists Roland Dixon, Alfred
Kroeber, Clark Wissler, Robert Lowie, and Livingston Farrand throughout
the continent to study tribes which Boas believed were in danger of imminent destruction. This corps of anthropologists represented a new generation of professionals, trained in linguistics and ethnology in the seminars

57. Franz Boas, "The Indians of British Columbia," *Bulletin of the American Geographical Society* 28 (1896): 242–243.
58. William F. Fitzhugh and Aron Crowell, *Crossroads of Continents: Cultures of Si-
beria and Alaska* (Washington: Smithsonian Institution Press, 1988), p. 15.
59. Boas to M. K. Jesup, 21 March 1898, 1898 Central Archives, American Museum of
Natural History.
60. Boas to Baron Ferdinand von Andrian-Werberg, 8 August 1898, Boas Professional
Papers.

of Columbia and the study collections of the American and Peabody museums. "The time is past," wrote Boas, "when anthropological work may be entrusted . . . to a man whose scientific judgment and knowledge in other branches of science can stand in place of a good training in anthropology."[61] With hopes for this new generation, his plans were becoming ever more encompassing, including designs on California and even China.[62]

By this time, Boas's plans for institutionalizing American anthropology were finally beginning to congeal. He had wedged himself into a joint appointment at Columbia and the American Museum, merged the Anthropological Club of New York with the American Ethnological Society to rejuvenate local interest, organized anthropological investigations all over the continent, and developed a cooperative program with Putnam at Harvard.[63] (Putnam of course had been critical to Boas' success, as Boas had literally followed in his footsteps from Chicago to New York.[64]) "If my activity continues to develop," he wrote his parents in 1899, "I will soon have an institute as large and as significant as Washington's Bureau of Ethnology." And in time, he hoped, "almost all of the American ethnologists of the next generation entirely or partly will come from my school."[65] Boas finally had the institutional foundations and professional networks which seemed to ensure success. If twelve years earlier Perthes had embodied a German model for his plans for geography, then the BAE clearly represented the American model for anthropology. Boas had merely transposed his plans and ambitions from one discipline to the other.

Within a few years, however, rifts formed in his institutional base. He had been slow to put up exhibits at the American Museum, subordinating

61. Boas to Zelia Nuttall, 20 November 1901, University of California file, Department of Anthropology Archives, American Museum of Natural History.

62. Boas to Zelia Nuttall, 16 May 1901, Boas Professional Papers.

63. George W. Stocking, Jr., "Franz Boas and the Founding of the American Anthropological Society," *American Anthropologist* 62 (1960): 1.

64. Putnam's role in this tradition is unfortunately beyond the limits of this essay. See Darnell, "Development of American Anthropology," pp. 159, 165–176; Joan Mark, *Four Anthropologists: An American Science in its Early Years* (New York: Science History Publications, 1980), pp. 5–11, 14–21, 31–55; and Stephen O. Murray, *Theory Groups and the Study of Language in North America: A Social History* (Philadelphia: John Benjamins Publishing Co., 1994), pp. 38–39.

65. Boas to parents, 25 June 1899, Boas Family Papers.

administrative plans for current collections to the contingencies of his exacting research. After a bitter dispute over museum methods and departmental authority, Boas resigned from the American Museum in 1905.[66] Boas's resignation significantly reduced his opportunities for anthropological investigations.

During this time, museums not only provided the dominant institutional context for anthropological research, but also the impetus for collecting in the first place. The funding for anthropological surveys, in other words, came from museum philanthropy. Each of the surveys, except for the Vanishing Tribes project, was established with the purpose of adding to or creating museum collections. George Dawson's long term plans for the Northwest Coast Committee involved creating a seed collection for a national museum. The Jesup Expedition and the Vanishing Tribes surveys built collections for the American Museum. If a museum was not the impetus for founding a survey, then it was the ultimate destination for the accrued material collections.

Boas's successor at the American Museum, Clark Wissler, continued the research of the Vanishing Tribes surveys. Wissler placed special emphasis on Plains and Plateau groups, sending Robert Lowie to the Lemhi Reserve in Idaho and later to the Blackfoot of Southern Alberta, and Pliny Goddard to work with the Chippewa, Beaver, and Sarsi, among others. Kroeber, as well, would work with Wissler's survey in the southwest. Wissler's own interests centered on the Blackfoot and most of the American Museum work in the next decades concentrated on tribes east of the continental divide.[67]

By the turn of the century, Boas had established a reputation as a tireless fieldworker, museum curator, and survey organizer. He used his reputation and connections to place his students Kroeber and Sapir within

66. Ira Jacknis, "Franz Boas and Exhibits: On the Limitations of the Museum Method of Anthropology," in *Objects and Others: Essays on Museums and Material Culture*, ed. George W. Stocking, Jr. (Madison: University of Wisconsin Press, 1985), pp. 86–89, 105–108.

67. Wissler and Lowie arguably continue this Boasian anthropological survey tradition, but due to various constraints, we were unable to examine their research in depth. Nevertheless, they deserve inclusion in this tradition. See Fowler and Wilcox in this volume for more continuities. And for valuable reminiscences on fieldwork conditions and practices, see Robert H. Lowie, *Robert H. Lowie, Ethnologist* (Berkeley: University of California, 1959).

emerging anthropological institutions.[68] Kroeber, under the endorsement of both Boas and Putnam, was appointed instructor at the University of California in 1901. Nine years later, Sapir secured a job through Boas as director of the Anthropological Division of the Geological Survey of Canada (hereafter GSC). Without Boas's recommendations, it is doubtful if either of them would have landed positions in these institutions.

Anthropology at the University of California was organized as a museum-oriented department in 1901. Within two years, the department established the Ethnological and Archaeological Survey of California (beginning in 1903) under the direction of Kroeber. The survey of California, funded by philanthropist Phoebe Hearst until 1918, continued sporadically into the 1920s, but never officially ended.[69] The survey was designed to coordinate the disparate approaches of the four fields of anthropology in an attempt "to solve the great problem of the relationship of the numerous groups of Indians in California, and their relationship with peoples of other parts of the continent and possibly with certain tribes of Asia." This "great problem" was essentially the same one Boas articulated six years earlier, aimed at "obtaining a knowledge of the first peopling of the Pacific Coast and of the early migrations. . . ." In this sense, it was a continuation of Boas's plans for the Jesup Expedition, with Kroeber following similar methods of diffusion for "determining the distribution of a tribe."[70]

The initial fieldwork involved mapping the linguistic and ethnological diversity of Native California Indians. The purpose of the fieldwork, similar to that of the Jesup and Vanishing Tribes surveys, was to preserve linguistic and ethnological data for historical reconstructions of the pre-contact moment, data based on the "memory culture" of the last members of a gen-

---

68. Boas to Zelia Nuttall, 16 May 1901; Boas to R. W. Brock, 14 May 1910, Boas Professional Papers.

69. See Alex Long, "From Survey to Handbook: A. L. Kroeber and the Hearst Anthropological Survey of Native California, 1903–1918" (master's thesis, Simon Fraser University, 1998). Cf. Timothy H. H. Thoresen, "Paying the Piper and Calling the Tune: The Beginnings of Academic Anthropology in California," *Journal of the History of the Behavioral Sciences* 11 (1975): pp. 271–273. During the mid-1930s, Kroeber again pursued research related to the California survey, when he organized the Culture Element Survey of Native Western North America (1934–1938). See Harold Driver, "The Contribution of A. L. Kroeber to Culture Area Theory and Practice," *Indiana University Publications in Anthropology and Linguistics, Memoir* 18 (1962): 17–18.

70. Kroeber, "Survey of California," p. 571.

eration who still spoke their indigenous languages.[71] "Nowhere in America," wrote Kroeber, "has there been such a diversity of Indian languages, a condition which has long puzzled anthropologists. . . . These Indian languages are now fast disappearing. . . . and hardly a year passes without some special dialect, or even language, becoming extinct."[72] While many amateur anthropologists worked for the survey, the fieldworkers generally consisted of students trained by either Boas, Putnam, and/or Kroeber, including Dixon, Sapir, Samuel Barrett, J. Alden Mason, Nels Nelson, and T. T. Waterman. Pliny Goddard and Constance Goddard DuBois were notable exceptions. The work varied from studies of mythology and basketry to religious ceremonies and phonetics to geography and shellmound excavations, all of which were contextualized within a specified culture area.

What distinguished the California survey from Boas's surveys was the application of an areal approach to linguistics and the explicit formulation of the "culture area" concept. In linguistics, Kroeber and Dixon, as early as 1903, began cooperating on comparative studies of California Indian languages. Although Boas did not agree with this comparative work, noting to Kroeber, "that you should take up one group by itself and work it out thoroughly," they persisted by making areal, and then later, genetic classifications.[73] Between 1912 and 1919, in collaboration with Sapir, Kroeber and Dixon challenged Powell's classification of California by consolidating the twenty-two linguistic families into seven larger families.[74] In ethnology, beginning about the same time, Kroeber started mapping the distribution of culture traits into larger patterns of cultural types. He was essentially modifying Boas's diffusionist method, applying it not only to myths, but also a minutia of other cultural traits, like games, burial practices, house styles, and basketry designs. He then correlated the distribution of these traits into patterns which comprised cultural types, later arguing that "the most in-

71. John W. Burton, "Shadows at Twilight: A Note on History and the Ethnographic Present," *Proceedings of the American Philosophical Society* 132 (1988): 424.

72. Kroeber, "Survey of California," p. 571.

73. Boas to A. L. Kroeber, 6 January 1902, A. L. Kroeber Papers (Banc MSS C-B 925), The Bancroft Library, University of California, Berkeley.

74. Darnell and Sherzer, "Areal Linguistic Studies," p. 22; Dell Hymes, "Alfred Louis Kroeber," *Language* 37 (1961): 8–11; and Roland B. Dixon and A. L. Kroeber, "Linguistic Families of California," *University of California Publications in American Archaeology and Ethnology* 16 (1919): 47–118.

tensive development or greatest specialization of culture has occurred at the hearth."[75] With this method, Kroeber, as Thomas Buckley notes, "objectified culture as its content and simultaneously abstracted this content from its social context. . . ."[76] Kroeber's fieldwork culminated in the publication of his *Handbook of the Indians of California* (1925), a comparative ethnography illustrating his theory of culture areas.

In 1910, Edward Sapir, as chief ethnologist at the Anthropological Division of the Geological Survey of Canada in Ottawa, organized the Canadian anthropological survey (1910–1925) along Boasian lines. The purpose of the survey was mapping the aboriginal languages and cultures of Canada. In his circular announcement, he noted the BAE as an important example of government anthropology as well as the "early efforts" of Dawson, Boas and the Jesup Expedition.[77] Sapir employed the "culture area" concept from the beginning, dividing Canada into five distinct areas, and stressing intensive ethnological and linguistics studies including text collection. Overall, he was less interested in survey work than his specific work on Nootka and other Athabascan languages.[78] He mostly employed university-trained researchers, including not only Boas students, like Alexander Goldenweiser, Paul Radin, and Harlan Smith, but also Oxford students, like Marius Barbeau and Diamond Jenness, among others. Sapir also inherited and incorporated the anthropological research of the Canadian Arctic Expedition (1913–1918), which studied the Eskimo of Coronation Gulf and Victoria Island in Northwestern Canada.[79] Sapir's use of culture areas, emphasis on linguistic text collection, and concern for professionally trained anthropologists were all hallmarks of the Boasian anthropological survey

75. A. L. Kroeber, *Handbook of the Indians of California* (Washington, DC: Government Printing Office, 1925; New York: Dover Publications, 1976), p. 901.

76. Thomas Buckley, "The Little History of Pitiful Events": The Epistemological and Moral Contexts of Kroeber's Californian Ethnology," in *Volksgeist as Method and Ethic*, ed. George W. Stocking, Jr. (Wisconsin: University of Madison Press, 1996), p. 272.

77. Edward Sapir, "An Anthropological Survey of Canada," *Science* 34 (December 8, 1911): 789–790.

78. Darnell, *Edward Sapir*, 49, 63, 52, and 62; Regna Darnell, "The Sapir Years at the Canadian National Museum in Ottawa," in *Edward Sapir: Appraisals of His Life and Work*, ed. Konrad Koerner (Philadelphia: John Benjamins Publishing, 1984), pp. 163–167.

79. Morris Zaslow, *Reading the Rocks: The Story of the Geological Survey of Canada, 1842–1972* (Toronto: Macmillan Co., 1975), pp. 279–280, 319–321.

tradition. Even his research rationale echoed a recurrent ultimatum: "What is lost now will never be recovered again." [80]

Between 1912 and 1918, Sapir and Kroeber engaged in a productive, long distant collaboration. During these years, Sapir began to articulate a methodology for uncovering the history of the languages and cultures of North America.[81] At the urging of Kroeber "to grapple with the accumulating and unorganized evidence on the time element," Sapir wrote a synthetic statement on the historical methods of cultural reconstruction.[82] He did this at a time when chronological dating was not based on archaeology, because stratigraphic excavation, only recently developed, was not yet recognized as a way to determine cultural changes through time.[83] Sapir's essay on "Time Perspective in Aboriginal American Culture" was a paradigmatic statement of Boasian historical methodology.[84] He stressed how language could provide "a sort of stratified matrix to work in for the purpose of unravelling culture sequences," arguing that linguistics was one of the most important methods to cultural reconstruction.[85] This method led to his radical 1921 reclassification of North American Indian languages into six superstocks, summarizing the genetic contributions of a number of scholars (including Kroeber and Dixon) over the previous eight years.[86]

Neither Kroeber nor Sapir strictly followed Boas's diffusionist methods

80. Sapir, "Anthropological Survey," p. 793.

81. Victor Golla, "Sapir, Kroeber, and North American Linguistic Classification," in *New Perspectives in Language, Culture, and Personality*, ed. W. Cowan, M. Foster, and K. Koerner (Philadelphia: John Benjamins Publishing Co., 1986), p. 19.

82. Kroeber to Sapir, 7 December 1914, in Victor Golla, ed., *The Sapir-Kroeber Correspondence: Letters between Edward Sapir and A. L. Kroeber, 1905–1925, Survey of California and other Indian Languages* 6 (Berkeley: Department of Linguistics, University of California, 1984), p. 163.

83. David L. Browman and Douglas R. Givens, "Stratigraphic Excavation: The First 'New Archaeology,'" *American Anthropologist* 98 (1996): 80–95.

84. Edward Sapir, "Time Perspective in Aboriginal American Culture: A Study in Method," in *Selected Writings of Edward Sapir in Language, Culture, and Personality*, ed. David G. Mandelbaum (Berkeley: University of California Press, 1985), pp. 389–462; Regna Darnell and Judith Irvine, eds., "Introduction," vol. 4 *The Collected Works of Edward Sapir*. ed. Philip Sapir (New York: Mouton de Gruyter, 1994), pp. 27–29.

85. Sapir, "Time Perspective," p. 432.

86. Golla, "Linguistic Classification," p. 18; Edward Sapir, "A Bird's-Eye View of American Languages North of Mexico," in *Edward Sapir*, ed. Konrad Koerner (Philadelphia: John Benjamins Publishing, 1984), p. 140.

without modifying them in some way. On the one hand, they were "rebell-ing" from Boas personally and professionally, pushing their conclusions further than he allowed. On the other, they were refining their own ideas and theories, and taking anthropology in new directions and toward new conclusions.[87] Such developments do not disqualify their work from being Boasian; they continued to follow Boas's historical project, his rationale, and most of the tenets. Boas remained the critical link between these sur-veys. With Sapir in Ottawa and Kroeber in California, he was thereby able to extend his professional influence in anthropology.

While surveys merely formalized field research, especially in regard to securing funding, they facilitated its coordination by placing the adminis-trative authority in specific hands. The administrator, responsible for the success of the overall project, directed (and sometimes determined) the field research. Throughout this tradition, individual fieldworkers had to nego-tiate the constraints of fieldwork conditions with the priorities of admin-istrative demands. Boas, for instance, challenged the restrictions of Hale, preferring localized studies; and Kroeber, in turn, disregarded the recom-mendations of Boas, preferring comparative studies. This process of admin-istration and negotiation was a reoccurring pattern in survey anthropology.

Although fieldwork did not always continue under the formalities of the survey tradition, the extensive research model exemplified in Boas's BAAS work established a baseline for fieldwork practices. The short sea-sonal trips to specific native communities usually followed the cycles of an academic year and required return visits. They were necessarily provisional. Sapir particularly bemoaned this problem. In an attempt to deal with such constraints, Boas, Kroeber and Sapir sometimes hired native interpreters and collaborators to work on the spot and help with research.

Conclusion

For over thirty years, the Boasian anthropological survey tradition influ-enced the methods and practices of anthropologists in Canada and the United States. This tradition not only reflected Franz Boas' early ambitions

---

87. Stocking, "Basic Assumptions," pp. 17–18. Cf. Stocking, "Ideas and Institutions," pp. 124–127; and Darnell, "Development of American Anthropology," p. 416.

for building a geographical institute and later a school of anthropology, but evolved from his training in German geography and his experiences in anthropological fieldwork. Boas defined the parameters of a distinctive approach to anthropology, one counter to the evolutionary trends of his contemporaries and composed of a number of specific tenets. He instilled these tenets in many of his students and collaborators, including Kroeber and Sapir, who in turn organized anthropological surveys along similar lines. Anthropological surveys, which prefigured the more intensive and individualized model of participant observation of the 1920's, significantly reinforced a sense of collective identity and purpose in a corps of field workers. For Boas and his students they also fostered a shared project, the reconstruction of the cultural history of Native North America. This project, which presupposed the slow empirical development of a cultural and linguistic database for reconstructing pre-contact Native cultures, was one of the legacies of Boas's initiatives and something his students continued as research models and paradigms changed.

Acknowledgments: Alex Long would like to express his gratitude to Regna Darnell, Lisa Dillon, Ira Jacknis, and Wendy Wickwire for their critical comments on drafts of this essay. Christine Mullins generously provided support and access to Doug Cole's research notes and Boas biography manuscript. We gratefully acknowledge the courtesies of the archivists and staff of the American Museum of Natural History (New York), the American Philosophical Society (Philadelphia), and the Bancroft Library (University of California, Berkeley). In particular, we wish to thank Edward Carter II, Roy Goodman, and Elizabeth Carroll-Horrocks of the American Philosophical Society, and William Roberts and Lauren Lassleben of the Bancroft Library.

PART FIVE
LEWIS AND CLARK

STRATEGIES FOR FINDING THE NORTHWEST PASSAGE
The Roles of Alexander Mackenzie and Meriwether Lewis

Alexander Mackenzie and Meriwether Lewis were the first explorers who intentionally crossed North America.[1] Mackenzie's experience as a fur trader and Meriwether Lewis's as an Army officer shaped their searches for the Northwest Passage. Assessing Mackenzie's voyage in the context of a Fur Trade Culture and Lewis's in that of an Army Officer Culture will indicate how both explorers approached their tasks. Such an assessment focuses not so much on what they did, but *how* they did it.

The terms "culture" and "Northwest Passage" appear often in the inquiry and need some explanation. Culture here refers to the physical and mental constructs people create to cope with their environment. The phrase Northwest Passage arose from the search for a water route through North America.

The possibility of a passage through North America had intrigued Europeans since the days of Columbus. Two centuries of searching had eliminated the largest part of the continent from consideration. Only on the Northwest coast, roughly between the forty-second and the sixtieth parallels, did there still seem to be space for a waterway through North America.

---

1. As always Ellen W. Barth has improved my prose and thoughts.

The final searches for the passage were shaped by the 1788 geographic knowledge of the Canadian high north. It depended largely on the ideas of a Detroit-born Canadian fur trader, Peter Pond, who in 1787 as head of the North West Companies' operations spent his last winter in the vicinity of Lake Athabasca. Based on the experience of his travels he speculated that a river which flowed west from the Great Slave Lake, north of Lake Athabasca, emptied into the Pacific in an estuary which Captain Cook's third exploring expedition had sighted on the West coast of North America. Pond imagined that the Rockies came to an end at the sixtieth parallel and that a river ran north of the mountains a relatively short distance to the ocean. He, of course, did not know he underestimated the distance between Great Slave Lake and Pacific by about seven hundred miles.

Alexander Mackenzie, Pond's twenty-five-year old successor as director of the Athabasca district, set out to test this speculation, hoping to improve the economic situation of the Montreal fur trade. A navigable waterway to the Pacific would reduce the North West Company's staggering transportation costs and would also provide links to the North Pacific and China trade. Along such a waterway trade goods and furs could be shipped in bulk between Europe and the Canadian Northwest. The present movement of trade goods over miles and miles of water in small vessels and canoes between Montreal, Grand Portage (at the northwest corner of Lake Superior), and the distant posts of the high north cut heavily into the company's profit.

Mackenzie's introduction into the fur business in a Montreal counting house had acquainted him with the strategic locations of the competing Hudson's Bay Company's depots on the western rim of that bay. They were farther west and north than Grand Portage which gave the competitor the advantage of a much cheaper supply route by sea. The North West Company had to carry its trade goods through churning rapids, hidden rocks, and strenuous portages.

Mackenzie looked for alternatives. On his 1789 expedition he discovered that the river flowing out of the Great Slave Lake in a northwesterly direction soon turned almost due north. It skirted a massive mountain range to the west, a section of the Rockies, and ultimately emptied into the Arctic Ocean. Long before he reached the ocean he realized that his "River of Disappointment," as he called the stream that now carries his name, would not bring him to the Pacific. But rather than return at that point, his fascination with the high north geography lured him to pursue the river to the sea in that brief Arctic Summer. In one hundred and two days, "accompanied by five Canadians & three Indians," Mackenzie covered the 3,000-mile-journey to the Beaufort Sea of the Arctic Ocean and back to Lake Athabasca. "This expedition," he laconically stated after the return, "proved without a doubt that there was not a North West Passage" north of the sixtieth parallel.[2]

In 1792 Mackenzie searched for the Northwest Passage farther south, in the vast expanse west of Lake Athabasca. In the previous year he had bought survey instruments and astronomical tables in London which he used quite successfully to determine his position during the second voyage. Mackenzie followed the Peace River from Lake Athabasca to the range of mountains which had defied his earlier attempt to reach the Pacific. He wintered at Fort Fork, at the juncture of the Peace River and the Smoke River. In the next year, with three fur traders, four voyageurs, and two Indians, he traversed the rugged mountains. In one canoe or on foot, the group followed streams or portaged on Indian trails and trade routes on a course which generally responded to Mackenzie's sense of direction. The Bella Coola River brought them to the ocean, some distance north of Vancouver Island.

"Alexander Mackenzie, from Canada, by land," he wrote on the face of a coastal rock the party had slept on, "the twenty-second of July, one thousand seven hundred and ninety-three."[3] Mackenzie proved that there was no continuous waterway in the north that could qualify as the Northwest Passage. His accomplishment came about two hundred and fifty years after Álvar Núñez Cabeza de Vaca and his three companions first crossed North America far to the South in what was later called the border lands. Both parties succeeded with the help of Native Americans. In Mackenzie's case the Indians were already an integral part of the Canadian Fur Trade Culture.

---

2. T. H. McDonald (ed.) *Exploring the Northwest Territory: Sir Alexander Mackenzie's Journal of a Voyage by Bark Canoe from Lake Athabasca to the Pacific Ocean in the Summer of 1789* (Norman, 1966), pp. 117, 120.

3. W. Kaye Lamb (ed.), "Journal of a Voyage from Fort Chipewyan to the Pacific Ocean in 1793," *The Journals and Letters of Sir Alexander Mackenzie* (Cambridge, 1970), p. 378.

At the turn of the eighteenth century the Fur Trade Culture of the Canadian high north reflected the outcome of a two-hundred-year adjustment of Euro-American and Native American belief and behavior to a constantly changing environment. In the course of the cultural contact, white traders had come to terms with Indian morals and practices just as Native Americans had with Euro-American ones. The mutual adjustments ensured a measure of stability for people who constantly had to cope with an environment altered by circumstances beyond comprehension or control.[4]

The fur trade as a cultural partnership had a special significance for the traders staffing the North West Company's outpost at Lake Athabasca. It was an area of recent contact between traders and Native Americans where Indians not only adapted to the new conditions produced by the trade but also shaped them. At the northern-most fringe of that world, in 1778, Pond had built his post. In the winter of 1787 Mackenzie joined him to take over when Pond returned to his native United States in the spring.

About that time the two traders began their contact with the Subarctic Métis, a Canadian group of mixed descent from Native American and European ancestry who in the mid-nineteenth century established the "Métis Nation" in the Red and Saskatchewan river valleys. One of the Métis, François Beaulieu whose father was either French or Métis and his mother Chipewyan, attested to the multi-cultural world of the high north. As *coureur de bois* he knew Mackenzie and Pond, who had employed his uncle as interpreter. Beaulieu defended the North West Company's interests against the Hudson's Bay Company. As chief of the Yellowknife, he drove the Sekani, who also feared the guns of the Beaver and Cree, into the Rocky Mountains where Mackenzie found them in 1793.[5]

Across the mountains, Mackenzie met another multi-cultural world. Leaving the Parsnip, he crossed the divide to the Fraser River and the country of the Carrier Indians. Although they had never seen a white man before, he found that some already had European iron tools supplied by Shuswap,

---

4. My understanding of the Canadian Fur Trade Culture has benefited from Dean L. Anderson, "The Flow of European Trade Goods into the Western Great Lakes Region, 1715–1760," Jennifer S. H. Brown, W. J. Eccles and Donald P. Heldman (eds.), *The Fur Trade Revisited: Selected Papers of the Sixth North American Fur Trade Conference, Mackinac Island, Michigan, 1991* (East Lansing, 1994), pp. 93–94.

5. Richard Slobodin, "Subarctic Métis," William C. Sturtevant (ed.), *Handbook of North American Indians*, VI [June Helm (ed.), *Subarctic*] (Washington, 1981), pp. 363–64.

Bella Coola, and Tsimshian Indians who were in touch with the trading ships on the Pacific coast. The Carrier who had suffered from the knives and guns of the Shuswap also fought the Chilcotin to get direct access to the trade goods.[6]

As a young and ambitious fur trader, Mackenzie was finely attuned to and experienced at dealing well in these multi-cultural worlds. He had also mastered the rugged mountains, the dense forests, and the turbulent rivers. He and his men understood well that the advantages gained from trade came only with the skills of survival in the wilderness: and trade and survival were urgent essentials in their culture. Mackenzie embraced the rigors of fur trade life style and culture. He was considered a harsh taskmaster who at times drove his men to the limit of endurance as they battled strong currents and awesome rapids.

Exhausting and speedy travel marked the Canadian fur trade. In the summer of 1824, the Canadian head of the Hudson's Bay Company, George Simpson, traveled by canoe from Hudson Bay to the Oregon Country. His *voyageurs* rose at one in the morning, ate, and then paddled steadily until seven in the evening. In 1750, one of La Vérendrye's sons explained to a minister of Louis XV that his father arduously searched for the Northwest Passage "and made myself and my brothers travel with such a vigor that we should have reached our goal, whatever it was."[7]

When Mackenzie's voyageurs protested his decisions and refused to go on, he argued, berated, and pleaded with them, and they soon accepted the fact that without him they would be in worse shape. Their experience reinforced the customary Fur Trade Culture and told them that a hard-driving leader was needed to reach swiftly the next portage or group of Indians, better yet, both of them at once. On the Pacific Coast rock, the men waited anxiously while Mackenzie took his position and wrote his message on the face of the rock, even though they were surrounded by aggressive Indians in canoes. Their previous experience with coastal traders had taught them to consider white people as enemies and to intimidate them. Mackenzie's men, though shaking with fear of the Indians and anger at his delays stood

---

6. Catharine McClellan, "Intercultural Relations and Cultural Change in the Cordillera," ibid., p. 388.

7. Lawrence J. Burpee (ed.), *Journals and Letters of Pierre Gaultier de Varennes et de La Vérendrye and His Sons* (Toronto, 1927), p. 503.

their ground with him until he allowed them to climb into the canoe for the return voyage.

Mackenzie treated the Indians he engaged as interpreters like his other employees. He never seemed to have asked himself whether he liked them as long as they did his bidding. During the course of the voyage, however, he insisted on shaking hands with the many Native Americans he met and made sure that his interpreters explained the significance of the gesture. Steeped in the complex culture of the trade, as a sharp trader he kept a sharp eye on his interpreters to be sure that no vital information was kept from him and no deal cut without his approval. He gave sugar regularly to children to gain the good will of their parents and in the same spirit of the trade he collected an impromptu vocabulary of the Carrier and Shuswap languages.

Descending from the divide to the ocean, for the most part he was able to spot and follow well-marked Indian trade and travel routes.[8] Despite the tense encounters, harrowing rapids, and strenuous portages, the spirit of Mackenzie's journal made it clear that mountains, rivers, and trails were part of the world he shared with Native Americans and they with him. Ensconced in the Canadian Fur Trade Culture, he never usurped a part of the common environment by attaching his name or that of one of his companions to a river, mountain, or pass.

Captain Meriwether Lewis, chosen in 1803 by President Thomas Jefferson to lead the first United States exploring expedition from the Missouri via the Columbia to the Pacific Ocean, had little exposure to Native Americans and to a wilderness culture. His West ended at the Army posts in the Ohio Valley. The Army Culture of the opening nineteenth century sustained him and his men. It grew out of Revolutionary War experiences of men and officers and emerged in the two decades which provided the political and economic framework of the young nation.

In the Continental Army, American soldiers learned to support each other to hold a line. Touching the shoulders of a comrade on both sides helped men suppress their fears. Their conduct in combat became a matter of pride, and at times they fought just to uphold their regiment's reputation

8. Lamb (ed.), *Journals*, pp. 289–91, 320, 322, 338, 314, 319, 334, 351, 371.

for fortitude. Intrepid officers, dashing forward at the head of the troops, calling to their men to follow, helped soldiers facing likely death.[9]

The Continental Army disappeared in 1783, done in by peace, sectional interests, and the constitutional, economic, political, and ideological malaise of the Confederation. But there still remained, as part of the emerging Army Culture, an obligation of officers to obey their orders and of soldiers to follow their officers through thick and thin and to stand with their comrades.

The post-war officers created an unhappy image. Many young ones, with their wartime exploits fresh on their mind, boasted of their roles as patriots and officers. They bragged that their Army service as officers had achieved American independence. Citizens who treasured the egalitarian and libertarian potential of the Revolution regarded the swaggering ex-officers as remnants of European authoritarianism and militarism. In 1786, when Shays's Rebellion dramatized the military impotence of the Confederation, the Congress relied on the subterfuge of Indian danger in western Massachusetts to raise troops to deal with rebellious farmers.[10]

After the Federal Republic replaced the Confederation in 1789, the Federalists and Republicans gave voice to their different ideas of the nature of a standing Army. The Republicans were dismayed when the Federalists who controlled the executive branch and the Congress used a series of military crises to create a national military establishment. The Republicans held the Federalists responsible for the actual and imagined threats that a standing Army represents to a free society. Some members of the new Army officer corps, however, thought of themselves not as a professional elite but as citizens-officers, based on the Cincinnatus model. They were a presence the Republicans welcomed when they came into office in 1801.

When Meriwether Lewis joined the U.S. Army as an ensign in 1795, officers were trained to urge their men to follow them facing death, and men followed their duty to do just that. Although Lewis embraced the Army Cul-

---

9. Robert Middlekauff, *The Glorious Cause: The American Revolution, 1763–1789* (New York, 1982), pp. 502–04.

10. Richard H. Kohn, *Eagle and Sword: The Federalists and the Creation of the Military Establishment in America* (New York, 1975), pp. 41, 54, 89; Charles Royster, *Light-Horse Lee and the Legacy of the American Revolution* (New York, 1981), pp. 30–34.

ture, he personally never led a thinning line of soldiers against anyone. The following year, after he was transferred to the First Regiment of Infantry, he was either on furlough, recruiting men, or visiting the Army forts of the Ohio Valley as the regimental paymaster. He did well with his promotions. An ensign in 1795, he became lieutenant in 1799 and captain in 1800. His commanding officer, John Francis Hamtramck, had advanced on a slower track. He was captain in 1776, became major in 1786, lieutenant colonel in 1796, and colonel in 1802.[11] One year earlier, when the French Canadian veteran of the Revolutionary War angled for a higher rank, a Federalist friend reminded him that the party now in power offered little hope of becoming a brigadier.[12]

Lewis's quasi-civilian Army background may have been among the attributes which in 1801 attracted Thomas Jefferson to the young Virginian whom he knew as son of an Albemarle County neighbor. His career proved useful to Jefferson who during the campaign of 1800 had promised to reduce the size of the Army. As the President's private secretary Lewis's personal knowledge of the officer corps help Jefferson to trim the Army officer roster without losing Republican officers or competent ones with no party allegiance.[13]

In 1803, when Jefferson appointed Lewis as leader of an overland expedition, the Army Culture of the opening nineteenth century enabled Lewis to resolve the great problem that met the expedition in its planning stage. The civilian component of the Army Culture allowed him to create a command of two captains as co-leaders. He wanted to accommodate William Clark whom Lewis and Jefferson had promised a captaincy if he joined the expedition. The Army, however, claiming that there was no opening in that rank, commissioned Clark a second lieutenant of artillery.

Lewis insisted that Clark would nevertheless be in every respect his equal. Ignoring the official rank, Lewis introduced Clark as captain and al-

---

11. Francis B. Heitman (comp.), *Historical Register and Dictionary of the United States Army, from Its Organization, September 29, 1789, to March 2, 1903*, 2 vols. (Urbana, 1965), I, 496, 631. This is a facsimile reprint of the original edition published in 1903.

12. Kohn, *Eagle and Sword*, pp. 295–96.

13. Donald Jackson, *Thomas Jefferson & the Stony Mountains: Exploring the West from Monticello* (Urbana, 1981), pp. 117–19.

ways shared responsibility equally. He thus forged a partnership which was fundamental to the cohesion of the expedition and its ultimate success. It rested on a device from the world of business, sustained by an Army Culture with room for the citizen-officer, and it yielded results far greater than each man might have achieved alone.

The solution did credit to Lewis's intricate personality. His journal entries reveal him as a man of sudden mood changes who slipped quickly from euphoria to gloom. Eloquence and silence marked the poles of his perceptive mind. Some of his journal entries are like soliloquies reflecting not only the range of his mind but also identifying him as the citizen-officer who could fill the complex role of leader *and* partner.

As a newly formed Army unit in search of appropriate procedures, the expedition could look to the Continental Army precedents. These spelled out the chain of command, the regulations enforcing discipline, and the punishment for violating the rules; in short, the conduct of troops garrisoned in the U.S. military posts. The Corps' area of operation, however, would not be tied to a base in the United States. Its field of action stretched through parts of the continent unknown to captains and men, thus placing the new unit outside any Army convention. The Corps' orders to be at peace with everyone clearly set it apart from units and soldiers whose commitment and pride were recharged in combat.

Lewis and Clark took charge of their special, newly formed Army unit while continuing to assess what constituted appropriate military conduct for the expedition. They gradually shaped the motley party into an intrepid Corps of like-minded men. They combined the conventional tools of military authority with the spontaneity of expeditionary leadership using the citizen-officer as a model. One practice inherited from the Continental Army, courts-martial were considered a standard part of Army discipline. With the help of six courts-martial, the captains molded the mixed lot of soldiers, backwoodsmen, and guides into a special Corps, with sensible discipline, total loyalty, and respect for the captains' judgment. This latter was tested severely at the confluence of the Marias and the Missouri. Unsure which river to follow, Lewis and Clark did extensive reconnaissance which eventually supported the captains' strong convictions and led to the correct decision. Although their explanations at the time of doubt did not convince the men, they "said very cheerfully," Lewis recorded in his journal, "that they were ready to follow us anywhere."[14]

The shared hardships of the trail and the requisite self-sufficiency of the group also altered Army routine. Adapting regular procedure, Lewis and Clark insisted that enlisted men sit on the courts-martial while a sergeant presided, except in trials involving crimes punishable by death, when the captains took over. The first winter camp and the severe North Dakota temperatures enforced the physical closeness of the expedition. The arrivals and departures of Indian chiefs and white traders at the fort impressed the men with the special status of their Corps. The four months of shared experiences in tight quarters strengthened their loyalties to each other, their compliance with regulations, and their commitments to the goals of the expedition. Once they left Fort Mandan courts-martial were not again needed on the voyage.

The captains as citizen-officers found that a somewhat egalitarian approach to discipline united the expedition. At their request, two days after Sergeant Floyd's death on August 20, 1804, the soldiers held an election for his successor, and Private Gass was duly promoted sergeant. On another occasion, November 24, 1805, all members of the expedition, including York and Sacagawea, were given the chance to vote on the location of the winter quarters on the Pacific coast. Clark even recorded each vote in his account of the election.

Lewis acquitted himself superbly as citizen-officer in his vital encounter with the Shoshoni, while Clark was bringing canoes and most explorers up the last navigable stretch of the Beaverhead River. The Shoshoni were the first Indians the expedition had seen in three months and the only possible source of horses for crossing the Rockies. After their first contact with Lewis they became apprehensive, fearing they were being led into an ambush. They threatened to disperse before horse trading could be conducted with the goods that Clark was bringing. The dual nature of the citizen-officer helped to solve the crisis. Lewis as army officer acted decisively to counter the Indians' suspicions; as citizen he was unencumbered by concerns for an

---

14. Reuben Gold Thwaites (ed.), *Original Journals of the Lewis and Clark Expedition: 1804–1806*, 8 vols. (New York, 1904–05), II, p. 136.

officer's honor and free to entrust his gun to the Shoshoni chief Cameawhait. Thus, Lewis could make himself a hostage pledging the peaceful aims of the expedition, as did his three companions.

The expedition's sense of mission derived from its role as the first United States exploring expedition. It was the brainchild of President Thomas Jefferson. A high point in his fascination with the American West, the expedition produced the first officially deliberate encounter with the nature, people, and resources of a large part of the continent unknown to the young nation. The mouth of the Columbia, however, had already been explored by the turn of the eighteenth century. Jefferson's idea that only a short portage separated the Missouri from the Columbia was more than the last phase of a long search for the Northwest Passage. It was the harbinger of new geopolitical aspirations of the United States.

The expedition matched Jefferson's far-reaching instructions to Lewis. The Louisiana Purchase treaty of April 30, 1803, added major diplomatic tasks. Lewis and Clark derived pride from the President's charges. And so did the men. "Our little Community," as the citizens-officers called the party, was a distinct contrast to the solitary traders, free-wheeling trappers, canny interpreters, and cagey representatives of the Montreal-based North West Company whom the explorers encountered. Each of these men were pursuing their interests or those of their employers.

The explorers officially served their nation's policy. Their success indicated that the Army culture had created a strong expeditionary force by infusing a democratic spirit into military routine. Their practical adaptations gave scope to the men's creativity and sustained their confidence in each other. The Army culture linked the diverse groups of explorers into a national expedition. Fusing diverse men and methods, the captains exposed their search for unity as the essence of the American experience.

Alexander Mackenzie pursued his own design. He sought to solve the North West Company's need for a feasible water way to the Pacific which would reduce the operating cost of its far-flung western posts. Mackenzie directed just one canoe with nine employees of the Montreal fur company to the ocean and back without governmental support. In 1807, an open letter to Lewis by the publisher of Patrick Gass's journal snidely questioned the large size and support structure of Lewis's expedition comparing it to the small size of Mackenzie's, but made no mention of the larger goals and tasks of the U.S. expedition.[15]

Despite of its small size and private nature, Mackenzie's voyage eventually became a part of a commercial and political development that provided Canada with a major share of the Pacific Northwest coast. His arduous exploring and trading venture supplied the geographic base for dreams of a Canadian continental destiny. Fortuitously, the fur trade culture which sustained Mackenzie and subsequent Canadian explorers acted for a while to shield Indian nations in the Canadian West from the sudden onslaught of land-hungry settlers.

Two decades after Mackenzie's voyage to the Pacific, the North West Company profited greatly from his discovery as it thwarted the efforts of the rival Hudson's Bay Company to find a convenient water route to the Pacific. During the War of 1812, employees of the North West Company purchased Fort Astoria at the mouth of the Columbia in October, 1813. They were inspired by rumors of approaching British men-of-war assigned to seize the post established by John Jacob Astor's Pacific Fur Company in 1811 as the pivot of his projected world-wide fur empire. When an arriving British naval captain, chagrined to see his target already in the hands of his countrymen, raised the Union Jack over Fort Astoria he turned the acquisition into a conquest. And as such it was returned to the United States in accordance with the peace Treaty of Ghent of December, 1814, which annulled all territorial conquests of the belligerents. The captain's territorial escapade thus diminished the British claims to the mouth of the Columbia, although the North West Company still owned Fort Astoria and called it Fort George.

The Convention of 1818 between the United States and Great Britain guaranteed equal rights to the citizens of both nations in the Oregon country and further weakened the British dominance in the area. Three years later, the balance shifted when the Hudson's Bay Company absorbed the North West Company and skillfully protected the Mackenzie legacy of its former rival.

---

15. Donald Jackson, *Letters of the Lewis and Clark Expedition with Related Documents: 1783–1854*, 2 vols. (2nd, rev. ed., Urbana, 1978), II, 401–02.

Faced with the American determination to hold on to the Oregon Country below the 49th parallel, the invigorated Hudson's Bay Company stripped the country of its fur resources and in the early 1840s started a slow retreat to Victoria, B. C. When the Treaty of 1846 between Great Britain and the United States extended the existing boundary of the 49th parallel across the Rocky Mountains to the Pacific, Great Britain retained its coastal possessions between that line and the 54th parallel, the southern limit of the Russian territory in North America. Thus Mackenzie's vision finally materialized with the emergence of British Columbia as the Canadian gateway to the Pacific.

Mackenzie's familiarity with the Fur Trade Culture enabled him to move men, provisions, Indian presents, arms, ammunition, and three thousand pounds of baggage in a lightly built canoe, twenty-five feet long inside, twenty-six inches deep, and four feet nine inches wide, to the divide of the Rockies, portaging the divide, backpacking and canoeing to the ocean. In one hundred and eight days his men covered the two-thousand-three-hundred-mile distance from Fort Fork to the Pacific and back.

Meriwether Lewis, facing a much more complex task assigned by Jefferson, applied his knowledge of the Army Culture to forge a motley group of men into the first United States exploring expedition. Together with his co-captain and partner, William Clark, he set an example as citizen-officer who instilled a sense of mission into the twenty-nine man core of the expedition: two captains, fourteen Army regulars, nine young men from Kentucky, the interpreter, two French Canadian river men, and Clark's black servant York. A French Canadian interpreter, his Shoshoni wife Sacagawea, and their baby were added to the expedition at the Mandan villages. In eight hundred and sixty-three days (two years, four months, and ten days), the co-captains led the expedition of discovery and diplomacy on a seven thousand-mile voyage from the Mississippi to the Pacific and back.

The discoveries of the Lewis and Clark expedition turned a western wilderness of guesswork and rumor into a distinct part of the continent. Even though it demolished the last hope for a convenient water passage through North America, the Corps found a route from the Mississippi to the Pacific. By exploring the breadth of the Louisiana Purchase, the explorers proved its significance to the future of the young republic.

Unwittingly, the expedition reinforced the destruction of Native American nations. Following Jefferson's instructions, the captains tried hard in many, many Indian councils to bring Native Americans peacefully into white society through commerce. As a prerequisite for commerce, they repeatedly urged Indians to live in peace with each other and with white Americans. Lewis and Clark, of course, faced a hopeless task given the role of peace and war in Indian societies and the complex trade relations among Indian nations. The two successfully carried out their instructions in many other areas. They increased the sum of useful knowledge through collecting ethnological, geographical, zoological, and botanical information and traced the course of a future continental empire.

The expedition buttressed the United States claim to the entire Columbia basin. In subsequent decades, Americans derived their title to the "Oregon Country" to a great extent from the explorers' topographical descriptions and maps. Their reports about natural resources drew migrants to the Columbia. Trappers, traders, and settlers added to the legal niceties about "the rights of discovery" the brawn of conquest.

Guided by the Fur Trade Culture and the Army Culture Mackenzie and Lewis accomplished their tasks. They knew how to do them, and they did them well.

DO OR DIE, BUT THEN REPORT AND PONDER

Palpable and Mental Adventures in the Lewis and Clark Journals

There are two widespread and very strong American feelings that bedevil popular understanding of Lewis and Clark. One is a longing for wilderness, the other an admiration for tough guys out west.

In the Far West, and probably over a much wider range, the mention of vast open spaces, deep forests, hard-to-reach lakes, or big-game country is often answered by an exclamation of sudden yearning. Just five or seven words say it clearly: "I'd like to *be* there—right *now!*" These words sometimes spill out simply and touchingly, but they can bespeak several ranges of yearning. One is something like addiction. People who have worked outdoors, hunted, fished, camped, hiked, or even slept overnight in Montana, Oregon, or Wyoming, often find that they cannot accommodate that experience in other routines elsewhere. They have to go back. Returning may be hard; it can take years and end in frustrations; but it drives some men and women back across long distances nevertheless, and persists into late old age. "I'd like to *be* there" also expresses something very different, a need not to return but to go further, on a longer excursion, up a higher mountain, into a deeper isolation, than life has yet afforded. Finally, that longing can be projected onto the past. "I'd like to *be* there" means in fact, "I yearn to be *back* there," back in an America that no longer exists but that still seems almost within reach somewhere out west—a place beyond barbed wire, power lines, logging roads, and survey markers, a place immense, unexplored, abounding in wildlife, and inexhaustibly mysterious.

This feeling can be as powerful as an addiction or a religious zeal. There is no arguing with it. It drives some people's lives. It may spring from misguided primitivism, half-baked romanticism, a distorted view of history, or deep unhappiness with the stifling vulgarity of modern, urban civilization. But it is no use trying to say that, indeed it could be very dangerous to suggest it, to anyone burning his way west across the Plains on a motorcycle or swinging into the saddle with a hunting rifle.

Another strong feeling for the West has more evident sources in literature and art. This is the American reverence for Western heroes, a feeling developed in the twentieth century through hundreds of popular novels, films, and television serials. It is arguable that until the 1990s millions of Americans were indoctrinated in the code of such heroes: the code of the tough, lonely, silent, brooding, righteous individual, who tracks his adversary across rugged terrain, then faces him in a duel and thereby wins both the love of a doubting woman and the enduring respect of lesser men. The role has been played to perfection by Gary Cooper; both on screen and off, it has made John Wayne and Ronald Reagan into powerful political symbols in our time.

The grip of this appeal may have slipped a bit very recently. The Western has proliferated into too many forms, too many re-runs, too many battered paperbacks, too many musical versions, parodies, and children's serials, to be seen as anything but a stylized fiction. Meanwhile, wide open spaces that could be imagined, at least, a few decades ago, have manifestly yielded to modern development; to move across long distances by horse a current adventurer had better have an expensive backup system of trucks, trailers, and telecommunications. For these and many other reasons, the Western is no longer the staple product of Hollywood or of network television.

Nevertheless, the ideal of lonely courage in a spectacular vast setting still has its undeniable pull on American minds. A good case in point is Jane Tompkins's recent, very personal study of Westerns, in which she traces their beginnings to a rejection of everything feminine, a rejection of women and all that they stand for.

Tompkins sees the Western code as an exaggerated reaction to another form of literature, the sentimental, female-dominated, Christian best-sellers of the late nineteenth century. "The Western hero," she writes, "who seems to ride in out of nowhere, in fact comes riding in out of the nineteenth century. And every piece of baggage he doesn't have, every word he doesn't say, every creed in which he doesn't believe is absent for a reason. . . . The surface cleanness and simplicity of the landscape, the story line, and the characters derive from the genre's will to sweep the board clear of encumbrances."[1] Tompkins argues that from page one, the Western emphatically repudiates both civilization and civilized people, especially women:

> Given the pervasiveness and the power of women's discourse in the nineteenth century, I think it is no accident that men gravitated in imagination toward a womanless milieu, a set of rituals featuring physical combat and physical endurance, and a social setting that branded most features of civilized existence as feminine and corrupt, banishing them in favor of the three main targets of women's reform: whiskey, gambling, and prostitution. Given the enormous publicity and fervor of the Women's Christian Temperance Union crusade, can it be an accident that the characteristic indoor setting for Westerns is the saloon? (Tompkins, 44)

After taking these critical bearings, one might suppose that Tompkins, a modern woman and a civilized reader, would go on to criticize the genre severely, and perhaps see beyond it to some hopeful reintegration of men's and women's imaginative versions of America. But not so, not so at all. Instead, Tompkins celebrates the Western; she admits she cannot break free of its appeal. For present purposes that is the crucial point of her book. With every reason to repudiate the Western, she frankly admits that it holds her fascination and her loyalties. Her chapters go on to reveal that she watches Westerns avidly, reads and re-reads Louis L'Amour novels, overcomes her original revulsion to admire Buffalo Bill Cody, and celebrates men in her own life who live by silence, isolation, and cold courage. In the end, she writes frankly of her own "righteous ecstasy" when she moves into showdown moments against female rivals at academic conferences (229–33).

---

1. Jane Tompkins, *West of Everything: The Inner Life of Westerns* (New York: Oxford University Press, 1992), p. 39.

The Western has Tompkins in its grip, and if she is a fair example of this phenomenon she must speak for hundreds of thousands, because she explains very compellingly why she should not yield to such seduction.

For attentive readers of Lewis and Clark, these two attitudes toward the West should stir considerable uneasiness and apprehension. The year 2003 is fast approaching, the beginning date for bicentennial celebrations of the Corps of Discovery. Professional historians have had recent bitter tastes of such national commemorations—in 1976, 1987, the controversies over Columbus in 1992 and the Smithsonian exhibits in 1995. Because of these two passionate feelings we have been surveying here about the West, the Lewis and Clark years could be as bad or worse.

Lewis and Clark seem to embody both these American longings—the longing to *be* there and the longing to do or die in a men's world of natural danger and natural grandeur. There is already an enormous pressure to make these heroes over into objects of these desires. It will be impossible to evade that pressure in the years ahead.

For people who want to *be* there, or get back to a pristine wilderness, Meriwether Lewis and William Clark are bound to stand out. They touch the imagination of common people already. They are almost palpable even today at many sites in the northern tier of Western states. They are there in place names and monuments. And everyone knows they came first—first across what is now America, first across the Rockies, first all the way to the Pacific. What many long to do just once in a lifetime, they did again and again—stand still and dissolve into a new place, where no one can be seen for miles and miles around. To get *back* there can seem identical with getting right into the moccasins of Lewis or Clark.

For people who want a Western adventure, a men's tale, a soul-testing ordeal against life-or-death adversaries, these explorers also offer irresistible materials. Highlights include a confrontation with the Sioux, a gunfight with horse thieves, a boat capsizing in midstream, bizarre storms, grizzlies at close range, and daring passages through the rapids. Other dramas unfolded every month: sexual encounters with Indians during the long winter encampments, grumblings and desertions by subordinates, threats of starvation at high elevations, onsets of widespread illness, makeshift inventions in the face of sudden losses and surprises. Dozens of pages from the journals cry out to be dramatized as heroic moments of cool American courage displayed against a panoramic background.

There is no way around it. Such scenes and adventures are bound to be commercialized (that is the word) on a grand scale. They will be turned into fodder for superficial displays of patriotism. They will frame photo opportunities for celebrities. They will be blown up in extravagant productions and hammered into our ears in trite jingles and slogans.

This onslaught cannot be repelled, but it can be deflected, if only a little. It may, just may, offer scholars an opportunity to alter some attitudes about the West as we find our way into a new century. What truths or better-informed views can be used to counter yearnings for wilderness and brutal heroism? The Lewis and Clark records have one outstanding feature that deserves three years of steady repetition. It is a pivotal truth about both early America and the Far West. It cannot be emphasized too often. Lewis and Clark were literate, civilized, disciplined men of science. As a result, they never abandoned, rejected, or tried to escape from civilization. On the contrary, they devoted themselves to recording whatever they observed and relating it to the highest achievements of civilization as they understood it.

This is not to deny that they, too, felt awe and exhilaration when new vistas opened before them. They certainly did. But they did not go west to lose themselves; they went to make better maps. Their journals show them recording mysteries, but then working through them with patience, confidence, and rational skepticism. Whoever would stand in their moccasins should be urged to see the West fully in their terms, and reminded that, as Donald Jackson put it, these were "the writingest explorers of their time." "They wrote constantly and abundantly," Jackson explains, "afloat and ashore, legibly and illegibly, and always with an urgent sense of purpose."[2] Informed by science and years of wide experience, they worked not only to see but to see into the West and to make their findings intelligible for the best informed researchers in the world.

It is also true that these men withstood tests of endurance, sometimes used force and violence, and even resorted to some acts of ruthlessness and

2. Donald Jackson, ed., *Letters of the Lewis and Clark Expedition with Related Documents 1783–1854*, 2d ed., 2 vols. (Urbana: University of Illinois Press, 1978), 1 : vii.

cunning. But in moments of crisis they were governed by very different motives from those of typical Western heroes. They did not stand alone behind a gun to prove their manhood or to assert some measure of justice in a remote and isolated little world. From first to last their concerns were global—to explore the final link of communication between Europe and Asia, and to survey the resources of America as a country that might span a continent. They were willing to risk their lives for high purposes like these. If they inflicted severe corporal punishment on their men, took deadly aim at Indians, or lied or prevaricated in councils, it was always with an eye to these larger aims—to reach the Pacific without fail and to bring back full records for the advancement of science.

It is hard to overcome some initial prejudices about their skills and capacities. As everyone knows, the spelling in their journals is atrocious. They were not highly educated; neither captain ever prepared for college. Apart from this expedition they would have no renown as naturalists or geographers. They were young men, soldiers, woodsmen, with skills and lore picked up from experience—and in Lewis's case, a few months of intensive preparation. A reader may well balk at the terms of praise Bernard DeVoto uses in assessing their mental capacities:

> Lewis was the diplomatic and commercial thinker, Clark the negotiator. Lewis . . . was the scientific specialist, Clark the engineer and geographer as well as the master of frontier crafts. Both were experienced rivermen but Lewis acknowledged that Clark had greater skill and usually left the management of the boats to him. Clark evidently had the greater gift for dealing with Indians. But by chance Lewis was alone at two critical encounters with Indians, the Snakes and the Blackfeet, and he handled them with an expertness that no one could have surpassed. . . . Both were men of great intelligence, of distinguished intelligence.[3]

Yet DeVoto's assessment, published over forty years ago, has been confirmed and reinforced by subsequent studies. Look at these men's maps. Consider their insights into Western geography and river formation. Take note of Lewis's eager and exact descriptions of new flora and fauna in different regions. Or notice both captains' rapid discernment when faced with conflict-

3. Bernard DeVoto, ed., *The Journals of Lewis and Clark*, Sentry edition (Boston: Houghton Mifflin, 1953), pp. xliii–xliv.

ing evidence or piecemeal bits of information about what lay ahead. The conclusion is inescapable. Rough as they had to be to clamber over the Rockies, these men were gifted thinkers: "men of great intelligence, of distinguished intelligence."

There is likewise a deep-running prejudice against mixing intellectuals up with rough pathfinders. Call Lewis a "botanist" and you may seem to put him among the naive tenderfoot easterners who show up in Western novels for comic relief. "I once hunted owl eggs with a botanist from Boston," a joker tells his dupe in Owen Wister's novel *The Virginian*. "Chiropodist, weren't he?" another man interrupts. "Or maybe a somnambulator?" But no, the first continues: "The young feller wore knee-pants and ever so thick spectacles with a half-moon cut in 'em and he carried a tin box strung to a strap I took for his lunch till it flew open on him and a horned toad hustled out. Then I was sure he was a botanist."[4] The knee pants of a child, the thick bifocals of the aged, the clumsy box that holds a worthless toad—these are the typical encumbrances of a botanist.

But of course Lewis was a botanist; as a matter of fact he can be found dealing very tenderly and studiously with a number of delicate plants. He was also a zealous ornithologist, a perceptive zoologist, and a fair ichthyologist, if we want to call him hard names. At the same time, he rode hard, shot straight, endured starvation and dysentery with little complaint, and found intelligent ways around daunting dangers; he also wore buckskin, saw clearly without glasses, and gladly ate red meat. In short, he gives the lie to the idea that real men and botanists must live worlds apart. That is precisely the point.

To see this point in some detail, let us turn to one particular journal entry, an exciting moment on the way west. If Lewis did not exactly walk on water and raise a doubting disciple from despair, he did at least save a follower's life one day, by steady, even thinking at the edge of a precipice. But let Lewis tell the story in his own words, in full and without interruption:

Friday, June 7th, 1805

It continued to rain almost without intermission last night, and as I expected, we had a most disagreeable and restless night. Our camp possess-

4. Owen Wister, *The Virginian* (1902; reprint New York: Fawcett, 1963), p. 127.

ing no allurements, we left our watery beds at an early hour and continued our route down the river.

It still continues to rain, the wind hard from N. E. and cold. The ground remarkably slippery, insomuch that we were unable to walk on the sides of the bluffs where we had passed as we ascended the river. Notwithstanding the rain that has now fallen, the earth of these bluffs is not wet to a greater depth than 2 inches; in its present state it is precisely like walking over frozen ground which is thawed to small depth and slips equally as bad. This clay not only appears to require more water to saturate it, as I before observed, than any earth I ever observed, but when saturated it appears on the other hand to yield its moisture with equal difficulty. In passing along the face of one of these bluffs today, I slipped at a narrow pass of about 30 yards in length and but for a quick and fortunate recovery by means of my espontoon I should have been precipitated into the river down a craggy precipice of about ninety feet.

I had scarcely reached a place on which I could stand with tolerable safety even with the assistance of my espontoon before I heard a voice behind me cry out, "God, God, Captain, what shall I do?" On turning about, I found it was Windsor, who had slipped and fallen about the center of this narrow pass and was lying prostrate on his belly, with his right hand, arm, and leg over the precipice, while he was holding on with the left arm and foot as well as he could, which appeared to be with much difficulty. I discovered his danger, and the trepidation which he was in gave me still further concern, for I expected every instant to see him lose his strength and slip off; although much alarmed at his situation, I disguised my feelings and spoke very calmly to him and assured him that he was in no kind of danger, to take the knife out of his belt behind him with his right hand and dig a hole with it in the face of the bank to receive his right foot, which he did and then raised himself to his knees; I then directed him to take off his moccasins and to come forward on his hands and knees, holding the knife in one hand and the gun in the other. This he happily effected and escaped.

Those who were some little distance behind returned by my orders and waded the river at the foot of the bluff where the water was breast deep. It was useless, we knew, to attempt the plains on this part of the river in consequence of the numerous steep ravines which intersected and which were quite as bad as the river bluffs. We therefore continued our route down the river, sometimes in the mud and water of the bottom land, at others in the river to our breasts, and when the water became so deep we could not wade we cut footsteps in the face of the steep bluffs with our knives and proceeded.

We continued our disagreeable march through the rain, mud, and water, until late in the evening, having traveled only about 18 miles, and encamped in an old Indian stick lodge, which afforded us a dry and comfortable shelter. During the day we had killed six deer, some of them in very good order, although none of them had yet discarded their winter coats. We had reserved and brought with us a good supply of the best pieces; we roasted and ate a hearty supper of our venison, not having tasted a morsel before during the day; I now laid myself down on some willow boughs to a comfortable night's rest, and felt indeed as if I was fully repaid for the toil and pain of the day, so much will a good shelter, a dry bed, and comfortable supper revive the spirits of the wearied, wet, and hungry traveler.[5]

This entry is presented here word for word from the Moulton edition but in modern spelling and punctuation, to eliminate needless distractions. (After all, the explorers themselves expected their writings to be edited and proofread before being published.) The passage has also been broken up here into five paragraphs, to reveal the coherent stages of Lewis's thought. In good order, he considers, first, the discomforts of the night; second, the effects of rain on the clay of this place and its dangerous consequences; third, the adventure with Windsor; fourth, the day-long trek over very daunting terrain; and fifth, the encampment at day's end.

Each of these paragraphs makes good compact sense by itself. Yet if we blend them together, as Lewis does in fact, we should also notice two or three consistent lines of coherence running through them at the same time. One is a movement from a bad camp to a good camp, by way of a forced march across seemingly impassable plains and rivers. Another is an expansion of Lewis's concern for his men, once he discovers how treacherous the mud is at this place. He records his own close scrape with death, then that of one close follower, then the safe but hard passage he directs the whole party to make. Finally, there is a fluid merging between attention to geographical detail and attention to emergencies. Does the close description of western mud serve as a necessary explanation before Lewis recounts two

---

5. Gary E. Moulton, ed., *Journal of the Lewis & Clark Expedition*, 11 vols. to date (Lincoln: University of Nebraska Press, 1983–), 4:262–63, spelling and punctuation modernized.

close calls at a precipice? Or do the two close calls merely illustrate the scientific observation that this curiously saturated clay "is precisely like . . . frozen ground which is thawed to small depth and slips equally as bad"? There is no way to tell from the language here. Probably Lewis himself could not tell. The two observations both need to be recorded at day's end, and Lewis nicely balances them. He knows he just escaped death, just saved Windsor's life, and just brought the party safely through a very dangerous spot. But what needs to be reported is not heroism but mud, the steepness of these ravines, and the state of game killed at this season at this elevation.

Stepping back from this page, we should also note two further depths of Lewis's mind. One is his steady formality, with perhaps a glint of self-mockery or conscious understatement. "Our camp possessing no allurements, we left our watery beds at an early hour." Or: "Although much alarmed at his situation, I disguised my feelings and spoke very calmly to him." Or: "I directed him . . . to come forward on his hands and knees. . . . This he happily effected and escaped." (Just imagine John Wayne saying, "This he happily effected"!) Lewis's lofty, distanced tone, combined with the several coherences we have traced, suggests a mind very much in command. It seems of a piece with his quick thinking when faced with a man dangling over a precipice or his assured orders that the way forward is by wading through breast-deep waters and cutting footholds in the cliffs.

Yet we would be wrong to think that Lewis is absolutely confident here, or that we have now plumbed his reflections. A good but hard question to ask about any passage in the journals is: What is uppermost in this writer's mind right here? The answer might seem to be either safety and survival, or the topography of this locale, or progress to a better camp. But in context, these are really minor matters. This passage alone does not show it, but on this date Lewis was acutely puzzled. He was in what is now northern Montana at a crucial fork in the Missouri River. Which was the main stream, which a mere tributary?—that was the question on which the fate of the expedition depended, for a wrong choice could lead to nowhere, and cost precious weeks of wandering and backtracking. Since June 4, Lewis had been leading one party up the northerly branch while Clark explored the southern. A day earlier, he had concluded that this stream could not be the Missouri and the route west, but everyone with him was convinced otherwise and he still had not compared notes with Clark. His keen attention to mud and danger here has a very practical side, as a result. If Lewis was wrong about this river, this was the route the whole party would have to cross again, dangerous or not.

This is an exciting, dramatic scene, but to read it properly we have to bear in mind that what Lewis did in a day and what he wrote about in a day are separate things, with complicated interconnections. Heroism may stand out, if that is what a reader wants to find, but in Lewis's own construction of events it is only a subordinate part of the story. For this reason Lewis and Clark can never be adequately summarized on film or television, in picture books or panoramas. Their words have to be read—and read very attentively.

It may be not only justice but justice long overdue, to make these points and insist on them. About five years ago Arlen Large published a little article about references to Lewis and Clark in works of literature.[6] In one section of that piece, he noted close parallels and some definite borrowings between James Fenimore Cooper's novel *The Prairie* (1827) and Nicholas Biddle's 1814 narrative of the Lewis and Clark expedition. Large showed that at least in that second volume of the *Leatherstocking Tales,* Cooper was building a myth of the West out of Lewis and Clark materials. It would be tedious and misleading to suggest anything further about the origins and development of Natty Bumppo from this source; Cooper's famous hero probably derived from Daniel Boone, other woodsmen of the East, and Cooper's own memory of characters in early New York State. But just this much information about his work and Lewis and Clark marks a neat point of departure from history into Western legend.

From the opening novel of the *Leatherstocking* series, Natty Bumppo unfolds as a great ancestor to the lonely heroes of Western fictions. In *The Pioneers* (1823) he appears early on as a figure living apart from civilization by his choice, dwelling with a sole Indian companion, resisting artificial laws with the righteousness of his own conscience backed up by the power of his hunting rifle. At the end of this novel he heads west as an old man alone, running with his dogs to a land where game still abounds. "I'm formed for the wilderness," he cries; "if ye love me, let me go where my soul craves to be

6. Arlen J. Large, "Literary Borrowings from Lewis and Clark," *We Proceeded On,* 18, no. 2 (1992): 12–19.

ag'in!"[7] (In other words, "I want to *be* there!") Through the five-novel series a common plot pattern emerges. Allan Nevins once condensed it into
one phrase: "wilderness journey, conflict, capture, pursuit, and rescue,
sometimes culminating in a romantic reunion of hero and heroine."[8] (Add
"duel to the death" as part of "pursuit and rescue," and we have the ground
plan of most Westerns.)

Cooper is often regarded as the greatest early author of frontier tales.
He was certainly the first widely successful American novelist. He made
Natty Bumppo into a world-famous figure of the American pathfinder at
the turn of the nineteenth century. It may be impossible to overturn that
achievement and futile to try. But history has now caught up with American fiction. In place of Cooper's fictions and Biddle's inadequate narrative,
we now have shelves of documents and monographs about genuine heroes
exploring the West. What is more, we can demonstrate the workings of their
intellect. We can show that while they followed Indian trails just as bravely
as any Leatherstocking, they looked west much more perceptively and hope-
fully. In Cooper's novel *The Prairie*, Natty Bumppo dies in 1804, a worn-out
old trapper on the Plains. For Lewis and Clark, 1804 on the Plains was only
the beginning.

7. James Fenimore Cooper, *The Pioneers* (1823; reprint, New York: Penguin, 1988),
ch. 41, p. 454.

8. Allan Nevins, ed., *The Leatherstocking Saga* (New York: Pantheon, 1954), p. 5.

PART SIX
NEW THOUGHTS
ON THE WEST

TRAVERSING THE FORTIETH PARALLEL
The Experiences of Robert Ridgway, Teenage Ornithologist

In 1867, Clarence King, a renowned American geologist, invited Robert Ridgway, a sixteen-year old from Mount Carmel, Illinois, to join him and other noted scientists on the United States Geological Survey of the Fortieth Parallel. Backed by parental approval, Ridgway, an enthusiastic bird lover, readily accepted. For the next two years, he traversed the mountains of California, Nevada, and Utah as the expedition's zoologist, gathering animal specimens for the Smithsonian Institution. His journey laid the foundation for his emergence as one of America's premier ornithologists. A study of his years on the survey not only provides interesting information about the extraordinary experiences of a teenager on a government expedition, but also details one account of the training of a budding American naturalist in the nineteenth century.

Many events propelled Ridgway to both science and the West. On 2 July 1850, he was born to David and Henrietta Ridgway in Mount Carmel, a small town located on the Wabash River in southeastern Illinois. At an early age he was attracted to nature, especially birds, largely because of the influence of his father who often took him into forests surrounding the town. Sometime in his fourteenth year, he observed an unfamiliar bird. Intrigued, he took the advice of a friend's mother and wrote to the Commissioner of Patents in Washington, D. C., asking him to identify the creature. Although the Patents Office had earlier housed an extensive natural history collection, including many birds, the current commissioner knew nothing about ornithology, and forwarded the letter to Spencer Baird, Assistant Secretary of the Smithsonian Institution. Baird graciously answered Ridgway's query, and a correspondence between the noted naturalist and the young teenager ensued.[1]

Ridgway frequently sent Baird drawings of birds around Mount Carmel, asking the scientist to identify them by name. As Ridgway's letters became more frequent, Baird, who already carried on correspondence with several other amateur ornithologists, became increasingly impressed with Ridgway's artistic and descriptive talents. "[Your letters and drawings]," he wrote, "show an unusual degree of ability as an artist, and of intelligent attention to a scientific subject."[2] Thus, when Clarence King informed him of plans to survey the West along the Fortieth Parallel, Baird suggested Ridgway as the expedition's zoologist.[3] He then wrote Ridgway, asking him if he would be interested in such a position. "How would you like to go to the Rocky Mts. and California for a year or two as collector of specimens?" Baird asked.[4] Astonished at his luck and eager to accept, Ridgway could only hope that his parents would give their permission. At first unsure, David and Henrietta finally consented after Baird assured them that "there are no dangers whatever from hostile Indians."[5]

One can understand why Ridgway's parents would be so reluctant to

---

1. Robert Ridgway, "Biographical Memoirs: Spencer Fullerton Baird," in *Annual Report of the Board of Regents of the Smithsonian Institution, 1888* (Washington, D.C.: Government Printing Office, 1890), pp. 711–12; see also Harry Harris, "Robert Ridgway," *The Condor* 30 (January/February 1928): 7–16; F. Garvin Davenport, "Robert Ridgway: Illinois Naturalist," *Journal of the Illinois State Historical Society* 63 (Autumn 1970): 271–74; Alexander Wetmore, "Robert Ridgway, 1850–1929," *National Academy of Sciences Biographical Memoirs* 15 (1932): 57–59. *The Condor* was an ornithological journal popular in the early twentieth century.

2. Spencer Baird to Robert Ridgway, 23 June 1864, published in Ridgway, "Spencer Fullerton Baird," p. 712.

3. Harris, "Robert Ridgway," p. 16; Davenport, "Robert Ridgway," pp. 275–76; Wetmore, "Robert Ridgway," p. 59.

4. Spencer Baird to Robert Ridgway, 27 February 1867, published in Harris, "Robert Ridgway," p. 16.

5. Spencer Baird to Robert Ridgway, 30 March 1867, published in Harris, "Robert Ridgway," p. 18.

approve of Ridgway's appointment. The period between 1862 and 1867 was a bloody time in American Indian affairs, characterized by many skirmishes between natives and American troops. For example, on 29 January 1863, a group of California Volunteers led by Colonel Patrick Edward Connor attacked a Northwestern Shoshoni village on the Bear River in Washington Territory, killing 250 Indians, including many women and children. Likewise, on 29 November 1864, soldiers under the command of Colonel John M. Chivington massacred at least 150 Cheyenne at Sand Creek, Colorado. In retaliation, the Cheyenne twice attacked Julesburg, Colorado and halted overland travel to Denver. On 21 December 1866, eighty soldiers were killed by a force of Lakota, Cheyenne, and Arapaho in part because of the establishment of three U. S. forts on the Bozeman trail from Colorado to Montana. Because of this violence, the American public, including Ridgway's parents, was very concerned about Native American relations in the West.[6]

In addition to Indian problems, the American West in 1867 was relatively unknown, especially scientifically. Many surveys of the West had occurred throughout the 1850s, mainly by United States Army Topographical Engineers searching for practicable railroad routes, but Americans still regarded large portions of the area as mysterious wilderness. Despite the number of people who had emigrated to California, the Pacific Northwest, and other regions, many citizens still felt that the West needed extensive exploration. Indeed, numerous civilian scientists decided that fame and fortune awaited anyone who could document the region's geological, geographical, and natural features. With this in mind, Clarence King lobbied Congress for an appropriation to traverse the Fortieth Parallel where the Central Pacific Railroad would run.[7] Congress agreed, and placed the expedition un-

---

6. For a fuller discussion of Indian / White relations during this time period, see Clyde A. Milner II, "National Initiatives," in *The Oxford History of the American West*, Clyde A. Milner II, Carol A. O'Connor, and Martha Sandweiss, eds. (New York: Oxford University Press, 1994), pp. 177–83.

7. Clarence King (1842–1901) was a chemistry graduate from the Sheffield Scientific School at Yale. In 1863 he served as an assistant geologist to Josiah D. Whitney on Whitney's geological survey of California, and wrote the highly popular *Mountaineering in the Sierra Nevada* about his experiences. Although only twenty-four in 1866, King had no problems securing an appointment as Geologist-in-Charge of the Fortieth Parallel Survey. After he returned from the expedition, he was appointed the first director of the United States Geological Survey in 1880, but soon thereafter faced deteriorating health conditions and lived out the rest of his life in relative obscurity. For more information, see Thurman Wilkins's excellent

der the authority of General A. A. Humphreys of the Army Topographical Engineers.[8]

Humphreys and King concurred that the survey would study and describe all the natural resources of the country near the planned Union and Central Pacific railroad line. The exploration would traverse a belt of country from California to the Rocky Mountains one hundred miles wide, digressing at times to more fully investigate the regions which would soon be populated by Americans coming by train.[9]

With his appropriation and assignment in hand, King began recruiting members for the survey. Although focusing primarily on geological and topographical elements, he also wanted natural history represented. Thus, Spencer Baird was able to suggest Ridgway as the expedition's zoologist. Baird's recommendation of a young, inexperienced amateur to represent the Smithsonian was not unusual. Since ornithology was a relatively new scientific discipline, few Americans participated in it professionally. In the words of one historian, "The best known ornithologists were clergymen, doctors, lawyers, or wealthy landowners." In short, ornithology was mostly an avocation.[10]

---

biography, *Clarence King: A Biography* (New York: The Macmillan Company, 1958; reprint, Albuquerque: University of New Mexico Press, 1988); page references are to reprint edition.

8. Richard Bartlett, *Great Surveys of the American West* (Norman: University of Oklahoma Press, 1962), pp. xi–xii; William Goetzmann, *Exploration and Empire: The Explorer and the Scientist in the Winning of the American West* (New York: Alfred A. Knopf, 1966), p. 355. King's survey was the first of the four "Great Surveys" of the 1860s and 70s. Also under the direction of the United States Army was Lieutenant George Wheeler's geographical expedition of the One Hundredth Meridian from 1869–79. Ferdinand V. Hayden conducted his Geological and Geographical Survey of the Territories from 1867–78, while John Wesley Powell explored the Rocky Mountain region from 1869–79. These latter two excursions were under the direction of the Department of the Interior. Although King's survey is noted as the most scientific of the four, the other three also had a tremendous impact. Hayden's exploration promoted and romanticized the scenic beauty of the West through photographs and paintings and also helped persuade Congress to establish Yellowstone National Park. Powell's expedition brought back not only scientific knowledge, but also ethnographical information about Native Americans and data on the aridity of the West. Wheeler's survey was perhaps the least scientifically rewarding of the four, but still contributed maps and salient information. See Bartlett, *Great Surveys*, p. xv; Goetzmann, *Exploration and Empire*, pp. 466, 487, 528, 572.

9. See Goetzmann, *Exploration and Empire*, 392, 431.

10. Ernst Mayr, "Epilogue: Materials for a History of American Ornithology," in *Ornithology: From Aristotle to the Present*, by Erwin Streseman, trans. Hans J. and Cathleen Epstein (Cambridge, Mass.: Harvard University Press, 1975), p. 373; E. F. Rivinus and E. M. Youssef, *Spencer Baird of the Smithsonian* (Washington, D.C.: Smithsonian Institution Press, 1992), p. 2.

Indeed, in the mid-nineteenth century, interested novices pervaded the natural sciences. Fields such as botany and zoology consisted of many unschooled enthusiasts who worked independently of scientific organizations or government surveys. Gideon Lincecum, for example, was a "self-taught naturalist" who gathered fossils, plants, and ants around his residence in Texas in the mid-nineteenth century. Based on his observations, he became a corresponding member of the Philadelphia Academy of Natural Sciences, and contributed thousands of botanical specimens to the Smithsonian and the British Museum. He also published over two dozen articles in several scientific journals.[11]

Rather than rejecting such participants, Baird, like other professional scientists, embraced them and enthusiastically capitalized on their interests. He even exploited personnel of the United States Army, receiving throughout the 1850s both ornithological and zoological specimens from Army Medical Corps' doctors stationed in the American West.[12] Indeed, this system of amateur collectors fit perfectly with Baird's concept of ornithology. In this "Bairdian Period," which lasted from the 1850s to the 1880s, he placed great emphasis on the collecting, cataloguing, and naming of birds, since few museum specimens actually existed.[13] Amateurs could easily collect birds, and, with a little training, could even skin and preserve them. Consequently, Baird frequently used novices, whether they were teenage correspondents, army surgeons, or civilian naturalists.[14] An examination of Ridgway's experiences, then, provides rich insight into the workings and achievements of these amateurs.

In the early weeks of March 1867, Ridgway received a letter from King formally extending the invitation to accompany the survey. He excitedly agreed to King's offer of "fifty dollars per month in U. S. currency with transportation and subsistence in the field."[15] After hearing of Ridgway's acceptance, Baird counseled the youth to come to Washington, D.C., three

11. Jerry Bryan Lincecum, Introduction to *Adventures of a Frontier Naturalist: The Life and Times of Dr. Gideon Lincecum*, Jerry Bryan Lincecum and Edward Hake Phillips, eds. (College Station: Texas A&M University Press, 1994), p. xx.

12. Ridgway, "Spencer Fullerton Baird," pp. 703, 706.

13. Ibid., p. 706.

14. Rivinus and Youssef, *Spencer Baird*, p. 83.

15. Clarence King to Robert Ridgway, 28 March 1867, published in Harris, "Robert Ridgway," p. 19.

weeks before the expedition's departure in order to familiarize himself with western birds and learn about preserving animal skins.[16]

Soon after, Ridgway left Illinois to join Baird in Washington, D.C. On 18 April 1867, he reached the city, and the next day, plunged into his training. Not only did he learn skin preservation techniques, but also the art of identification. Because he brought a box of Mount Carmel birds, Baird had him study and compare Illinois and eastern birds. "Tell pa that I wish I had a hundred black-birds in my box instead of three," he wrote his mother. "Ours is a distinct species from the eastern one, and I have the honor of first pointing out the specific differences in the two."[17]

Yet Ridgway did not spend all his time studying. Baird also introduced him to important scientists, such as Henry Ulke, "the most celebrated Coleopterist in the Country."[18] Likewise, Baird gave Ridgway letters of introduction to several scientists in the West, thus enabling Ridgway to start building his own scientific network.

The time soon came for the expedition to depart. On 5 May, Ridgway received a letter from King asking him to come to New York on 9 May.[19] He complied, and on 11 May, he, along with King, Henry Custer (a topographic assistant), William Bailey (a botanist), and Timothy O'Sullivan (the group's photographer), set sail for the isthmus of Panama, the first stop on the journey.[20] Three large chests of equipment accompanied Ridgway. "My outfit could not possibly be any better than it is," he wrote his father. Aside from twenty-four animal traps and two Maynard rifles ("the best guns in existence"), he also carried many different preservation chemicals, such as arsenic, alum, saltpetre, tartar emetic, and carbolic acid. "Thus you see I want nothing: but will be amply provided for."[21]

---

16. Harris, "Robert Ridgway," pp. 19, 21.

17. Robert Ridgway to Henrietta Ridgway, 5 May 1867, in Robert Ridgway Papers, Special Collections, Merrill Library, Utah State University, Logan, Utah; hereafter cited as RRP. Unless otherwise noted, all of Ridgway's correspondence, both incoming and outgoing, is drawn from this collection.

18. Ibid. The *coleoptera* is an order of insects which includes both beetles and weevils.

19. Robert Ridgway to Henrietta Ridgway, 5 May 1867, in RRP.

20. Robert Ridgway to David Ridgway, 25 May 1867, in RRP. On 1 May, James Gardiner (a geologist), Arnold and James Hague (geologists), Samuel Emmons (a geologist), and F. A. Clark (a topographic assistant) had left for California as an advance group. See Bartlett, *Great Surveys*, p. 154; Goetzmann, *Exploration and Empire*, p. 438; Wilkins, *Clarence King*, p. 104.

21. Robert Ridgway to David Ridgway, 9 May 1867, in RRP.

Around 17 May, the group arrived in Panama and began crossing the isthmus by train. In this Central American region, Ridgway found flora and fauna more beautiful than any he had ever imagined, and he displayed a youthful sense of wonderment. "Little did I dream of *ever* seeing such a scene," he wrote while looking out of the train's window. The tropical vegetation entranced him, but the varieties of "regally-colored birds," including the "fiery scarlet ibis . . . snowy-white herons, and golden-plumaged snipes" were even more engaging.[22] Ridgway had entered an ornithological heaven.

After crossing the isthmus, the group embarked on a steamer headed for California. Although the wind blew Ridgway's hat overboard, the journey was relatively uneventful,[23] and in the early hours of 3 June the boat reached San Francisco Bay. After two days in the city, members of the expedition boarded a river steamer, the *Yosemite*, and sailed for Sacramento. There they located the advance party of James Gardiner, James and Arnold Hague, Samuel Emmons, and F. A. Clark at an established camp.[24] After a voyage of twenty-three days, Ridgway had finally made it to the West.[25]

Although expressing delight in the mountains surrounding Sacramento, Ridgway experienced an intense longing for home in this unfamiliar terrain. His first letter from the region showed a desire to find anything familiar on the landscape. "Casting my eyes on the ground I see nothing but dog-fennel, dog-fennel: just as it is about Mt Carmel," he declared. Likewise, he noted the abundance of orchards around the area: "Here, figs and oranges are as common as peaches and apples are at home."[26] More important, however, were his clear feelings of homesickness. Whereas in Washington, D.C., he had stated, "I am not the least bit home-sick,"[27] he now proclaimed, "Ma I cannot get along without about a dozen more *Photographs*." Speaking about his baby brother, he poignantly wrote, "I could almost walk home just to see him."[28] Although enjoying his new surround-

22. Robert Ridgway to David Ridgway, 17 May 1867, in RRP.

23. Robert Ridgway to David Ridgway, 25 May 1867, in RRP.

24. For more information on these individuals, see Bartlett, *Great Surveys*.

25. Robert Ridgway to Henrietta Ridgway, 24 June 1867, in RRP. See also Bartlett, *Great Surveys*, pp. 154–55; Goetzmann, *Exploration and Empire*, p. 438; Wilkins, *Clarence King*, p. 106.

26. Robert Ridgway to Henrietta Ridgway, 24 June 1867, in RRP.

27. Robert Ridgway to Henrietta Ridgway, 5 May 1867, in RRP.

28. Robert Ridgway to Henrietta Ridgway, 24 June 1867, in RRP.

ings, the sixteen-year-old—like most teenagers away from home for the first time—yearned for his family.

Yet Ridgway had little spare time for his homesickness to fester. Camped in Sacramento, he finally had the chance to test his zoological training. Indeed, the region abounded with collecting opportunities. "Althoug [*sic*] nothing of importance was expected from this locality I have nevertheless obtained 4 or 5 of the desiderata," he wrote his mother, later explaining that he acquired specimens of yellow-billed magpies ("a rare and very beautiful species"), owls, and hawks. Additionally, he collected at least 140 bird eggs. "As far as hunting is concerned I have enjoyed it greatly," he confided, while also expressing a wish for a new locale, since he had gathered all that he desired from the area.[29]

Ridgway would not have to wait long. On 4 July, the expedition moved east across the Sierra Nevada mountain range into Nevada, observing the construction of the Central Pacific Railroad along the way.[30] Because the company never stopped to make camp, Ridgway had no time to collect along this route. "A number of additional species and many valuable observations were thus lost to the collection and archives of the exploration," he lamented. Finally, on 24 July, the survey set up a working camp at the Big Bend of the Truckee River.[31] Settled here for the next twenty-five days, Ridgway gained some valuable ornithological and survival experience, especially on a trip to Pyramid Lake.[32]

In August, Ridgway, O'Sullivan, and H. G. Parker, Indian Superintendent of Nevada, began a journey down the Truckee River to the lake where

---

29. Ibid.

30. Robert Ridgway to Henrietta Ridgway, 11 August 1867, in RRP.

31. *Report of the Geological Exploration of the Fortieth Parallel*, by Clarence King, Chairman (Washington, D.C.: Government Printing Office, 1878), 4:310. The expedition only made stops when the topographers and geologists wanted to explore the country, since the primary purpose of the survey was to "examine and describe the geological structure, geographical condition, and natural resources" of the region. See Wilkins, *Clarence King*, p. 102; Bartlett, *Great Surveys*, p. 162. The Truckee River flows out of Lake Tahoe in California into the Truckee Meadows near Reno. It drains into Pyramid Lake. James W. Hulse, *The Silver State: Nevada's Heritage Reinterpreted* (Reno: University of Nevada Press, 1991), p. 12.

32. Pyramid Lake, a deep desert lake, is fed by the Truckee River and is the "largest, deepest and most picturesque of all of the lakes in western Nevada." John C. Frémont named it in 1844. Effie Mona Mack, *Nevada: A History of the State from the Earliest Times Through the Civil War* (Glendale, Calif.: The Arthur H. Clark Company, 1936), 28; Hulse, *The Silver State*, p. 41.

Ridgway hoped to collect bird specimens while O'Sullivan took photographs. Sailing in the *Nettie*, "a very good fair-vaned Batteaux, 21 feet in length," the trio soon ran into trouble on the "tortorus" river. Rounding a bend too quickly, the boat "went slap broadside against a fallen cottonwood, through the middle of which ran about a 5 mile current." To prevent the vessel from capsizing, O'Sullivan and Ridgway jumped to its lower edge while Parker, thinking he could pull it to shore, leapt into the water. While O'Sullivan put all his weight on the edge of the craft, Ridgway bailed out the water and Parker pushed the boat loose.[33] Although exciting enough at the time, Ridgway later remembered the journey only as being "sufficiently difficult, not to say risky, in places."[34] Memory also affected O'Sullivan's reconstruction, as he later greatly exaggerated his role in the adventure:

> Our photographic friend, being a swimmer of no ordinary power, succeeded in reaching the shore, not opposite the *Nettie*, though it was but forty yards from the shore, for he was carried a hundred yards down the rapids. A rope was thrown to him from the boat, and thus he rescued the little craft with her crew from the perilous situation. The sharp rocks had torn the little clothing of which he had not divested himself, and had so cut and bruised his body that he was glad to crawl into the brier tangle that fringed the river's brink.[35]

With such an exciting beginning, one wonders how the rest of the Pyramid Lake expedition could possibly compete. Yet at least in terms of ornithology and scenery, the lake itself satisfied Ridgway. Traversing its shores, he and Parker shot pelicans "too heavy to carry," so only the skins were preserved and transported back to camp. Likewise, he marveled at the still,

---

33. Robert Ridgway to David Ridgway, 1 September 1867, in RRP.

34. Harris, "Robert Ridgway," p. 24.

35. John Samson, "Photographs from the High Rockies," *Harper's New Monthly Magazine* 39 (September 1869): 467. According to William Goetzmann, John Samson was probably a pseudonym for Timothy O'Sullivan. In their accounts of the boat trip, both Goetzmann and Richard Bartlett accept O'Sullivan's account as accurate. Goetzmann also places James Hague on the trip. See Goetzmann, *Exploration and Empire*, pp. 439–40; Bartlett, *Great Surveys*, p. 165. Ridgway's description, however, exposes O'Sullivan's exaggerations and shows that only Parker, O'Sullivan, and himself were on the boat. James Hague and Samuel Emmons, Ridgway relates, rode their mules down to the lake later on.

deep water, and the willows and aquatic shrubs so thick they reminded him of Central America.[36]

Soon, however, the group returned to the main camp. There they rejoined the survey, and on 25 August, the entire expedition departed, heading east to the Humboldt River.[37] Upon reaching it, they decided to camp at the Humboldt Sinks, a place where the air reeked with sulphur and "millions of blood-thirsty mosquitos" constantly attacked. These insects quickly transported malarial fever to the party, Ridgway being the first to contract it. He later recollected,

> It was near noon, and I was probably a mile, perhaps farther, ahead of the rest of the party, when feeling sick and "queer" I dismounted, tied my mule to a sage-bush, and lay down in his shadow. I never knew when they picked me up and placed me in the ambulance, nor was I conscious at all until camp was reached.[38]

At the time, however, he only wryly commented to his parents that "after living all my life in a place reported as the worst part of the U. S. for this infernal disease," he, in Nevada for the first time, suffered from "the abominable fever and ague." [39]

The disease soon affected most of the party,[40] and they moved to "healthier water and purer air" in the West Humboldt Mountains. At first recuperating at Wright's Canyon, the group relocated to Buena Vista Canyon by the town of Unionville. Ridgway found both places teeming with birds, especially Buena Vista which "prov[ed] to be the best locality, for birds, yet visited." The group stayed until the middle of October. After once again passing through the Humboldt Marshes, they then journeyed to Carson City and established winter quarters.[41]

36. Robert Ridgway to David Ridgway, 1 September 1867, in RRP.

37. The Humboldt River flows northeast to southwest for 280 miles, and drains the northern third of Nevada. Hulse, *The Silver State*, p. 13.

38. Harris, "Robert Ridgway," p. 25.

39. Robert Ridgway to David Ridgway, 15 October 1867, in RRP.

40. In his report to General A. A. Humphreys, chief of the Army Engineers and King's supervisor, King reported that three-fourths of the expedition contracted the fever, wasting at least twenty percent of the survey's effectiveness. Bartlett, *Great Surveys*, p. 168; Goetzmann, *Exploration and Empire*, p. 442.

41. *Report of the Geological Exploration*, 4:311.

Unfortunately, little is known about the survey's activities from January to May of 1868. King spent much of his time exploring mining shafts such as the Comstock and, along with Emmons and the Hagues, gathering geological data of the Carson City region. Custer and Clark, the topographers, revised their maps. Ridgway, meanwhile, spent some time at the Truckee Reservation with Parker, who assisted him with his collections.[42]

Finally, in May, King decided that the time had come to resume the expedition. On 14 May, Ridgway once again journeyed to the Truckee Reservation. Here, as was his custom, he visited a small pond "for the purpose of studying the several species of Swallows which came there in large numbers every evening." He also found time to make another excursion to Pyramid Lake, accompanied by Parker and several Paiute Indians. "Large collections were made here," Ridgway reported, and he secured "very rare eggs of several species of water-fowl breeding on these islands."[43]

Soon after Ridgway's return, the expedition left for the Toiyabe Mountains in eastern Nevada. Along the way, Ridgway made careful notes and acquired many important specimens. Indeed, as a zoologist exploring new western regions, there was no time to relax. He constantly listened for the songs of new birds, even at night and in the early morning. He also tracked the creatures, often hiding among mountain rocks to observe their movements.[44]

From the Toiyabes, Ridgway and the rest of the expedition moved on to the Ruby Mountains, which they reached in the middle of July. Here Ridgway supposedly had an "Indian scare." On the way to Thousand Spring Valley, he, O. L. Palmer (Clarence King's bookkeeper), and a cook had a party of fifty or sixty Indians gallop towards them, "yip-yiping as if pandemonium had broken loose." Palmer and the cook drew their revolvers "and expected

---

42. Goetzmann, *Exploration and Empire*, p. 442; *Report of the Geological Exploration*, 4:311. Parker, as Indian Superintendant, ran the Truckee Reservation which housed Northern Paiute Indians. It was located near Pyramid Lake just off the Truckee River. Ridgway, because of the considerable time he spent at the reservation, made numerous friends with the Indians. In fact, one of his letters contains Paiute names for birds, one of the more valuable contributions of his writings. See Robert Ridgway to David Ridgway, 15 October 1867, in RRP.

43. *Report of the Geological Exploration*, 4:311, 445.

44. Ibid., 4:469, 564.

the 'exercises' to begin," but the natives merely reined in their horses and approached more leisurely, enjoying the fear they had caused.[45]

Ridgway may have exaggerated this story, for he never mentioned the incident in any letters at the time and only gave this account sixty years later. Additionally, he had earlier stated that "unless shamefully treated by white men there is no danger whatever from [the Indians]." Six decades later, like others recalling journeys to the West, he probably thought it necessary to include a story about wild natives to satisfy his audience.[46]

At the end of August the expedition moved northward along the East Humboldt Mountains. By the end of September, they reached their most northern locality, the "City of Rocks" in southern Idaho. "When opportunity permitted," Ridgway reported, "small collections were made" along the way. From the City of Rocks, the group journeyed south-eastward, arriving in Salt Lake City, Utah, early in October.[47] There, they stored their equipment at Camp Douglas, a military establishment close by the city, and, on 20 October, traveled by stagecoach to Green River, Wyoming, where they caught the Union Pacific Railroad and headed east for a month's vacation.[48]

Ridgway must have felt a great deal of excitement as he rode the train back to Mount Carmel. For the first time in almost nineteen months he would see his family, including his baby brother Jodie whom he was sure had forgotten him.[49] The reunion was short-lived, however, and Ridgway soon left for Washington, D.C., where, under the direction of Spencer Baird, he examined and prepared the specimens he had collected.

Yet soon after his arrival in Washington, Ridgway heard disturbing news. Because the survey's original congressional funding had run out, Clarence King was forced to lobby diligently for another cash allotment.[50]

45. Harris, "Robert Ridgway," p. 23.

46. Robert Ridgway to Henrietta Ridgway, 11 August 1867, in RRP. Clyde A. Milner II discusses this phenomenon of "false memory" in "The View from Wisdom: Four Layers of History and Regional Identity," in *Under an Open Sky: Rethinking America's Western Past*, William Cronon, George Miles, and Jay Gitlin, eds. (New York: W. W. Norton and Company, 1992), pp. 209–215.

47. *Report of the Geological Exploration*, 4:312.

48. Goetzmann, *Exploration and Empire*, p. 445; Bartlett, *Great Surveys*, p. 175. At this time, the terminus of the Union Pacific was in Green River. By the time of the survey's return in May of 1869, the Union Pacific and Central Pacific had been joined at Promontory Point in Utah. Harris, "Robert Ridgway," p. 21.

49. See Henrietta Ridgway to Robert Ridgway, 4 August 1867, in RRP.

50. Goetzmann, *Exploration and Empire*, p. 446.

Although successful, King informed Ridgway that his new appropriation was not as generous as the previous one, and therefore, he was "forced to drop the Zoology and the Botany from the Exploration." Knowing of the fine work Ridgway had already accomplished, however, King offered to let him accompany him back to Salt Lake City in the spring, although Ridgway would receive only subsistence pay. After discussing it with his father and taking some time to think it over, Ridgway decided to accept King's offer.[51]

Thus, in May of 1869, after another short visit to his family, Ridgway boarded the recently completed transcontinental railroad and traveled again to Salt Lake City. Along the way, he busied himself by taking notes on various birds observed outside his window.[52] By 15 May he had reunited with the rest of the survey, and on 20 May he resumed collecting in the Salt Lake region.[53]

During the last week in May, King gave Ridgway, Sereno Watson (a botanist), F. A. Clark, and a Mr. Davis (a topographer) the assignment of exploring the massive Great Salt Lake. The group visited several islands in the lake, including Antelope, Stansbury, and Carrington Islands, and obtained eggs from a few bird species. Upon completion of this exploration, King sent Ridgway and Watson to the western spurs of the Uinta Mountains where they remained until 8 July. These excursions proved particularly fruitful, and Ridgway informed his mother, "I am enjoying myself as I never have before and having great success in my work."[54]

---

51. It is not known exactly when Ridgway made the decision to accompany King, but apparently it was not until at least April. Up until then, he planned on returning to Mount Carmel for the summer. Why Ridgway accepted is also unclear, but it is probable that Spencer Baird, anxious for more bird specimens for the Smithsonian, influenced him to continue his explorations in the West. See Robert Ridgway to David Ridgway, 20 January 1869, in RRP; Henrietta Ridgway to Robert Ridgway, 31 January 1869, in RRP; Henrietta Ridgway to Robert Ridgway, 13 February 1869, in RRP; Henrietta Ridgway to Robert Ridgway, 13 March 1869, in RRP.

52. One wonders how accurate Ridgway's account of observing birds from the train is. Historian Anne Farrar Hyde has stated that from a train, most western scenery for travelers was hazy. "The blurred foreground isolate[d] the traveler from the landscape close to the train and only allow[ed] him to see the general outline of the far distance. All detail near the train disappear[ed]. . . . The scenery . . . bec[a]me a boring blur from the window of a train. . . . The train actually prevented sightseeing." Anne Farrar Hyde, *An American Vision: Far Western Landscape and National Culture, 1820–1920* (New York: New York University Press, 1990), pp. 117–19.

53. *Report of the Geological Exploration*, 4:487.

54. Ibid., 4:312; Robert Ridgway to Henrietta Ridgway, 14 June 1869, in RRP.

Indeed, several letters from Spencer Baird concurred with Ridgway's statements, showing how experienced the youth was becoming. "The birds came all right, and were splendid in preparation," Baird praised. "The capture of *Helminthophaga virginiae* is a very important one." Baird also related how some of Ridgway's discoveries were shattering previous ornithological perceptions of bird range: "I see you are at your old tricks of capturing eastern birds out of usual range."[55]

Throughout July and early August, Ridgway stayed at the main camp in Salt Lake City writing field notes. On 16 August, however, his adventures in the West came to an end. That day, he and Sereno Watson packed up their equipment and headed back to Washington, D.C. to work on their reports.[56] Although Ridgway must have experienced some feelings of sadness, the joy of returning home probably engulfed him, for he had earlier informed his father, "I am literally homesick, and would like to collect at home next spring and summer."[57]

However, Ridgway would never again reside at his home in Mount Carmel. Upon his return to the Smithsonian, he became Baird's "unofficial assistant" and commenced a plethora of tasks.[58] Not only did he work on the survey report, but he also assisted Baird and Thomas Brewer in preparing their book, *A History of North American Birds*. Providing them with firsthand information about western birds, Ridgway also drew several pictures for the publication.[59] Nevertheless, Ridgway's writing, not his artwork, gained him the most attention in the upcoming years.

Ridgway's publishing career began with his work on the Fortieth Parallel survey. Two articles appeared while he still labored in the field. One, "A

55. Spencer Baird to Robert Ridgway, 22 June 1869, in RRP. Ridgway first observed *Helminthophaga virginiae*, more commonly known as Virginia's Warbler, on the eastern slope of the Ruby Mountains. Although not found west of that mountain range, the bird was especially abundant among the scrub-oaks on the foothills near Salt Lake City. See *Report of the Geological Exploration*, 4:428.

56. Goetzmann and Bartlett, both examining Clarence King's papers, give different dates for Ridgway's departure. Goetzmann places it at the end of September, while Bartlett claims he left on 1 September. Ridgway himself, however, stated it was 16 August. Goetzmann, *Exploration and Empire*, p. 448; Bartlett, *Great Surveys*, p. 178; *Report of the Geological Exploration*, 4:313.

57. Robert Ridgway to David Ridgway, 20 January 1869, in RRP.

58. Davenport, "Robert Ridgway," p. 278.

59. See Spencer Baird, Thomas Brewer, and Robert Ridgway, *A History of North American Birds*, 2 vols. (Boston, Mass.: Little, Brown and Company, 1874), 1:vii.

True Story of a Pet Bird," was more of an entertaining tale of the West than a scientific treatise.[60] The other, "Notices of Certain Obscurely Known Species of American Birds," became an important scientific work. Based exclusively on Ridgway's observations on the survey, it, in the words of one scientist, expressed "the dawning realization that geographic variation had to be taken into consideration" when classifying species.[61] According to Ridgway,

> when we have traced a species through all its variations to a certain point where the discrepancy from the typical style is too great and uniform to be accounted for by any physical cause, it becomes us as naturalists to assign to such extreme conditions a specific rank.[62]

Charles G. Sibley, a California ornithologist, declared that Ridgway's arguments showed the growing influence of Charles Darwin's theory of evolution because it moved away from the belief in the immutablity of species.[63] Ridgway's paper, influenced by Baird who had earlier discussed geographic variation, was a significant step towards an understanding of the classification of species.[64]

In a similar way, the book which advanced Ridgway's scientific career most directly arose from his adventures in the West. Clarence King commissioned Ridgway to write the section on ornithology for the eight-volume *Report of the Geological Exploration of the Fortieth Parallel*. This volume, simply entitled *Ornithology*, "attracted at the time the favorable notice of the entire scientific world." [65] The book consisted of extensive and lucid descriptions of birds Ridgway had encountered in the West. Writing about the western kingbird, for example, he stated, "It is of an even more vivacious and quarrelsome disposition, continually indulging in aerial com-

---

60. Robert Ridgway, "A True Story of a Pet Bird," *The American Naturalist* 3 (August 1869): 309–312.

61. Charles G. Sibley, "Ornithology," in *A Century of Progress in the Natural Sciences, 1853–1953*, by the California Academy of Sciences (San Francisco: California Academy of Sciences, 1955), p. 632.

62. Robert Ridgway, "Notices of Certain Obscurely Known Species of American Birds," in *Proceedings of the Academy of Natural Sciences of Philadelphia* 21 (June 1869): 126.

63. Sibley, "Ornithology," p. 632.

64. Mayr, "Materials for a History of American Ornithology," p. 368.

65. Harris, "Robert Ridgway," p. 27. See also Goetzmann, *Exploration and Empire*, p. 460; Bartlett, *Great Surveys*, p. 210.

bats, sometimes to such an extent that half a dozen or more may be seen pitching into each other promiscuously."[66] With such clear descriptions of birds, and a full catalogue of birds encountered, Ridgway's report became an important work on ornithology in the American West.

Based on the strength of this publication, and with an education gained entirely in the field, the twenty-four-year-old Ridgway became officially employed at the Smithsonian in 1874 as an ornithologist.[67] His ascension to this post, however, contradicted changes trickling into other sciences at the time, and showed the continuing amateur makeup of ornithology. Whereas Ridgway's prowess enabled him to enter the profession without the basis of formal schooling, scientists in other fields in the 1870s, including natural science, found it increasingly necessary to gain a college education. The experiences of C. Hart Merriam illustrate this growing professionalization.

Merriam, much like Ridgway, accompanied the Hayden Geological Survey of the West in 1872 as a sixteen-year-old zoologist. Upon his return, he worked at the Smithsonian Institution. After Merriam expressed a desire to perform fieldwork on another survey, Spencer Baird counseled him instead to study at the Sheffield Scientific School of Yale where he "would have the advantage of laboratory work and lectures." He could then become "a trained naturalist" rather than merely "a *collector* of natural history specimens." Merriam followed Baird's advice and became a famous zoologist.[68]

Other scientific disciplines followed the same route in trying to produce a professionalized cadre of scholars. According to historian Robert V. Bruce, by the mid-1870s, several universities, such as Johns Hopkins, Harvard, Yale, and Pennsylvania, offered graduate programs in many different areas such as geology and chemistry. Because of these developments, research in scientific fields began shifting to universities and colleges. By 1900, "most universities required the Ph.D of their teachers and made publication of research a weighty factor in their promotion." Indeed, at the turn of the century, universities had become the centers for most scientific research,

---

66. *Report of the Geological Exploration*, 4:407, 528.

67. Wetmore, "Robert Ridgway," p. 60; Davenport, "Robert Ridgway," p. 278; Harris, "Robert Ridgway," p. 31.

68. C. Hart Merriam, "Baird the Naturalist," *Scientific Monthly* 18 (June 1924): 593–94 (emphasis in the original).

rather than other institutions such as the Smithsonian.[69] Ornithology, however, lagged behind most other disciplines in its academization, presumably because most professionals still focused completely on collecting and describing specimens and did not establish graduate programs until the early twentieth century.[70]

The experiences of ornithologists in the late nineteenth century accentuate this lack of schooling. Edgar Alexander Mears, like Ridgway, developed a love for birds early in his life. By 1875, at the age of nineteen, he carried on correspondence with some European collectors. Throughout the 1870s he published a few works on birds in scientific journals and presented a paper before the prestigious Linnaean Society in New York, even though he had no real training in ornithology. Mears's main occupation was Assistant Surgeon of the Army Medical Corps, but he still participated in the organization of the American Ornithologists' Union and was considered an important ornithologist.[71]

Likewise, James Denver Glennan, another surgeon with the army, attracted much attention for his work. In 1888, Glennan headed west as part of an army dispatch to the Indian wars. There he fell in love with birds and began studying them intensely. He delivered several papers based on his observations and ultimately became an Associate of the American Ornithologists' Union, a position he held from 1898 to 1902. With no formal schooling, Glennan still contributed a great deal of information to the field.[72]

Thus, Ridgway's professional emergence was not an anomaly in ornithology, although it was becoming more unusual under the general framework of science. Yet his achievements still stagger the imagination. Historians today recognize him as "America's foremost professional ornithologist during the period from about 1890 to the 1920s," and note his tremendous influence on the field.[73] Indeed, after his work on the Fortieth Parallel Sur-

---

69. Robert V. Bruce, *The Launching of Modern American Science, 1846–1876* (Ithaca, N. Y.: Cornell University Press, 1987), pp. 325, 334–35. See also Nathan Reingold, "American Indifference to Basic Research: A Reappraisal," in *Nineteenth-Century American Science: A Reappraisal*, George H. Daniels, ed. (Evanston, Ill.: Northwestern University Press, 1972), p. 55.

70. Mayr, "Materials for a History of American Ornithology," pp. 373–74.

71. Edgar Erskine Hume, *Ornithologists of the United States Army Medical Corps* (Baltimore, Md.: The Johns Hopkins Press, 1942), pp. 297–98.

72. Ibid., pp. 162–63.

73. Ibid., p. 368.

vey, he published many notable books, including *A Nomenclature of Colors for Naturalists and Compendium of Useful Knowledge for Ornithologists* (1886) which established a color nomenclature for scientists, and *The Birds of North and Middle America (1901–1919)*, his magnum opus which drew on his field adventures to produce a massive catalogue of birds.[74] The latter study garnered him several awards, including the Daniel Giraud Elliot Medal and Honorarium from the National Academy of Sciences, and the Brewster Medal of the American Ornithologists' Union.[75]

Ridgway served a long and distinguished career as an ornithologist. After working a number of years at the Smithsonian Institution, he became curator of birds at the United States National Museum in 1886. He was also one of the founding members of the American Ornithologists' Union. Ridgway died in 1929 in Olney, Illinois, only a few miles from his childhood home of Mount Carmel.[76]

Soon after his arrival in California on the Fortieth Parallel Survey, Ridgway wrote to his family, "I hope [my letters] may give you some pleasure but I hardly have reason to think they will."[77] Today, historians can gain much enjoyment and salient information from Ridgway's accounts of his experiences in the West. Through them, we see the influence of a western expedition on one teenager's life and career, as well as the contributions of the survey to nineteenth-century American ornithology. We observe the Central Pacific and Union Pacific railroads chugging along towards Promontory Point, Utah. We can better imagine the landscape of nineteenth-century California, Nevada, and Utah after reading Ridgway's descriptions

74. Robert Ridgway, *A Nomenclature of Colors for Naturalists and Compendium of Useful Knowledge for Ornithologists* (Boston: Little, Brown and Company, 1886); Robert Ridgway, *The Birds of North and Middle America*, 9 vols. (Washington, D. C.: Government Printing Office, 1901–19).

75. See E. A. Abbot to Robert Ridgway, 24 March 1921, in RRP; Wetmore, "Robert Ridgway," p. 67.

76. His numerous successes in his profession notwithstanding, Ridgway's personal life was scarred by sickness, death, and sadness. On 12 October 1875 he married Julia Evelyn Perkins from Washington, D.C., and soon after their only child, Audubon Whelock, was born. Audubon, however, passed away at the young age of twenty-four, and Ridgway's wife, unable to handle the death spent the remainder of her life weak and sickly. She died in 1927. Ridgway passed away soon after on 25 March 1929. Harris, "Robert Ridgway," pp. 34–35; Wetmore, "Robert Ridgway," p. 60; Frank M. Chapman, "Bird Haven: The Robert Ridgway Wild-Life Sanctuary," *Bird-Lore* 29 (January–February 1927): 1–3.

77. Robert Ridgway to Henrietta Ridgway, 24 June 1867, in RRP.

of the majestic Sierra Nevada, pristine Pyramid Lake, and horrible Humboldt Springs. We get a glimpse of the survey through the eyes of a common teenager destined for scientific greatness. Indeed, Robert Ridgway's experiences on the Fortieth Parallel Survey are historically rich. Whether or not his family derived pleasure from hearing about them, historians today can certainly appreciate them for their contribution to the understanding of science and youth in the American West.

THE ROMANTIC AND THE TECHNICAL IN EARLY NINETEENTH-CENTURY AMERICAN EXPLORATION

Introduction: Humboldtian Science and Exploration

During his 1842 expedition to the "country lying between the Missouri River and the Rocky Mountains," Lieutenant John Charles Frémont and some of his expeditionary corps ascended what they thought was the highest peak in the Rocky Mountains. Frémont provided an extended description of the event which included the following:

> Putting hands and feet in the crevices between the blocks, I succeeded in getting over [a buttress], and . . . in a short time reached the crest. I sprang upon the summit, and another step would have precipitated me into an immense snow field five hundred feet below. . . . I stood on a narrow crest, about three feet in width, with an inclination of about 20° N. 51° E. . . . We mounted the barometer in the snow of the summit, and fixing a ramrod in a crevice, unfurled the national flag to wave in the breeze where never flag waved before. . . . A stillness the most profound and a terrible solitude forced themselves instantly on the mind as the great features of the place. Here on the summit . . . we thought ourselves beyond the region of animated life; but while we were sitting on the rock a solitary bee (*bromus, the bumble bee*) came winging his flight from the eastern valley, and lit on the knee of one of the men.

It was a strange place . . . for a lover of warm sunshine, and we pleased our-
selves with the idea that he was the first of his species to cross the mountain barrier, a solitary pioneer to foretell the advance of civilization. I believe that a moment's thought would have made us let him continue his
way unharmed, but we carried out the law of this country, where all animated nature seems at war; and seizing him immediately, put him in at
least a fit place, in the leaves of a large book, among the flowers we had collected on our way. The barometer stood at 18.293, the attached thermometer at 44°, giving for the elevation of this summit 13,750 feet above the Gulf
of Mexico, which may be called the highest flight of the bee.[1]

This is an extremely rich and revealing entry and it's not surprising that it has
frequently been discussed in the history of American exploration. The combination of the romantic, sublime silence, the literary transformation of the
bumble bee into a metaphor for expansion, unfurling the flag, listing general direction bearings, and taking barometer readings—all of these were
frequently meshed together in early nineteenth-century travel narratives. I
want to use the quotation to illustrate some of the themes for my talk in
which I will characterize exploration as a science of place. My contention is
that scholars have made romantic representations and technical knowledge
appear to be incompatible; by examining exploration as a process I hope to
show how both functioned in the production of *knowledge about* America.

William Goetzmann cited the passage to show how what he called Humboldtian scientists broadened their gazes "to include the widest possible
range of experience." They were, he argued, nationalistic romantics who believed that the universe was a dynamic interrelated system. The sheer magnitude of what they gathered with their capacious gazes overwhelmed their
ability to generalize. In the end, they fell back on the grandeur and mystery
of the cosmos. Frémont, Goetzmann states, "carried this to extreme when
he climbed what he thought was the highest peak in the Wind River Moun-

1. John Charles Frémont, *A Report on an Exploration of the Country Lying between the
Missouri River and the Rocky Mountains on the Line of the Kansas and Great Platte River*
[1843], in *The Expeditions of John Charles Frémont*, ed. Donald Jackson and Mary Lee Spence
(Urbana: University of Illinois Press, 1970), 1: 260–270. Frémont's first and second expeditions were published as *Report of the Exploring Expedition to the Rocky Mountains in the
year 1842, and to Oregon and North California in the Years 1843–44* (Washington, DC: Gales
and Seaton). There see pp. 60–70 in the August 15 entry.

tains and commented chiefly upon the habits of a bumble bee." The fact that Frémont did nothing of the sort will be addressed below.[2] Goetzmann's discussion of Humboldtian science in part led Susan Faye Cannon to challenge and refine the definition. Downplaying romanticism, she used the concept to provide a name for the nineteenth-century attempt to include "astronomy and the physics of the earth and the biology of the earth all viewed from a geographical standpoint, with the goal of discovering quantitative mathematical connections and interrelationships—'laws' if you prefer." Humboldtian scientists were professionals, fascinated by instruments and measurement. They observed, but not indiscriminately. Their theories, not a cosmic romanticism, guided their researches.[3]

I mention this debate because the topic has been revisited recently and, following Cannon, most researchers have privileged the rational, instrumental side of Humboldtian science over its romantic or cosmic side.[4] Recent scholars of exploration, such as Mary Louise Pratt and Bruce Greenfield have resurrected an interest in romanticism, but they ignore the technical aspects in favor of the narratives. Romanticism, they argue, should be placed in its colonial context. During the nineteenth century the landscape was naturalized—depicted as dynamic, majestic, and, most important, as *empty*. These textually pristine landscapes allowed travelers to legitimize bourgeois values of conquest and "improvement." This would seem to accord well with Goetzmann's argument that explorers were programmed by the urban center, importing its goals and values into the landscape.[5]

2. Wiliam Goetzmann, *Army Exploration in the American West, 1803–1862* (New Haven: Yale University Press, 1959), p. 19. The discussion of "Humboldtian" science can be found on pp. 17–21, 423, 431. ———. *Exploration and Empire: The Explorer and the Scientist in the Winning of the American West* (1966; Monticello Edition reprint, New York: History Book Club, 1993), pp. xi, 53, 159.

3. Susan Faye Cannon, *Science in Culture: The Early Victorian Period* (New York: Dawson and Science History Publications, 1978), p. 77. Humboldtian science is the subject of chap. 3, pp. 73–110; see esp. pp. 75–78, 87–88, and 95–96.

4. See, for example: R. W. Home, "Humboldtian Science Revisited: An Australian Case Study," *History of Science*, 33 (1995): 1–22; Trevor H. Levere, "Elements in the structure of Victorian Science or Cannon revisited," *The Light of Nature: Essays in the History and Philosophy of Science presented to A. C. Crombie*, ed. J. D. North and J. J. Roche (Dordrecht: Reidel Publishing Company, 1985), pp. 433–49.

5. For general accounts of these explorations see: Bruce Greenfield, *Narrating Discovery: The Romantic Explorer in American Literature, 1790–1855* (New York: Columbia University Press, 1992); Mary Louise Pratt, *Imperial Eyes: Travel Writing and Transculturation* (New York: Routledge, 1992); Christopher Looby, "The Constitution of Nature: Taxonomy

All of these approaches have their merits, but none of them address the romantic and the technical together even though historically they were thoroughly mixed. The romantic was not simply the sublime, although it was that, to be sure. These engineers refused to let their training stop them from seeing the infinite in a barometer reading. Their attempt to uncover the regularities of a dynamic cosmos through its daily patterns, its fossilized relics or its immemorial processes fits many of the conceptions of romanticism. In addition, the expedition leaders were represented as the best of American society—technically trained but cultivated men of feeling. They fused the romantic and the technical into a nationalist project which they made even the common bumble bee proclaim. The natural sublime, as David Nye has recently put it, became the American sublime.[6]

What has gotten lost in the current debates is the sense of exploration as a process. Euro-Americans defined and redefined nature even as they were transforming it. Understanding discovery, Richard White has argued, requires that we examine those transformations along with an analysis of the representations from any given period.[7] Beginning with Lewis and Clark in 1803 and ending with Frémont in the 1840s, these expeditions helped transform lands west of the Mississippi into places which are often comprehended under that weighty term, "The West."

Exploration: The Science of Place

When Lewis and Clark or Zebulon Pike made their western travels, Euro-Americans knew very little about their newly purchased territory. They set

as Politics in Jefferson, Peale, and Bartram," *Early American Literature*, 22 (1987): 252–75; Charlotte M. Porter, *The Eagle's Nest: Natural History and American Ideas, 1812–1842* (Tuscaloosa: University of Alabama Press, 1986); Goetzmann, *New Lands, New Men: America and the Second Great Age of Discovery* (New York: Penguin Books, 1986); John C. Greene, *American Science in the Age of Jefferson* (Ames: Iowa University Press, 1984); Donald Jackson, *Thomas Jefferson and the Stony Mountains: Exploring the West from Monticello* (Urbana: University of Illinois Press, 1981).

6. David E. Nye, *American Technological Sublime* (Cambridge: MIT Press, 1994), chap. 2, esp. 38–59. Also see: Carl Woodring, *Nature into Art: Cultural Transformations in Nineteenth-Century Britain* (Cambridge: Harvard University Press, 1989), esp. 6–18; Greenfield, *Narrating Discovery*; and Leo Marx, *The Machine in the Garden* (New York: Oxford University Press, 1967).

7. Richard White, "Discovering Nature in North America," *The Journal of American History*, December (1992): 875–91. Goetzmann, *Exploration and Empire*, p. xi; Pratt, *Imperial Eyes*, pp. 28–30 and 119–125; Greenfield, *Narrating Discovery*, pp. 77–84.

out with specific instructions into what they often referred to as "the Wilderness." Pike, writing to General James Wilkinson, assured him that he would be able to meet all obstacles successfully, "although those inseparable from a Voyage of several hundred leagues through a Wilderness inhabited only by Savages may appear of the greatest Magnitude, to minds unaccustomed to such Enterprizes."[8] That sense of emptiness, that the lands were nothing more than a "Wilderness inhabited only by savages," involved a set of conceptual changes that reflected the growth of American colonization.

The transformation of wilderness into a place involved exploratory technologies which combined the techniques of surveying, civil engineering, natural history, geology, ethnology and travel writing. Some of these technologies existed in the eighteenth century, especially in ocean exploration, while others were developed only in the nineteenth century.[9] Eighteenth-century accounts included categories such as geographical and cultural translation, narrative interpretation, and the assessment of particular regions in terms of their future utility (for settlers, mining, or trade). In other words, the field experience of travel had to be translated into generalized, global categories. Instruments became the nineteenth-century key to trans-

---

8. Zebulon Pike to James Wilkinson, 24 October 1806 in the *Journals of Zebulon Montgomery Pike, with Letters and Related Documents*, ed. Donald Jackson (Norman: University of Oklahoma Press, 1966), 2: 156.

9. Many of the techniques of measurement and instrumentation were borrowed from ocean explorers and land surveyors. See Richard Sorrenson's "The Ship as a Scientific Instrument in the Eighteenth-Century," *Osiris* 11 (1996): 221–36. Also see the introductory essay to that volume by Henrika Kuklick and Robert E. Kohler, 1–14. Prof. Kohler is in the process of working on notions of place as well. My work has benefitted from a preliminary talk he gave to the History and Sociology of Science department in the Fall of 1996. I have described eighteenth-century modes of making places in my "A Place in the Wilderness: Utility and the Native in Early American Exploration," delivered at the History of Science Society Meeting in 1994. The literature on travel writing is growing rapidly, but there is still too little attention paid to scientific travelers. See, for example: Philip Edwards, *The Story of the Voyage* (Cambridge: Cambridge University Press, 1995); S. Schwartz, ed. *Implicit Understandings: Observing, Reporting, and Reflecting on the Encounters between Europeans and Other Peoples in the Early Modern Era* (Cambridge: Cambridge University Press, 1994); Anthony Pagden, *European Encounters with the New World: From Renaissance to Romanticism* (New Haven: Yale University Press, 1993); Greenfield, *Narrating Discovery*; Pratt, *Imperial Eyes*; Pamela Regis, *Describing Early America: Bartram, Jefferson, Crevecoeur and the Rhetoric of Natural History* (Dekalb: Northern Illinois University Press, 1992); Mary Campbell, *The Witness and the Other World: Exotic European Travel Writing, 1400–1600* (Ithaca: Cornell University Press, 1988); Charles Batten, *Pleasurable Instruction: Form and Convention in Eighteenth-Century Travel Literature* (Berkeley: University of California Press, 1978).

lating local knowledge into what Bruno Latour has called immutable and combinable mobiles—data, descriptions, measurements, and specimens which were portable and comparable to other similar mobiles in "centers of calculation" like Washington, D.C., Paris or London.[10] The process was complicated by the fact that direct experience was often translated in a variety of ways, both in the field and after the return. Given that explorers examined each other's works it was also a cumulative and a referential project—a "protean conversation" as White described it.[11] In addition, explorers always combined projections of the future with analysis of the past and present: the landscape was never simply what was currently "there."

Beginning with the Lewis and Clark expedition both the size and the methods of scientific travel changed. The average size of expedition groups from 1800–1850 was roughly 25 and most of these were under military supervision.[12] The groups were assembled based on requisite skills so that they could be self-sufficient, which also made them potentially more insulated from the kinds of interactions earlier travelers experienced.[13] Exploration was also becoming a disciplined set of practices with routinized training. What started out as the "Corps of Discovery" was bureaucratized in the Army Corps of Topographical Engineers. The Lewis and Clark expedition

---

10. Bruno Latour, *Science in Action: How to Follow Scientists and Engineers Through Society* (Cambridge: Harvard University Press, 1987), pp. 219–232.

11. White, "Discovering Nature," p. 877.

12. Lewis and Clark listed 18 members (including themselves), which increased after the winter at Fort Mandan. Gary E. Moulton, in the recent edition of the Lewis and Clark journals, lists 37 members and 12 *engagés*, in addition to Sacajawea, Toussaint Charbonneau, Jean-Baptiste Charbonneau, and Jean Baptiste Lepage. See Lewis and Clark, *The Journals of the Expedition under the Command of Captains Lewis and Clark*, ed. Nicholas Biddle (New York: Heritage Press, 1962), 1:1; Gary E. Moulton, ed., *The Journals of the Lewis and Clark Expedition* (Lincoln: University of Nebraska Press, 1986), 2:509–29. Pike's 1806 expedition had 24 members; Long's 1819 Rocky Mountain expedition had 24. See Zebulon Montgomery Pike, "Diary of an Expedition made under the orders of the War Department . . . to explore the Internal Parts of Louisiana," in *Sources of the Mississippi and the Western Louisiana Territory* (Ann Arbor: Readex Microprint facsimile ed. of both reports, 1966), 111; on Long's expedition see Roger L. Nichols and Patrick L. Halley, *Stephen Long and American Frontier Exploration* (Newark: University of Delaware Press, 1980), pp. 76–77. Non-military expeditions could also be fairly large, such as Bradbury's 1809 trip into the Louisiana Territory with fur traders. The group began with 16 men and was augmented at times with as many as 60 people traveling for various reasons. See John Bradbury, *Travels in the Interior of America* (1817; Ann Arbor: Readex Microprint facsimile ed., 1966), pp. 23, 46.

13. For example, see Greenfield, *Narrating Discovery*.

had provided a model for these developments. Lewis, as other scholars have pointed out, received training from some of the best known scientists of the time.[14] Goetzmann's study of the Army Corps documents the technical training explorers received from the 1810s until the program at West Point was fully in place in 1838. For example, both Stephen Long and Frémont were college graduates, taught mathematics, were skilled engineers, and gained field experience before commanding their own expeditions.[15]

Increased training and division of labor are reflected in changes in the official reports. Geographical translation in the form of narrative description and interpretation did not disappear. They were, however, overshadowed by grids of calculation: meteorological data, latitude and longitude charts, mileage estimates, statistical tables of Native American populations, fur company data, and cost analyses for settlers all began appearing in travel reports in the early nineteenth-century. The novelty of statistics (at least in the United States) can be seen in an 1803 letter from University of Pennsylvania mathematics professor, Robert Patterson to Thomas Jefferson. Patterson wrote, "I recommended to Capt. Lewis, the use of a *Statistical Table* in which to set down his astronomical observations . . . as an expedient that would save a great deal of time, and be productive of many other obvious advantages."[16] Although recent editions often omit the tables or present them in prose format, tabulated information regularly appeared even in published editions of the time. In addition, recalling a tradition from seventeenth-century travel books, specialized chapters summarizing flora

14. The literature on Lewis and Clark is substantial. Perhaps the best account of their training can still be found in Paul R. Cutright, *Lewis and Clark: Pioneering Naturalists* (Urbana: University of Illinois Press, 1969). Also see the introductory materials and notes in Moulton, *The Journals of the Lewis and Clark Expedition*; and the letters in *Letters of the Lewis and Clark Expedition*, ed. Donald Jackson (Urbana: University of Illinois Press, 1962), p. 56. Also see: Albert Furtwangler, *Acts of Discovery: Visions of America in the Lewis and Clark Journals* (Urbana: University of Illinois Press, 1993); Silvio A. Bedini, "The Scientific Instruments of the Lewis and Clark Expedition," *Great Plains Quarterly* 4 (1984): 54–69.

15. On the training of members of the Army Corps see Goetzmann, *Army Exploration*, pp. 12–17. Brackenridge, Bradbury, and Nuttall were some of the last solitary naturalists to produce accounts in the nineteenth-century, but it is important to note that this mode of scientific travel continued. On the decline of the solitary naturalist in favor of corporate or military exploration, see Porter, *The Eagle's Nest: Natural History and American Ideas, 1812–1842*, esp. chaps. 11, 12.

16. Robert Patterson to Jefferson, 18 June 1803, in *Letters of the Lewis and Clark Expedition with Related Documents*, p. 56.

and fauna were often included.[17] For example, Edwin James's account of the Long expedition to the Rocky Mountains included chapters on the geological formations of the region, an account of the diverse Native American peoples, natural history, latitude and longitude tables, and meteorological tables.[18] The reports also contained lithographs, detailed maps, illustrations of fossil and botanical specimens, and, in the case of James's report, even vertical sections of the geological formations.

Even so, specialized chapters on Native Americans declined after 1820. This resulted due to reasons that I can only briefly mention here. Greenfield has suggested that particular Native American peoples were increasingly reduced to the blanket categories of "Indian" or "savage." That might be expected from the chauvinism of the Indian Removal era, but that only partially accounts for the shift. Native Americans were also being studied by a growing community of ethnologists who were analyzing languages, comparative anatomy, mythology, and population statistics.[19] Some of that language and population data appeared in tabular form in the travel reports by Pike and James, for example. What is true, is that Native Americans were disconnected from their lands in a number of ways. United States expansion diminished and then eliminated their territorial sovereignty. Accounts furthered this process by stressing their migratory life and their supposed in-

17. Those seventeenth-century works were tied more to the traditions of composite narratives. See Pratt, *Imperial Eyes*, 41–49. The nineteenth-century accounts reflect a specialization of knowledge which had very distinct roots that have little to do with apparent similarities in the texts.

18. Edwin James, *Account of an Expedition from Pittsburgh to the Rocky Mountains* (Philadelphia: H. C. Carey and I. Lea, 1823). I have made use of the Readex Microprint facsimile edition of 1966. James was the compiler of the expedition which included long quotations from other members of the expedition, such as Thomas Say, the naturalist. See Nichols and Halley, *Stephen Long and American Frontier Exploration*.

19. Henry Rowe Schoolcraft is an interesting intermediate example of this trend. He served as an Indian Agent in the Michigan Territory and was dispatched by Lewis Cass in 1830 to search for the source of the Mississippi River, in addition to mediating disputes between the Chippewas and the Sioux. He included statistical data on the fur trade and on Native American populations. See Henry Rowe Schoolcraft, *Schoolcraft's Expedition to Lake Itasca: The Discovery of the Source of the Mississippi*, ed. Philip P. Mason (East Lansing: Michigan State University Press, 1958). Later the state of New York and the Federal government hired him to undertake censuses of the Native American population. The federal study resulted in a six-volume study entitled *Historical and Statistical Information Respecting the History, Condition, and Prospects of the Indian Tribes of the United States* (1851–1857). For a brief account see: Richard G. Bremer, *Indian Agent and Wilderness Scholar: The Life of Henry Rowe Schoolcraft* (Mount Pleasant, MI: Clarke Historical Library).

ability to understand private property. Equally important, after 1820 their reputed "nature" or "character" was often asserted to be a racial attribute rather than being a product of the climate, environment, or mode of subsistence. Thus, Greenfield is correct in part, but fails to acknowledge the more specialized discussions among the ethnological community.[20]

Unlike the decreasing use of narrative in favor of other specialized reports and numerical data, the assessment of future utility remained important. Projecting settlements, assessing existing settlements, plotting railroad routes, and advising future settlers about what to expect were included in nearly every account of the period. Even the Long expedition report, which was criticized for supporting the notion that the southwest was a "Great American Desert," included numerous examples of favorable regions, such as the following description of a tributary of the Missouri:

> There are no settlements on its banks, except at the mouth where is a trading house. . . . The lands are, however, of a good quality, and the adequate supply of timber, and numerous springs of water, will ensure their speedy settlement.

Frémont included descriptions of settlers in his reports and noted that he was instructed to find "some convenient point of passage for the road of emigration" through the Rocky Mountains to "the usual ford of the Great Colorado."[21]

Description and interpretation, as I noted above, were not eliminated from the narratives. Lewis and Clark generally utilized pastoral imagery, but later explorers turned to the romantic rhetoric of the sublime. Powerful natural forces, great vistas, and profound stillness were just some of the recur-

---

20. Greenfield, *Narrating Discovery*, pp. 104–11. I am currently writing about the transformations in early American ethnology in my "The Varied, The Average, The Type: The Naturalization of Humanity in Antebellum America, 1800–1860." Also see: Robert E. Bieder, *Science Encounters the Indian, 1820–1880: The Early Years of American Ethnology* (Norman: University of Oklahoma Press, 1986); and William Stanton, *The Leopard's Spots: Scientific Attitudes Toward Race in America, 1815–1859* (Chicago: University of Chicago Press, 1960).

21. James, *Account of an Expedition from Pittsburgh*, 1: 98. For a negative assessment, see Ibid., 1: 37–38; Frémont, "Report of the Exploring Expedition of Oregon and North California in the Years 1843–44," in Jackson and Spence, *The Expeditions of John Charles Frémont*, 1: 451. See also 1: 445.

ring themes. The Frémont quotation with which I opened is just one example of meshing together the romantic and the technical (more will be said
about this below). The two definitions of Humboldtian science noted above,
suggest that somehow the romantic and the technical were incompatible.
Clearly, for these scientific travelers they were not. The question is not
whether they were guided by their romantic, cosmic conception of nature,
as Goetzmann suggests. Nor am I willing to reduce grids of calculation and
narrative rhapsodies to mere tropes or narrative strategies. The romantic
and the technical were a dialectical presentation of the process of globaliz-
ing the earth which were, as I will suggest, unified by equating the grand,
nationalist enterprise with the dynamic forces of nature. For the remainder
of my paper I would like to describe briefly some of these issues and discuss
how *knowledge about* places was a complicated, referential process involving methods of gathering data, social negotiation, and power relationships.

The Romantic AND the Technical: Making Places out of the Wilderness

Between 1800 and 1850, the United States expanded to the Pacific Ocean.
Western lands were transformed from an arena of competing European
and Native American interests into a wilderness of disorderly, majestic nature destined to fall into American hands. Lewis and Clark asserted the sovereignty of the United States throughout the Louisiana Territory. At the time
that sovereignty was often more symbolic than actual. By the time Frémont
traveled through the West, his account sounded as much like an entertaining hunting trip as it did a surveying mission. Greenfield has pointed to this
nicely, suggesting that traveling west shifted from being a trip to distant
lands and became "a trip into the future of the United States."[22]

22. Ronda, *Lewis and Clark Among the Indians*; Greenfield, *Narrating Discovery*, pp. 82–
83. In general see: James P. Ronda, *Astoria and Empire* (Lincoln: University of Nebraska
Press, 1996); David Dary, *Entrepreneurs of the Old West* (New York: Alfred A. Knopf, 1986);
Richard Slotkin, *The Fatal Environment: The Myth of the Frontier in the Age of Industrializa-
tion, 1800–1890* (New York: Atheneum Press, 1985); Michael Paul Rogin, *Fathers and
Children: Andrew Jackson and the Subjugation of the American Indian* (New York: Vintage
Books, 1976); Robert A. Trennert, *Alternative to Extinction: Federal Indian Policy and the
Beginnings of the Reservation System, 1846–1851* (Philadelphia: Temple University Press,
1975); John A. Hawgood, *American's Western Frontiers: The Exploration and Settlement of the*

Given all of these transformations and the influx of settlers, it might be difficult to see how any travel narrative could produce reliable data. In addition, explorers studied natural changes, the geological past, and the human past. Romantic nature and technical knowledge can be seen as two poles of representation merging human history and natural dynamism. Rather than merely focusing on apparent changes or even vast geological catastrophes, they sought for the underlying law-like regularities of the cosmos. Instrumental knowledge and the vast catalogues of data and specimens were combined with other data to uncover global regularities. Places, as I noted above, were never simply the accurate representation of what was "there."

The tables filled with numbers obscure the complications of determining even a single latitude or longitude. Silvio Bedini suggested that Lewis might have required at least three assistants using sextants or octants to measure altitudes and distances of the moon and a nearby star as many as four or five times. Lieutenant J. D. Graham of the Long expedition, repeated his measurements near Council Bluffs fourteen times before he was satisfied with a latitude of 41° 25′ 03.9″. He required "forty-two distances of the moon from the sun and stars, together with three eclipses of Jupiter's Satellites" to obtain a longitude of 95° 43′ 53.″[23] In addition to fixing their positions, they were, of course feeding themselves, checking the temperature and the barometric pressure three times per day, collecting noteworthy flora and fauna, and recording important events.

The more an observation or a measurement could be re-confirmed the more stable it might become, but additional claims often led to further revision. In the Frémont quotation with which I opened, he continued, stating that "from the description given by Mackenzie . . . with that of a French officer still farther to the north, and Colonel Long's measurements to the south, joined to the opinion of the oldest traders of the country, it is presumed that this is the highest peak in the Rocky Mountains." His contention could only be challenged by further climbing and measuring else-

---

Trans-Mississippi West (New York: Alfred A. Knopf, 1967); Goetzmann, *Exploration and Empire.*

23. Bedini, "Scientific Instruments," pp. 57–58 and 63–64. James, *Account of an Expedition from Pittsburgh*, vol. 2, "Astronomical and Meteorological Records," preface, p. vii following p. 442.

where in the Rocky Mountains. Frémont marshaled his own measurement and the testimony of traders as well as explorers, including Stephen Long, to produce not just an accurate elevation, but also the highest peak and the highest flight of the bumble bee.[24]

Technical skills were not simply tools for defining a place. They were also crucial for navigating *in* a region. Explorers had to avail themselves of other skills as well. They employed guides, boatmen who had practical knowledge about the behavior of rivers, and interpreters who made it possible to gather information from Native Americans. When these sources of information were unavailable, scientific travelers had to fall back on past experience and their skills. On June 3d, 1805, Lewis and Clark's Corps of Discovery found themselves at a fork where the Missouri met an unknown river. The problem was "which of these two streams is what the Minnetarees call Ahmateahza or the Missouri, which they described as approaching very near to the Columbia. On our right decision much of the fate of the expedition depends." If they chose incorrectly and had to retrace their path they might find themselves crossing the Rocky Mountains in the winter.[25]

Over the next six days they used a variety of methods to determine whether the south or north fork was actually the Missouri. The Minnetarees had assured them that the Ahmateahza contained a set of waterfalls where the water was clear. Lewis and Clark examined the clarity of the water in both forks, the quality of the riverbeds, the consistency of the air, and the currents. Men were dispatched down each fork for a day to get a better sense of their general bearing. Still uncertain Lewis and Clark each ascended a fork and were separated for five days. On the ninth of June they consulted with each other about the proper course. They re-examined Aaron Arrowsmith's map of the region which was based on Peter Fidler's calculations. Fidler *may* have entered the area on behalf of the Hudson Bay Company in 1792. Lewis and Clark were already suspicious of the Arrowsmith map at Fort Mandan (their winter quarters in 1804). They doubted its accuracy even more after reconnoitering the two forks. Next, they communicated their conclusion that the south fork was in fact the Missouri. Some of the

24. Jackson and Spence, *The Expeditions of John Charles Frémont*, 1:270–71. James, *Account of an Expedition from Pittsburgh*, 2:362.

25. Lewis and Clark, *The Journals of the Expedition under the Command of Captains Lewis and Clark*, 1:149, entry for 3 June 1805.

corps disagreed, arguing that the north fork was correct. They were basing their argument on the testimony of boatman Pierre Cruzatte, who was experienced on the Missouri but not that far west. Finally, it was decided that Lewis would pursue the south fork until he reached either the falls or the mountains. He did reach a set of falls on 13 June, and recorded one of the more romantic descriptions in the journals.[26]

The Missouri, according to Native American testimony and a previous map, was a river which contained a set of falls, which continued to be navigable to the Rocky Mountains, and which ran close to the Columbia. Both sources of testimony could have been incorrect (indeed, Arrowsmith's map was incorrect). What perplexed Lewis and Clark was that "the Indians" had not told them about the fork. What I want to stress is the multiplicity of methods the corps employed to resolve the situation. When Lewis reached the falls he relied on Native American accounts that they were part of the Missouri. The events which led to their decision and celestial observations at the fork helped to transform the Ahmateahza into the Missouri and substantiate it with an immutable mobile.

Returning to previously explored places showed just how quickly they could change. On July 30th, 1804, Lewis and Clark reached a plain separated by a "woody ridge about seventy feet above it" which gave them a "beautiful view of the [Missouri] River, and the adjoining country." They camped there and waited "with much anxiety" for a council with representatives from the Ottoes and the Missouris. After a successful meeting they named the spot, Council Bluff. They further described it as a location "exceedingly favourable for a fort and trading factory, as the soil is well calculated for bricks and there is an abundance of wood."[27]

On September 19th, 1819, three miles below Council Bluff, the Long expedition decided to establish their winter camp. They were about a mile above Fort Lisa, which had been constructed by the Missouri Fur Com-

---

26. Lewis and Clark, *The Journals*, 1:149–160, 3 June 1805–14 June 1805. In the Biddle edition, Lewis and Clark discussed their considerations of the Arrowsmith map at Fort Mandan in the entry for 3 June 1805. They do not mention the Arrowsmith map by name in the letter from Fort Mandan, but state " The map, which has been forwarded to the Secretary of War, will give you the idea we entertain of the connection of these rivers . . ." (*Letters*, 233). They based that map on Arrowsmith, conversation with the Mandans, and their own calculations.

27. Lewis and Clark, *The Journals*, 1:22, 24; 30 July 1804 and 3 August 1804.

pany. There they studied the strata which contained "numerous relicks [sic] of marine animals" and took the measurements required for establishing the latitude and longitude.[28] Their description of Council Bluff was similar to that recorded by Lewis and Clark: "This is a most beautiful position, having two important military features, security and a complete command of the river." By that time, however, the abundance of wood was gone, "there being little within a mile above and much farther below."

Frémont ended his narrative of the 1842 expedition near Council Bluff as well. He made no mention of the bluff itself, but he did note an establishment owned by the American Company. On his last entry for October first, he recorded, "I rose this morning long before daylight, and heard with a feeling of pleasure the tinkling of cow bells at the settlements on the opposite side of the Missouri."[29] The region surrounding Council Bluff had been transformed from its initial moment in the assertion of United States sovereignty into a pleasing pastoral landscape.

The romanticized, pastoral setting was only one of the common tropes of the period. The expedition reports also reveal the growing appeal of the sublime and its equation with nationalist vision. Examining popular rather than scientific views, David Nye has suggested that Americans did not appreciate the sublime until the 1820s. These cultivated men of feeling, however, appreciated it even if they did not privilege it. The violent power of nature, profound silences, and majestic landscapes were equated with the sublime. When Lewis reached the secondary falls, below the Missouri's Great Fall, he found a "shelving of rock, which without a single niche and with an edge as straight and regular as if formed by art" produced an "uninterrupted sheet to the perpendicular depth of fifty feet." This fall was "singularly beautiful, since without any of the wild irregular sublimity of the lower falls, it combined the elegances which the fancy of a painter would select to form a beautiful waterfall." Two and a half miles from there, Lewis found a smaller cataract where, on the opposite shore "on a cottonwood tree an eagle had fixed its nest, and seemed the undisputed mistress of a spot, to contest whose dominion neither man nor beast would venture

28. James, *Account of an Expedition from Pittsburgh,* 1:146.
29. Jackson and Spence, *The Expeditions of John Charles Frémont,* 1:285.

across the gulfs that surrounded it."[30] The Great Falls were sublime because they were wild and irregular while the secondary falls recalled the art of the stonemason and the pictorial art of the painter. The former shapes and produces order, the latter softens disorder to make the irregular symmetrically beautiful. Both images linked human improvement to nature just as the process of exploration was meant to reveal order in apparent disorder. Beyond the wild irregularity was an eagle, the recently adopted symbol of America, and here a symbol of dominion. Measurements fixed points for future reference and were keys to uncovering law-like relations in nature. Together the descriptive narrative and dynamics of nature were unified in a nationalist vision.

By the time of the Long Expedition of 1819, references to the sublime power of nature were depicted with a greater sense of awe. After describing strata in the Rocky Mountains, James wrote:

> It is difficult, when contemplating the present appearance and situation of these rocks, to prevent the imagination from wandering back to that remote unascertained period, when the billows of the primeval ocean lashed the base of the Rocky Mountains . . . and endeavoring to form some conception of that subsequent catastrophe which has so changed the relative elevation of the two great formations. . . .

The ephemeral quality of human enterprises compared with nature also led to similar moments. Contemplating the burial mounds near St. Louis, James said, "We cannot but compare their aspect of decay, with the freshness of the wide field of nature . . . with the majestic and imperishable features of the landscape. We feel the insignificance and the want of permanence in every thing human. . . ."[31]

With Frémont's expeditions in the 1840s, the sublime landscape was fully invested with the sense of manifest destiny. The complete silence of the Wind River Mountains was shattered by the sounds of Frémont's bumble bee pioneer, his fluttering United States flag, and the sound of the barom-

---

30. Lewis and Clark, *The Journals*, 1:161; 14 June 1805. On the appreciation of the sublime, see Nye, *American Technological Sublime*, pp. 17–20.

31. James, *Account of an Expedition from Pittsburgh*, 2:2 and 1:66.

eter being fitted into the rocks. The quotation with which I opened, how-ever, also reveals the beginning of the decline of the Romantic vision as his corps "carried out the law of this country," as he put it, "where all animated nature seems at war" and killed the bee. Frémont did not comment on the habits of the bumble bee. He borrowed a metaphor which had already ap-peared in other travel narratives. John Bradbury, who traveled in the Louisi-ana territory from 1809–1811, noted the following on 6 April 1809:

> Bees have spread over this continent in a degree and with a celerity so nearly corresponding with that of the Anglo-Americans, that it has given rise to a belief, both amongst the Indians and the whites, that bees are their precursors, and that to whatever part they go the white people will follow. I am of the opinion that they are right, as I think it as impossible to stop the progress of the one as of the other.[32]

Progress and manifest destiny broke the sublime silence. The vision of na-ture at war may signal the transfer of the natural sublime to the technologi-cal sublime of the railroad, a colossal symbol of human ingenuity. In any case, the thousands of measurements, the lengthy lists of plant species, and the mixture of barometer readings with nationalism show that in the United States at least, the technical reinforced the progress symbolized by the com-mon bee. What we should make of its demise, flattened in the pages amid botanical specimens, is another question.

---

32. John Bradbury, *Travels in the Interior of America*, p. 34.

THE SECOND COLORADO RIVER EXPEDITION
John Wesley Powell, Mormonism and the Environment

In surveys of great nineteenth-century American scientific explorers the story typically ends with John Wesley Powell, the last of the breed. After him, there was nothing significant left to explore in the great West. The nation's map was complete. Powell himself remarked in 1874, just five years after his harrowing first expedition, that "exploring expeditions are no longer needed for general purposes."[1]

Powell, like many of his contemporaries, was strongly in the grip of a romantic ideal of scientific exploration in which rugged, self-reliant, often lone men went manfully into the wilderness and came back with spectacular new facts. Indeed, he was so affected by that ideal of what an expedition must be that he decided to omit from his writings all mention of his second expedition down the Colorado River, though it was a major undertaking in its own right and pivotal in Powell's thinking about the West, its land and settlement. In 1875 he published, as a government report, *The Exploration of the*

---

1. John Wesley Powell to Secretary of the Interior, April 24, 1874, in "Geographical and Geological Surveys West of the Mississippi," 43d Cong., 1st sess., House Report 612,10.

Colorado River and Its Canyons. It is still in print, and thousands who have read it must have assumed that here was an account, in Wallace Stegner's words, of "the last great exploration within the continental United States, and an exploit of enormous importance in opening the West after the Civil War."[2] But the report covers only the first three-month voyage Powell made, with nine other men, in the spring and summer of 1869. It omits completely any reference to the second expedition, which began from the very same spot as the first—Green River Station in Wyoming Territory—and ended either on August 1, 1872, at Kanab Creek in the Grand Canyon, where they took their boats out of the water for good, or on February 16, 1873, when one of the expedition members, Frederick Dellenbaugh, arrived in Salt Lake City with a completed topographic of the plateau province in his hand.

Why did Powell fail to mention this much longer, and far more scientifically productive, expedition, not only in his report but throughout his life? The men of that second expedition, including Powell's second in command, his rather jealous brother-in-law Almon Thompson, resented the slight, so much so that Dellenbaugh felt compelled to try to rectify the injustice by publishing his own account, *A Canyon Voyage* (1908), a readable account which also is still in print, though it has never enjoyed the popularity of Powell's own work.

Dellenbaugh was an artist, hired because he could draw lovely maps, and one gets from his belated account little of the second expedition's real significance. Like Powell, he was a romantic idealizer when it came to narrating exploration, always looking for the dramatic and the heroic. He ends his story with these words: "The Major and Prof. [Thompson] repose in the sacred limits of Arlington. Strew their graves with roses and forget them not. They did a great work in solving the last geographical problem of the United States."[3] But that too leaves the question of the second expedition's significance back with "exploring nature"—going into the wild, making a map,

2. Wallace Stegner, "Introduction," *The Exploration of the Colorado River and Its Canyons* (New York: Penguin, 1987), p. vii. The original title was *Exploration of the Colorado River of the West and its Tributaries* (Washington: Government Printing Office, 1875).

3. Frederick S. Dellenbaugh, *A Canyon Voyage: The Narrative of the Second Powell Expedition down the Green-Colorado River from Wyoming, and the Explorations on Land, in the Years 1871 and 1872* (1908; Tucson: University of Arizona Press, 1962), p. 267.

managing a topographical survey. What Dellenbaugh left out of his account was exactly what John Wesley Powell overlooked in his definition of exploration: the rich social and human ecological dimension which characterized the second expedition.

The second expedition was, like the first, ostensibly about going down the Colorado River, puzzling out how this most sensational of North America's landscapes had been made. But it was what was happening *on* the land, the surrounding Colorado Plateau, that presented Powell with some of his most lasting discoveries. He discovered the people called Mormons, and they opened his eyes to the problem of how American society in general might rethink its relation to economy and ecology. This discovery tended to be unsystematic, casual, disjointed, and unfocused, yet one could no more separate it from the canyon voyage than one could separate the canyon wall from the waters flowing past them.

Undoubtedly, scientific exploration has never been simply a matter of delving into the facts of nature; with every explorer, either in some open or hidden way, the process of discovery has been one of learning not only how the earth is organized but also of thinking about how one's society is organized or might be reorganized. Going into nature, the explorer is often thinking about human culture, human values, human ways of livelihood. Lewis and Clark certainly were explorers in this richly layered sense, not only in meeting and thinking about the Indian peoples along the way but also in carrying in their heads the dreams of American commercial empire.

Scientific exploration is also shaped by, and responsive to, the infrastructure of a society, its production of goods and service, its organization of labor, its deployment of technology. This does not make exploration merely a reflex of that infrastructure, but it does require us to examine how all these social factors, mental and material, help give meaning to an expedition and affect its outcome.

Powell, tutored in a narrative convention of intrepid explorers entering unknown lands, did not acknowledge that complex social context. He assumed that it didn't really matter; the voyage alone mattered or had purpose. "Expedition" must refer only to the thrilling saga of first entering a wild land. As Stegner wrote, the second expedition "doesn't make a story. It hasn't the thrill or the suspense, the fear, the fateful climax, . . . it doesn't come to us with either the terror or triumph of the first . . . Exploration like seduction puts a premium upon the virgin."[4]

Here in a few words is how the second trip went. They came down the Green River until, in mid-July, 1871, they reached the mouth of the Uinta River, whereupon Powell departed for a nearby Indian agency and then went on to Salt Lake City where his wife and new daughter were staying in a boarding house. Six weeks later he rejoined his men downstream, at Gunnison Crossing, having spent the interim unsuccessfully looking for a way to get more provisions to the most remote parts of the river. Then together he and his band continued down the Green and the Colorado, until mid-October when Powell left them behind once more, passing though the village of Kanab in southern Utah and on to Salt Lake City and, by railway, to Washington, D.C. His men had instructions to triangulate the terrain from the Grand Canyon northward into Utah and over toward Nevada. When Powell rejoined them in November, they worked together on the map, though Powell spent considerable time going into both Mormon and Indian communities. It was not until the next August that they put their boats back into the river, at Lee's Ferry, and raced through the Grand Canyon. The river was high that year and very treacherous, so Powell changed the original plan and pulled them out in early September, deciding that neither science nor his men's welfare would be well served by further risk. He then took a wagon back to Salt Lake City, leaving, as noted above, Dellenbaugh and others to complete the expedition. They stayed until mid-winter, 1873, finishing the grand topographic map of the entire Colorado Plateau.

As Stegner said, it is not a neat, dramatic story like the first expedition, but the reasons why it is not are themselves interesting and revealing. Powell's first expedition had no government funding; this time, however, he had funding from Congress, though it was not secure and he now had to become a lobbyist in Washington as much as an explorer in the field. On the first trip three of his men had mutinied, in part because they were nearly starving. Their food supply had diminished considerably, and there was little in the way of game to be had from the country. Climbing out of the canyon the mutineers were killed, probably by Indians. Feeling personally respon-

---

4. Wallace Stegner, *Beyond the Hundredth Meridian: John Wesley Powell and the Second Opening of the West* (Boston: Houghton Mifflin, 1954; Lincoln: University of Nebraska Press, 1982), p. 137.

sible for that tragic outcome of his first expedition, Powell was determined, the second time around, to reduce the risks of exploration by insuring ample food supplies along the way.

Most importantly, he had, almost unknowingly, joined his own expedition for the pursuit of science to the forward march of Mormon settlement in the Great Basin, a march that by 1870 had advanced southward onto the Plateau and soon would leap across the Colorado River in Arizona. During the first trip Powell had virtually ignored the Mormons, but two years later they could not be ignored. They were everywhere around him. They had built primitive roads down to the river, established a settlement and crossing point at Lee's Ferry, even stretched a telegraph line to a point only a couple days' ride to the Canyon rim. In valley after valley throughout southern Utah, they had begun to plow the soil and plant their crops, pushing the native peoples aside, and to set up their sawmills, banks, churches and printing presses. This fast growing network of economic services became an integral part of Powell's second expedition. In a sense, the Mormon community was riding along with him in his frail wooden boats. No wonder then that the very idea of exploration, that saga of "undaunted courage" patterned by Lewis and Clark some sixty years earlier, courage exercised far from the settlements and independent of them, no longer seemed to apply.

The Mormons had begun arriving in the Great Basin in 1847, refugees from an unfriendly America. Almost all of the land they encountered was mountainous or desert, but their leader Brigham Young (1801–1877) meant to have it for his people and make the best of it. He set in motion a systematic program of exploration that would have "every hole and corner from the Bay of San Francisco to the Hudson Bay known to us."[5] Mormon-sponsored exploration has never been given its due, mainly because the explorers were simple, ordinary men who wrote down little of what they saw. But they reported faithfully back to the Church authorities, and sitting at the head of the Church, President Young turned that knowledge to the task of building up the Kingdom of the Saints. His grand scheme was to create a fully self-sufficient economy in Utah, with lines running all the way to the West Coast. As the United States government bore down on his

5. "Journal of Wilford Woodruff," cited in Leonard Arrington, *Great Basin Kingdom: An Economic History of the Latter-day Saints. 1830–1900* (Cambridge: Harvard University Press, 1958), p. 42.

independent-minded leadership, Young became increasingly determined to create a Mormon world free of outside dependency.

Immediately before Powell's first expedition, Young succeeded in incorporating the lower Colorado River into his grand scheme. In 1864 he sent a band of the faithful down to the banks of the Virgin River, a tributary of the Colorado, to set up there a new colony called St. George with the purpose of raising cotton for textiles. That same year he announced that he would soon have steamboats chugging up the Colorado from the Gulf of California as far as they could go, opening a route of access from the ocean to the Salt Lake. Using the river route would lower the costs of bringing in both supplies and new emigrants from America and Europe. Beginning in 1866 the Mormons brought goods from San Francisco to the mouths of the Colorado, then six hundred miles up that river to the "port" of Callville, about twenty miles southeast of present-day Las Vegas.[6] The man after whom this port was named, Anson Call, was seining in the river when Powell's first expedition emerged from the Grand Canyon, and it was Call who took them out of the river, fed them on melons, and sent them north to see Brigham Young. The entire Mormon hierarchy in Salt Lake City was intensely interested in Powell's exploratory efforts, for he was helping them fill in a very large piece of their own topographical understanding.

Preparing for his second expedition, Powell sought Brigham Young's personal advice and support. They met in Salt Lake City in the summer of 1870. The great explorer needed a guide, and Young recommended Jacob Hamblin, the famous "buckskin apostle" to the Indians, a man whom Powell would come to depend on along with several other frontier scouts who knew the land where he knew only the river. Along with Hamblin would come other guides, teamsters, packers, horses. Hamblin also provided an introduction to the Native American tribes, the Utes, the Shivwits and other Paiutes, the Hopi, and the Navajos. By 1870 virtually all these peoples had been gathered into reservations, relinquishing their claims on the scattered valleys where food could be grown. Powell's second expedition would be fed by virtue of the Mormons' agricultural conquest of the Indians, iron-

---

6. Leonard J. Arrington, "Inland to Zion: Mormon Trade on the Colorado River, 1864–1867," *Arizona and the West* 8 (Autumn 1966): 239–250.

ically so since he would develop a lifelong interest in the fate and cultures of these defeated peoples.

After his 1870 meeting with Young in Salt Lake City, Powell and his reconnaissance party went south to examine the land-side of the river they would navigate. Along the road they were overtaken by President Young, who, despite his nearly seventy years of age, had decided to go on still another inspection tour of his far-flung settlements. Their combined parties started over the mountains for Kanab, a journey that Powell used to advantage to extract still more information from the Mormon patriarch. Later that same month Powell was led down to the Colorado's edge by the scout Hamblin, who wrote a report to Young illustrating precisely the linkages between the Church and the expedition:

> I have been to the Colorado with Maj. Powel [sic], found a place where we can get supplies to the River for his exploring party another season, yet it will be with concidrable difficulty. This point is sixty miles south of Pipe Springs, at Windsor Castle, two watering places. abundence of grass, & dwarf sage the most the way. we visited the small band that killed two or three of Maj. Powels men, last season. I gathered them together & explained to them Maj. Powels business, sent one of them over the River to visite the remainder of the band, and left our Hourses, & most or our lugage with them while we climed down to the River. The Maj. expressed some anxiety about his goods & Horses, found on our return, that every thing was right, being absent nearly two days, The Maj. & 3 of his men will go the Navyos with me. There is a small flat boat being built at the river, at the mouth of the Pahreah. This will be don mostly at the expence of Maj. Powell. I will communicate to you on my return.[7]

This was how Powell prepared, with Mormon help, to undertake his second expedition, and the dependency of the Powell party on the Mormon network continued through the next several years.

When the second expedition made a pause in fall 1871, Powell and his men, along with Mrs. Powell and Powell's sister Nellie, settled down to spend the winter in canvas tents on the outskirts of the Mormon town of Kanab.

---

7. Letter from Jacob Hamblin, Santa Clara, Sept. 30, 1870, Brigham Young Papers, Historical Department, Church of Latter-Day Saints, MS 1234, reel 63, fd 11.

Here all the party's men and women were drawn further into the bustling frontier world of their hosts. They went to community dances, made close friends among the Mormons, drank local whiskey, hung around the post office daily. Powell himself was very tempted to settle his family in this little outpost. When Brigham Young made another visit to the town, he got an offer on some of his extensive real estate holdings. "Maj. Powell," he wrote, "has desired a lot of Kanab and says he will improve it and seems much interested in developing the country."[8]

What Powell saw in frontier Mormon villages that made him want to stay and settle was a spirit of cooperative enterprise that would remain central to his social philosophy for the rest of his life. In contrast to the individualistic, laissez-faire society that he had known growing up in Ohio, Wisconsin, and Illinois, he found among the Mormons a remarkable degree of social harmony. Working together in what he later called a system of "cooperative labor under ecclesiastical organization," these people were turning a harsh land into a prosperous, virtuous society. Where most non-Mormon observers saw the evils of polygamy or patriarchy in Utah, Powell saw an organic society in which individuals were all united in a common cause. Much of the second expedition was spent, without any planning to that end, observing that society up close and watching its energy at work. Powell would continue coming back to Utah to do field reconnaissance on geology and ethnology for several years, until at last (however reluctantly we can only guess) he bought a house in Washington and took a permanent position with the federal government; but it was that second expedition that made a great and lasting impression on his imagination.

Brigham Young's economic principles lay at the very heart of Mormon society. They mixed a commitment to economic growth and progress with a strong distrust of any moneyed class which would threaten social unity. Instead of encouraging private capitalists, most of whom happened to be non-Mormons, Young promoted the idea of "cooperatives" both for production and marketing. From 1868 to 1884 as many as 200 separate cooperatives were founded in Mormon country, the most famous of them be-

8. Brigham Young to Hon. Daniel [J.?] Wells, Dec. 16, 1870, Brigham Young Papers, Historical Department, Church of Latter-Day Saints, Box 73, FD 33.

ing the Zion's Cooperative Mercantile Institution, or ZCMI, in Salt Lake City, though every ward was expected to set up its own cooperative general store, with shares available to the poorest member. These cooperative enterprises were to be the foundation of a virtually classless society. Few of the cooperatives survived the intense pressure from the U.S. government during the 1880s to open Utah to free enterprise. Most of them were bought out by local businessmen. But for a while they thrived, they expressed an intensely egalitarian ideal of frugality and virtue, and they left a profound impression on the social thought of John Wesley Powell.

According to Leonard Arrington, what was sought in Mormon Utah was "a system of relationships in which self-seeking individualism, and personal aggrandizement would be completely replaced by common action, simplicity in consumption, relative equality and group self-sufficiency." [9] The most thorough application of this system came in southern Utah, not far from Kanab, in the years 1873–74, just after the second expedition had completed its work. It is highly likely that Powell heard something about its preparation. Following the model laid out by Joseph Smith back in 1831, as well as the admonitions of Brigham Young, a group of colonists formed themselves into a joint-stock corporation called the United Order and founded an experimental village called Orderville. They pooled all their economic resources and organized their lives on a thoroughly communitarian basis. The town's entire economy was divided in various departments—the Store, the Grist Mill, the Shoe Shop, the Farming department—and everyone in the town worked for one of these departments, receiving compensation according to their needs. The experiment lasted less than a decade, but while it lasted it illustrated in the most rigorous form the utopian socialist tendencies of Mormonism. [10] And it was precisely that utopian socialism that deeply impressed the scientific explorer Powell, more it would seem than the Colorado River and all its glories did. He went west with the intention once more of studying the landscape, but he ended up dwelling

---

9. Leonard Arrington, *Great Basin Kingdom,* p. 323.

10. Joel Edward Ricks, *Forms and Methods of Early Mormon Settlement in Utah and the Surrounding Region, 1874–1877.* Utah State University Press Monograph Series, XI (January 1964): 105–114. See also Arrington, *Great Basin Kingdom*, pp. 323–349; and Leonard J. Arrington, Feramorz Y. Fox, and Dean L. May, *Building the City of God: Community and Cooperation among the Mormons*, 2nd ed. (Urbana: University of Illinois Press, 1991).

among the Mormons, observing their peculiar ways, and discovering a new approach to organizing frontier society.

The southern Utah villages of Orderville, Kanab, St. George, and Tacquerville all shared a common challenge: how to build a self-sufficient, cooperative community in a very arid land. They had no trained scientists to tell them how to do that, though by the early 1870s they had over two decades of experience in the Great Basin to guide them. They knew they must capture the small flowing streams, prone to sudden flooding, and irrigate their crops with them, using only their own capital and labor for the work. The rest of the arid country was wide open, after the Indians were out of the way, for the grazing of their livestock. Both kinds of agriculture encouraged the cooperative spirit. They worked together to build dams and canals on the smaller streams that they could control, and they often ran their cattle and sheep together on the mountain pastures. Powell had done some farming as a boy in Wisconsin, though he did not like it much, but he was particularly fascinated by how the Mormons had adapted agriculturally to their environment, especially the Colorado Plateau.

The Mormons preached careful stewardship over their fragile environment, but historians have not agreed on how effective that stewardship really was. Richard Jackson concludes that nineteenth-century Mormons were more concerned than other American settlers to minimize their destructive ecological changes; as careful pragmatists, they respected the limits of the land and adjusted their practices accordingly.[11] On the other hand, Dan Flores argues that, despite their ethic of stewardship and communitarianism, the early Mormons "quite clearly overstrained the . . . environment," especially by overgrazing their animals.[12] But what Powell would have mainly seen of their land practices, on a still new frontier in the early 1870s, was not the destructive side, but rather a picture of humble men and women working together to make homes for themselves in desert conditions. He would have seen neat, tidy villages springing up on every hand.

11. Richard H. Jackson, "Righteousness and Environmental Change: The Mormons and the Environment," *Essays of the American West, 1973–74*, ed. Thomas G. Alexander (Provo, Utah: Brigham Young University Press, 1975), p. 38.

12. Dan L. Flores, "Zion in Eden: Phases of the Environmental History of Utah," *Environmental Review* 7 (Winter 1983): 331.

He would surely have agreed with Dellenbaugh, who wrote from his experience that winter in Kanab: "As pioneers the Mormons were superior to any class I have ever come in contact with, their idea being home-making and not skimming the cream off the country with a six-shooter and a whiskey bottle." [13]

Powell left the second expedition completely out of his 1875 report of exploration, but without any acknowledgment he drew substantially on that experience when he came to write his very important *Report on the Lands of the Arid Region*, published in 1878.[14] Most of the report is about Utah, and the radical reforms in the nation's land laws that Powell proposed in the report all came out of his experience with the Mormon economic and ecological order. In effect, he argued that the entire country west of the hundredth meridian ought to follow the Mormon pattern of settlement: "cooperative labor," but not under "ecclesiastical organization." The federal government would make its land available to private citizens under a communitarian regime, carefully adapted to arid conditions, and the citizens then would organize themselves into a secular society. Without much exaggeration one could say that this 1878 document, with its blueprint for a new American West, was the missing report of the second expedition.

Nineteenth-century exploration was always more than "pure science," whatever that may be. It was highly mythologized in the popular culture, and several explorers, including Powell, used their mythic standing to win political or government careers for themselves. Exploration commonly expressed a diverse cluster of social goals, including conquest and wealth, as much as scientific interests. The explorer carried those social goals, whether idiosyncratic or common, into the country with him and mixed them among his collections, sketches, notebooks, and other natural data. How the social context of exploration affected the ideas and purposes of science per se is not a question I have tried to open here, though it merits attention.

---

13. Dellenbaugh, *A Canyon Voyage*, 175.

14. J. W. Powell, *Report on the Lands of the Arid Region of the United States*, 45th Congress, 2d sess., House Executive Document 73. Wallace Stegner (op. cit., p. 219), called this report "quite as revolutionary and original, and a solution more practicable" than Henry George's famous single tax on landed property. Perhaps so, but like the tax Powell's land reforms were never put into practice.

How that context shaped the very process of exploration, however, has been my theme. In the case of John Wesley Powell the role of context is clear: in the process of organizing an expedition to the Colorado River, he became an explorer among the Mormons, and thence he became an explorer of his own society's future possibilities.

Appendix: Conference Program

SURVEYING THE RECORD: NORTH AMERICAN SCIENTIFIC EXPLORATION TO 1900

A CONFERENCE OF THE AMERICAN PHILOSOPHICAL SOCIETY
14–16 MARCH 1997
Benjamin Franklin Hall
427 Chestnut Street, Philadelphia

FRIDAY MARCH 14

REGISTRATION: NOON
SESSION I: 1:00–1:45 p.m. Welcome and Overview
Edward C. Carter II (American Philosophical Society) *"Welcome"*
John L. Allen (University of Connecticut) *"Where We Are and How We Got There"*

SESSION II: 2:00–3:30 p.m. The Cartographic Record
CHAIR: John L. Allen (University of Connecticut)
John Rennie Short (Syracuse University) *"A New Mode of Thinking"*
Clifford M. Nelson (United States Geological Survey) *"Completing a Reliable
    Geologic Map of the United States"*

REFRESHMENT BREAK

SESSION III: 4:00–6:00 p.m. Oceanic Exploration
CHAIR: Harold D. Langley (Catholic University of America)
Elizabeth Green (Indiana University) *"Science as a Landed Activity"*
Barry Alan Joyce (San Diego State University) *"Elisha Kent Kane and the Eskimo of Etah:
    1853, 1854, 1855"*
Dean C. Allard (Naval Historical Center) *"Spencer Baird and the Scientific
    Exploration of the Northeast Atlantic, 1871–1887"*

Reception APS Library: 6:00–7:30 p.m.

SATURDAY MARCH 15

REGISTRATION: 8:00 a.m. Continental Breakfast
SESSION IV: 8:30–11:45 a.m. The Artist as Explorer, The Explorer as Artist
CHAIR: Elizabeth Johns (University of Pennsylvania)
Kenneth Haltman (Michigan State University) *"Geologic Landscape Paintings by Samuel Seymour"*
Katherine Manthorne (University of Illinois Urbana-Champaign) *"Image as Text: Reading Expeditionary Art"*

BREAK

Ron Tyler (Texas State Historical Assoc.) *"Illustrated Government Publications Relating to the American West"*
Debora Rindge (New Mexico State University) *"Science and Art Meet in the Parlor: The Role of Popular Magazine Illustration in the Pictorial Record of the 'Great Surveys'"*

BOX LUNCHEON

SESSION V: 1:00–2:45 p.m. Lewis and Clark
CHAIR: Gary E. Moulton (University of Nebraska-Lincoln)
Gunther Barth (University of California at Berkeley) *"The Roles of Alexander Mackenzie and Meriwether Lewis during the Final Searches for the Northwest Passage"*
Albert Furtwangler (Mount Allison University) *"Do or Die, But Then Report and Ponder: Palpable and Mental Adventures in the Lewis and Clark Journals"*
Gary E. Moulton *"Reconstructing the Herbarium of the Lewis and Clark Expedition: New Discoveries"*

BREAK

SESSION VI: 3:00–5:00 p.m. Exploration and Anthropology
CHAIR: Anthony F. C. Wallace (University of Pennsylvania)
Don Fowler (University of Nevada) and David Wilcox (Museum of Northern Arizona) *"From Thomas Jefferson to the Pecos Conference"*
Richard Veit (Monmouth University) *"Montroville Wilson Dickeson, Pioneering American Archaeologist"*
Douglas Cole and Alex Long (Simon Fraser University) *"Surveying, Salvaging—or Savaging?—the Indians"*

REFRESHMENT BREAK

SESSION VII: 5:15–6:45 p.m. Works in Progress
CHAIR: Howard R. Lamar (Yale University)
Howard R. Lamar *"Stephen H. Long's 1820 Expedition: Responses to Native Americans"*
Marc Rothenberg (Joseph Henry Papers) *"The Smithsonian Institution and Scientific Exploration, 1846–1878"*
Lisa Strong (Columbia University) *"Collecting Oneself: Karl Bodmer, Alfred Jacob Miller and the Indian Sketch Collection"*
Ben Huseman (Amon Carter Museum) *"New Research on John James Young, Enigmatic Government Expeditionary Artist and Draughtsman"*
Donald C. Dahmann (U.S. Department of Commerce) *"Placing the Career of the Geographer Henry Gannett (1846–1914) in a Context That Relates to Our Own Time"*

SUNDAY MARCH 16

REGISTRATION: 8:00 a.m. Continental Breakfast
SESSION VIII: 8:30–10:00 a.m. A Biography of Explorers
CHAIR: Edward C. Carter II (American Philosophical Society)
Matthew Godfrey (Utah State University) *"Traversing the Fortieth Parallel: The Experiences of Robert Ridgway, Teenage Ornithologist"*
James Fleming (Colby College) *"The Mexico Boundary and the Boundaries of Science: Jean Louis Berlandier and the Politics of Exploration"*

SESSION IX: 10:00–1:00 p.m. New Dimensions of Exploration Studies
CHAIR: James P. Ronda (University of Tulsa)
Donald Worster (University of Kansas) *"The Second Colorado River Expedition: John Wesley Powell, Mormonism, and the Environment"*

BREAK

Lucy Jayne Kamau (Northeastern Illinois University) *"What Constitutes Science? William Maclure, The Academy of Natural Sciences, and the Nature of Science in the Early Republic"*
Brad D. Hume (Indiana University) *"The Romantic AND the Technical in Early Nineteenth-Century American Exploration"*
James P. Ronda *"Looking Backward—Looking Forward: Thoughts on the Meaning and Contributions of 'Surveying the Record'"*

CONCLUDING REMARKS
Edward C. Carter II (American Philosophical Society)

PROGRAM ADVISORY COMMITTEE

CHAIR, Edward C. Carter II (American Philosophical Society)
John Logan Allen (University of Connecticut)
James P. Ronda (University of Tulsa)
Martha A. Sandweiss (Mead Art Museum, Amherst College)

The Conference is supported by the American Philosophical Society
Andrew W. Mellon Library Endowment Fund.

All sessions will be held in Benjamin Franklin Hall
427 Chestnut Street, Philadelphia
Telephone Inquiries: (215) 440-3400; During Sessions: (215) 440-3103

Notes on Contributors

DEAN C. ALLARD is the former Director of United States Naval History and author of *Spencer Fullerton Baird and the U.S. Fish Commission: A Study in the History of American Science* and co-author of *The United States Navy and the Vietnam Conflict*.

JOHN L. ALLEN is Professor of Geography at the University of Connecticut, the author of *Passage through the Garden: Lewis and Clark and the Image of the American Northwest* (Choice Book Award and Lewis and Clark Trail Heritage Foundation Award of Meritorious Achievement) and the editor of the three-volume *North American Exploration*.

GUNTHER BARTH is Professor of History Emeritus at the University of California, Berkeley and the author of *City People: The Rise of Modern City Culture in Nineteenth-Century America* and *Fleeting Moments: Nature and Culture in American History*.

EDWARD C. CARTER II is Librarian of the American Philosophical Society, Adjunct Professor of History at the University of Pennsylvania, Editor in Chief of the ten volume edition of *The Papers of Benjamin Henry Latrobe* (co-winner English-Speaking Union Ambassador Book Award for *Latrobe's View of America, 1795–1820. Selections from the Watercolors and Sketches*), and the author or editor of four other books.

The late DOUGLAS COLE was Professor of History at Simon Fraser University, Vancouver, British Columbia, the author of *Captured Heritage: The Scramble for Northwest Coast Artifacts* and co-author of *An Iron Hand Upon the People: The Law Against Potlatch on the Northwest Coast*.

DON D. FOWLER is Mamie Kleberg Distinguished Professor of Anthropology and Historic Preservation at the University of Nevada, Reno, author of *The Western Photographs of Jack Hillers: "Myself in the Water"* and coeditor of *Others Knowing Others: Perspectives on Ethnographic Careers*.

ALBERT FURTWANGLER is an Independent Scholar living in Salem, Oregon and the author of *Acts of Discovery: Visions of America in the Lewis and Clark Journals* and *Answering Chief*

Seattle. Prior to his 1996 move to the United States Northwest, Furtwangler was Professor of English at Mount Allison University, Sackville, New Brunswick.

MATTHEW GODFREY is a doctoral candidate in American History at Washington State University who recently completed his master's thesis on the topic of his conference paper and is currently writing a history of the Montana National Guard during the Mexican Border Campaign and World War I.

ELIZABETH GREEN MUSSELMAN is a doctoral candidate in History and the Philosophy of Science, Indiana University, and will be a Mellon Postdoctoral Fellow in the History of Science at the University of Oklahoma. She is the author of "Swords into Ploughshares: John Herschel's Progressive View of Astronomical and Imperial Governance."

BRAD D. HUME is a doctoral candidate in History and Philosophy of Science, Indiana University, a history Instructor at the University of Dayton, author of "Anthropometry" in *The Readers Guide to the History of Science*, and a presenter of a number of conference papers.

BARRY ALAN JOYCE is a history Lecturer, San Diego State University, a former American Philosophical Society Library Mellon Fellow, the author of *A Harbor Worth Defending* and is now working on a study of the ethnological work of the Wilkes Expedition.

ALEX LONG is a recent graduate in History at Simon Fraser University, Vancouver, British Columbia, where he wrote his master's thesis on A. L. Kroeber and the Hearst-sponsored anthropological survey of Native California. Currently he is extending his research on this latter topic and helping edit Douglas Cole's biography of Franz Boas.

KATHERINE E. MANTHORNE is Academic Programs Coordinator, National Museum of Art, Smithsonian Institution in Washington, District of Columbia and author of *Tropical Renaissance. North American Artists Exploring Latin America, 1839–1879* and *The Landscapes of Louis Remy Mignot: A Southern Painter Abroad*.

CLIFFORD M. NELSON is Staff Geologist, History Project at the United States Geological Survey (USGS), Reston, Virginia and the author of articles about the geosciences and their history, and is at work on a manuscript-based study of the USGS's origin and early years.

DEBORA RINDGE is Assistant Professor, Department of Art, New Mexico State University, author of *The Painted Desert: Images of the American West from the Geological and Geographical Surveys, 1867–1879* and contributing author of *The Paintings of Frederic Edwin Church*.

JOHN RENNIE SHORT is Professor of Geography, Syracuse University and the author of *Imagined Country* and *New Worlds, New Geographies* and a former American Philosophical Society Library Mellon Fellow.

RON TYLER is Professor of History and Director of the Texas State Historical Association, University of Texas at Austin and author of *Prints of the West and Audubon's Great National Work: The Royal Octavo Edition of the Birds of America* (Best Book of the Year Award of the American Historical Print Collectors Society).

DAVID R. WILCOX is Senior Research Archaeologist and Special Assistant to the Deputy Director, Anthropology Department, Museum of Northern Arizona at Flagstaff and author of *The Mesoamerican Ballgame* and "A Hemenway Portfolio" constituting an entire issue of *The Journal of The Southwest*.

DONALD WORSTER is Hall Professor of American History, University of Kansas, the author of *Nature's Economy: A History of Ecological Ideas* and *An Unsettled Country: Changing Landscapes of The American West* and was awarded the Bancroft Prize for *Dust Bowl: The Southern Plains in the 1930's*.

Index